Poor Man's Golf

POOR MAN'S GOLF

David Lunt

First published by David Lunt 2021

Cover Design and typeset by BookPOD Pty Ltd

Typeset in Garamond Premier Pro and ITC Avant Garde Gothic

ISBN: 978-0-6452270-0-0 (paperback) 978-0-6452270-1-7 (e-book)

 A catalogue record for this book is available from the National Library of Australia

Front cover image: The front cover depicts a top knur and spell player in the early 1860s. The implement he is holding looks very similar in design to other illustrations in this book which show pummels from the early 1600s and the late 1900s.

Back cover image: The photo on the back cover shows the contents of a modern-day poor man's golf bag. The most important piece of equipment is the ball retriever which ensures that golf balls do not ever need to be purchased. The work horse of the three clubs shown is the driver. Most days every shot played is with this club including the putts. The seven iron and the sixty-two-degree wedge are mostly there to make the bag carrier look like a real golfer! Every few months the wedge comes in handy when the wielder finds himself stranded on the beach.

For my beautiful mother Kathleen (7.4.1923 – 19.1.2021)

I am so sorry that I could not be with you when Covid took you from us.

Contents

Foreword...xi

Introduction..xv

Chapter 1
Scottish, Dutch, French, Chinese, Roman, Swiss, Anglo-Saxon,
Norse or English?..1

Chapter 2
Let's go Dutch...5

Chapter 3
Put it in writing..31

Chapter 4
Romans, Vikings, pubs and Roger Bannister....................................37

Chapter 5
What a load of old balls..49

Chapter 6
World champions, footballers and cricketers....................................81

Chapter 7
Great golf matches, knur and spell, rabbits and lawnmowers......... 105

Chapter 8
Spells, pins, pummels and Grammar School boys........................... 121

Chapter 9
Kings, queens, aristocrats and other bludgers................................ 145

Chapter 10
Dead Poet's Society and paintings.. 165

Chapter 11
Trapball, kilts, a surgeon's son and lots of meanderings................ 179

Chapter 12
Golf starts in Baildon (Yorkshire) almost three hundred
years after knur and spell 185

Chapter 13
The Old Troon clubs 201

Chapter 14
Every man and his dog, but don't use your own name 237

Chapter 15
Pub sports rule...cockfighting, bear-baiting, prizefighting and
arrow-throwing 241

Chapter 16
Vikings and Anglo-Saxons 249

Chapter 17
Blame it all on the Roman Emperor Constantine 253

Chapter 18
More Romans, Dutch balls, a special Derbyshireman and the bard 261

Chapter 19
Knur and spell, the Danelaw, MUFC, slaves and potteries 269

Chapter 20
The Lunt, Lunt Meadows, Lunts and more Lunts 303

Chapter 21
Knur and spell and early golf in the Antipodes, Articles of
Agreement and handicaps 311

Chapter 22
Four hundred years and gone nowhere 333

Chapter 23
Cloth caps, clogs, Aborigines, the rise and fall of knur and
spell and stolen holly trees 345

Chapter 24
Royals, Rich Landowners, Bell's Life and Freemasons 365

Chapter 25
The publicans have it 379

Chapter 26
Did those English chappies really invent golf? 389

Chapter 27
Did golf come after knur and spell? 403

Chapter 28
Why? 417

Chapter 29
This will really piss off the Scots! 433

Chapter 30
Now is the time to say goodbye. Goodbye! Fartatata! Fartatata!
(As Peter Cook and Dudley Moore would say) 441

Afterword 443

Acknowledgements 444

Foreword

Thanks to my good friend David Lunt for inviting me to do the foreword of this book. It is indeed a privilege!

Two years ago, I had never heard the words knurr and spell! Nor did I have any knowledge of it as a game! David mentioned the name in passing while we were talking about golf history! It intrigued me that all the golf history books I had ever read never mentioned Knurr and Spell as an 'early stick and ball game' which could have been associated with the evolution of golf! How could this be? When, in so many ways, it has uncanny similarities to golf!

Immediately I was fascinated, hooked, and determined to find out more about this ancient sport! Fortunately, I did not need to do the investigating! David was doing the hard yards, leaving no stone unturned in his quest for information about a sport he knew as a boy! A sport he had seen being played in his hometown of Colne in the UK.

In this book, David leads you on a fascinating journey through the twists and turns of places, events and history of a game often referred to as 'poor man's golf'. Played in so many towns and villages across northern Britain by thousands of people! The pubs, the sports meetings and the betting associated with the game, will all keep you captivated!

Whether you are a keen golfer, a sports historian, or just love a good history read. I commend David's book 'Poor Man's Golf' to you!

Ross Baker
Traditional Golf Club Maker and Golf Historian.
Surrey Hills Victoria, Australia.

One has to be careful with history; it might be wrong. We've surely all heard the old chestnut, 'History is written by the victors', and in many respects this is true. There was a time, and not so very long ago, when people did believe in history, by which I mean they just naturally and instinctively trusted that what was written was true.

Now, thankfully, we're all so much wiser and far less gullible. We are aware that, like newspapers, history can be discriminatory, biased, prejudiced, partisan. This allows us, now, to exercise a certain amount of discrimination of our own: to read between the lines and make up our own minds.

But how alarming to find that something has been forgotten by history. No, not written out of history through the clever rearrangement of facts, but just simply not mentioned, not referred to, not spoken of. Forgotten and abandoned.

This is precisely what happened to knurr and spell. What! You've never heard of knurr and spell? Of course you haven't...it's been forgotten. It's been discriminated against so thoroughly, so well, that few and far between are those who have even heard of it. And yet it was once far and away more popular than golf and played by many thousands of people across northern Britain in what was once known as the Danelaw.

Knurr and spell was a stick and ball game of great antiquity; its origins may go back to early Viking days...and beyond that who can say? The story of knurr and spell is not only intriguing, it is full of intrigue: regal, religious, sociopolitical, moralistic and, with the advent and the increasing prominence of the game of golf, outright jealousy and class conflict from golf.

If, with hindsight, it seems to us extraordinary, that one could be arrested, imprisoned, tortured, pilloried, and ostracized for merely playing a game which, despite these dire threats to one's well-being, was indulged in by many thousands of people and attracted thousands more over many centuries, then it is surely even more extraordinary that such a game could be nigh completely forgotten, both by history and by people. What happened? And why?

In a remarkable and painstaking piece of research Mr. David Lunt has pulled the story of knurr and spell out of the past in which it had been allowed to sink. In a piece of sleuthing which would have been the envy of the venerable Holmes himself he has produced for us a most remarkable and remarkably unbiased story, thereby shining a light on a forgotten piece of history.

This is not just a book for golfers and historians, or champions of social justice, this is a book which will intrigue and delight everyone.

In its search for the truth, this book touches on and highlights many fascinating tales from antiquity which have heretofore been buried in the warp and weft of history, the tapestry of time. That it frequently does this with both sparkling humour and a delicious disrespect, makes the whole process doubly delightful. *POOR MAN'S GOLF* not only intrigues and delights, but it also informs on so many unexpected levels. It will be a quirky and worthwhile addition to your shelves.

Timothy St Julien Barber
Poet, aesthete, wordsmith.
April 2021

Introduction

The best description of what you are about to read is that it is a long rambling rant about the evolution of golf.

No attempt has been made to fine tune or give any real structure to the story. It is merely a collection of thoughts just as they popped into my head. At times it is somewhat incoherent. It is extremely self-indulgent and verbose. If you can fill the unforgiving page with an abundance of superfluous words, why strive to write a miserable *haiku* with only three lines and seventeen syllables or a whimsical clerihew with just four lines? Long live circumlocution!

There is duplication, no shortage of oxymorons, and a plethora of solecisms throughout, for which I make no apologies. There could be a sprinkling of profanity or coarse invective. I am definitely not a closet scatologist! Because there would have been far too many of them, I have avoided the use of footnotes. So be prepared for a 'jerky' read with constant tangential excursions.

At the end of the day, in common with every other book I have ever read on this subject, there are no firm conclusions. I cannot pretend to know exactly where golf came from or how it began. However, if we accept that the first commandment when we talk about golf is that it is a game invented in Scotland, then I must confess at the outset that this book may be considered transgressive in nature.

About two years ago I was talking to a good Australian friend of mine called Ross Baker. Ross is a traditional golf club artisan based in Surrey Hills, Melbourne, who still makes golf clubs exactly how they were made in the 1800s with wooden heads and shafts. He exports these all over the world to hickory golf club *aficionados*. Even the world's best ever golfer, Mr Jack Nicklaus, has received some of Ross's clubs. Apart from his amazing club making talent, Ross is extremely well versed in the history of Australian golf and golf in general. He also has an impressive collection of old golf clubs dating back to the 1800s.

During one of our many discussions I asked Ross what part he thought knur and spell may have played in the evolution of golf. To my great surprise he told me that he had never even heard of knur and spell. When I told him what knur and spell was and that competition knur and spell had been played in Australia long before The Australian GC, Royal Melbourne GC or Royal Sydney GC were even dreamt about, he almost fell off his chair. Even his faithful old dog, Jigger, pricked her ears up! Of course, Jigger was named after an old-fashioned golf implement and not after an electrical device used to trick racehorses to run faster! I have also spoken to several current and former golf professionals in Australia about knur and spell and none of those had ever heard about knur and spell either.

I knew about knur and spell from my boyhood days in Lancashire in the 1950s. However, by then it was already almost extinct, and I never knew just how big the game had been in its heyday. For most of my life I have always thought about knur and spell as being just a minor fringe sport played by a handful of cranks. Subsequent research has shown me that I had it very wrong. Throughout the 1800s knur and spell was much bigger than golf, on a par with cricket and probably bigger than football. And I don't mean the tinpot, headbanging game of AFL (Australian Fumbleton League) played in Australia. I am talking about the world game!

There is nothing new about knur and spell being talked about as a game which may date back to Viking or Anglo-Saxon days or as being a forerunner to the game of golf. Its colloquial name of 'poor man's golf 'is testimony to that. Books and videos about the game of knur and spell, most of which refer briefly to poor man's golf and to Vikings, are also available. However, none of these have attempted to explore the possible linkage between knur and spell and golf in any depth. The possible connection between knur and spell and Vikings likewise does not appear to have been closely studied. This book is an attempt to rectify the situation.

The crux of this book is to bring into sharper focus the role which this very ancient north of England game may have had in the development of golf. Despite all its shortcomings I hope that some of the things discussed may prove of interest to golf history enthusiasts.

Above all, it will hopefully encourage further debate and maybe inspire others to research the subject more fully. With absolute certainty there will be a mountain of additional information just waiting to be unearthed in the libraries, museums and local history societies scattered throughout the former Danelaw area of England and probably more to find in Australia and Scotland too!

Chapter 1

Scottish, Dutch, French, Chinese, Roman, Swiss, Anglo-Saxon, Norse or English?

Golf has been around for five or six hundred years, but where did it come from? What were the origins of this great game which captivates millions of people world-wide?

From what I could find out there seems to be general agreement that the game of golf as we know it today was developed by the Scots. This nation of male skirt wearers, bag-pipe blowers and haggis eaters has been playing the game since the 1500s and would almost certainly have played it from the early 1400s if King James **II** had not banned it because he didn't want his archers to waste time playing golf when they should be practising their archery skills. In fact, they had probably played the game for about four hundred years before the very first Open Championship was held in 1860. There is also fairly general agreement that the Scots didn't develop the game of golf from scratch and that they just took another existing golf-like game (or several games) and refined the rules into what we now play. However, which game they adapted, or if it was a compilation of several different games, has been the subject of much speculation over many years. The Scots themselves seem to believe that the game evolved out of the Dutch games of colf or kolf and the similarity of these names to the word 'golf' certainly sounds very plausible. However, many different countries have stuck their hands up claiming that golf came from one of their games.

It has been well documented that the first custom-made golf clubs were in fact made by Scottish bowmakers. For the first two or three hundred years of golf's existence there was a very close link between golfers and archers. There is even a suggestion in some circles that not only the golf clubs but maybe even the game itself could possibly have evolved from the sport of archery. Bows and arrows were invented at least ten thousand years ago, and archery was still very much a major activity in Scotland at the time golf had started to appear. Bowmakers traditionally used yew wood to make their long bows from, but sometimes they would also use ash, hazel or elm. Both ash and hazel were also commonly used in the early golf clubs.

It has surprised me somewhat that I never saw any reports about either golf club or knur and spell pummel shafts being made from yew wood. Apart from long bows, yew was also used to make spear shafts from, and this would not be too dissimilar to a golf shaft or a knur pummel. Yew is a very tough and durable wood which has high elasticity. It will spring back after bending. In the old days yew trees were generally planted in church yards where, unlike the residents, they thrived and had great longevity. Both golf and knur and spell were initially played in or around church yards. Most parts of the yew tree are however poisonous to both humans and animals so maybe this restricted its use. It probably meant that the supply of yew wood was very limited because they could not plant any yew trees anywhere where horses, cows, goats and sheep etc could get at them. Demand for yew wood to use in long bows would have been high. Golf and knur and spell would not get a look in. Keeping the army supplied would have had top priority. Knur and spell? What the hell is that I can hear everyone asking. No rubric on knur and spell will be provided at this stage but read on. All will be revealed eventually.

There had been a big surge in British archery activity after the Norman conquest in 1066 where William the Conqueror had far more skilled archers in his army than the English. The archery sport of 'roving clout' which is still played in Britain today, dates to those very early days. This is at a time when other sports were banned, and men were encouraged to amuse themselves on their way to church by wandering through the fields and firing their long bows at clouts. A clout was any kind of a random marker such as a clump of grass or a tree. The word came from the Viking *clud* which meant a piece of cloth. Incidentally, the oldest surviving bows were found in a peat swamp in Holmegaard, Denmark where some of the Vikings also came from.

The long bows could shoot the arrows around one hundred and eighty yards and they moved from clout to clout. The trajectory of an arrow fired from a long bow would be similar to that fired from a golf club. It would be much higher than the flat trajectory of short distance target archery. One can imagine that being an adjudicator for such a contest would have been rather dangerous with lots of men firing arrows. Maybe flying golf balls are marginally safer than flying arrows? I don't suppose there would have been injury insurance for toxophilites in the Middle Ages! If anyone wonders, it is from the Greek.

Just as golf balls are being hit longer because of technology improvement in both clubs and balls, the same thing has happened in archery with high-tech bows and high-tech arrows. In golf, we have long driving competitions where no target is involved. In archery, there is Flight Archery where only distance covered is what matters. The interesting thing is that the archers easily have it over the golfers in this discipline. At the time of writing, the world record for an arrow travelling from a hand-held and hand-pulled bow is 1,222.01 metres. Please don't forget that last centimetre! Compare this with an average PGA tour drive of maybe three hundred metres. Even with a following wind and a bone dry, rock hard downhill fairway in the thin atmosphere of Denver, a golf drive couldn't travel half the distance an arrow can. The archers could shoot a double condor with a single shot! There are no other non-extinct birds of prey larger than a condor so let's go pre-historic and call it a teratorn. Of course, if Alan Shephard had hit a Big Bertha on the moon's surface during the Apollo 14 mission in 1971 instead of his six iron, he could probably have easily hit a double teratorn! With zero air resistance and only one sixth of the earth's gravity on the moon, the ball would literally go out of sight! Sadly, for Alan there were no Big Berthas around in 1971. At least none that would fit in a golf bag!

We have also heard about the Irish playing hurley possibly back to pre-Christianity days. The Scots did likewise with their game of shinty. The English played a game called bandy and there is a stained-glass window in Canterbury Cathedral from the 1200s which appears to depict this game. The Romans played a couple of ball games called *harpastum* and *paganica*. The Chinese have told us about *chuiwan* which was popular during the Song Dynasty between 960- 1279 AD. In Holland, the Dutch played *colf* and kolf from the 1200s onwards. From the 1200s – 1400s the French and Belgians played games called *soule* and *chole*. When King Edward **III** was on the English throne in 1327 a game called *cambucca* was all the rage. He even banned the game in 1369. This game had been around at least from the 1200s and involved hitting a small wooden ball with a curved stick. Sir Guy Campbell, a renowned British golf course architect after the First World war, advocated that *cambucca* had been a pre-cursor to golf. Then in France during the 1400s and 1500s, *jeu de maille, paille maille* and *chicane* were practised. *Chicane* was a game which involved hitting a ball in the least number of strokes to a church or garden door. Not to forget the Swiss who still today play *hornussen* (farmer's golf) which apparently goes back to the 1500/1600s. In fact, the 1625 records of the *Consistory (Roman Catholic Council of Cardinals)* in Lauperswil, Berne Canton gives details of two men being fined twenty francs for playing *hornussen* on a Sunday. In Persia they had *chaugán* and much older than any of these is the game of *gulli-danda* which is played in India, Pakistan, Sri Lanka, Nepal and Bangladesh and is thought to go back two thousand five hundred years. The Pharaohs could also perhaps make a case with their several thousand-year-old ancient carvings in Egyptian tombs of what appears to be a golf-like game. In the area bordering France and Belgium, they still have a game called *jeu de crosse* which dated back to the 1300s or earlier and which also had a very golf-like swing. They use one multi-purpose club, and a ball called a *choulette*.

It was really drawing a long bow (pardon the pun) to suggest that some of these games were golf-like just because they involved the use of both a ball and a stick (or in some cases a stick and a wooden peg). Many of them were more akin to games like hockey, lacrosse, and croquet. *Chole* was a strange comparison because it was a game played between two teams who played end-to-end like a soccer or rugby game. In fact, in medieval times *chole* was played in Cornwall, just across the English Channel from Northern France, and there the *chole* name eventually became known as football. Of all these games, the ones which to my mind are most like golf are *hornussen* and *jeu de crosse* although they are perhaps the least mentioned of any of the games as possible forerunners to the golf we all know. *Hornussen* is very much like a golf long driving competition and like another seldom mentioned game called knur and spell which is discussed in much more detail later.

Chapter 2

Let's go Dutch

The Dutch games of colf or kolf appear to be the firm favourites to have been at least one of the chief forerunners to golf. According to the explanation *From Colf to Kolf* by Geert and Sara Nijs, these two games were not one and the same thing. They say that colf was the older of the two games and was played with a smaller ball and a shorter stick and was played long distance over open land, after initially having been a short form game. Colf had been played in the Netherlands and its neighbouring country, Belgium, from the 1200s. Kolf on the other hand was played with a much longer and heavier stick and a bigger ball. The stroke in kolf seems to be a push stroke and not a free swing. According to Nijs the playing of colf, for some unknown reason, ended abruptly almost exactly in 1700. Kolf then took over and was played mostly indoors on relatively short playing areas. Sometimes these games used a hole but often they just used a pole or some other marker as a target. The club they played kolf with was called a *kleik* which of course sounds like the word cleek used by the early Scottish makers of iron headed golf clubs.

It all sounds plausible and there is plenty of evidence, both documentary and recovered artefacts, to support the early playing of colf in Holland. Geert Nijs has uncovered an enormous amount of information on both the games as played in Holland. There is also plenty of written evidence about the 'kolf' part of the story but that doesn't help much because kolf at that time had very little in common with golf except that it was played with a stick and a ball...just like lots of other games. The problem comes in definitively linking colf to Scotland. As far as I know colf itself was never played in Scotland. Yes, the Scots had probably heard about colf, but they had also probably heard about dozens of other ball and stick games as well. Yes, Dutch traders were often going to Scottish ports and indeed there were significant numbers of people of Dutch origin living in the Lothians.

However, the Dutch traders were also often going to English ports too where there was a far greater Dutch diaspora than in Scotland. Kolf in Holland is said to have replaced colf in 1700. However, before that date the two games must have existed side by side for quite some time. Certainly, kolf appears to have been played in Holland decades before 1700. It didn't just start when colf ended.

If we look at Rembrandt's sketch of *The Kolf Player* dated 1654, we can see that the short version of the game was already being played. This date is when the sketch was done. Kolf could have been played long before 1654. The sketch also confirms that kolf bore little resemblance to golf at that time. The ball they used was considerably larger than a golf ball. The stick they used was much longer, up to shoulder height, and the grip by the player, with his hands about two feet apart on the club, would have been far more conducive to making a push stroke than a golf swing. There were also other people sitting around in the sketch within a very short distance of the striker which strongly suggested that he didn't expect to propel the ball any great distance. What sounds as if it was the same type of kolf game was also reported as early as the 1614 – 1674 period in the USA, where Dutch settlers had introduced the game into New Amsterdam which later became New York. If Geert Nijs's explanation of colf / kolf is correct whereby the short form of the game superseded the long form, this is exactly the opposite of what happened with both golf and knur and spell. Golf started off as a short game played with wooden balls around churches before expanding to five or six holes and eventually to eighteen holes when they got better balls. Knur and spell also probably started off as the short version, known as trap-ball, which was also played around churches and which also later evolved into a longer form game.

When we consider colf or kolf as being forerunners to the game of golf in Scotland, we must also be aware of what was happening generally in the Netherlands and surrounding countries in that period. In fact, it doesn't do any harm to look at the period four of five hundred years before the approximate 1450 golf start-up date in Scotland until about four hundred years after that time. We may even go back as far as the Romans. Cities in the Netherlands such as Maastricht and Utrecht were first developed after the Romans had arrived. So, we can safely assume that they would have brought the *harpastum* and *paganica* balls with them. These were hair filled leather balls which the Dutch probably copied later and sold lots of to Scotland prior to 1618 for golf playing.

The Romans ruled the Netherlands for over four hundred years and were there for about the same time that they were in England. Most of the Roman settlement areas were in the south of the country. They regarded the ancient Frisians who lived in the north part of the Netherlands as barbarians. These people had been Germanic tribes who had moved to the northern coastline about four hundred years before the Romans turned up. Although the Romans governed the north of the Netherlands from an administrative viewpoint, the Frisians always maintained their independence. In other words, there was a suzerainty established between the Romans and the Frisians. This required the Frisians having to provide recruits into the Roman army. Some of these recruits were probably used by the Romans to help them man the garrisons along Hadrian's Wall around the year 200 AD. Although the Romans left Britain in about 410 AD, many of the forts along Hadrian's Wall still had people occupying them well into the 500s. Frisians?

Between 250 and 450 AD the sea levels on the northern coast of the Netherlands rose dramatically and most of the ancient Frisians had to scarper. Many of them re-settled into England (Kent, Yorkshire, East Anglia etc). Later on as the climate settled down again Frisia became inhabited again but it was not necessarily by the same people. These were referred to as the New Frisians and were probably Angles, Saxons and Jutes.

Although many people tend to talk about the Netherlands and Holland as being one and the same place, we should remember that Holland is just a province within the Netherlands. Although it boasts the three main cities (Amsterdam, The Hague and Rotterdam), Holland occupies only about eighteen per cent of the total area of the Netherlands and is home to about one third of the population. Friesland (Frisia) is the biggest province in the Netherlands with about 5,750 square kilometres, but only about fifty-eight per cent of this is land area. The 2019 population of Frisia is about 648,000 which less than four per cent of the population of the Netherlands.

If we jump from Roman times up to the ninth century, we will find that a Danish Viking called Rorik was conceded all the north part of the

Netherlands in 850 including Dorestad (Wijk bij Duurstede) and all lands north of the River Maas (Meuse). During that period, a warlord from Frisia called Ubbo had fought on the side of the Danish Vikings when they first invaded Northumbria in England. Many Danish Vikings settled in Frisia during that period. Most of Frisia is in the north part of Holland. Frisian merchants had set up trading posts in many places during the time when the Vikings occupied England. One of those places was York, which was the Viking capital of the Danelaw region. What we must remember during this period is that Northumbria was a much bigger area than it is today. Basically, it included all the land from north of the River Humber up to the Firth of Forth. More importantly, the area of Scotland where golf started, Edinburgh and Leith links in particular, were all part of England back in the Viking days. For those interested in reading more about the Vikings in Holland, France, Spain etc there is an excellent source of information in the *Viking Society Web Publications*. The Viking Society was formed in 1893 and is continually unearthing new information about where the Vikings went and what they did.

This could be significant for two reasons. Firstly, it is known that the north part of the Netherlands was the main region where colf and kolf were played. In 2019 the game still survives in the Netherlands and virtually all the existing clubs are in that area. Secondly, the Viking connection may prove to be very important. This is because the previously mentioned very ancient game of knur and spell (discussed in minute detail later) was played almost exclusively in the part of England which was ruled for several hundred years by the Danish Vikings in an area known as the Danelaw. Thus, it is not impossible that the Vikings could be the common link between golf, colf and knurr and spell. In other words, let's not just restrict ourselves to pondering about whether or not golf emanated from colf. Let's also ask the question where did colf come from? Did the Dutch invent colf or did the Romans, the Saxons and the Vikings etc all have an influence on this game too? Probably! At the very least we already know that the Romans were playing around with little leather balls long before the Dutch and the Scots were playing colf / golf with their little leather balls!

The next significant part of the Dutch history is the period when the Netherlands were ruled by Spain. Spanish rule had started in 1556 but the Dutch never really accepted the Spanish intrusion and there were continual wars between 1568 – 1648 even though the Dutch had already been granted independence by 1588. From a colf and kolf standpoint the significance of Spanish rule would have been the adverse effect of religion on the playing of sports. We know from very early on in the piece that the Pope didn't like people to enjoy themselves playing sports. He wanted them to spend all their leisure time praying in church or repenting. We also saw that from sporting bans in England, Scotland and many other European countries. However, the Spanish monarchs were very strong Catholic supporters and for all the time when they ruled the Netherlands (and Belgium) they were also running the infamous Spanish Inquisition. This had started in 1478 and didn't officially end until 1834 although its power had declined long before that. Jews and Muslims were ordered to convert to Catholicism or leave the country. Many people pretended to convert rather than go through all the hassle of moving countries. Anybody caught expressing heretical views after their conversion could well end up being executed. The Pope didn't muck about in those days.

About four-hundred and seventy-five years later in the late 1970s I personally had an indirect experience of this religious oppression. I was travelling on business in Turkey. Our agent in Istanbul at that time was a gentleman by the name of Victor Mesulam. During our daily meetings in his office, I quickly learned that he could speak seven or eight languages fluently as he spoke by telephone with suppliers in many countries. Actually, this was not all that unusual. Many of our overseas agents were similarly gifted. However, one evening he invited me to his home for dinner. During the evening I heard him conversing with his family and was very surprised to hear him speak to them only in Spanish. Although my Spanish is serviceable, I was struggling to understand everything they said. When I questioned him about this his explanation amazed me. His ancestors had been driven out of Spain in the early 1500s by the Spanish Inquisition. For almost five hundred years, and across many generations, they had maintained Spanish as their main language in the family home. I expect that Istanbul was known by its previous name of Constantinople in those days. The reason I had limited understanding is because they were still talking medieval Spanish and not modern-day *castellano*!

As far as the Netherlands were concerned in the 1500s and 1600s, during Spanish rule, the country became divided from a religious viewpoint. The south of the Netherlands, geographically nearer to Spain, was mostly Catholic and the north Netherlands mostly Protestant. It would have been far more relaxing to play sport in the north than in the south whether it be colf, kolf, knur and spell or any other sport because there would have been far less hassle from the church.

Despite this, after the independence from Spain, the Netherlands very quickly became the most prosperous country in Europe. The 1600s were a fabulous time for them economically and the above-mentioned Rembrandt sketch was just one of many which we can see today. All the old Dutch Masters such as Rembrandt van Rijn, Johannes Vermeer, Jan Steen and Franz Hals to name only a few, were extremely prolific. They painted and sketched every conceivable kind of subject. Works by earlier Dutch painters such as Pieter Brueghel who died in 1569 can also be found. What a great pity that Lawrence Stephen Lowry had not been around in Lancashire when knur and spell was at its peak! Lowry specialised in painting everyday activities of the ordinary working man. He didn't die until 1976 however, so there is still a possibility that he painted a knur and spell scene or two during its declining years.

If we compare the population of the Netherlands to that of England, we can see that England is several times greater. If we assume that colf/kolf was mostly played in the north of the Netherlands and compare this area with the size of the Danelaw in England, we can also see that the latter is bigger in area and with a much larger population. Therefore, it is not unreasonable to assume that there were far more knur and spell players in England than there were colf and kolf players in the Netherlands. What is more, the knur and spell players spoke the same language as the people in the Lothians and were only a few miles away from Scotland just over the English border. With only a few lusty blows they could have driven a wooden or staghorn knur well into Scotland with their hand-made pummels! To my mind the average Scot would have known far more about knur and spell than he knew about colf or kolf at least from the 1600s onwards and probably even earlier than that!

The comparison we have just done between Danelaw England and the Netherlands is based on how these two areas look today in 2019. We should not forget that back in the 1500 and 1600s, and earlier, the Netherlands looked nothing like it does today. The Spanish name for the Netherlands is *los Países Bajos* (the Low Countries). Much of the Low Countries was completely under water in those days and another big chunk was marshy, boggy land. The country has long been in a continual battle over many centuries against inundation from the North Sea. It is also located in the delta area of three river systems, the Rhine, the Meuse and the Schelde. As such it is also prone to flooding. Since the 1200s or maybe even a bit earlier, the Dutch have been reclaiming vast areas of land from the sea. The reclaimed land is called a polder and they control the water level using a system of dikes and canals. In the early days they used windmills to pump the water around. These days they use pumping stations and sluices to control the water. There are over three thousand polders in the Netherlands. The biggest polder is about five hundred and forty square kilometres, but the average polder size is only five square kilometres. A high percentage of modern Netherlands lies below sea level and most of the rest of it is below ten metres above sea level. Back in the Rembrandt days (about 1650) the actual dry land area of northern Netherlands was about twenty-five per cent less than it is today and, besides this, much of the country would have also been very marshy and quite unsuitable for playing colf. In the 1550-1700 period there was a very big increase in the urbanisation rate of the coastal cities such as Amsterdam and Rotterdam. Those places would have been very overcrowded with polders, dikes, canals and windmills everywhere. Space would have been at a premium as the rapid process of urbanisation took place. They would not have been ideal places to play the long form colf. This could perhaps help to explain the rise of the short form kolf which needed less space? Although the amount of dry land in the Netherlands is significantly more in 2019 than it was in the 1500s, golf played there today is far less than in the other big European golf playing countries, both in absolute terms and on a per capita basis.

	Population (millions)	Number of Golf Courses
England	56.0	2270
Sweden	10.23	62
Scotland	5.5	614
Ireland	5.0	494
Denmark	5.8	346
Netherlands	17.3	330

These figures were taken from the *Golf Around the World 2019 R&A Report*. How reliable these stats are may be questionable. The number of courses in any country varies considerably depending on which source is used. e.g. the Netherlands figure varied from only sixty-five to three hundred and thirty. England varied from eighteen hundred to two thousand five hundred.

The only thing we can say for sure is that no matter which statistical source is used Netherlands always come way down the list. In fact even the tiny country (principality) of Andorra in the Pyrenees, with only seventy-seven thousand people, has almost seven times more golf courses per capita than the Netherlands!

Apart from the rapid urbanisation process, which was happening in the Netherlands at that time, we should maybe also mention the thing which most people think about when they think of the Netherlands and Holland in particular. i.e. tulips from Amsterdam! (Good old Max Bygraves!) Tulips had been imported into the Netherlands from Turkey in the late 1500s. By the early 1600s the country had gone berserk about tulips and the infamous Tulip Mania so-called bubble occurred in 1637. Prior to 1637 the old smoke and mirrors trick had been the order of the day. Much like the 'dot. com' shambles in the late 1900s and maybe like the 'bitcoin fad' which is all the rage today. Ridiculous prices were being paid in the marketplace for things which had nothing substantial behind them. This was a big part of what was happening in the Netherlands at the time golf was starting to rear its head in Scotland. This may have been yet another reason why land to play colf on was becoming less available during that era.

Despite the Tulip Mania collapse in 1637, today in modern Netherlands, the flower market is still a very big industry. These days the majority of the big tulip fields are situated in Flevoland which is land that was entirely reclaimed from the massive Zuiderzee inland sea. All of this land is at least six metres below sea-level. It is interesting to note that there are at least four hundred and fifty known shipwrecks scattered around this immense re-claimed land area.

To get an idea about just how significant the flower growing and bulb business in the Netherlands is, when it comes to the availability of land for golf courses, just consider this. The Netherlands is the number one producer of flowers and bulbs in the world. They have about fifty-two per cent of the global market which is worth many billions of dollars to them. In 2019 over three million acres of land in Holland is used just for flower and bulb production. The size of an average 18-hole golf course is about one hundred and fifty acres. Thus the Dutch flower and bulb acreage alone would be enough land to build 20,000 golf courses!

For the Netherlands it doesn't end with them being the world's biggest flower and bulb producers. They are also the world's second largest producer by value behind the USA of most other agricultural products as well. This is absolutely incredible when we note that the Netherlands only have about forty-one thousand square kilometres of land and the USA has close to ten million square kilometres. They achieve this amazing output by growing most things in greenhouses where they drastically reduce the need to fertilisers and pesticides etc and also ensure extremely efficient water usage.

Of course all the above takes no account of Dutch Farmers golf (Boerengolf) which was started by a Dutch cheese farmer in 1999 at his farm in the small village of Lievelde. This game is quite different to Swiss Farmer's golf (hornussen). It is played with just one 'golf stick' which has a head shaped like a Dutch clog and is played with a big, six-inch-diameter rubber ball. It is played on ordinary farmland and uses bucket size holes over a ten-hole course. Expensive course maintenance does not apply. However, penalty strokes are incurred if you hit a cow with your ball! In the past twenty years this game has grown much faster in the Netherlands than regular golf. It is an organised sport with structure and competitive leagues throughout the country. There are now about twice as many registered places in the Netherlands where this game can be played than there are golf courses. It has also spread to other neighbouring European countries such as Belgium, Germany, Sweden, Austria, France etc.

In one of his write-ups, Geert Nijs shows a map of places in Holland where he found colf to have been played when at its peak. If I were to try to produce a similar map of the Danelaw area of England where knur and spell was played at its peak it would take me years to compose. Knur and spell was played over a much bigger area, in hundreds or even thousands of more places and by considerably more players. I concur with the point Geert Nijs makes about the places he shows not being the only places where colf was played. i.e. they were just the places where he found written evidence about the game. Exactly the same applies to the game of knur and spell in Danelaw England. I personally know of many places where it was played which didn't appear in the press. In fact, if I were to hazard a complete guess, I would think that the Danelaw knur and spell players at their peak would have outnumbered all the early English / Scottish golfers and Dutch colf players put together!

The big difference between colf in Holland and knur and spell in northern England during those early years was the kind of people who were playing these games. Colf in Holland during the 1500s and 1600s seems to have been played by gentlemen. To garner this kind of information we just need to look at the way the players in the old Dutch paintings were dressed. They were generally very well dressed. They could afford to commission the paintings which the Dutch Masters were churning out. This was the Golden Age for the wealthy Dutch.

In all European countries at that time there would have been far more poor people than rich people. However, it would generally only have been mostly the rich people who featured in the paintings etc. The number of paintings and drawings of knur and spell players in northern England which have surfaced are very few. This is despite the fact that there were probably far more knur and spell players in northern England than there were colf players in Holland. Unfortunately, they didn't have the casherooney to pay for fancy paintings!

One thing which Geert Nijs and I fully agree on is just how small the game of golf in Scotland was until after the guttie ball appeared on the scene. He came up with an estimate of not more than five hundred players between 1750 and 1850. I have assumed that this number would be his estimate of golfers associated with an actual club or a golfing society because it would be impossible to know how many Jocks had a stick and a ball and who just had the odd *ad hoc* bash around the links or up and down paddocks which didn't have holes and flags (which I myself have done on many occasions). If we add thirty or forty Blackheath (BHGC) members in about 1830 to this total plus ten or twelve at the original Manchester GC, we can see that the eleven hundred golfers playing at Dum Dum GC in Calcutta around that time (as reported to BHGC by Major Playfair himself and mentioned in the *Blackheath Chronicles*) easily made India the biggest golf playing nation in the world! I say that tongue in cheek because very few, if any, of the eleven hundred players in India would have been wealthy Indians. Most would have been ex-patriot employees of the British East India Company. This was a massive English company headquartered in London which even had its own army. They employed large numbers of Scots. In 1800, around ten percent of the company's civil servants were Scots, at least fifty per cent of their soldiers and one third of their officers. For about one hundred years between 1757 and 1858 this company virtually ruled India. At one point over a quarter of a million soldiers were employed by the company in their private army. It is quite easy to envisage that there was more golf played in India than in Scotland during those days. Most of the ex-pats in India were 'living the life of Riley' with servants and *punkah-wallahs* etc. They would have been financially much better off and much better able to afford playing golf than most of the general Scottish population still living in Scotland. Of course, after 1850 the number of golf clubs and courses in Scotland started to increase sharply when the guttie ball came on the scene.

With eleven hundred golfers playing golf in India in the 1830s and 1840s it is obvious that they would have needed lots of featherie golf balls. Whether this supply of balls were all imported from their Scottish homeland, or whether the enterprising Indian entrepreneurs would have started to make featherie golf balls, with their very cheap labour costs, I don't know. This may be something worth further investigation. If these balls were supplied from Scotland, and presumably golf clubs too, then such a high demand at that time would have been a big shot in the arm for the Scottish club and ball makers, because for the period extending from the end of the 1700s to at least 1830, golf in Scotland had been floundering.

While we are talking about the Netherlands, I should briefly mention another game which is still played today in Frisia called *klootscheiten* which can also be traced back to the 1600s or earlier. It has nothing directly to do with either golf or knur and spell, but it is another very old ball game. It has been played with iron balls and maybe earlier with flintstone balls. It is played along remote country lanes. The players bowl the ball as far as they can. The contest can be the longest single bowl wins, or more commonly they can nominate a location several miles away and the winner is the one to reach that place in the least amount of bowls. In other words, it is similar to how both golf and knur and spell started but without the stick. Maybe golf / colf / knur and spell evolved out of this game? *Klootscheiten* translates as 'ball shooting'.

The reason why this game is interesting to me is because, when I was a young boy in the 1940s, my father played a very similar game in Lancashire called 'road-bowling'. This game was probably also played in other northern counties. I never saw dad play knur and spell, but he often played road-bowling. I heard from other old people in the village that he was apparently very good at this game. He was a blacksmith with a strong arm! Apart from having a strong arm, the skill of the game was trying to keep the stone on the road surface as long as possible. Players tried to prevent the bowl from running into the grassy ditches on either side of the road and negotiating bends in the road was where the greatest skill was needed. Generally, they used an under-arm bowl but occasionally they would also bowl over-arm depending on the camber in the road etc. In Lancashire they didn't use a ball. They used a hard stone which had been fashioned into the shape of a small tyre or do-nut, but solid without the hole in the middle. It was about the size of a thick Eccles cake! I don't know which kind of stone these bowls were made from. They were very hard and were probably made from flintstone, granite or millstone grit. The hardness probably came from the quartz content (chemically silicon dioxide). From memory, I think the stones would have been about ten centimetres diameter and about four to five centimetres thick with rounded / bevelled edges but don't hold me to these measurements. I probably haven't seen dad's bowling stone for about seventy years. Like knur and spell, it was also a game associated strongly with drinking and gambling and the Northern English pub scene. They were always on the lookout for anyone in authority, so I guess it was illegal to play this game on public roads. This game disappeared a long time ago in Lancashire, but I understand that road-bowling is still played and flourishes in Ireland in 2019.

In late 2019 I had the great pleasure of meeting with Jack Greenwood at the Trawden Community Centre 'old farts club'. Jack was into his nineties by that time. Over the years he has published several fantastic books of old Trawden photos. In one of those books, *Trawden Another Glance*, he included a photo of five old bowling stones which also had a twelve-inch ruler as a reference point. All five stones were different sizes. They were all smaller than what I had remembered. Diameters ranged from about five and a half centimetres to almost seven centimetres. The only reasons I can come up with to explain these different sizes are the following. Firstly there was probably no regulation in this sport governing the initial size and weight of these stones when new. Secondly, with frequent use, the stones would without doubt abrade slightly as they came into contact with the rough road surface which generally would have been a bitumen layer with small stone chippings embedded into it using a rolling technique when the bitumen was still hot and semi-molten. So the older the stone, the smaller it would become.

A very good account of the game still played in Ireland can be found in a book written by Fintan Lane called *Long Bullets - A History of Road Bowling in Ireland*. Fintan is a Cork-born historian. He has traced the game back at least to the 1700s and he believes that it was brought to Ireland by British (Lancashire) weavers who migrated there. The Colne, Nelson and Trawden area where my dad played was dominated by cotton mills in those days. Apparently, the Irish play with a twenty-eight-ounce iron ball. This is much heavier than the kind of donut shaped stone bowl which my dad used in the 1930s and 1940s in Lancashire. My best guess is that this may have weighed eight ounces maximum. Although this may seem like a very big weight difference between the Irish and Lancastrian balls, the size of both balls would have been approximately the same. Both of them would fit comfortably into an adult hand. The reason for this is the big difference in specific gravity between cast iron and millstone grit sandstone. Cast iron ranges from 7.0 – 7.13. Millstone grit ranges from 2.0 – 2.6 depending on the degree of porosity in the sandstone. Thus if dad's bowling stone had been made of cast iron it may have also weighed 27 -28 ounces.

There is a chance that road-bowling in Lancashire may have been adapted from the Dutch game of *klootscheiten*. The textile industry in Lancashire had been going long before the Industrial Revolution started. Hundreds of years before factory mechanisation and mass production of textiles (both cotton and woollen) started to appear in the late 1700s, there was a widespread cottage industry of hand-loom weavers in Lancashire and other northern counties. They had been there at least since the 1300 and 1400s and probably earlier. Many of these hand-loom weavers were small holding farmers who combined both occupations. They are thought to have originally arrived there from Flanders which is the Dutch speaking area of modern-day Belgium. In about 1350 Edward **III**, the Plantagenet king of England, had banned the export of wool to Flanders. He wanted the English to weave their own cloth and to support this he encouraged Flemish weavers to migrate to Manchester and other surrounding towns. It turned out that Lancashire had an ideal climate for spinning and weaving natural fibres...the key factor being the favourable relative humidity. It is also quite possible that a further wave of weavers from the Flanders area arrived later when the Spanish were persecuting religious protestant dissidents in the Low Countries during the Spanish Inquisition.

In the early days they only used small amounts of cotton in their cloth production. Mostly they made linens (flax), woollens and fustian. The latter was a cloth which had a linen warp thread and a cotton weft. i.e. linen going along the length of the cloth and cotton going across it. These hand-loom weavers eventually achieved notoriety in history as the infamous Luddites when in 1811 - 1812 they tried to oppose the new automated weaving technology for fear of losing their livelihoods. They also gave a new word to the English dictionary, 'luddite', which refers to anyone who opposes new technology.

For anyone interested in finding more detailed information about these Dutch speaking weavers in Lancashire there are great sources of information...*University of York, The National Archives and the Humanities Research Institute, University of Sheffield.* In 1440 the English Parliament ordered a census of all non-English-born residents. This census included their names, their countries of origins and their occupations. There were about twenty thousand foreign residents on this list which accounted for approximately one per cent of the total English population at the time. They were of course spread throughout England and came from all over the place between the mid-1300s and the mid-1500s. The purpose of this census was ostensibly so that the government could levy a new tax on the foreigners to help the country pay for the high cost of the Hundred Year's War with France which was just coming to an end. Apart from all the detailed information about what these migrants were doing, where they had come from and where they had settled, these old tax records also must give a very good indication about how they had been received by the English born people. Multi-culturalism was obviously well and truly in vogue in medieval England! It is interesting to note that even in 1901, four hundred and fifty years later, the number of non-English born residents in England was still only hovering around the one per cent mark.

Fast forward to 2020 and we find that about fifteen per cent of the UK population were not born there. Just like here in Australia, I can go into some suburbs in England, and I can't even read the signs in many of the shop windows. They are written in Pakistani or Vietnamese or some other language with a completely different alphabet, so I can't even make a guess at what they are selling. I expect to have that problem if I am strolling around Islamabad or Saigon but not if I am trying to find a coffee in a small village on the outskirts of Bradford in my own country. I suppose we call it multi-culturalism. As I write this section I have been bunkered down at home for several months, self-isolating and physically distancing, on account of something called corona virus. I guess this is yet another benefit from multi-culturalism and globalisation? It may be interesting to note that at least two-thirds of this fifteen per cent figure has occurred since 1968 which was the year when Conservative MP Enoch Powell made his infamous anti-immigration speech in Birmingham UK. So for nineteen hundred years it never got past one per cent. In the next fifty years it got to about five per cent and in the last fifty years it has already reached fifteen per cent. Is this a good thing or a bad thing? Either way, we can say for sure that the world is now more or less unrecognisable from the pre-1968 days! It seems to me that in future, as cultures disappear or at best get severely diluted, there will not be any multi-culturalism...only one boring mono-culture, which will bear no resemblance whatsoever to any of the original cultures. I wonder if that mono-culture will turn out to be one of the existing cultures which has emerged and grown to dominate all other cultures. God forbid!

I don't suppose that reading the shop signs would have been a big issue for Enoch Powell. He already spoke thirteen languages and even at the time he died he was learning yet another language...Hebrew. This may indicate that he must have had quite a keen interest in other peoples' cultures, even though he was anti-immigration. In his early life, before WW2, he had probably been the youngest ever professor at an Australian university (Sydney) when he became professor of Greek at age twenty-five. Not bad for an Englishman who had Welsh ancestry. Apart from anti-immigration, Enoch was also very strongly against the UK going into the European Union. In 2020 he would have been looking down with a smile on his face. He had been a member of the UK Conservative Party for almost thirty years when he resigned in 1974 mostly because the Tory PM Ted Heath had taken Britain into the EU without a mandate from the people.

One of the frequently used Colne and Nelson road-bowling 'tracks' was a two mile stretch of country lane starting at the Shooters Arms near the tiny hamlet of Catlow Bottoms and ending at the Coldwell Inn. Catlow Bottoms has a very long history going back to at least the Bronze age. The Shooters is on a hillside above Nelson very close to Marsden Park public golf course where my early golfing 'talent' developed in the late 1950s. Son Jonathan and I played a few games there in the summer of 2017. It is also only about half a mile away from the Castercliff Hillfort ruins which predates the Roman occupation of Britain. A very good summary of the Roman history in and around Colne is given in *The Annals of Colne and Neighbourhood* by James Carr (1878). The Coldwell Inn was on a remote backroad which eventually goes over Widdop Moor past Hardcastle Crags to Hebden Bridge and Halifax. There are dozens of tiny hamlets in this general area where knur and spell was also played. Pecket Well which is two miles outside Hebden Bridge is one such hamlet. This tiny village, also close to Halifax, hit the national UK headlines in 1920 when a coach load of thirty-two knur and spell supporters from there crashed near Oxenhope en route to watch a knur and spell match in Laneshawbridge. There were several fatalities. In October 2020, the *Keighley News* ran a tribute to the five people who had lost their lives to commemorate the 100th anniversary of the tragedy. The five, which included a married couple and three men, were all from Wadsworth. The article included an old photograph of the decimated open-topped charabanc. All thirty-two fans were patrons of the Robin Hood Inn at Pecket Well. This pub, which had undergone major renovation in the 1800s, had been a coaching inn from the 1600s. It is still in operation in 2021.

The Shooters Arms also still exists today. It has been there since about the year 1660 and earlier had been called the Shooters Inn. I had a beer there with my son Jonathan in 2017 just after we had completed our epic eight- or nine-hundred-kilometre trudge across the Pyrenees from St Jean Pied de Port in France to Santiago de Compostela and Fisterra in Galicia on the French Camino. The Coldwell is now a charity-run activity centre close to Thursden Valley. Jonathan and I walked past it during one of our pre-Camino training hikes which had involved climbing the nearby Boulsworth Hill in the South Pennines. *En route* to Boulsworth we had passed through the very old hamlet of Wycoller which existed before the tenth century. As kids, my younger brother Richard and I spent many happy hours playing in the beck there tickling trout. Rick was always much more adept at this particular pastime than I. The ruins of Wycoller Hall can still be seen. This Hall was built in the 1500s and is believed to have been the inspiration for *Ferndean Manor* which Charlotte Brontë wrote about in her famous *Jane Eyre* novel in 1847.

The vicarage where the Brontës lived in the village of Haworth, and is now a museum, is about ten miles away. The famous sixty-nine-kilometre Brontë Way which starts at Oakwell Hall in Birstall, Leeds and ends at Gawthorpe Hall in Padiham is one of Britain's many walking tracks. It passes through the tiny hamlet of Wycoller. Today Wycoller has a population of about fifty. At its peak in the early 1800s about three hundred and fifty lived there ... mostly hand-loom weavers and farmers. According to John Bentley's *Portrait of Wycoller*, in 1557, a large crowd of men, including John and Peter Hartley of Wycoller, were fined for playing at the prohibited game of scoles. I have no idea what 'scoles' was all about. However, it does confirm that illegal sports playing was happening in this area in the 1500s. The court records for the Halmote of Colne show that the first Inquistion of the Forest of Trawden was held in May 1510. After the White Swan pub was built in about 1716, the Colne Halmote Court was held there for over two hundred years. This pub was eventually demolished in 1938. The Court Rolls for the Manor of Colne which includes the Forest of Trawden date to at least 1425 and are held in Clitheroe Castle. Halmote Courts were in fact a Saxon legacy and therefore pre-dated the Vikings. They administered both criminal and civil cases.

Several vaccaries for cattle breeding already existed in Trawden in 1323. A very good insight into the early game playing and other 'naughty' activities throughout England is also given by Marjorie Kenniston McIntosh's book *Controlling Misbehaviour in England 1370 – 1600*. I suspect that many of the illegal games at that time were much more widespread than what we are given to believe by written accounts. People who played these games did so under the fear of retribution or punishment. Consequently they didn't make a song and dance about their game playing. They kept a low profile and indeed made every effort to conceal their game playing and NOT to be seen.

Knur and spell, pidgeon shooting, rabbit coursing and starling shooting were also very old sports associated with both the Shooters Arms and the Coldwell Inn. Pidgeon shooting was a particularly big money sport in England in the 1800s. In 1860 there was a two-man shoot held in Birmingham for four hundred pounds. This would equate to about forty-nine thousand pounds purchasing power in 2019! However, I suspect that road-bowling was maybe even older than knur and spell. It seems to me more logical that a game which just involved propelling a stone by hand would have evolved before they had the idea of using an implement to hit it with. Rabbit coursing was older than any of these other games. It was a very big sport throughout England and Scotland in the 1800s which attracted very large crowds of spectators and big numbers of participants. For instance in 1879 the Open golf championship was held at St Andrews GC and attracted just forty-seven entries who were probably all Scotsmen. In the same year, according to the *Shields Daily Gazette*, just about one hundred and eighty miles away at a small place called Hebburn on the south bank of the River Tyne in Northumberland, a small nondescript rabbit coursing event attracted seventy-four entries. There were hundreds of rabbit coursing events taking place all over England in 1879. The Hebburn meet would have been one of the smaller events! Quite often rabbit coursing and knur and spell would both be on the same pub programme played on the same day and some men would enter both events. There would have even been more snakes and ladders players in the world in 1879 than there were golfers. Snakes and ladders evolved from the very ancient game of *Moksha Patam* which has been played in India since the second century.

The Coldwell Inn was quite isolated on the edge of the moors. It was notorious for any games which lent themselves to gambling. Road bowling, knur and spell, cock fighting, rabbit coursing, pitch and toss etc. In the late 1700s and early 1800s it was used by travellers who were taking their cloth by packhorse from the hand-loom weavers in Colne and surrounding hamlets over the moors to the famous Halifax Piece Hall. This massive ten thousand square yard quadrangular building had been built in 1779 as a Cloth Hall where the hand-loom weavers could trade their wares.

I am not clear why the hand-loom weavers around the Colne and Trawden area would make the long packhorse trip over the moors to Halifax because Colne had its own Piece Hall. It was opened in August 1775 which was four years before Halifax and only five years after Captain Cook arrived in Botany Bay. In fact even as early as 1731 there was a newspaper report that the 'free-sale' of linen cloths were being sold at the Cloth Hall in Colne during Fair time. So maybe the 1775 Piece Hall was just a bigger and better one. Colne Piece Hall changed its name back to Colne Cloth Hall in 1810. Maybe it was because the Colne Piece Hall was originally dealing in woollen and worsted fabrics such as shalloons and calimancoes? From the early 1800s it mostly dealt just in cotton fabrics as the cotton industry took off. Colne Cloth Hall was bulldozed and demolished in 1953 which was the year of Queen Elizabeth **II**'s coronation. The only thing remaining from the old Cloth Hall building in Colne is part of its bell tower which can still be seen close to St Bartholomew's Church in Colne which was originally built in the 1200s.

When they were involved in all their illegal activities, the Coldwell Inn always employed plenty of guys to keep a watch out for any policemen in the area. For a long time, they managed to keep one step ahead of the law. Eventually, in the early 1900s, the police organised a massive raid on the pub with over one hundred policemen. It was interesting to note that those arrested were not just poor working men. Some doctors, solicitors and dentists were also amongst the ones nabbed. Gambling and alcohol addictions don't discriminate between rich and poor men! Of course, the raid may have slowed things down for a while, but it didn't stop them. This raid had been carried out when my dad was just a baby or maybe even before he was born. By the time he was young man it was already 'business as usual' again at the Coldwell Inn!

When dad played road-bowling in the 1940s there would have been very few cars on all the country lanes around Colne and Nelson. As a young boy in the late 1940s I remember that we used to play cricket all day in the main street in Trawden village. In summer, the days were very long. At ten o'clock in the evening there was still daylight. If we saw two or three cars pass through the village in a day that would have been a record number. Those cars would have belonged to the rich cotton mill owners. In fact the first car ever seen in the village of Trawden in the very early 1900s was a Belgian made Minerva which had been bought in Manchester by a local Trawden mill owner. This was a luxury vehicle almost in the Rolls Royce class but at a cheaper price. Cars had been around from the early 1900s, but they were generally only bought by wealthy individuals and mostly seen in the big cities and not so often in remote country villages like Trawden. Just before World War II in 1939 only about one person in three hundred in the UK owned a car. It was early to mid-1950s before dad was able to buy his first car, a second-hand lime green Austin A40 Devon (FFR 542) with a column gear change, by which time he would have been already in his thirties. This was the car I passed my first driving test in. After that dad had a few different Saab 96 cars which were powered by 841 cc three-cylinder two-stroke engines. Although it was like driving a little sewing machine, I still thought that I was Erik Carlsson the Sub-African

Safari car rally champion, haring around the local country lanes near the village. Sixty years earlier, in 1880, the police were already hounding road-bowlers for illegally playing the sport on the road, even though cars hadn't yet been invented! The *Burnley Gazette* December 1880 reported on two men charged at Colne Petty Sessions with bowling stones on the highway between the Shooters and Coldwell. Even without cars it could apparently still be a dangerous game. In 1888 the *Burnley Gazette* reported that a Trawden man called Charles Bannister, who lived in Smithy Lane, had mysteriously died in an accident while playing road bowls up Job Lane in Trawden. Maybe he had copped an errant road bowl on the noggin? The coronial inquest for Mr Bannister was held at the Black Rock Inn in May 1888. Smithy Lane eventually underwent a name change in the late 1800s and became Church Street where I used to live and where my ninety-six years old mother still lives in 2019. I don't know if Charles Bannister was related to the Ralph / Roger Bannister clan, but he certainly lived in the same street around the same time. Don't bother looking for Job Lane on a current map either. In 2019 the old Trawdeners like myself still talk about Job Lane as if it still existed even though its name was probably changed to Burnley Road in the 1800s!

The other thing to note about those days is that just because cars hadn't been invented yet didn't mean that you couldn't get a speeding ticket! In 1884 the *Preston Herald* newspaper reported that the landlord of the Red Lion pub in Colne had been summoned before the magistrate charged with 'furious driving' of his horse drawn buggy on the three mile stretch between Colne and Laneshawbridge. He could even have been returning from a knur and spell contest which were commonplace events in Laneshawbridge in the late 1880s and early 1900s at the Alma Inn, the Emmott Arms, or the Hargreaves Arms over Monkroyd. Needless to say that we never called it Laneshawbridge. To locals it was always pronounced 'Lansherbrig'. Apart from speeding tickets you were just as likely to get a parking fine! In the *Burnley Gazette* of September 1874 two men were summoned for allowing their horses and carts to stand on the highway near the Commercial Inn which still stands in Colne's main street. Fundraising in the nineteenth century was already in vogue just as it is today!

Using a shaped stone as the centre point of a game was not restricted to the Lancashire road-bowlers. The Scots had been using a large stone for one of their main leisure activities from at least the mid-1500s in the very old game of curling. Curling is still a big sport in Scotland in 2019 and indeed all around the world. In fact today there are more curling clubs in Scotland (593) than there are golf clubs (550). It is also an Olympic sport. We also know from Dutch Masters paintings that curling was also played in the Netherlands in the 1500s. However, there is no suitable granite source in Holland so maybe the Dutch copied this game from the Scots?

The curling stone and the Lancashire road-bowling stone are roughly the same shape. The big difference is in the size and weight. Curling stones are in the thirty-eight to forty-four pounds range whereas the Lancashire stones would have been less than one pound. The Lancashire stone was effectively a miniature curling stone without the handle. The other big difference was in the way the stones were used. The curling stone is propelled by sliding on its side across the ice, but the Lancashire stone is bowled on its edge and rolled along the road like a small tyre or wheel. Although I can only guess what the Lancashire bowl was made from, I can say for certain that curling stones are definitely made from granite. There are only two sources of suitable granite in the world. One is in Scotland and the other is in Wales. About sixty per cent of the world's curling stones are made with granite from the small rocky island of Ailsa Craig which lies about twelve miles off the Ayrshire coast from the Trump Turnberry GC, twenty-six miles from Prestwick GC and twenty-seven miles from Troon GC. Three different types of granite come from this island. All of them can be used to produce curling stones but the blue variety is generally accepted as being the best quality. Ailsa Craig is uninhabited. The stones are all manufactured at a small village called Mauchline which is about eleven miles east of Prestwick GC. The curling stones are polished when finished but the Lancashire road bowls were probably matt finished. No point in a polished finish because the tarmac road surface would very quickly have destroyed the polished surface! In fact in the 1800s maybe many of those roads were not even sealed.

Before the Ailsa granite had become the standard in the early 1800s, granite from other Scottish sources had been used to make curling stones at umpteen different villages throughout the Scottish Lowlands. For more than three hundred- and fifty-years curling had been a winter sport which was played on frozen ponds and lakes. These days it is a year-round sport after the first artificially frozen ice rink (based on natural ice) opened in London in early 1876. The first long lasting artificial rink opened in Glasgow in 1907. Australians will be pleased to learn that indirectly they had an input into the development of ice rinks. The refrigeration process used to make the rinks was initially found by a guy in London who was trying to find a way he could import frozen meat into England from Australia and New Zealand.

I doubt very much that the Lancashire bowling stones were made from granite or flint because there is very little of these stones in Lancashire or Yorkshire. Most of the old rocks there are either sandstone or limestone. Flint is a type of chert and is a polycrystalline quartz. Some nodules of chert would be found in the limestone of Yorkshire, but flint is usually found in chalk deposits so would need to come from other areas of England. My best guess is that the road bowling stones were made from millstone grit which is a coarse-grained sandstone formed in the Carboniferous Age over three hundred million years ago. There are many thousands of miles of dry-stone walls in Lancashire around all the farmers' fields and most of these would have been made with locally quarried millstone grit. Dry-stone walls go back a very long way. There was not much done by the Anglo-Saxons, but the Vikings were very prolific wall builders. Apart from the walls, millstone grit was also used for gate posts, animal drinking troughs and maybe very relevantly for cornmill grinding stones. Bear in mind that if a curling stone was about forty times heavier than a Lancashire bowling stone, then a typical cornmill grinding stone was about eighty times heavier than a curling stone! This reminds me that the Old Stone Trough public house at Kelbrook on the main road from Colne to Skipton was a frequent venue for knur and spell matches when I was a boy. This pub got its name in 1824 after new turnpike roads had been built. Prior to that it had still been a pub which for many years was called the Wilson Arms.

Millstone grit deposits are abundant throughout Yorkshire and Lancashire. Apart from the large size cornmill grinding stones which could weigh up to fifteen hundred kilos each, the same type of stone had been used in this area, for hundreds if not thousands of years, to make much smaller hand-operated grinding stones known as quern-stones. i.e. long before the Romans invaded Britain. Quernmore Crag near Lancaster and Whernside in the Yorkshire Dales are two places which readily spring to mind. Another very famous one in Yorkshire is at Wharncliffe Crags which is a few miles north-west of Sheffield in the vicinity of Deepcar and Stocksbridge which is in very strong knur and spell playing heartland. The latter was a very major quern-stone production site which now has National Heritage protection following a serious moorland fire which had destroyed a large section of the area in 1996 and revealed thousands of abandoned quern-stones which had previously never been seen.

I don't know where my dad got his bowling stone from. I have no recollection of him making it himself although being a blacksmith probably means that he would have had the tools and the skill to do it. Maybe there was a cottage industry of stone bowl makers in the local villages just as there was for wooden knurs used in knur and spell?

The Irish road bowlers use a cast iron ball. The early *klootscheiten* players also used a cast iron ball which was between five- and eight-centimetres diameter and weighed about two pounds (thirty-two ounces). Thus the Irish and the early Dutch balls used were about the same weight. The other name for the game in Ireland, 'long bullets', tells us where these balls originated. They would have been versions of cannon balls used in medieval warfare. Gunpowder was invented about 1000 AD. Guns arrived in the mid-1300s. Iron or lead cannon balls were first used in the 1300 and 1400s. Before cast iron cannon balls, the 'round shot' in guns and cannons had been made from stone (granite). Even in the 1600s some stone balls were still being fired from cannons.

Because the Irish / early Dutch balls were cast iron and the Lancashire bowls were stone, it may suggest that the Irish game really came from the Dutch and not from the weavers of Lancashire. Also since the Lancashire bowlers used a small wheel shape rather than a ball shape which was made from stone and not iron, this may suggest that their game was the older. Afterall, the Iron Age was several hundred years BC, but the Stone Age was several thousand years BC. It may also be significant that the Dutch game is called *klootscheiten*. *Kloot* sounds to be very similar to the English word 'clout' which was mentioned earlier when archery was discussed, and which is thought to have come from the Viking word 'clud'. The Vikings could hold the key to many things. As mentioned earlier they were responsible for a great many of the drystone walls still found today all over the north of England. Also remember that *klootscheiten* is still mainly played today in Frisia where at one time the Vikings were in charge! The Vikings, through Halfen's son, were in Frisia as early as 807 AD. They steadily gained traction through Rorik in the mid-800s until the death of his successor, Godfrid, in 885 AD. During this period they also had a strong connection to England. We also know from one of the oldest surviving pieces of Old English literature, the Anglo-Saxon written *Beowulf* poem, that the Vikings had been plundering Frisia as early as the mid-500s. What a pity that the Vikings themselves were not literary giants. They left very little written evidence and we have been kept guessing about so many things.

Chapter 3

Put it in writing

The big problem linking any of these games to the golf played in Scotland is providing documentary evidence. The first actual golf club in Scotland, generally accepted to be the Honourable Company of Edinburgh Golfers, which evolved into the current day Muirfield GC, was established in 1744. We also know from the Carnoustie GC website that they formed in 1839 and claim to be the oldest artisan golf club in the world. However, we already know that golf in some form or another was around in Scotland in the 1400s played in an unstructured ad hoc manner. So, any games which golf may have emanated from had to be shown that they were around before that date. It then had to be shown that the Scots had seen or at least heard of those games.

Coming up with documentary evidence for anything prior to about 1500 is not easy. In 1500, Britain was essentially an illiterate country with ninety per cent of all men and one hundred per cent of women being unable to read or write. This had not always been the case. In fact, after the Romans invaded Britain in 43 AD the literacy in England improved to quite a high level. Unfortunately, after the Romans withdrew in 410 AD, the place went to the dogs, and by 1500 AD the *hoi polloi* were virtually illiterate. Please excuse the perceived tautology used in *the hoi polloi*. I do know that in Greek the word 'hoi' means 'the' but I think it sounds better that way. When I think of it, I still refer to an ATM (automatic telling machine) as an ATM machine! Incidentally, ATMs in some form or other have been around since before 1970 but in 2019 I have still managed to survive quite well without ever using one! However, I must confess that as ATM's are gradually being replaced by the 'Tap and Go' system, I have succumbed to this latest technology. I must also admit that my silent protest against ATMs, which had started because my wife Kathleen was a bank teller before she retired, has been fairly meaningless!

Between 410 AD and 1500 AD literacy in England was mostly limited to churchmen. When the famous *Magna Carta* was drawn up in 1215 AD for King John, it was drafted by the Archbishop of Canterbury and/or his lackeys. A few decades earlier, when King William **I** ordered the *Domesday Book* it was also prepared by churchmen. Both these documents were written in Latin which was the *lingua franca* in that period. The 800th Anniversary of the signing of the *Magna Carta* was held in Lincoln Castle in 2015 where one of the four original copies is held. Kathleen and I were lucky enough to visit Lincoln that year and saw this awesome piece of world history. Lincoln Castle is also the home of another even more game changing document. i.e. King Henry **III**'s *Charter of the Forest* from 1217 which was also written in Latin. Lincoln Castle is the only place in the world where both these documents can be seen in the same place. This Charter was abolished by the dastardly UK Conservative government in 1971 after serving the common people well for over seven hundred and fifty years. The castle was built before the year 1100 by William the Conqueror not long after he had ousted the Vikings from the city of Lincoln.

The *Domesday Book* had a very big impact going forward. It looked as if it was just a big tax audit of England. In reality it was much more than that. It facilitated a massive transfer of land ownership from the English to the Normans. It allowed King William to legally gift all his lords and barons security of tenure over the lands he had bestowed on them. Effectively it gave William total control of all England.

Thank goodness things started to change quickly after 1500. German Johannes Gutenberg had invented his printing press in 1440 and Englishman William Caxton got cracking in the 1470s. The first printed book in English was in 1474. It was sold at Sotheby's auction house in 2014 by the Duke of Northumberland for just over one million pounds. Shortly after, in 1476, the *Canterbury Tales* were also printed in English. These had been written almost one hundred years earlier by Geoffrey Chaucer who is probably regarded as the Father of English Literature. Only ten confirmed original copies of the *Canterbury Tales* are known to exist. When Chaucer was born in 1343 the two main languages in England were Latin and French. He was one of the first English poets to write in Middle English. Just about five years after Chaucer was born the Black Death plague wreaked havoc in the UK and all across Europe. He was one of the lucky ones who lived to tell the tale. In his case the *Canterbury Tale*! Chaucer operated in the south of England. If knur and spell was played when he was alive there is every chance that he would not have heard of it. Although he may well have been aware of one of the awesome stained-glass windows in Canterbury Cathedral which was thought to represent a bandy or a cambucca game. The so called 'Miracle Windows' in the Trinity Chapel are thought to have dated to about 1180 which is about two hundred years before Chaucer wrote his famous book and of course long before any golf was played in Scotland.

The first newspapers and newsletters started to appear in the early to mid-1500s. However, the first daily newspaper, the *Daily Courant,* didn't appear until it was launched in 1702 during the reign of Queen Anne. The reason that it took over two hundred years for this to happen was because up until the late 1600s there had been strong censorship whereby anything printed had to be sent to the Government censor for approval prior to printing. Only a very small number of printers were allowed, and all of these had to be appointed by the Archbishop of Canterbury or the Bishop of London. Just imagine all the bureaucracy printers would have to wade through before they could publish anything! Censorship was allowed to lapse in 1695 and soon after that things started to take off.

With these game-changing developments, the picture changed rapidly as can be seen in the following table which shows percentage illiteracy in England at the start of each century.

	Men	Women
1500	90	100
1600	70	90
1700	50	70
1800	40	60
1900	5	5
2000	1	1

Public records were not all that flash in those days. The above table is not from just one source. It is an average of figures taken from various sources. Nevertheless it gives a rough idea of how things have evolved over the past five hundred years.

The change in literacy and the advent of newspapers fuelled an even bigger change in England.

Up until 1500 the most powerful man in Europe was the Pope. There was still a feudal system operating in England with a very strict hierarchy in place. Beneath the Pope came the King. Then a big list of hangers-on including dukes, earls, barons, knights, squires, and lords before we get to the masses who were classed as peasants. After 1500 the feudal system began to change and eventually developed into what we know today.

To explain why this major change came about we can revert to the old tried and tested reason of 'cherchez la femme'. King Henry **VIII** had decided he wanted to get rid of his first wife Catherine of Aragon and bunk down with Anne Boleyn. Problem was that for the marriage to be annulled he needed the Pope's blessing. But the Pope would not play ball. Henry's right hand man, Cardinal Wolsey, the top Roman Catholic in England, failed to facilitate the annulment and ultimately paid the price. He died on his way to London where he was to be tried for 'accepting the authority of the Pope above that of the Crown'. Henry **VIII** didn't like playing second fiddle to the Pope. The English Reformation Protestants surged and by the mid-1500s the English Church had broken away from the Catholic Church. There was a brief setback when Queen Mary **I** (Bloody Mary) tried to push the Catholicism barrow and burnt two Archbishops at the stake between 1553 -1558. But along came Elizabeth **I** in 1559, the daughter of Henry **VIII** and Anne Boleyn, and fought off the Catholic challenge. The last ever Roman Catholic Archbishop of Canterbury was in 1558.

So, after 1500 it is not so much a problem to find mention in books or old newspapers about any game you care to mention. Prior to 1500 the best chance of finding documentary evidence of ancient sporting activities is either in church records, in old government records prepared by churchmen or in old paintings. The latter is an especially rich source of information.

There are many old paintings, particularly in Continental Europe, which depict what appear to be golf-like games.

After the Vikings left in 1066 there had been a resurgence of handwritten manuscripts and chronicles. Many of these have survived. They were generally written by church scholars and nearly always in Latin. The reign of King Henry **II** (1154-1189) was a productive period for biographers of famous people and chroniclers. In fact, when Henry banned English students from attending Paris University it had a beneficial effect on English learning - at least for the wealthy one per cent or less of the population. Oxford University had existed before this but after the ban came into effect it flourished. Cambridge University wasn't far behind, firing up in 1209.

One of the better-known chroniclers from that period was William Fitzstephen who died in about 1190. He wrote biographies in Latin on several famous people and about the times in general. Translations of his works have revealed that there were many different ball games and ball/stick games being played in England at that time. They were often played at Easter or at other times during the Christian calendar. He especially mentions games being played on Shrove Tuesday which was known as carnilevaria in those days. And just like modern accounts of old sports talk about them going back in history many centuries, Fitzstephen, even when he wrote in the 1100s, also talked about them going back centuries before then. At that time in history, Easter and Lent had already been celebrated for over one thousand years, so it is not inconceivable that many of the games had been played before the Vikings arrived. In John Stow's book *A Survey of London* published in 1598 he extracts much from Fitzstephen's chronicle *Description of London* written in 1173. It doesn't specifically mention knur and spell because knur and spell was not played in the London area, but it does confirm that stick and ball games were well established in Norman England at least on Shrove Tuesdays.

The above only represents a very simplistic view of what was happening during that period. Even the very definition of what constituted 'literacy' and 'illiteracy' is often questioned by the experts. Long before the printing press some people could read but they couldn't write. We do know for sure that from about 1500 onwards there was a big expansion of the English language vocabulary. This was followed in the 1600s by the first

English language dictionaries and books on pronunciation. For a far better understanding of just where the English public were during that period read Adam Fox's book *Oral and Literate Culture in England 1500-1700*.

Whether the Scots could have seen or heard about games being played in other countries is not an issue. Sailors of many nations were crossing seas and doing trade long before the Roman Empire existed. For instance, if the Chinese really did have a golf-like game called chuiwan during the Song Dynasty, news of this game could quite easily have reached Europe. The famous Silk Road trade routes between China and Europe had started during the Han Dynasty (207 BC to 220 AD) and were in operation from about 130 AD to 1453 AD. Marco Polo didn't go to China until the 1200s but Roman ambassadors had been going there since around 200 AD.

It is very conceivable that sporting activities may be mentioned in church records because many of the games which were passed down through the ages started off as church rituals. Some of these rituals had even been adopted by the Christian church from much older pagan rituals. Easter was one time when it was traditional to play games. But there were also other dates in the Christian calendar which were linked to game playing. This probably means that some of the games probably went back to older pagan cultures too. It certainly sounds as if 'paganica' as played by the Romans could have been one such game.

Since the nineteenth century the playing of games at Easter Time has been restricted to Easter Monday. However, this wasn't always the case. Back in the Middle Ages people used to take a full two weeks to celebrate Easter. It was King Alfred The Great (849-899) who decreed that people didn't need to work during the fourteen-day period surrounding Easter. Generally, people did their religious thing during the first week before Easter and their partying / game playing in the week after Easter. Gradually the partying and games time was eroded. In 1552 Parliament decided that the full week after Easter was too much. They reduced it to Easter Monday and the following day. This remained the same until sometime in the 1800s when it was further reduced to Easter Monday only.

Chapter 4

Romans, Vikings, pubs and Roger Bannister

The other way many of the games developed was through the British fascination with pubs, taverns, ale houses and the like. This part of British culture dates to the Roman invasion around the start of the first millennium (43-410 AD). When the Romans started to build roads in England they also built taverns where the marching armies could stop to rest and refresh themselves. Initially they were just wine bars but since the brewing of beer by the Celts started before the Romans arrived, they quickly got the taste for beer as well. This was verified in the 1980s when some wooden tablets were dug up at in Northumbria very close to Hadrian's Wall. These tablets showed a hand-written record of domestic and military accounts which included beer purchases by the Roman fort at Vindolanda from a local brewer. By the 1500s England was one gigantic brewery. In the 1577 census, there were fourteen thousand ale houses in England, over sixteen hundred inns and over three hundred taverns. An ale house just sold ale and beer. An inn provided bed and board as well as beer. Whereas a tavern could sell liquor as well as ale and beer. Although beer drinking had happened before the Romans arrived, it was probably the Vikings who were most responsible for the big surge in boozing in England. The word 'ale' probably came from the Danish word for beer which is 'øl'.

If anyone is in any doubt about just how boozy the English were in the 1500s we can compare the number of pubs throughout the ages adjusted for population.

1500	16,000 pubs for 3.2 million people (one pub per 200 people)
1950	70,000 pubs for 41 million people (one pub per 586 people)
2020	40,000 pubs for 56 million people (one pub per 1400 people)

It is accepted that the 1500 population estimate maybe inaccurate. The first proper Census in the UK was only conducted in 1801 and has been done every ten years after that apart from 1941 when WW2 intervened. I also accept that these figures don't necessarily mean that people are drinking less today than they did then. It probably just reflects the fact that we are buying much of our grog these days from Dan Murphy's and consuming it at home rather than being sat in the pub!

The Vindolanda museum, which I visited two years ago with my eldest son Jonathan, is an incredible place. It lies close to Hadrian's Wall and is not far from Haltwhistle, Hexham and Haydon Bridge. Apart from the writing tablets it also has a magnificent collection of old Roman leather sandals, shoes and purses which have been very well preserved in the oxygen free soil in that area and even a pair of old leather Roman boxing gloves! If leather articles under the right anaerobic soil conditions can survive at least eighteen hundred years without disintegrating, there could still be a slight chance of finding old featherie leather balls on golf courses since some of these would only be maybe less than two hundred years old. Over the last forty or fifty years of archaeological digging at Vindolanda they have uncovered thousands of leather articles in a very good state of preservation. I am not suggesting that they will find featherie golf balls at Vindolanda but maybe one of these days they will find an old *paganica* or an old *harpastum* leather ball as used by the Romans. The digging is a continual process, and they are still uncovering new artefacts just about every single day. Both these games used leather balls filled with hair. *Harpastum* used a small ball and *paganica* a larger ball. Using hair (animal or human) to fill leather balls is not all that different to the leather golf balls used by the Scots which were filled with feathers. Hair and feathers are close to being the same thing. Chemically they are both keratins (see a fuller explanation of this later).

Hadrian's Wall is about seventy-three miles long and stretches from Wallsend in the east to Bowness-on-Solway in the west. In addition to Vindolanda there are fifteen other major Roman forts along the wall and also check-points (called milecastles) every Roman mile. A Roman mile was a bit shorter than a standard English mile. There were at least ten thousand Roman soldiers and their recruits stationed across the country keeping those pesky Scots under control. The exciting finds at Vindolanda will probably represent just a tiny fragment of what is still waiting to be uncovered. Hadrian's Wall does not represent the boundary between England and Scotland. Although it is close to the actual boundary on the west side, it is over sixty miles from the boundary on the east side. It was probably built where it is because it was the shortest distance from east to west at that point.

Archaeologists may not yet have found any Roman paganica or harpastum balls near to Hadrian's Wall, but they have found some balls. In the year 207 AD the Romans were doing some repair work to Hadrian's Wall. They extracted the stone needed for this repair work from a stone quarry close to Brampton which is about two miles south of the Wall and eleven miles from Carlisle. In the 1700s archaeologists found some graffiti in a quarry at Gelt Woods depicting a large phallus complete with some impressive testicles. Apparently this phallic symbol represented good luck for the Romans in those days. There were also several Latin inscriptions at the site which gave a clear explanation of what it was all about.

Along Hadrian's Wall is not the only place in England where these suitable soil conditions can be found. Leather boots and shoes which belonged to the Vikings in the 800s, have also been unearthed in York. They can be seen in the York Museum. Vindolanda is not the only place in England where Roman wooden tablets with writing on them have been found. As recently as 2010 – 2013 a very large hoard of tablets were found in London, within a stone's throw of London Bridge, at a building site which was being cleared to construct a new building for the Bloomsbury Company. These tablets, which had been written using a metal stylus to scratch words on fir-wood slabs which had first been coated in beeswax, were several decades older than the Vindolanda tablets.

By the twentieth century there were maybe seventy thousand pubs in Britain which is almost thirty times the number of golf courses. The games which were linked to pubs not only enticed the masses into a drinking culture, but they were also associated with gambling throughout their history. People often indulged in some form of gambling long before the Romans arrived in England. Even ancient Egyptians in 3500 BC had dice games. The strong link between games such as Australian Rules football and beer swilling / gambling is certainly not a modern phenomenon. The Saxons and the Danish Vikings were very fond indeed of gambling. Gambling was not just a rich man's pastime. It was also very common among the peasants. We know that there were many attempts to ban the playing of sports, especially on Sundays, by the church and the monarchs. Similar edicts were also issued to try to curb gambling. Henry **II**, Richard **I**, Henry **III**, Edward **III**, Richard **II** and Henry **VII** all had a go at this ...but to no avail.

The games which were linked to pubs could be played inside the pub or even outside the pub in nearby fields and on moors. One such game, not often mentioned as being a possible pre-cursor to golf is knur and spell. This game was played mostly in the northern counties of England for several hundred years before it all but disappeared about 1992. It was found mostly in Lancashire and Yorkshire but was also played in Lincolnshire, Shropshire, Cumbria, Westmorland, Northumberland, Cheshire, Durham, Staffordshire, Derbyshire, Nottinghamshire, and Worcestershire. How far this game goes back is a mystery. The name is believed by many to trace back to an old Norse word called *nurspel* which I have been given to believe simply means ball-play. If it did come from that source, then it could conceivably date back to when the Vikings ruled England between 793 AD and 1066 AD. When I say Vikings, I should really say Norsemen because the word 'Viking' is an occupation meaning sea traveller or warrior and not a nationality. The Danes had in fact been coming to England long before 793 AD. Even in 568 AD the *Peace of Nottingham* was concluded between King Ethelred and the Danes. Most of the Norsemen who conquered the north of Britain were Norwegians or Danes. However, this was not a lay-down *misère*. An occasional Swede also turned up and even the odd Dutchman fighting on the side of the Danes. The Danes generally landed on the east coast of Yorkshire, Lincolnshire, and East Anglia. They worked their way across from there. The Norwegians went to Ireland and Scotland first but after being kicked out by the Irish they sailed across to the Wirral and the Irish Sea / Fylde coasts between Liverpool and Knott End. The attractions here were the estuaries of the River Dee / River Mersey / River Ribble and River Wyre which the Viking longboats could sneak in and find a safe haven. The Wirral in particular was very heavily settled by Norwegian Vikings. This was a great location for them and very convenient for plundering the old Roman walled city of Chester. Many historians believe that the famous Battle of Brunaburh in 937 AD took place on the Wirral near the modern-day town of Bromborough. This is not far away from the Stanlow Oil Refinery at Ellesmere Port where I worked in the 1960s at a carbon black manufacturing plant. The River Ribble was also a very important entry point because it provided a good way for the Norwegian Vikings to get across the country and attack the Danelaw capital of Jorvik (modern-day York).

The Old English word for a gnarly protuberance on a tree was called a knur and the first known use of this word was in the 1300s. Certainly by the late 1400s /early 1500s, which was the time when golf in Scotland was rearing its head, the use of the word 'knur' as a kind of wooden ball used in ball games was already part of the established lexicon at that time. In the first Latin-English dictionary published in 1538 by Oxford scholar Sir Thomas Elyot (1490-1546) this word was already well entrenched.

Some people have also suggested that it may be a Viking game because the participants were usually referred to as 'laikers' (a common Lancashire / Yorkshire word meaning 'players') and that this word probably originated from an Old Norse word called *leika* which apparently means sport-play. However, from my boyhood in Lancashire, I know that the word 'laiker' was not just used for knur and spell. It was a local word used for a player in any sport. It was also a common word used in everyday life. For example, if as a boy I called at a friend's house and said to him 'Atter laikin' out?'... that would translate as 'Are you coming out to play'? The word 'Atter' is an abbreviation or contraction of the medieval English words 'art thou' which means 'are you'. In some phrases the word 'atter' was further contracted. For instance, in the sentence 'Weer'ter barn?' This translates as "where are you going?". More literally it said, 'where art thou bound?' Weer was a corruption of where. The 'at' was dropped from 'atter', leaving the 'ter' to be joined up with weer. 'Barn' was a corruption of bound. Yet another example was 'th'at nobbut a lad' which translates as 'you are only a boy'. Nobbut is a contraction of 'nothing but'. Th'at was a contraction of thou art.

Of course, although we often spoke like this, we never or rarely wrote these words down on paper. I have just made a crude attempt to write them as they were spoken phonetically. These are just a few examples of the everyday language we spoke. Naturally, when I arrived at Colne Grammar School as an eleven-year- old in 1954, I was not allowed to speak like this. The teachers there had a terrible job trying to get me to speak properly 'LIKE WHAT THEY DID!' I never could pronounce 'the rain in Spain stays mainly in the plain' to their satisfaction and I used to dread the regular elocution lessons because I was always made to feel inferior! Headmaster AJ Phillips used to conduct these elocution lessons. He was not my favourite man since I had felt the sting from his flailing split bamboo cane on my backside on more than one occasion! When Mr Philips retired and French master JP Allison replaced him, known affectionately to us younger inmates as Jim Crow, my life took a decided turn for the better! How we arrived at this cognomen I have no idea, other than his first name being James. It certainly had nothing to do with racial segregation or the rhyming slang connotations which may still have applied at the time in the southern states of the USA.

These days my Lancashire accent is stronger than ever despite having lived in Australia for almost forty years. Moreover, I am now proud of my accent and no longer self-conscious about not speaking 'Queen's English' i.e. not speaking with a plum in my gob! One learns eventually, doesn't one?

The old Trawden way of speaking has mostly disappeared these days although older residents like my dear old mum still come out with some of the old phrases and a few old words are still heard from some of the younger folk. Mum is also the absolute classic Mrs Malaprop, but we could fill another book on that subject! Like the time when there was a house fire in the village and, according to mum, the police suspected 'arsenic'. Or during the long CV19 lockdown in the UK, mum told us that being able to keep in touch with all her extended family using Zoom is one of the few things which have helped to keep her 'insane'! George W Bush would come out looking like Shakespeare compared with mum! However, if truth be known, Shakespeare probably invented more words than any man (or woman) in history! Malapropism is something which must run in the family. I still remember when my four years old daughter, Jennifer, with a mischievous look in her eye, told me that the capital of Bolivia was 'Newton John'.

The Vikings did regularly play ball games. There were three main games they played which were called *Knattleik, Soppleik* and *Skofuleik*. At least one of these games was a stick and ball game. From various stories about these games it seems they were very rough affairs which often resulted in injury and occasionally death. However, it is interesting to note that they all contained the *leik* connection and one of them also has the 'kn' connection. Maybe knur and spell evolved from one of these games as a less rough, more civilised game? In Denmark there is also a surname called '*Knørr*' and in Germany there is a surname called '*Knurr/Knauer*'. So, between the Danish Vikings and the Saxons they have knur and spell covered. When I travelled a lot on business during the 1970s throughout Scandinavia the letter 'ø' became a firm favourite as I quickly learned how to ask for a beer (En øl, tak).

Both the Danes and the Norwegians throughout history also ruled Iceland for long periods. For six hundred years prior to Iceland becoming independent in 1944 the Danes predominated. The Icelanders had a place called *Leikskálavellir* where they played games including a ball and stick game similar to knur and spell.

We do know that in the 1700s, 1800s and into the 1900s knur and spell was traditionally played at Easter time, especially on Shrove Tuesday which marked the start of Lent. The practice of fasting during Lent has been going on since at least 200 AD. At first there was no widespread agreement about the 'rules' of Lent. But after the legalisation of Christianity in 313 AD the practice became more standardized. Just when Knur and spell first became associated with Easter and Lent is not known (or at least not known to me!) Maybe an extensive search of church records could uncover this? In the *Northern Star and Leeds General Advertiser* dated 6 March 1841, it mentioned that young men had been playing at knur and spell for almost two hundred years on a plot of land in the city. This would suggest that the custom dates to at least the 1600s and would support the 1618 Baildon Manor find (see this story later). Baildon is just twelve miles away from Leeds. What we don't know is whether or not the long Easter celebrations decreed by Alfred The Great also applied in the area of England which at the time was ruled by the Danish Vikings. Alfred had successfully prevented the Vikings from conquering most of the South of England, but they did hold a very big chunk of England which was known as the Danelaw.

Although no substantial evidence for knur and spell emanating from the Viking days has come to light, there is definite evidence for other Shrovetide 'sports' dating back to when the Danes were in charge. One such 'sport' was called the Threshing of the Cock. It may sound rather rude, but it was very brutal. It probably started in just one town in Cumberland or Westmorland but eventually was practised throughout England by everyone from the nobility to the poorest peasant. The custom started after some Englishmen had formed a plot against the Danish intruders. For some unknown reason, the plot involved the use of some cocks. Unfortunately, the plot went awry when the cocks crowed when they should have been silent, and the Danes were alerted. The Englishmen decided to bash the cocks on the head in retribution and this became an annual custom at Shrovetide. All a bit gruesome really!

Although traditionally played on Shrove Tuesday, knur and spell was still always linked to the English pub scene and was played at any time of the year. Prior to a match being played, players would first congregate in a local pub before going out on to the moor or into an open field for the contest. After the match was over, the players would always adjourn back to the pub for a few pints and some conviviality. There was inevitably a bookmaker at the match and large amounts of cash would be changing hands. In its heyday, several thousand people could attend a match. Many more people than the total attendance at the last three Victorian PGA Championships in Melbourne! In England it was common for pubs to be named after different sporting activities e.g. Cricketers Arms, Hare and Hounds, Dog and Gun etc. The *London Gazette* dated 12 July 1861 announced a match to be played at the Knurr and Spell Inn, Batley. This Batley pub was already operating in 1841. There was also a Knor and Spell Inn at Northbridge, Halifax in 1868. In the very early days golf was also very closely associated with pubs and drinking. In the days when the Scots played on such places as Leith Links there were no established golf clubs or very few of them. Most people would play on the links and then adjourn to their favourite watering hole. In fact, the eating and drinking associated with a day's golf in those days seemed to be more important, or at least equally important, to the golf itself! There were many pubs, especially in Scotland, which made a reference to golf in their name e.g. The Nineteenth Hole. Some of them survive to this day. When researching knur and spell matches, most of the match reports are centred on pubs. There were literally hundreds and hundreds of pub names throughout the whole north of England which featured in these matches. Far too many to list in this book.

The observation of Lent would not of course have applied to the Vikings. For much of the two-hundred and seventy-five years they were in England they were basically still of the pagan persuasion. Towards the end of their time in England, Christianity had been introduced to Scandinavian countries. Danish Vikings were the first to convert to Christianity. Norwegian Vikings were maybe one hundred years behind them. Swedish Vikings saw the light a while after that.

In fact, it was not just the Vikings who were pagan. Although Emperor Constantine had legalised Christianity in the 300s AD that did not mean that all English people had become Christians. Many of them stayed with their paganism until after the Norman Conquest.

The reason I know quite a bit about the game of knur and spell is because Colne, Lancashire, where I was born, was probably the Lancashire centre for the sport. Even in the small village of Trawden where I was raised, which is only two miles away from Colne, I recall from my early teens seeing some of the adult villagers practising knur and spell on the village recreation ground. Even the word 'recreation' came into the English language because of the church influence. The church encouraged sport at Easter Time as a way in which a person could spiritually re-create himself! The older men often let me try hitting the knur but all I could do at the time was produce 'air shots'. One of the regular Trawden players in the 1950s was a big man called Leonard Shuttleworth who answered to the nickname of 'Pin'. I always knew him as Pin Shutt! I don't know if this name was because he played knur and spell from the pin and not the spell (see explanation later). The official name for the Trawden recreation ground was the Jubilee Grounds. It received this name after Queen Victoria's Golden Jubilee in

1887. However, in my time I never heard it referred to by that name. I only ever knew it as 'Trawden Rec' and, apart from my hopeless knur and spell efforts, I spent many hours there as a young boy playing football, cricket, practising my golf shots and training for fell races (running). Since it was fairly isolated from the rest of the village it was also a favourite courting place, but the least said about that the better!

Colne has a very long history, possibly dating to the Roman era after some Roman coins were found there in the 1600s near Castercliff Hill fort. The forerunner to Colne Grammar School, where I spent my youth, was in existence from the 1500s. Probably the school's most famous pupil was John Tillotson who was Archbishop of Canterbury, Primate of All England, between 1691 – 1694. Sadly, Colne Grammar School doesn't exist today. It was sold and turned into luxury apartments in 2009.

Dr Roger Gilbert Bannister, the first man in the world to run a four-minute mile, also has a strong link to Colne and Trawden. His father Ralph was born there in 1894, and the Bannister family had several hundred years of history in Colne and Trawden before him. In or around 1860 Dr Roger's grandad, David Bannister, lived in Trawden at 31 Church Street. His wife Jane was living at that address in May 1918 when she died. Most of Ralph's siblings were weavers in the cotton industry. There is no evidence that any of the Bannister clan played knur and spell, but the probability that some of them did is quite high. Since knur and spell was booming in the village around 1900 and the family lived only fifty yards away from the Rock Hotel, a place where knur and spell was regularly played at that time.

My ninety-six-year-old Mum has lived at 54 Church Street since the early 1950s, having lived at other addresses in Trawden since before the start of World War II. David and Jane had eleven children and one of those was Ralph. Trawden was, and still is, too small to have its own maternity hospital, so Ralph, like myself, may have been conceived in Trawden but born in Colne. Like me, Ralph would have attended Trawden Primary School as a junior albeit about forty-five years earlier. In the 1911 UK Census Ralph was listed as a seventeen-year-old boy clerk working in the Civil Service and lodging in London. That was the start of the upward movement in the fortunes of his family. Not only was Ralph's son Roger a great runner but he went on to become an eminent neurologist.

The Bannister family can maybe trace their ancestry back to a gentleman called Robert de Banastre, a Frenchman, who had fought under William the Conqueror in 1066 and had been given big chunks of land in Wales as a reward. A *banastre* was a basket-maker. In 1857 one of the Bannister family ran the old cornmill in Trawden very close to where I lived as a boy. In the 1940s and 1950s when I was growing up, another Bannister (Harry) also operated Hollin Hall (known by Trawdeners as Floats), one of the biggest cotton mills in the village which had originally been built around 1850. Yet another famous Bannister was Fred Bannister who also lived in Trawden. In 1922 he wrote *The Annals of Trawden Forest* which to this day is still the best historical account of our village history.

Chapter 5

What a load of old balls

A Colne man called Stuart Greenfield was twice knur and spell world champion. He hit the knur two hundred and twenty-five yards in 1970. That may not sound like a big hit until you realise that the knur, which was the size of a large marble and made of ceramic, had a smooth surface without dimples. If Tiger Woods hit a modern golf ball which had no dimples he would be lucky if it travelled one hundred and thirty yards. It is easy to find a demonstration of this on YouTube with specially made smooth Pro VI balls being hit by a number of top 2020 professionals. Using drivers, some of them hit significantly less than one hundred and thirty yards! The dimples are there to make the ball climb and to reduce drag. Before they switched to ceramic knurs they used wooden ones or ones carved from staghorn. These wooden knurs must have been a bit heavier because they flew further. They were hand carved out of a hardwood such as holly, boxwood, or lignum vitae. The wooden knurs also lent themselves to quite a bit of jiggery-pokery, akin to present day ball-tampering in cricket (not sure if they had sandpaper in those days...ha ha). Players used to etch or carve different patterns on their wooden knurs to reduce drag and improve the ball flight. Most likely the forerunner of dimples on a golf ball? The wooden knurs had a rough surface which enabled them to be hit up to a record three hundred and seventy-two yards. This was happening at least two centuries before the featherie was replaced by the guttie ball. The featherie had mostly a smooth surface, at least when new, although the stitching probably stood a little 'proud' which would have influenced the flight. Understandably, as the featherie ball became somewhat damaged, which could occur quite quickly, the damage would have influenced the ball's performance which may well have made the featherie fly further. In 1990 a featherie ball made by Allan Robertson in 1840 sold at Christie's Auction House for close to fifteen thousand pounds.

Even today in Geordie-land the wooden knur legacy is still alive in their everyday language. Because they were often carved out of lignum vitae wood and criss-crossed with lines, the knurs were called 'liggies' in that region of England. One Newcastle article described the wooden liggies as being 'ribbed', which suggests that changing the knur surface to improve ball flight was being used many decades before the golfers got in on the act. They were even still called liggies after the change was made to ceramic balls. Geordies also extended the use of the word liggie when they spoke about marbles used in the very popular kids' game. They also used the word liggies as a slang word for testicles. I suspect that the use of the word liggies in the Newcastle area started from at least the early 1800s or even before that. The *Illustrated Sporting and Dramatic News* 24 April 1880 talked about lignum vitae knurs being 'tooled all over with concentric circular lines'. Articles in the *Newcastle Chronicle dated 1887* were talking about 'white pot liggies' being used in a knur and spell match on Sunderland Moor. Thus it seemed by then that wooden lignum vitae knurs were already a thing of the past in that area. Of course lignum vitae knurs were not just restricted to the Newcastle area, although they were particularly popular there. In October 1840 *Bell's Life* reported on a match in Leeds between Jagger and Lax which specified lignum vitae nurrs.

The main reason lignum vitae was popular for knur making all-around north-east England was probably due to the ship-building industry. Ships had been built in this area from at least the 1200s in ports all around Tyneside and Teesside at places such as Newcastle, Sunderland, Stockton, Hartlepool, Hendon, Thornaby, Jarrow, Wallsend, North and South Shields etc. Lignum vitae, which was also known as guayacan or guaiacum, was extensively used in old sailing ships for things like belaying pins and other parts used in the rigging process. When sailing ships were replaced by modern engine-powered ships, lignum vitae continued to be used at least until 1960 to make water-lubricated shaft bearings. Even for the high-tech Nautilus nuclear-powered submarine in 1955, parts on the main shaft still used lignum vitae. These days, all around the world, lignum vitae is an endangered species. For sure, many of the shipbuilders would have been knur and spell players and they would have had no shortage of small scrap pieces of this amazing wood to supply their needs. There was probably also some lignum vitae used as an engineering material in mines which were littered all around the north of England.

The use of lignum vitae wood throughout history was not just reserved for knur and spell 'balls'. It was also used extensively for bowling alleys and lawn bowling which were major sports played throughout England, Scotland, and Wales long before anyone had the idea to play golf. In the very early days, 1100s and 1200s, they probably started off using stone bowls. In the 1400s they were using boxwood and holly to make their bowls with, just like knur and spell. They started to use lignum vitae from the 1500s and until the mid-1930s this was the chief material used to make bowls from. Around this time, bowlers in the Antipodes were complaining that lignum vitae bowls suffered from cracking in hot weather, especially on outdoor flat-green lawns. So local bowls makers came up with synthetic alternatives. These first involved a rubber compound which was later replaced by melamine formaldehyde thermosetting resin. The Melbourne based Henselite company are probably still the world leaders in this field. In 2019 the synthetic bowls dominate the market for both flat-green and crown-green bowling. However, the true traditionalists can still today buy lignum vitae bowls from the sole remaining UK manufacturer in Liverpool albeit at a ginormous price of about five hundred pounds sterling per pair. In the same way traditional golfers can still buy hickory shafted and long-nosed wooden clubs from my good friend Ross Baker in Surrey Hills. Today bowling is a major sport in Scotland which arguably could rival golf as their national sport. In fact on a world-wide basis, if we combine the lawn bowlers with the ten-pin bowlers, the number of participants would easily be two or three times the number of golfers.

Ten-pin bowling alleys, which took off in a very big way in the USA from the 1820s, also used lignum vitae bowls for well over a hundred years. These bowls were a much bigger and heavier bowl and needed holes in the bowl for one or two fingers and the thumb in order for the bowl to be gripped. In the 1900s, as newer synthetic resins were invented, lignum vitae for these kinds of bowls also disappeared as it was replaced by polyester and later by polyurethane.

Guttie golf balls only started to have patterns on after the moulding process had been introduced, whereas the patterned wooden knurs were used in the 1700s and probably much earlier (Taylor's balls with moulded-in dimples didn't arrive until 1908.) The other kind of tampering which happened with wooden knurs was weight changing. It wasn't uncommon for unscrupulous players to drill holes in the wooden or staghorn knurs, insert some lead into the ball, and then carefully seal it again to make it look like a normal knur. There was very big illegal gambling taking place at knur and spell matches so all kinds of skulduggery were taking place. Once the potty ball was introduced ball tampering became much more difficult. I suspect that the ceramic ball would have started to appear in the second half of the 1700s after Josiah Wedgewood had started up his world-famous fine China pottery factory in Stoke on Trent in 1759. The change from wooden or staghorn knurs to ceramic ones was not a sharp one. This was quite different to the transition to guttie balls from the old featherie leather balls in the golfing world which was very rapid indeed during the early 1850s. Even in the early 1900s there were still knur and spell matches being announced in the newspapers which stated that wooden knurs would be used. An article in the *Manchester Evening News dated 1877* reported the theft of some box-wood trees from a garden nursery. These trees would be on-sold to manufacturers of knur and spell equipment for both knur and pummel head manufacture. In fact, there were regular newspaper reports throughout the 1800s of court cases involving the theft of boxwood or holly trees, both of which could be used to make knurs.

In *Bell's Life* 11 December 1853 they reported on a match where they played with 'hazel heads and holly split nurrs'. I saw this reference to 'holly split nurrs' in several matches over a period of years in the 1800s but I must confess I don't know what 'holly split nurrs' really means.

In Joseph Wright's *The English Dialect Dictionary* covering the period between 1700-1905 it refers to a knur and spell ball as a 'nigney-knur' in West Yorkshire, but I have no idea what this means either. Unless it was a typo and should have said 'ligney-knur' in which case it may have been a kid's way of describing a lignum vitae knur.

The ceramic balls were probably never made specifically for the game of knur and spell. They were first made to use in kettles and maybe industrial boilers to prevent lime-scale deposition (usually referred to as furring) in areas of England which had 'hard' water i.e. water which had high levels of dissolved calcium and magnesium carbonates. Furring still occurred but the deposit stuck to the balls and not the kettle. It could then be easily got rid of by removing the balls and just rubbing them together.

As far as I know most of the pot knurs were glazed. However, when the Bolsterstone Archaeology and Heritage Group were digging in about 2008 at an old building in that village which had been a blacksmiths smithy from at least the 1600s, they found some unglazed knurs which they dated to the late 1700s and early 1800s. Bolsterstone is a tiny village on the edge of the Derbyshire Peak District in South Yorkshire, just about ten miles north-west of Sheffield.

Its population is only a few hundred, but it has existed as a village even before the Vikings arrived in Yorkshire. i.e. pre-799. In the same dig they also found pottery shards from the late 1400s and early 1500s. The building had survived as a smithy well into the 1900s but had been demolished in 1958.

Many blacksmiths' smithies disappeared in the first ten or fifteen years after World War II, including the Lunt family smithy in Trawden which I believe closed up in about 1947. Actually, it wasn't closed down. It was destroyed by a big fire. Was it an accident or a deliberate act? I have no idea, but I can say that the reason for most of these closures was purely economic. The traditional blacksmith's business from the local farmers was disappearing fast. There were far fewer magnificent shire horses to shoe, and no new carts being made as tractors and hay baling machines gradually, but relentlessly, took over. There had been a smithy on the site, behind the current Trawden Arms, since at least the early 1800s and probably much earlier than that. However, I believe that the Lunt family only became involved with that smithy from the late 1800s or very early 1900s. They had moved to this part of Lancashire from the area close to the Irish Sea / Fylde Coasts between Liverpool and Southport in West Lancashire. This is the area where the Norwegian Vikings had landed when they were kicked out of Ireland.

Old Dick Lunt who owned the smithy was a legendary character in the village. Apart from being the village blacksmith he was a lay preacher at the local Wesleyan Chapel and also served for a long period on the village council. As a blacksmith there were many family stories. One which always made me smile was that he used to pull out red-hot glowing embers from the forge fire between his forefinger and thumb and use them to light his cigarette from. His hands must have been as tough as leather with the constant forge heat and callouses formed from all the heavy manual work. As a councillor, back in the good old days when village councillors had some autonomy and could make decisions about things which happened in their village, he was once involved in a debate about a new bridge which was to be erected over Trawden beck. The story goes that the council committee were discussing several tender offers to construct this bridge. Old Dick apparently thought that all the offers were ridiculously over-priced which prompted him to comment that the beck at that point was very narrow and he could even 'piss that far'. When the chairman of the committee ruled him out of order old Dick quickly retorted 'Yes, I AM out of order. Otherwise I could piss twice that far!'

The ceramic balls had a smooth surface and were generally referred to in the newspapers as 'common pot knurs'. They did not have patterns on them like the wooden balls. At least all the ceramic knurs I ever saw were smooth. But later I read in *Bell's Life of London* 14 October 1865 about two knur and spell matches to be held at Newhall near Sheffield in November that year. One match was over thirty rises for £50 a side using wooden knurs. And the other match was for £35 a side over thirty rises using RIBBED pot knurs. What is very interesting is that it used 'ribbed' ceramic knurs, and this is long before golf balls had dimples on them. I am aware that some golfers were manually making indentations into their guttie balls by hammering them to improve the flight characteristics. This probably occurred for twenty or thirty years before the dimples were later built-in at the manufacturing stage in the 1880s. But doctoring by the players could not happen with ceramic knurs. The knurs would just shatter if they were tampered with. The ribs on ceramic knurs would have had to be done at the kiln firing stage. So clearly the knur and spell guys were well ahead of the golfers when it came to ball technology...at least in the flight aspect department. Even in *Bell's Life* 12 December 1868 I was still seeing matches where ribbed pot knurs were specified. It is also very interesting that there were thirteen hundred spectators watching the match with ribbed pot knurs in 1865. To put this into some kind of context we must consider that England's population in 1850 was about fifteen million compared to the fifty-six million in 2018.

Some newspaper reports referred to the ceramic knurs as china knurs. In *Bell's Life* 19 June 1869, there was a match which stipulated half-ounce china ribbed knurs. This report also gave a rise-by-rise account of the distances achieved with these knurs and over fifty rises the winner averaged about ten score (two hundred yards) per rise with a longest strike of two hundred and forty yards. The player involved was not one of the prominent superstars of the day. So, it seems that the ribbed knurs did indeed give an advantage over the common pot knurs which were smooth surfaced.

I also saw reference to some matches where stone knurs were played in the 1860s and wondered whether or not stone was just another way of referring to the ceramic pot knurs. However, in a match described in *Bell's Life* 29 April 1860, one combatant played with china knurs and the other played with stone knurs. This suggested that stone and ceramic knurs were not the same thing. Maybe stone was another way for describing the jet pot knurs? (see later)

Ceramic materials were generally a mixture of metallic silicates and metallic oxides. The exact composition of the ceramic balls is unknown, but it is highly likely that the material used had a specific gravity at least twice as high as any wood used. Therefore, if the ceramic knur had the same diameter as the wooden knur it would be much heavier. However, I have seen reference to half-ounce pot knurs being used in big matches and wooden knurs varying in the range of threequarters to one ounce. This suggested that the diameter of the wooden knurs must have been significantly larger than the pot knurs. In *Bell's Life in London and Sporting Chronicle* dated 3 October 1852 it mentioned that holly nurrs were 1.5 / 1.75- inch diameter. This indeed is much larger than ceramic knurs which were about an inch in diameter. It is maybe no coincidence that golf balls have generally been in the 1.62 / 1.68-inch diameter range which just happens to be about the middle of the holly knur range! I suspect that holly knurs were around long before featheries. I do have an old wooden knur in my possession. However, it is only 1.38 inches diameter and weighs twenty-six grams. Although this is much smaller diameter and under sixty per cent the weight of a golf ball, it is still significantly bigger that the half-ounce, one-inch diameter common pot knurs. It is very dark brown in colour and sinks very quickly in water which may indicate that it is made from lignum vitae. The surface of this wooden knur is rough, with the carving marks clearly evident. (see photo 6 in Chapter 8) I am pretty sure that 1.38 inches diameter and twenty-six grams weight were not the definitive dimensions for all wooden knurs. I have seen many reports where significantly larger diameters than this were used. Probably the weight was more closely controlled than the diameter.

It is interesting that either holly, boxwood or lignum vitae wood was mostly used to make the early wooden knurs because there is a very big difference in the specific gravity of these various woods. English holly is generally in the 0.50/0.65 range whereas lignum vitae, which generally comes from the Caribbean or South America, is in the 0.99/1.30 range. Boxwood is normally in the 0.72/0.88 range. This means that if balls of the same diameter were made with these three woods, they would all weigh differently. I suspect that the weight was the important parameter to be controlled and the diameter varied according to the type of wood used. Of course this is all guesswork! The lignum vitae knur would travel further than the holly knur. Lignum vitae is also a much harder wood and would have been less likely to split on impact. Knurs made with holly or boxwood would not be as resistant as lignum vitae to playing in wet weather. However, if the holly or boxwood knurs were hit into a pond they would float and be easy to find. Whereas the lignum vitae knurs would sink to the bottom and most likely disappear forever. I have an old 1800s wooden knur on my desk. It does very quickly sink straight to the bottom when immersed in water. I have never had the wood type analysed but I suspect that it will be a lignum vitae knur. Some of the boxwoods would also probably sink but maybe not so fast as a stone.

The use of boxwood and holly to make ancient knurs from, just like the 'featherie' leather golf balls used by the early Scottish golfers, probably owes its origin, at least indirectly, to the Romans. The Egyptians were also big fans of boxwood several thousand years before the Romans, but they didn't rule England for four hundred years. Both boxwood and holly trees / shrubs were extensively used in the landscaping of Roman gardens. The woods obtained from these trees were also widely used by the Romans to make all kinds of everyday articles such as musical instruments, combs, shuttles for hand-loom weaving, writing tablets, holders for augers etc.

Although the Romans most commonly used boxwood for their writing tablets, the approximate five hundred tablets found at Vindolanda in the 1970s and 1980s were not boxwood. They were made from woods locally sourced close to Hadrian's Wall such as oak, alder and birch. The use of boxwood in particular is frequently referred to in Roman literature. Mark V Braimbridge's book *Boxwood in Roman Times* is a must read on this subject. There are dozens of varieties of boxwood trees and shrubs around the world. One of the favourite types used in England is *Buxus Balearica*, originally from Turkey and other places around the Mediterranean.

When knur and spell playing with boxwood knurs was at its peak in the mid-1800s, one of the other common uses for boxwood was making chess pieces. The oldest chess pieces ever found in the UK also gave us a Viking connection. They were found on the Isle of Lewis in the Outer Hebrides in 1831. They were dated by the British Museum to be from the 1100s. At that time Scotland was still ruled by the Norwegian Vikings. Most experts believe that these chess pieces had been made at Trondheim in Norway. Although they were carved in walrus tusk ivory and not boxwood, this was yet another example of the Viking legacy in the UK. In 2019, just one single chess piece, which had been missing from the 1831 find, turned up unexpectedly in Edinburgh. It sold at Sothebys for £735,000. That's a nice cheque, mate!

In the 1700s and 1800s holly trees were quite important in Westmorland (now part of Cumbria). Farmers there would often plant whole woods of holly trees. They used to trim the new shoots from the tops of these trees and feed them as fodder to their sheep and other animals.

The staghorn knurs are somewhat perplexing. I have never seen a stag knur, but there are many newspaper reports from the first half of the nineteenth century where stag knurs were commonly used in challenge matches. Staghorn is a bony kind of material with high calcium and phosphorus contents. Male deer (stags) grow structures from their heads known as antlers just prior to the mating season every year. After mating they shed the antlers and then re-grow them for the next mating season.

Staghorn was, and still is, used in the manufacture of knife handles. Sheffield in Yorkshire was a major knife making centre dating back to long before golf started in Scotland. It has long been accepted that Sambar staghorn is the most suitable type of antler for making knife handles because they are the densest (less porous) and therefore the toughest. The Sambar antlers grow up to forty-three inches long and the cross section would probably be big enough to allow knurs to be carved from them.

Antlers which are shed and re-grown each year are quite different in structure to bovine animal horns (cows, goats, rams etc) which are generally never shed and just continue to grow while the animal lives. Ram's horn in particular was used in thin sections to improve the durability of the face of the old wooden headed golf clubs.

When animal horn is used for this application there are two important things to consider. It contains keratin layers which are extremely insoluble in water. However, it will absorb moisture and this absorbed moisture is important to its impact resistance. If the horn dries out too much the impact strength falls away somewhat. The other important thing to note is that the impact strength is not the same in both directions. To maximise strength the sliver of horn should be cut in the longitudinal direction and not the transverse direction. i.e. it should be cut parallel to how the horn grows out of the animal's head.

Keratin is a fibrous structural protein with amino acid chains. X-ray diffraction patterns have shown it to contain both crystalline and amorphous (non-crystalline) phases. The strength and rigidity of alpha keratin is due to it containing a significant amount of cysteine in its chemical make-up and also has two polypeptide chains twisted together in a coil arrangement. This contains sulphur which leads to di-sulphide linkages in the molecular structure which are present in addition to both intra and intermolecular hydrogen bonds. Keratin is actually a dead tissue, and its strength is also derived from the fact that it forms overlapping layers which stack on top of each other. Animal horns generally have a density in the 1.28 to 1.33 range and on average would be a bit denser than even lignum vitae.

I did wonder if the old stag knurs were not carved from antler horn at all and were really made from bovine horn. Afterall, the description of the two types of horn may have been easily confused in those days because the complex chemical nature of their structures which we know today would not have been fully known at that time. However, I don't believe this to be the case because I can't imagine that ram's horn would have been available in a big enough cross-section for a one and a half-inch diameter knur to be carved from it. My guess is that the Sheffield knife industry were using Sambar antlers and that their workers were stealing bits to make knurs with. These antlers may well have been imported because the Sambar deer is mostly found in India and SE Asia. It is not native to the UK.

Having said this, I may need to have a re-think. In an article in the *Illustrated Sporting and Dramatic News*, 24 April 1880, it mentioned that stag knurs were always smaller than wooden knurs. They were apparently made by carefully filing and then boring through and through before filling the holes with lead. So if the overall weight was always achieved in this manner when using staghorn, it could well be possible that smaller cross section, locally available staghorn may still be a suitable raw material. It could also mean that maybe lead-filling these knurs was NOT a 'ball tampering' exercise but was how all the stag knurs were made. Difficult to be sure because I have never seen a stag knur. That is unless the knur shown in the Baildon Hall equipment photos in chapter 12 proves to be a stag knur...which is quite likely.

Knife making in Sheffield, Yorkshire, dates to the 1200s and it really took off in the 1600s and 1700s as improved steel making technology started to evolve. Sheffield (and its surrounding villages / hamlets) was also one of the earliest epicentres for knur and spell playing. There would have been plenty of supplies of staghorn around in those days and there would have been plenty of workers around who had experience of working with staghorn.

My first impression was that staghorn would have been one of the earliest materials used to make knurs...maybe in the 1300s, 1400s, 1500s and 1600s or even earlier. However, it seems that some staghorn knurs were still being used for some knur and spell matches even in the 1800s.

In *Bell's Life in London and Sporting Chronicle* dated 6 January 1828, it mentioned a match to be played at Darnall in Leeds which involved the famous Yorkshire cricketer, Tom Marsden, where stag knurs had been stipulated. In various other match reports involving Marsden from around that date, stag knurs were also used. In *Bell's Life* dated 20 September 1840, Joseph Lax, also from Sheffield, used staghorn nurrs in a £100 a side challenge match. The same man was still using stag nurrs in March 1842. In 1834, the annual salary for a police constable in Colne was fifteen pounds. These guys were gambling about six years wages on one knur and spell match!

Staghorn was still being used in the manufacture of knife handles in the Hallamshire area around Sheffield as late as the late 1800s and early 1900s. For a very good account of this industry it is well worth reading *Continuity and Change in a Pennine Community: The Township of Stannington circa 1660 – 1900* by JE Hatfield in her Sheffield University doctoral thesis. Focussing on the Hallamshire areas of Sheffield, Bradfield and Ecclesfield it gives a very detailed account of the cutlery making evolution. Hallamshire was in fact one of the earliest areas settled by the Danish Vikings who were skilled blacksmiths and had a long tradition of knife, axe, sword, and agricultural implement making before they invaded England. Maybe this industry is a Viking legacy? The Egyptians, Indians and Chinese were well ahead of the game when it came to carbon modified iron, but the Hallamshire boys did have the last laugh when, in 1913, a man from Sheffield discovered serendipitously how to make stainless steel using an alloy with chromium. After that at least one hundred different types of stainless steel have been developed using a range of other alloying metals such as nickel, titanium etc, including both magnetic and non-magnetic versions. Curiously enough, stainless steel had been used by humans at least as far back as King Tut in about 1325 BC. A stainless-steel knife had been found in his tomb. But it wasn't from man-made steel. It had been fashioned from an iron meteorite which already had some nickel contamination in it when it landed on earth. The same explanation has been given for King Arthur's legendary sword, Excalibur, in the fifth and sixth centuries. The Sheffield boys had also invented a process for silver plating in 1743 and were commercially making Sheffield Plate in 1761.

Another great article on this subject is *Knife Handle Making-the subsidiary trades in the Sheffield Cutlery Industry* by Joan Unwin, Archivist to the Company of Cutlers in Hallamshire. The cutlery industry in Sheffield had a craft guild which had been ratified by an Act of Parliament in 1624.

This is just about the same time that George Villers had been playing golf at Therfield Heath with Sir Robert Deale...full story on this later. I suspect that staghorn knurs would have been used at least from around this date, and maybe even earlier because by 1624 knife making in Hallamshire had already been happening for over three hundred years. The last date I saw staghorn knurs mentioned in newspaper match reports was 1842 which suggest that staghorn knife handles were maybe not as important by that time. Staghorn was mainly imported from Africa and India. According to the *British Census* of 1861 the number of staghorn workers in the whole of the Sheffield area was only thirty-one out of a total of four hundred and twenty-one workers knife handle workers .i.e. less than eight per cent. The other ninety-two per cent plus of the knife handle workers were working with other materials such as bone, bovine horn, pearl and ivory. So it is maybe understandable that staghorn to make knurs with was not as easy to get hold of as previously. In 1850 Merrill, Jarvis and Merrill were still listed as staghorn merchants in Sheffield and Chester Brothers of Sheffield were still dealing in staghorn in 1871.

Several reports I have read about staghorn knurs mention that they were generally drilled with a criss cross of small holes which were then filled with lead and carefully sealed. If this is the case then it would have been very difficult to control the weight distribution from knur to knur. This would have given these staghorn knurs some very interesting flight characteristics!

The circle is complete when we learn that knur and spell player and famous Yorkshire cricketer, Tom Marsden, was born in Sheffield in 1803. He died young of consumption in 1843. It would not surprise me if his father worked in the cutlery industry. A very high percentage of Sheffield workers in those days would have been employed in that trade.

In *Bell's Life* 1852 it also mentioned that 'cast metal' knurs were sometimes used in the Sheffield area, but I have never seen any evidence of this in any actual match reports. Another report mentioned that zinc was the metal used, but I never saw any of these knurs, nor do I know how often they were used. Maybe they suffered the same fate as Dennis Lillee's famous aluminium cricket bat? Zinc had been discovered in 1746 so this suggestion is feasible. Aluminium came along much later so that can probably be ruled out.

In the *London Evening Standard* dated 17 October 1834, I also read about knurs made from oak and in another newspaper dated 31 January 1863 about knurs made from hawthorn wood. However, I never saw any match reports using either of these woods. Actually, it would not surprise me if, over the many centuries knur and spell was played, all manner of different woods had been experimented with. If not in the big money 'professional' matches, then certainly by the average Joe Hacker who only ever played in games where the loser bought the beer!

Whichever type of knur was used for a match there would have been very large theoretical variation in the distance they could be hit. They may have been able to closely control the ball diameter, but the weights would have been all over the place between different knur types. Pre-match agreement on which kind of knur they would play with was essential. On most occasions, players would use the same kind of knur in their match. However, in some of the handicap matches different players could opt to play with different knurs. When this happened, the players with the common pot knurs would receive an advantage of maybe five to ten score over the players who used wooden knurs, a fact which confirmed that wooden knurs, with their carved pattern surface, could be hit significantly further than the smooth surfaced common pot knurs. Indeed, when we see mention of record hits by various champions, the common pot knurs were usually in the two hundred yards range whereas distances well over three hundred yards have been recorded with wood knurs.

In fact, the longest hit ever recorded for a wooden knur was achieved in an 1899 competition at the Lightcliffe Gun Club ground near Halifax by a gentleman called Fred Moore. His hit was measured at 18 score, 12 yards and 1 foot eight inches. i.e. just over 372 yards! One can readily understand that, when hitting a small, dark coloured knur these kind of distances, both players and ball-spotters alike would certainly need to be accipitral. Or as we say in Lancashire they would need to have eyes like a toilet rodent! Or shithouse rat if you can tolerate crude language!

The top knur and spell players were very aware of the weight of their knurs. One player used to control his weights to one ounce plus the weight of fifteen pennies for his wooden knurs. Another player used to only use green boxwood for his competition knurs and dried box-wood knurs for his practice knurs. Yet another player used to harden all his box-wood knurs prior to use by pickling them in a mixture of salt and sand.

This process also reminded me that the moisture pick-up during play in wet conditions would have been significantly different for all the various knur types. The pot knurs were generally glazed so would have had relatively little moisture pick-up. The stag knurs would absorb more moisture than the pot knurs, but it would be a slow up-take. However, the wood knurs would probably have absorbed moisture fairly quickly and this absorption would vary depending on whether boxwood, holly or lignum vitae was used. It is possible therefore that increasing the weight of the wood knurs by pre-soaking them may have been used as an underhand way of achieving extra distance. I never read anything about knur weights being checked prior to competition, but I can't believe that shrewd Lancashire and Yorkshire men would fall for this potential form of trickery. Top players also had their own individual preferences when it came to the patterns carved on the surface of the wooden knurs.

Irrespective of the kind of wood used to make the knur and of the variation in moisture pickup, and no matter how closely the weight of the knur was controlled, every single wooden knur would have performed differently. This is because every wooden knur was made by a hand carving process and it would have been totally impossible to replicate the rough wooden surface of the knur. For sure players would have had 'favourite' knurs which they knew from experience would fly further through the air because of their individual surface characteristics. Of course it would be done on a trial-and-error basis and was not something which they could easily control. Once they had identified any high performing knurs they would do their utmost to avoid losing them during play. I imagine that having all their knurs made by the same man, and not buying from different sources, may at least help a bit with the consistency.

Most of the common pot knurs appear to have weighed half an ounce (about 14.2 grams), but I also saw match reports where three-quarter ounce pot knurs were specified and occasionally even one-ounce pot knurs. Golf balls weigh 1.62 ounces which is nearly forty-six grams. I even saw a few articles which mentioned two-ounce and four-ounce pot knurs, but I suspect that this must have been a printing error. The two-ounce may have been a possibility, but a four-ounce knur would have been more than twice the weight of a modern golf ball and the impact would probably have smashed the pummel head to smithereens or at least have transmitted quite a shock to the fingers through the shaft. In 1916 there was a newspaper advert by the Regent Pottery Company of Hanley near Stoke on Trent in the region of England known as the Potteries (Staffordshire). They were offering a large assortment of pot knurs to knur and spell players. No details were given about what the assortment consisted of, but at least this does seem to indicate that various sizes were available. In the early 1900s I also read that a clay pipe (ceramic) manufacturer called Naylor's in Cawthorne near Barnsley were also supplying some pot knurs to the local knur and spell players. This company had been founded in 1890 and still exists today.

In the second half of the twentieth century, as knur and spell was just about sunk, a small ceramic kiln business in the very old Ivegate area of Colne also had a go at producing ceramic knurs. By that time pot knurs were in very short supply. Problem was that by then the number of knur and spell players could probably have been counted on one hand so it would hardly have been a commercial proposition for them and would only have been done as a favour to a friend.

The knur type used would dictate which pummel head construction the player would opt to use and maybe even influence which shaft material and which shaft length he would use. In modern day golf both the ball diameter and the ball weight are rigidly controlled. I don't know how well the featherie and guttie balls performed in this regard. I do know that the leather featherie balls were never completely round in shape because all the segments had to be stitched together. The ball flight characteristics of the featherie must have been very interesting.

In the 1950s I only ever saw the ceramic knurs and they were always coloured white. In a newspaper article in 1861 from Sheffield there was a reference to 'tinted pot knurs' being used. I don't know if these were still white or if other colours had been used. I never actually saw any of the staghorn knurs, but maybe they were painted white to assist finding them after they had been hit. Long before the 1950s the public would have grown tired of rogues illegally chopping down their beloved boxwood and holly trees to make knurs with. In any case, mass produced ceramic knurs would always have been much cheaper to buy than hand carved wooden knurs! And all types of knurs would have been much cheaper to produce than the very expensive featherie golf balls. I did see newspaper reports from both 1885 and 1910 which talked about 'jet pot knurs'. I have no idea what they were. I can't imagine anyone playing with black knurs because they would have been very difficult to find after being hit.

The only thing I can think of in relation to 'jet' knurs, and it is maybe a long shot, is that jet mining was very popular in Yorkshire especially in the 1800s. Throughout history, going back over four thousand years, jet has been regarded as a minor gemstone. It lends itself to polishing. Ornaments and other artefacts carved from jet have been found in burial mounds in many parts of England. Jet is really a mineraloid which is effectively fossilised wood from the Monkey Puzzle tree created by high pressures over the past two hundred million years. There are two forms of it found. A hard variety and a soft one. The main area where it was mined are in Yorkshire at places such as Swainby, Guisborough and Cleveland close to the North Yorkshire Moors. It was very popular during Queen Victoria's reign and the main processing area was Whitby where Captain Cook sailed from. Fifteen hundred people in Whitby worked in the jet industry in the 1800s. This was a big percentage of the Whitby population which was only about eight thousand at that time. It had also been popular when the Romans were in charge. It was often found in conjunction with ironstone and mudstone. These days it is no longer mined in Yorkshire, but it is often found on the beaches near Whitby where it occurs through natural erosion of the coastline from Boulby down to Robin Hood's Bay. Knur and spell was played in every single place mentioned in this paragraph and many others in the same vicinity. So it is maybe not such a ridiculous idea that some knurs could have been carved out of this material by the miners who mined the jet. Jet usually has an SG between 1.2 and 1.40. Lignum vitae is also similar, so this would fit in quite nicely from a weight and size viewpoint. Not sure how the brittleness of jet would survive the impact from a knur and spell pummel. Maybe the 'soft' variety of jet would be OK? The miners certainly had plenty of 'form' when it came to nicking a pickaxe handle or a lump of lignum vitae from their employers to fashion a nipsy stick or a liggie knur, so a bit of jet would have been no problem to get hold of. There again this could all be a red herring. I just don't know. The Whitby Museum in Pannett Park has a very extensive collection of artefacts made from jet. Maybe a jet knur could be found there?

In 2020 there is still a pub called the Jet Miners Inn in the village of Great Broughton near Stokesley on the edge of the North Yorkshire Moors. I don't know if knur and spell matches were ever hosted there. However, they most likely were because quoits matches were definitely held there, and these two games were often played on the same programme. Also travelling in any direction from Stokesley, dozens of knur and spell playing places can be found within a short distance. These days Great Broughton is perhaps better known as a stopping off place along Blackburnian Alfred Wainwright's famous Coast to Coast walk which starts at St Bees, traverses the Lake District, the Yorkshire Dales and the North Yorkshire Moors, and ends on the east coast at Robin Hood's Bay not far from Whitby (and passing through lots of knur and spell playing places on the way!)

Although the ceramic knurs were much cheaper than the wooden or stag knurs, one of their draw backs was that they frequently split or shattered when being hit. This often led to disputes between players. Broken ceramic knurs reminds me of a very interesting story. When researching knur and spell I discovered that the game had been played behind the Rock Hotel in Trawden, Lancashire in the late 1890s and very early 1900s. This was only about twenty-five yards away from where I lived as a young boy. When I read about this I was somewhat puzzled because there was never enough land immediately behind the Rock Hotel to accommodate a knur and spell hit. I therefore assumed that the players must have been hitting their knurs, over the village beck which runs closely behind the pub emanating from nearby Boulsworth Hill, and uphill into a local farmer's field. In March 2021, my suspicions were confirmed in a quite unusual way. My brother Richard, who still lives in the village, was taking his boxer dog, Rocky, for his daily walk in the field in question when quite by chance he stumbled across a broken ceramic knur. (see photos below) This partial knur, which would have been languishing there at least one hundred and twenty years, was located just across the beck in an area where the valley floor just started to slope steeply upwards. It was only about thirty yards away from where the striking area would probably have been confirming that when ceramic knurs split they carried only a very short distance. Of course, if a knur split on impact, the player was able to hit another knur without penalty. So split knurs were never retrieved. No doubt there will still be many thousands of knur fragments, and also lost whole knurs, littering fields behind thousands of village pubs all across the former Danelaw area...remembering that this area, at the time, was larger in size than all the Scottish golf playing regions combined.

The knurs didn't always split in two equal halves. In the case shown in the photograph, the knur split in a 60 /40 or a 65 /35 ratio. The 'half' we found was the smaller of the two fragments.

Fragments of 120-year-old pot knur found in field behind Trawden Arms

The wooden knurs would also split occasionally but not as often as the pot knurs. Boxwood and holly were the most easily split. Lignum vitae was considerably tougher but much more expensive. Staghorn knurs would have been just about impossible to split but were very difficult to come across after the early 1800s. Being white, the pot knurs were easiest to find after they had been hit. I am unsure as to whether the wooden or stag knurs were ever painted white. The wooden knur I have in my possession is dark brown in colour and on microscopic examination I could not find any trace of its ever having been painted.

It seems that throughout the years the knur used by the knur and spell players varied much more that the various balls used by golfers. Knurs could be made from staghorn, holly, boxwood, lignum vitae, oak, stone, zinc, ceramic or maybe even jet. The wooden knurs could have an infinite number of patterns carved on them. The ceramic knurs could weigh half ounce, three-quarter ounce or one ounce. They could be glazed or matt finish, and they could be smooth or ribbed. Ceramic knurs were usually about one-inch diameter, but wooden knurs could be in the 1.4 – 1.75-inch range. When Strutt wrote his book on sports in the late 1700s which was published in 1801 he talked about the knur being made of leather. Now isn't that interesting? I never saw any match reports talk about leather knurs. I wonder if they came before stag and wood knurs? I wonder if leather knurs came before leather golf balls. Or was Strutt merely confusing knur and spell with golf? Very likely!

Golf balls have changed over time: wooden, leather (hairie and featherie), guttie, wound and solid core balls. However, within each era the variation available was probably always less than what happened with knurs. The imported Dutch leather balls filled with cow hair came before the featheries. It is difficult to know when they took over from the wooden balls, but it is possible that the hairies were around from the mid-1400s to 1618. Featheries were generally available in four different weights ranging between 27 and 31 pennyweights (42 – 48.2 grams). i.e. up to 1.70 ounces. According to the *Cassell's Book of Sports* 1891, gutties were also supplied in four different weights between 27 and 29 drams (47.84 – 51.38 grams). i.e. up to 1.81 ounces. These guttie weights seem very heavy compared to a modern ball at 1.62 ounces (45.9 grams). If the gutties really were as heavy as 1.81 ounces, or even 1.70 ounces, it may explain why they caused a lot of damage to wooden clubs. I suspect that the Cassell units should be pennyweights and not drams. This would reduce the Cassell range from 42 – 45.1 gms. Apart from the question mark on weight, it is interesting to note that for most of the guttie ball era, there was no rule which stipulated the actual diameter of a golf ball. The golfers probably copied the knur and spell boys in this respect. This only changed in 1897 when the R & A took over the rule making for the game of golf and came up with 1.62 inches MINIMUM diameter and 1.62 ounces MAXIMUM weight. Featheries were used over a period of about two hundred and fifty years from the early 1600s to around 1850. Gutties were only around for a relatively short period from about 1848 to the late 1800s and early 1900s. For the approximate fifty-years history that the guttie balls were in use, the chemical nature of the ball didn't change. Gutta Percha is a latex which comes from a tree. It is a polyterpene known as trans-1,4 polyisoprene. As opposed to natural rubber which is the cis-1,4 polyisoprene version. Both gutta percha and natural rubber each have five carbon atoms and eight hydrogen atoms in the basic monomeric unit. The difference is in the way these atoms are configured. The 'trans' form enables much closer packing of the individual molecular chains which results in a material with higher crystallinity. This in turn gives gutta percha higher rigidity which makes it more severe on wooden clubs. So when we see different descriptions of these balls such as gutta, guttie or gutty, this is just semantics. They all refer to the same thing.

The story about wooden balls preceding hairy or featherie balls in the game of golf is an interesting one. Here we have to be careful to recognise what separates actual facts from factoids. According to the *Scottish Golf History* (SGH) website ' the use of wooden balls in golf in Scotland is an assumption, but without any definite evidence'. SGH go on to describe other games in Europe using wooden balls and have concluded that 'the spherical wood balls were smooth and did not have good handling properties' and 'the distance they could be hit was only about seventy-five metres'. Indeed most photos of old wooden balls shown in golf ball articles have generally been 'smooth' balls. This estimate of hitting distance may well be a true statement for 'smooth' wooden balls, but it is way off the mark for hand-carved wooden balls (knurs) which were far from smooth and which had been used for many centuries in England. For at least as long as golf had been played and probably longer! If the Scots had wanted to see how far a non-smooth wooden ball (a knur) would travel they did not need to travel to continental Europe to see it. All they needed to do was to venture a stone's throw over the border into northern England and they could have watched thousands of Southrons playing knur and spell and regularly smacking little wooden balls two or three hundred yards (record hit was three hundred and seventy-two yards!) with relatively crude knur and spell pummels. No super-duper stainless steel or carbon fibre shafts or titanium heads were necessary to hit these kind of distances. The Scots didn't even need to go over the border into England. They could have seen the same thing in Ayrshire and in the county of Angus! What is more, in 2020, if they want to actually see examples of the knurs which were travelling those distances, all they need to do is visit any one of dozens of museums around the former Danelaw of England where holly, boxwood or lignum vitae knurs can readily be seen. Or alternatively they can just refer to the photograph section of this book! If they get very lucky they may even see a staghorn knur which possibly pre-dated the wooden ones! Scotland probably still has more stags than anywhere else in Europe. If they care to look seriously in their own backyard, they may even find example wooden knurs or an odd pummel or two in Dalry or Dundee where knur and spell was played in the 1850s and 1860s...long before the big worldwide explosion in golf occurred! As I write this section I have a carved wooden knur staring back at me now from the top of my desk here in Australia! Yes, wooden knurs were used here too before the golf craze hit the road!

I wonder why the Scots chose not to use carved wooden knurs like the ones used for many centuries in the English game of knur and spell in favour of the hairie and later the featherie balls? It doesn't make a lot of sense. If we check the *Blackheath Chronicles* we see that in June 1813, one of their members, a Mr Laing, had laid a bet that he could drive a featherie ball five hundred feet during the course of the season, he having the chance of ten strokes to accomplish it. Five years later, in 1818, Laing won the Knuckle Medal and the Silver Club Medal at Blackheath GC which suggests that he was an above average player, albeit not one of the top echelon. Five hundred feet is close to one hundred and sixty-seven yards. At that time in the early 1800s there were hundreds if not thousands of knur and spell players who could hit a carved wooden knur well over two hundred yards. Indeed, the record hit for a wooden knur made before the end of the 1800s was well over three hundred yards! I suspect that this would have been considerably longer than most of the Scottish golfers were driving featheries in those days. There are accounts to be found of some of the top golfers in Scotland hitting featheries over two hundred yards. Also the record hit in 1836 with a featherie, aided by a strong tail wind, was said to be three hundred and sixty yards, which is almost as long as the longest knur and spell hit. Despite this, it is fairly clear from the available data on this that long hitting with featheries was the exception rather than the rule. On the other hand, winning distances for knur and spell contests were ALWAYS reported in the newspapers so we have an abundance of accurate information on this subject. These reports clearly show that there were large numbers of knur and spell players who could regularly hit wooden knurs well over two hundred yards, with the star players often averaging close to three hundred yards. Reports on distances hit by golfers are not as readily available, because most competition reports generally focussed more on how many strokes had been taken. Comments on driving distances were relatively rare. Whatever the case, we can say with absolute certainty that knur and spell distances, using wooden knurs, were at least as long as featherie hits and, if measured across the range of different playing abilities, were probably significantly longer. To be honest, this should not really be all that surprising when we realise that during the 1800s there were far more knur and spell players in England than there were golfers in Scotland...by several orders of magnitude!

It is true that the carved wooden knurs were probably a bit smaller than the size of a featherie, but a slightly larger rough surfaced knur would probably have made a good compromise. The undeniable advantages of the carved wooden knur, in addition to the likely longer hitting distance, are that the price would have been a tiny fraction of the featheries, and the durability would have been considerably better...particularly in wet conditions.

Although I have talked about knurs being hit a certain number of 'yards', this was not the measurement term used by the knur and spell players themselves. Their hits were always denoted by a number of score. One 'score' was twenty yards. Thus a two hundred yards hit was recorded as 'ten score'. The word 'score' is perhaps a much older one than the word 'yard'. We recall that the Bible referred to ' three score years and ten' for someone who lived to seventy years of age. Whereas it was King Henry **I** in the early 1100s who first fixed the yard as being the distance from the tip of his nose to the thumb of his outstretched hand. This is perhaps another indication that knur and spell is a very old game?

We must also consider that golfers were starting to get creative with golf club design and had things like ram's horn inserts on their club faces etc. Compare this with the very pummel design used by the knur and spell players which basically hardly changed between 1600 and 1990 apart from variation in the shaft length and type of wood used to make the shaft. Carved wooden knurs would have been a far better option for the golfers than featheries or gutties, even if it meant plumping for a slightly smaller diameter ball.

It may also be pertinent at this stage to ask the question why the SGH and other golf history writers didn't make any comment about wooden balls (knurs) being used in England for centuries before the guttie ball arrived? Surely it couldn't be possible that they had never heard about knur and spell and its colloquial name of 'poor man's golf'? Surely the history of wooden knurs, staghorn knurs and ceramic knurs would have been relevant information to have included in the overall discussion on the history of stick and ball games? Surely there must at least have been some degree of curiosity aroused in the Scots as to what 'poor man's golf' was all about? How could it be that the Scots seemed to know all about 'smooth' wooden balls being used in stick and ball games on the European Continent, but they didn't seem to know about hand carved 'rough' surface knurs being used by thousands of players just a few miles away over the border in England? Even though thousands of Scots were actually living and working in all the northern English counties! Things do not add up! One can only reasonably assume that there was a deliberate decision to ignore this part of the story.

Maybe the Scots *did* use these kind of knurs before the hairie and featherie balls arrived? Maybe they intentionally wanted to eradicate wooden knurs from the golf story because of their absolute hatred of everything English in those early days of continual conflict? Far stranger things than this have happened through the ages. One thing is quite clear. There are many reports in Scottish documents which refer to 'golf' being played in and around churchyards...a situation where holes and flags would not have been used. Although I can't claim to have seen one of these reports referring to any particular type of ball being used, there is a strong likelihood that balls hit in and around church yards, probably by common people and not by aristocrats, would be wooden balls which didn't travel great distances. Common people would not have had the wherewithal to buy expensive handcrafted leather balls. And if they could, they wouldn't waste them by bashing them into church walls, an act which would instantly make them unfit for further use. The *National Library of Scotland* has an article which mentions 'In 1632, Thomas Chatto was killed by a flying golf ball in Kelso churchyard.' Although this was fourteen years after the featherie ball first appeared on the scene, I suspect that this incident would have involved a wooden ball. Maybe this wooden ball was a carved knur? Kelso is a Scottish border town and very close to England. The nearest English village to Kelso is Carham in Northumberland which is only about six miles away. About one in every three persons living in Carham were born in Scotland. Rock on Tommy!

Here is some very good news for my Scottish friends. It's never too late! You don't have to take my word for it or indeed you don't have to believe any of the thousands of old newspaper reports available on-line. Last time I looked, boxwood, holly and lignum vitae trees were still being grown. Just chop a branch off one of your neighbour's trees when he is away on holiday, hand carve yourself a few beautiful rough surface wooden knurs, and bash them up and down the practice fairway at your local golf club. If those wooden knurs don't travel considerably further than the seventy-five metres mentioned earlier, I will bare my arse on the town hall steps! A word of caution. Last time I issued a similar challenge, on a completely different, non-golf related subject, I lost, and I still have the photograph to prove it! Not a pretty sight! (No, this photograph has NOT been included in the book!)

There were in fact only two significant changes made to the guttie balls across their fifty-year history. The first related to the ball's surface. The first guttie balls made had a smooth surface and they didn't perform too well when hit. i.e. they flew erratically and not very far. However, as they became scuffed or damaged during play, players noticed that their performance improved. This led to new balls being deliberately and systematically disfigured prior to use, by a crude hammering process. The second significant change related to the manufacturing process used. The early guttie balls were made by heating up the resin and then simply rolling the balls by hand against a hard flat surface. Eventually, probably in the early to mid-1860s, some whizz kid came up with the idea of developing a simple single-cavity compression mould. This made it much easier to achieve the same ball size every time and also gave infinite opportunities to score a pattern into the mould face with different markings which altered the resultant ball surface and helped to optimise ball flight characteristics. It was probably into the 1860s, almost twenty years after gutta percha first started to be used, before moulds with patterns on them began to appear. Until then all the moulds were smooth surfaced. A fine example of an 1860s smooth ball mould and press was seen in the Roberto Family Trust Golf Collection at Bonham's auction house in 2017 which had apparently been used by professional John Allan at Westward Ho GC in Devon. These ball surface and manufacturing process modifications were ostensibly the only permanent changes made during the fifty-year period.

There were several different types of compression mould available. The earliest models tended to use a hand-operated screw arrangement to apply the required clamping force. Later models, still being offered in 1895, used more of a lever / pincer movement to apply the pressure. As far as I am aware, none of the gadgets had direct built-in capability to heat up the mould itself. Electricity had not yet been invented when these moulds were being used. Gas was being used for street lighting from the early 1800s but did not come into common use by the general population until near the end of the 1800s.So I am guessing that the gutta percha would need to be heated up in a wood fired oven prior to the pressing process, to soften it up and make it pliable. I have only ever seen single cavity versions. I don't know if multi-cavity models were ever used in guttie ball manufacture, although of course these did come later for other types of balls. Maybe the mould itself was also pre-heated in an oven. The charge loaded would always be a few grammes heavier than the final ball. The excess would be squeezed out as the pressure was applied and the resultant 'flash' would be trimmed off later.

A good example of the mould being sold in 1895 can be seen in the *Golf Far and Sure* advert from that era (see below). One of these moulds can still be seen in the Jeparit Museum in north-west Victoria. Jeparit is a tiny village three hundred and eighty-seven kilometres outside Melbourne with only three or four hundred population. I did read that pre-1850 some wooden moulds had been used at Musselburgh Links, but most of the moulds would have been made in cast iron. Nowadays they will be all made in hardened steel. History buffs will know that Jeparit was the birthplace of Australia's longest serving prime minister, Sir Robert Menzies.

GOLF. October 18, 1895.

"HOME" GOLF BALL PRESS.

Thousands in Use.

PATENT

For making and re-moulding Golf Balls. In two sizes, "27" and "27½." Highest Testimonials from Leading Golfers.
EVERY PRESS GUARANTEED. PRICE 10s., POST FREE 10s. 6d.
Special "Elastic" Paint for Golf Balls. Warranted not to Chip or Crack. Price 1s. 6d. per Tin, Post Free 1s. 9d.
Sole Agents for HULBERT'S GOLF BALL CLEANER (Patent), For use on the round. Price 1s. 6d., Post Free 1s. 7d.
"HOME" GOLF BALL PRESS COMPANY, 24, Howard Street, GLASGOW.

Golf Far and Sure 1895 advert of Jeparit Museum's golf ball mould

There were several attempts over the years to improve the 'kindness' of gutties towards wooden clubs by experimenting with various additives incorporated into the gutta percha. That is, make the gutties less damaging by making them a bit softer. Many additives were trialled such as cork powder, bits of leather, metal powders etc. However, the process of mixing additives into rubber, or into resin, was very much in its infancy. Also the critical importance of optimal dispersion was not yet fully understood. As far as I can see, none of the modification attempts appear to have been successful from a commercialisation standpoint. This does not mean that examples of some of these trial balls will not still exist in someone's cupboard, garage or loft. Just like a few of the wooden golf balls made during the WW2 natural rubber shortage continue to surface from time to time (see below) Apart from these totally wooden WW2 golf balls, experimental Dunlop 65 golf balls were also made at that time which had a solid wooden core with a balata cover. One of these balls sold at the June 2018 *US Open Memorability Auction* for ninety dollars.

Despite the relatively short life span of the guttie balls, significant numbers of them were made. In the last few decades of the nineteenth century golf was starting to explode all across the world and guttie balls played a very important role. In 1892 alone, about five hundred tonnes of gutta percha was used in this application, which equated to about eleven million golf balls.

Wooden golf ball offered during WW2 Natural Rubber shortage

The wound balls, starting with the Haskell, survived in some form or other from about 1900 to late 1990s. i.e. just about one hundred years. Both the gutties and the wound balls were made with natural polymers which came from trees until at least the 1960s. i.e. natural rubber and gutta percha / balata. As such they would have had all the variable quality limitations which are found in naturally occurring substances. Not the least of which could be caused by the natives pissing in the latex after they had extracted it from the tree! From that time onwards these natural polymers have gradually been replaced by a whole range of synthetic (man-made) polymers such as ionomer resins, polybutadiene, synthetic polyisoprene, urethanes etc. This coupled with very advanced computer-controlled manufacturing processes has resulted in vast improvements in the quality consistency of golf balls. The Titleist Pro V1 was probably the first solid core multi-piece ball to be widely accepted by professional golfers in about 2000, even though solid core balls had been first developed quite a bit earlier than that, maybe late 1960s or early 1970s. In the very early days of the wound balls, the weights from big suppliers such as Dunlop or Slazenger were quite a bit heavier than modern balls. In 1909, Basque golfer Arnaud Massy, who won an Open Championship in 1907, used to meticulously weigh his golf balls. The weights he recorded ranged from 1.665 ounces (47.17 grams) to 1.713 ounces (48.55 grams). This weight of ball was around between 1900 and 1922 prior to the introduction of the 1.62 -ounce standard. The Americans also dallied with a 1.55-ounce ball in 1931 but it was short-lived. I noticed that the latest Titleist Pro VI has a thermoset urethane coating on its cover (i.e. it is not thermoplastic). This means that in some way the polymeric chains must be cross-linked, probably using organic peroxide, and therefore these balls do not lend themselves to recycling and are not environmentally friendly. At least they are not single use, throw away items, and can be reused many times providing that they are not lost during play. Unlike the earlier balata covered balls which could be totally wrecked by one single off-centre hit, the modern ball has a cut and scuff resistant outer jacket which is relatively very difficult to damage.

Although the weight of the golf ball has remained constant for quite a long time now, the same cannot be said for the physical diameter of golf balls. In the 1920s everyone in the world played with a 1.62 ounce / 1.62-

inch diameter ball. Then in the early 1930s the Americans decided they would move to a 1.68-inch ball. Various reasons for this move were put forward, but mostly likely it was done so that the Americans could have a big commercial advantage. The R&A resisted the change for many decades after that but eventually they lost the battle. They switched over to the 1.68-inch ball for professional tournaments in 1974 and finally banned the 1.62-inch ball for ordinary club golfers in 1990. We must be aware however that 1.68 inches is a minimum size for a golf ball. There is no restriction to making a bigger ball than this provided the density of the core material is reduced so that the overall maximum weight of 1.62 ounces is maintained. Hence today in 2020 we can find balls on the market like the Callaway Super Soft Magna which has a 1.732-inch diameter. Knur and spell never had the close regulation for knurs which applied to golf balls and this may have been one of the reasons for its demise.

Whereas the size, weight, and some performance characteristics of the golf ball off the club face are tightly regulated, the same does not apply to the materials used in its manufacture. Golf ball makers closely guard their exact raw material specifications. The other thing they fiercely protect is their dimple design. This includes the size, shape, and number of the dimples. It also includes the depth of the dimples and the pattern in which they are arranged on the ball surface. The number of dimples is generally somewhere between three hundred and five hundred. The dimples need to be arranged in a symmetrical fashion to ensure that the ball flies properly. Dimple shapes often have a polyhedron shape, such as tetrahedron, octahedron, dodecahedron, and icosahedron. Often on the same golf ball we can see different size dimples. Even back in the 1960s and 1970s I remember that my old friend Mike Shaw, who spent his working life with Dunlop golf balls in the UK back in the days when the 'Dunlop 65' golf ball was king, spent many hours crossing backwards and forwards over the Atlantic in a big white bird involved in court cases fighting infringements by US golf ball makers of Dunlop's dimple design. Two things are for certain. Firstly, the ball surface technology has come a long way since knur and spell players began to carve patterns on their wooden knurs many moons before golfers started to use a hammer on their guttie balls. Secondly, the Americans were very smart back in the early 1900s when they grabbed the commercial initiative with the ball size. Today the world golf ball market is over one billion balls per year and is worth well over one billion dollars. Titleist alone probably manufacture over one million balls per day. Just a few more than the five or six featherie golf balls per day which Allan Robertson was making in the 1840s!

Chapter 6

World champions, footballers and cricketers

For centuries golfers have used a range of different clubs to play their game. It probably started off with just one club before some bright spark had the idea of digging a hole. Earlier on in the piece it increased to about six clubs and by the early 1930s this number rose to over thirty clubs. Eventually the law was brought in to permit a maximum of fourteen clubs. Knur and spell players only ever played with one pummel. However, the top players would carry a box of different pummel heads and different flex shafts from which they would choose according to the weather conditions. They had some pummel heads which tended to hit the ball high to take advantage of tail winds and others which tended to hit it lower when hitting into a head wind. As far as I know all the pummel head faces were always flat and did not have different degrees of loft like golf clubs. Having said that, I did notice that on one of the loose Ted Griffiths pummel heads, which I had access to in late 2019, the dowelling piece going into the head had been inserted at an angle. Maybe this had been done deliberately to create an angle for the pummel head face?

I didn't know it at the time, but I recently discovered that world champion knur and spell player, Stuart Greenfield, used to work as an electrician at a company called Burroughs & Green in Trawden where my brother Richard did his engineering apprenticeship in the 1960s before embarking on a career as an officer in the merchant navy. During the second world war this company was converted to an ammunition making factory and my mother also worked there making bullets after she had been evacuated from Kingston-Upon-Hull in the East Riding of Yorkshire as a sixteen-year-old to escape the heavy bombing by the Germans. Apart from

London, Hull was one of the most heavily bombed cities in England during the last war.

Another Colner, called Billy Baxter, was also world champion in 1937. In an interview which Billy gave many years later, he recalled that they took seventy-five pounds gate money from admission fees. Since they only charged sixpence for the entrance fee, it meant a crowd of at least three thousand people were watching. I say 'at least' because the matches were played on open parkland or open moorland. It would have been impossible to control the entry points properly and stop many people from sneaking in to watch the contest for free. In actual fact entrance fees to watch knur and spell matches hadn't changed all that much since the famous Marsden and Lax contests in the 1820s when spectators were charged threepence to watch. In relative purchasing power terms the 1828 fee would have been quite a bit more expensive than the 1937 fee. Bear in mind that the total population of Colne in 1937 would have been about twenty-five thousand and about half of those would be women who would not be attending a knur and spell match! An article in the *Nelson Leader* newspaper dated 18 April 1957, gave a reproduction of the advertising bill from the 1937 match. Billy played against the reigning world champion, Jim Crawshaw from Stocksbridge in Sheffield. The match was played at the Alma Inn Grounds at Laneshawbridge just outside Colne. It was played for £100 over twenty-five rises with only the longest knock to count. Both players used three-foot nine-inch pummels and half ounce pot knurs. Entry fee for spectators was indeed advertised as sixpence. Baxter's winning strike was 188 yards and one foot. After a very close match his opponent was only three yards shorter.

According to various old timers I was able to interview, on the same day that this 'world championship' was being played at the Alma, a Colne and Nelson local derby Lancashire League cricket match was also being played just over one mile away at Colne's Horsfield Ground. This match had attracted a sell-out crowd, but it was still significantly less than the knur and spell crowd, despite the fact that men, women, and children were at the cricket match and only men were at the knur and spell. Having more spectators at a knur and spell match in 1937 than at a Lancashire League cricket match derby was not a new thing. Almost fifty years earlier in 1889, the *Burnley Express* newspaper, had an article where the Nelson CC were bemoaning the fact that their ground takings at a Seedhill derby cricket match were considerably down that year because a tipping match (knur and spell) had been held that day at Blacko, which is a small village about three miles away from Nelson. There were plenty of examples to show that, in the north of England at least, knur and spell was equally as popular as cricket, if not more popular during the 1800s and early 1900s. Just as a matter of interest, Blacko was the village where my old friend and work colleague Ivan Hipperson used to live before emigrating to New Zealand. It was Ivan who had invested jointly with me in a half share of an old bag of golf clubs back in the days when we were both junior laboratory assistants at the Pioneer Oilseals factory. Ivan's dad operated a family-owned sheet metal working business in Nelson.

Very interesting to note that when Sir Henry Cotton won the second of his three British Opens at Carnoustie in 1937 he picked up the same prize money as Billy Baxter (£100). After four hundred- and eighty-seven-years golf had finally caught up with knur and spell ! This may in fact have been one of the last knur and spell matches where significant prize money was on offer. After the second world war none of the knur and spell events which I saw advertised appeared to be big money challenge matches between two combatants. They seemed to be long knock handicap events where lots of players entered and there would be elimination heats. There was never much prize money. I suspect that they were mostly playing for a championship cup and the bragging rights which went with it. I also suspect that by then the number of spectators watching would have dropped considerably and they would not have been charging to watch. By that time football would have been the big paying spectator sport in winter and cricket in summer. When Billy Baxter played in 1937 there were probably around five hundred men regularly playing the game in Colne and the surrounding villages. This would have been at least ten times the number of members playing at Colne GC. When I regularly caddied there in the mid-1950s I never saw more than three or four groups on the course on any given day. In the very early 1900s even knur and spell events held at relatively minor pub locations such as the Old Duke Hotel in Waterside Colne and the Cottontree Arms at Winewall near Trawden with fairly modest prize money, would regularly attract seventy or eighty entrants. By 1970 the knur and spell playing numbers would have been very small.

Baxter is a name of Scottish origin meaning 'baker'. Billy himself had been born in the small village of Foulridge, just a few miles outside Colne, in 1909. After his world championship win in 1937 he served his country during the second world war. Had it not been for the six-year hiatus Billy may have been able to win more world championships. During my 2019 visit to Trawden I was lucky enough to meet with Stephen Coupe who is the head chef at the Trawden Arms. I was there on 'poppy' day which is the second Sunday in November. Stephen was proudly carrying his 'Uncle Bill's' war medals. He also had some old war photos which showed Billy wearing a Tam O'Shanter Scottish beret which indicated that he must have served in a Scottish regiment such as the Black Watch, Royal Scots, or Cameron Highlanders. A knur and spell world champion with Scottish connections. Fancy that!

By coincidence, the Alma Inn, which was built in 1775, is just a few hundred yards away from Colne GC where I first got my interest in golf as a caddie at the age of twelve. It is also close to Bluebell Farm which is run by my brother's daughter Jane and husband Russell as an activity centre for handicapped children. Bluebell Farm is a place where the children can get tremendous therapeutic benefit from working with all kinds of animals, at the same time giving welcome respite to their devoted parents. Eldest son Jonathan and I spent some 'relaxation' time there before and after our Camino walk in the European summer of 2017, helping to build new stables for the horses. We also enjoyed a nice beer (or two) at the Alma pub! Both Colne GC and Bluebell Farm are only about one mile from Noyna Hill where knur and spell was also regularly played in the 1800s and 1900s. And just to cap it all off, I was in Noyna House when I attended Colne Grammar School in the 1950s. All the school 'houses' were named after local hills in the surrounding area...Pendle, Boulsworth and Noyna. Pendle Hill was the most famous of these having been associated with the famous Lancashire witch trials in 1612.

Sometime prior to Colne GC being started in 1901, in the 1700s and early 1800s, Bluebell Farm was probably the original site for a pub called the Bluebell Inn. This pub had existed even before the Alma pub had been built.

It was mentioned in the *Leeds Intelligencer* newspaper of November 1763 in an article about turnpike roads between Colne, Haworth, Keighley and Bradford. It was also mentioned in *The Statutes at Large from the Magna Carta To the End of the Eleventh Parliament of Great Britain* by Danby Pickering in 1761, amending an act which had been passed in 1755 in the twenty-eighth year of the reign of King George II. According to a story in *Backthenwhen – Odds and Ends of the History of Colne,* the Blue Bell Inn also featured in a famous bigamy case which happened in 1787. It probably was there in the first half of the eighteenth century and maybe even earlier. However, some sources mention that the Blue Bell Inn had been on the site where Colne GC now stands. Either way we are in the right vicinity. Blue Bell Farm and Colne GC are only about a hundred metres apart. At least one other pub in the main street of Colne, which is still open for business in 2019, was selling the amber liquid back in the 1700s. This was the Hole in the Wall pub which was mentioned in the *Manchester Mercury* newspaper in July 1776 and in fact had been built in the very early 1700s. The same pub also appeared in the *Burnley Gazette* in April 1863 where it was listed as one of the regular stopping places for a daily omnibus service (horse drawn bus) operating between Burnley, Marsden, Nelson, and Colne. The first omnibus service in Britain had opened in 1824 in Manchester. The Hole in the Wall name hasn't survived, but the pub has. These days it is has the very unimaginative name of Market Street Tavern. What a travesty!

On the site of the current Bluebell Farm there had also been a blacksmith's smithy. The remains of this can still today been seen in the form of a 1702 date inscription on a lentil above a blocked-in door which is now a window. Hammer and tong symbols plus upturned iron horseshoes, the common blacksmith's shop signs, can also be seen carved into the stone.

I found no evidence that knur and spell was ever played at the Bluebell Inn. However, there are several fields directly behind the current Bluebell Farm which would have been ideal for knur and spell playing. Couple this with the fact that virtually every other pub within a few miles radius of the Bluebell did hold knur and spell events, this would make it highly likely that knur and spell was also played there. Pubs such as the Alma Inn and the Emmott Arms at Laneshawbridge, the Hare and Hounds at Black Lane

Ends, the Herders Arms on the old Haworth moor road and the Hargreaves Arms at Monkroyd all held knur and spell events.

The Colne GC (9 holes) on Skipton Old Road, which had been founded in 1901, was for a long time not the only golf course in Colne. A second nine-holes course, St Andrews GC Colne, had been formed in 1912. They played on a course laid out alongside the stream which runs from Laneshawbridge to Wycoller and close to the Old Emmott Hall site. Colne GC and St Andrews GC were less than two miles apart. Just prior to WW2, St Andrews GC had 140 members. However, in the *Barnoldswick and Earby Times* 31 December 1948 they were already being referred to as a 'former' club and had disappeared.

Certainly by the time I had found an interest in golf in my early teens, the St Andrews course had already reverted to ordinary farmland. The Alma Inn, Emmott Arms and Hargreaves Arms where knur and spell was played regularly, were all less than one mile away from both these golf clubs. It is also interesting to note that in 1957 a knur and spell handicap event was actually held on the land where the St Andrews GC had been.

In 1971 knur and spell was featured on BBC TV and Freddie Trueman, a Yorkshire and English cricketer, took part in the competition. Freddie had been born in the coal mining community of Maltby, Yorkshire which is only a few miles away from Barnsley where knur and spell playing was extremely popular. Apparently, although Freddie was a great fast bowler at cricket, he wasn't much cop at knur and spell! Another Yorkshire and England cricketer, Geoff Boycott, also turned up to this event. However, he didn't play because he was carrying a cricketing injury which had probably been caused by too much stonewalling!

The last World championship was held at Bradshaw's Tavern, Halifax in 1991. Stuart Greenfield also played on that occasion, but he didn't win. But another man from Colne, Len Kershaw, did win. This was the last time the World Championship was held, so to this day Len is probably still the reigning world champion!

Between 1970 and 1991 there were several attempts to revive the old game of knur and spell. In total during this twenty-one-year period there were about six world championships held. In addition to the BBC TV showing some interest a few other sponsors put their hands up from time to time with some prize money, but they didn't hang around. These included the Gannex Raincoat company who were based in Elland near Leeds and the Webster's Brewery Company from Halifax. The Gannex raincoat had been popularised by prime minister Harold Wilson and later by Queen Elizabeth. Webster's were the most frequent sponsor of the event and as a consequence most of the championships were held in or around Halifax in Yorkshire, apart from 1973 which was played at Dodworth Colliery Sports Ground. What made these championships different from ones that had been played in the 1800s and early 1900s was that the players were playing for a cup in addition to some prize money. For this reason they liked to think that these were 'official' world championships. The prize money was usually in the £200 - £500 range. But I suspect that that the winner didn't take everything and that the first three may all have received some prize money. The world champions in that period and their winning knocks were as follows.

1970	Eric Wilson	Sheffield	197 yards
1971	Stuart Greenfield	Colne	225 yards
1972	Len Kershaw	Colne	200 yards
1973	Stuart Greenfield	Colne	171 yards
1979	Frank Lenthal	Barnsley	210 yards
1991	Len Kershaw	Colne	175 yards

These distances seem to be quite short when compared with many of the distances recorded in the 1800s and early 1900s. For example, according to the *Manchester Mercury* 12 June 1821, over one hundred and fifty years earlier, Baker played Gragg for ten guineas a side over thirty rises. Baker shot 301 score and Gragg 275 score. So Baker, who was NOT a world champion, was averaging over two hundred yards per strike over thirty hits and not just one lucky long knock hit. Certainly, it was acknowledged that the wooden knurs would travel much further than the pot knurs. Reasons for this are well known. The wooden knurs were heavier and also had a rough surface. However, some of the pot knur distances recorded in the distant past were also much longer. In some cases ribbed pot knurs may explain some of this. Maybe also some of the older pot knurs were heavier. Supply of pot knurs in the later years was problematical and they had to use whatever quality they could get hold of. Unlike the massive evolution which has occurred with golf clubs, especially drivers, this did not happen with knur and spell pummels. Photos of both 1860s and 1990s pummels show them to appear virtually unchanged, at least as far as shape is concerned. So significant distance changes due to the pummel itself would not be expected.

I never had the opportunity to meet with Len Kershaw even though he is a member of a club in Colne where I have frequently visited over the last thirty-six years on my annual visits back to Colne and Trawden from Melbourne, Australia. This is the Royal British Legion Club near the top of Carry Lane in Colne. My brother Rick is a member there. We invariably spend an afternoon there on the snooker tables playing our once-a-year challenge match. Rick is a decent snooker player and always kicks my backside! In local snooker circles he is known as 'The Grinder'. His claim to fame is that he once played the 1980 World Snooker Champion, Canadian Cliff Thorburn (also known as The Grinder), in a friendly match. Apart from being world knur and spell champion, Len Kershaw was also a very handy football, cricket, and snooker player. Len's longest ever knock at knur and spell was two hundred and ninety yards with a pot knur. He did this in the 1960s against a champion Yorkshire player called Selwyn Schofield, but still only came runner-up. Maybe there was a big tail wind that day.

All this may sound a bit like the Roald Dahl story *Danny, The Champion of the World* where Danny excelled at poaching pheasants. But Colne was, and still is, a small town with about twenty thousand inhabitants. If you became world champion at anything you made a name for yourself. Even when Stuart Greenfield won in 1971, Billy Baxter was still hanging around the knur and spell scene and was still dining out free on his world championship win in 1937.

It is difficult to know exactly when the knur and spell boys first had the idea of calling their big matches 'world championships'. Prior to that they had held matches which were billed as the 'championship of England'. As early as 1841 in the *Leeds Times* one of the contenders was boasting that he was the champion knor and spell player of all England. Another such event took place on Doncaster Racecourse in November 1861 and was reported in newspapers all over the country and not just in knur and spell playing areas. The winner of that event picked up £100. By comparison, the first truly Open golf championship which was held at Prestwick GC in 1861 involved ten professionals and eight amateurs. The winner, Old Tom Morris, picked up a championship belt but zero cash! A match at Abbey Hey, Manchester in 1878 which was billed as 'Great Knur and Spell Match for £300 and Championship of the World' in the July 20 *Sheffield Independent* newspaper may well have been the first time this description had appeared.

In addition to these big money knur and spell events, All England knur and spell handicap events were also being held annually over the 1850 -1960 period. These events catered for the less skilled players and generally offered a cup and much smaller prize money. Hundreds of players often participated in these handicaps. Almost every year between 1860 and 1920 many events were also held which were billed as 'Great Knur and Spell Matches'.

About six miles away from Colne is the slightly bigger town of Burnley. Knur and spell was very popular in and around Burnley in the nineteenth and early part of the twentieth century. It gradually took a back seat to football after 1888 when Burnley became one of the original twelve teams which formed the first ever football league in England. One of the most prominent Burnley footballers from that era was a locally born lad called Jerry Dawson who played goalkeeper for Burnley between 1906 to 1929. He still holds the record for the greatest number of appearances for Burnley (522) and he was in the 1914 team which gave Burnley their one and only win to date in the FA Cup, beating Liverpool 1-0. He was also part of the 1920/21 team which gave Burnley one of only two Division One league championships and he won two England caps in the 1921/22 season. Why is all this relevant to the story? Because when he wasn't playing football, Jerry Dawson was also an East Lancashire champion knur and spell player! In fact, he could almost certainly earn much more money in those days from playing knur and spell than he could from playing football! In 1920 the maximum weekly wage paid to top football stars was about nine pounds sterling. By 1961 the maximum wage paid by Manchester United to their star players was still only £50 per week. Average players of course received significantly less than this. In 1927 Jerry Dawson challenged the reigning world champion, Jim Crawshaw, at a long knock contest for fifty pounds. He lost, but only narrowly, by a seven-yard margin.

Even in 1850 a single match between two knur and spell players could be for £200 or more with winner take all. This was a lot of money considering that in 1850 a new house cost £75, an average yearly wage was £20, and a modest house could be rented for less than £5 per year. Quite remarkable in fact when we factor in the general parsimonious nature of northern men, especially Yorkshiremen, which still persists even today. Also remembering that apart from the £200 prize money, much more could be made on the illegal gambling side plus they would sometimes get a percentage of the gate money if a big crowd attended. Just also consider that one hundred years later in Melbourne, Australia in the 1950s, Jack Harris would often play for total golf purses of £100 or even less where, even if he won, he would only receive part of the purse, and the rest would go to the other place getters. In its heyday, knur and spell (poor man's golf), was a big money sport! In fact, for hundreds of years' knur and spell paid much more money than golf did to the winners. The winner of the British Open did not receive £100 until they played the British Open at Royal Liverpool GC, Hoylake in 1930. One of golf's greatest ever legends, Bobby Jones, won on that occasion but of course he was an amateur so could not receive any prize money. Three months later he completed the first ever Grand Slam and retired from golf at only 28 years of age. He is still the last amateur to win the British Open.

For another good indication of just how big the sport of knur and spell was in years gone by consider this. When the first ever *Wisden's Cricket Almanack* was published in 1864, part of it was devoted to explaining the rules of knur and spell. It sold for one shilling. It continued to be published throughout the war years but because of the paper shortage the number printed were very restricted and copies are very rare. If anyone has a complete set of *Wisden's* in good condition from 1864 to 2018 pull them out now, dust them off, and pick up at least five hundred monkeys from some mad keen cricket memorabilia collector. In 1963 when they published the hundredth edition, they named Six Giants of the Wisden

Century which included WG Grace, Sir Jack Hobbs, Tom Richardson, Sid Barnes, Victor Trumper and Sir Donald Bradman.

There had been a strong synergy between knur and spell and cricket long before 1864 which may well have dated back into the 1600s or 1700s. Each had developed along a similar path. Both games had been encouraged by owners of public houses and both had attracted very heavy gambling... especially cricket! From the time *Bell's Life* first appeared in 1820s both games featured regularly and prominently, with details on both stake moneys and betting odds etc. The first super-star of Yorkshire cricket was a Sheffield man called Tom Marsden. Sheffield was one of several epicentres for knur and spell in Yorkshire. Marsden was equally adept at both cricket and knur and spell. On July 24, 1830 in the *Sheffield Mercury*, Marsden had an advert where he challenged to play any man in England either at single wicket (cricket) or knur and spell. In May 1827, according to the *Sheffield Independent* newspaper, Marsden played knur and spell against Royds at Darnall for £40 a side. Admission was three pence to be returned in drink.

This may not sound like much money but to put it in context consider this. The average worker in that year earned about twenty pennies per day. There were 240 pennies in a pound. Therefore, the winner at Darnall collected the equivalent of about three years wages. The star knur and spell players could play many challenge matches every year so if they were successful, they could get quite rich. For most of the 1800s many top cricketers also dabbled at knur and spell. It was rather like many footballers, cricketers, and other sportsmen today who play golf in their free hours. The *Newcastle Journal* 17 January 1870 reported on a match which Robert Proctor, a top Northumberland cricketer of the day, had played in. *Sporting Life* dated 24 March 1880 detailed a match which famous Lascelles Hall and Yorkshire county cricketer, Billy Bates, played in. Cricket had been played on the Lascelles Hall ground as far back as 1698 and the Lascelles Cricket Club had been formed in 1825. Another Yorkshire county cricketer called Irwin Grimshaw also played knur and spell in the late 1880s. Even two Surrey county cricketers played knur and spell in about 1880. One of them was Emmanuel Blamires who also played in an England XI. In his case it should be noted that he had been born and raised in Bradford, Yorkshire which had always been a knur and spell hotbed!

In Tom Marsden's day, apart from a handful of players at Manchester GC and a few dozen at Blackheath GC, golf in England did not yet exist whereas knur and spell was everywhere. Both cricket and knur and spell often involved just two men challenging each other with big money at stake. In knur and spell it was just a case of which man could hit the knur the furthest either in a single strike or a series of strikes. In cricket it was also just between two men in a game known as single wicket cricket. Both men just both batted and bowled against each other and the one who scored most runs won. They could have a common team of any pre-agreed number of fielders but none of these batted or bowled. None of the fielders could be chosen by the combatants themselves. They had to be appointed by the independent umpire. Single wicket cricket matches for big money stakes were still being played in and around the Leeds area in 1864.There were even several attempts at reviving single wicket cricket in England throughout the 1900s but not for the big money challenge matches.

Of course, team versions of both cricket and knur and spell also existed. In July 1831 even the *American Turf Register and Sporting Magazine* was writing articles about Tom Marsden and Nurr (not knur) and Spell!

The synergy between knur and spell and cricket didn't just end with the gambling side of things. It was not unusual in the 1800s for both knur and spell matches and a cricket match to be held simultaneously at the same event. In fact it was not unusual for cricket clubs to actually organise the knur and spell part of the event. Often other games were also played at the same time. In 1840 another Sheffield man was issuing challenge notices in *Bell's Life* to play any man in England over three different games i.e. knur and spell, single wicket cricket and quoits.

My home-town of Colne had a cricket club about seventy or eighty years before they had a golf club. In fact they are the oldest club in the famous Lancashire League, having been formed in 1830. During the 1800s they folded and re-formed several times before they became a founding member of the Lancashire League in 1892, along with twelve other North East Lancashire mill towns. Most of the other Lancashire League teams had also existed long before 1892 when the League formed. E.g. Burnley (1833), Todmorden (1837), Ramsbottom (1840), Accrington (1846), Clitheroe

(1860), Nelson (1861), Rishton (1865), Lowerhouse (1869), Walsden (1870), Haslingden (1883) etc. Todmorden and Walsden are now just over the border in Yorkshire but up until 1888 the administrative Lancashire / Yorkshire border ran right through the middle of the Todmorden ground. Colne CC play at the Horsfield Ground which is about one and a half miles from where I used to live. Seedhill Ground, the home of Nelson CC, is about four miles away from that.

All the Lancashire League clubs employed professional cricketers from 1892 onwards. From the mid-1920s / 1930s onwards they tended to employ international players. The list of famous players who played in this League is like a who's who of world cricket. E.g. Sir Clive Lloyd, Sir Learie Constantine, Sir Viv Richards, Sir Everton Weekes, Sir Wes Hall, Sir Charlie Griffith, Shane Warne, Allan Border, Dennis Lillee, Steve Waugh, Ray Lindwall, Michael Holding, Kapil Dev, just to name a few.

The best cricketer of all-time, Sir Garfield Sobers, also played a couple of guest professional appearances in 1961 when he played in a Rishton v Colne match. Yes, I do know that Sir Donald was a great batsman. But to win a test match you have to make runs AND take wickets. Sobers averaged about 58 with the bat (which was just about as good as any specialised batsman of his era), took more test wickets than Merv Hughes (117 times more than Bradman) and took 77 more catches than Bradman (three times more than Bradman)! Depending on pitch conditions Sobers could also bowl medium-fast or spin. If Bradman was ever pitted against Sobers in a single wicket cricket match he would have lost every time.

The two best Australian players never to play for their country, Bill Alley and Cec Pepper, also played in the Lancashire League. Bill Alley was my hero at Colne CC when I was a boy. Both these colourful Australians went on to have successful umpiring careers in addition to long playing careers. Then we had the fast bowler who has taken more test wickets than any other fast bowler in the whole history of the game. Jimmy Anderson, aka the Burnley Express, also started off his long career at Burnley CC in the Lancashire League.

Nelson CC have in fact won the Lancashire League more than any other club. When Learie Constantine went to Nelson in the 1930s he was paid £800 a season which probably made him the highest paid sports star in England at that time. When he retired from cricket he became Trinidad's High commissioner to the UK. He became a barrister, was knighted in 1962 and also became the first black peer as Baron Constantine of Nelson.

Nearly all the Lancashire League cricket clubs are located in a very small area of Lancashire. Virtually all of them are between five and fifteen miles from Burnley and many of the towns which play in the league have less than 20,000 population. In its heyday the Lancashire League thrived on the back of the booming Lancashire cotton industry. As that industry declined and eventually disappeared, the mill town Lancashire League teams started to struggle. They could no longer pay the money required to attract the top world stars and they had to lower their sights and make do with players of lesser calibre such as James Brayshaw from Australia, one of the current AFL commentators in 2019. He played for Nelson in 1989.

All through the 1800s and well into the 1900s knur and spell matches often attracted bigger crowds than cricket matches. Every single one of the Lancashire League playing towns also had lots of knur and spell players. Plenty of the cricketers also played knur and spell. Some of the cricketers also played football.

The Burnley goalkeeper in the 1914 -1925 era played football for Burnley, cricket for Burnley CC and was also the East Lancashire knur and spell champion. Tommy Lawton, who played centre forward for England between 1938 and 1948, played both football and cricket for Burnley at one stage at the Turf Moor ground.

The only book I have been able to find which was written specifically about knur and spell was the one entitled *Colne Giants* by Paul Breeze and Stuart Greenfield which has been mentioned several times in this book. Maybe other books exist but I still haven't found them. The men who called themselves the Colne Giants were really only involved in the game from the 1950s until the games total extinction in the mid-1990s. Although that period in the game's history is obviously important, it was in reality a very small fraction of the overall knur and spell story. i.e. covering only about the last forty or fifty years of a game which had been going for at least four hundred years and probably longer than that. Certainly, after WW2, knur and spell was in serious decline.

Probably the first Colner to reach the dizzy height of being a 'world champion' was Billy Baxter when he beat the reigning world champion, Ernest 'Jim' Crawshaw in 1937 at the Alma Inn Grounds in Laneshawbridge. The war cut short Billy's time in the limelight. However, after serving in the war, he did continue to make appearances at handicap events until the late fifties by which time he was fifty years old. In fact at age forty-eight he won a long knock event at the Tempest Arms by beating another Colne Giant, Ted Griffiths. I said Billy Baxter was 'probably' Colne's 'first' ever world champion, but I don't say that with any great conviction. After the first world war, in the period before Billy Baxter arrived on the scene, Colne had another star player called Jimmy Bullock. I suspect that he may also have taken the odd world championship from the Yorkshire boys sometime in the 1920s. In fact in 1927 Jimmy beat the legendary Joe Edon in a match which may have been for a world championship. Joe may even have been the reigning world champion at the time. Jimmy was playing at least as early as 1921 and he was still turning out in handicap events twenty-five years later in 1946.

The other partners in crime from the *Colne Giants* posse were Stuart Greenfield, Len Kershaw and Ted Griffiths all of whom only became involved with the game from the mid to late fifties onwards during one of the many revival attempts. Such is the age of the game of knur and spell that no matter when it was being written about, it was often described as an ancient game which was enjoying a revival period. Even in the early 1800s this was still the case.

Greenfield and Kershaw each held the world championship on multiple occasions. Ted Griffiths never won the world title but did win many big money individual challenge matches. Each time they won they had to beat each other as well as fight off the best rivals from across the Yorkshire border. When I was in Colne in late 2019 I tried to set up meetings with both Stuart and Len, but in the end I ran out of time. Shortly after returning to Australia I received the news that Stuart (1934 – 2020) had died in early 2020. Their chief Yorkshire rivals during that period were probably Frank Lenthal, Eric Wilson and Selwyn Schofield. The first two of these players also held the world title at one time or another. Not sure about Selwyn Schofield, but more than likely he did too. Frank Lenthal was also a talented nipsy player. His old nipsy stick can be seen on display in Barnsley Museum. Elsewhere in this book will be found a photo of a nipsy stick which I have in my collection of artefacts.

As keenly fought as all these post-war knur and spell championships no doubt were, the strength of depth of the playing talent was only a shadow of what it had been at its peak in the 1800s or even early 1900s. i.e. there were only a handful of top players left in the game. Consequently there were far fewer events for them to compete in. Most of the competitions were handicap events involving relatively small prize money. Big money head-to-head challenge matches were few and far between. Many of the players turning up at the handicap events were older men who were already in their 50s, 60s or 70s.

When Bill Baxter won in 1937 he was twenty-eight years old. The man he beat was forty-six years old Jim Crawshaw who hailed from the Yorkshire villages of Bolsterstone and Deepcar which are close to the Derbyshire Peak District. Prior to losing to Bill Baxter, Jim had held the world title for most of the 1920s and 1930s. After losing in 1937, Crawshaw regained the world title in 1939 at age forty-eight when he beat Archie Robinson at the Flouch inn Grounds in Penistone. Jim Crawshaw was one of the biggest superstars the game of knur and spell had ever seen. And that is very high praise indeed because throughout the 1800s and early 1900s, there were dozens of great players who could perhaps lay claim to that title.

Not least of these great players was Jim Crawshaw's father, Herbert Watson Crawshaw, who played at the highest level from about 1883 to about 1913. During that period Herbert also held the world title on multiple occasions. He was still winning long knock events in 1906 at age forty-five. One of his last championship knocks, at age fifty-two, was in 1913 for £100 when he lost to Joe Edon, another young superstar of the game from Barnsley. Joe Edon was born in 1890 and was only two years older than Jim Crawshaw. By the time he was only seventeen or eighteen years old Edon was already playing regularly in big money challenge matches. In 1908 he beat Tom Pearson in a match for £100. In 1913 he played Herbert Crawshaw for £100 and the world championship. Joe Edon would have been Jim Crawshaw's biggest rival in the 1920s. When Billy Baxter beat Ted Griffiths in a long knock event in 1957/58 at the Tempest

Arms Elslack near Skipton, the *Nelson Leader* newspaper reported that both sixty-eight years old Joe Edon and sixty-six years old Jim Crawshaw both turned up as spectators from Stocksbridge to watch the revival event. Edon was said to be only a slight man. He was also a very avid gambler. When he was twenty-two in 1912 he was already part of a pitch and toss gambling circle which played at the Queen's Ground in Barnsley.

At the same time as Herbert was strutting his stuff, another Yorkshire man from Grenoside, Sheffield, was also lighting up the knur and spell scene. His name was Joe Machen, and he was arguably an even better player than Jim Crawshaw. When Joe died in 1926 at age seventy-four he had won over £4000 playing knur and spell. This was very useful money for any working man to win in those days, bearing in mind that most of them would have had full-time jobs. Knur and spell was only a pastime or hobby for most of them. In the 1800s there may have been a few men around who tried to earn a living from the game. But these were probably men who were adept at most of the other pub-based sports which involved prize money and gambling. i.e. quoits, single wicket cricket, arrow throwing, pedestrianism, prize fighting, pidgeon shooting, wrestling, rabbit coursing etc. These men would regularly compete for prize money at several different sports and would also regard gambling as a profession. One of Joe Machen's last competitions was in 1922 when he was seventy years old, when he beat Joe Beaumont with a strike of eleven score (two-hundred and twenty yards) using pot knurs. His career spanned almost fifty years. His longest hit at long knock with a pot knur was about 305 yards (fifteen score 14 feet to be precise). This is probably the record hit for a pot knur. It was achieved at the Queen's Ground in Barnsley in 1892 playing against Joseph Fleetwood. Joe was forty years old at the time. In March 1898 Joe played against Walter Driver from Colne at the Craven Heifer pub grounds in Cullingworth in a long knock competition for ninety pounds. It was a close match which Driver won by 13+ score (267 yards) to 12+ score (257 yards) using wooden knurs. In August 1901, at age forty-nine, Joe hit an aggregate seventy score over five rises playing with wooden knurs (14, 15, 15, 13, 13), averaging two-hundred and eighty yards per strike, with two strikes at three hundred yards. Apart from knur and spell Joe Machen was also involved in dog training for greyhound coursing.

Only a few years before Herbert Crawshaw and Joe Machen hit the big time, the two standout performers around 1860 were Kirk Stables of Leeds and Job 'Nelly' Pearson of Baildon. They were both Yorkshiremen who both held the All-England title several times.

Two other Yorkshiremen who featured in what may have been the first ever competition dubbed 'World Championship' held at Abbey Hey, Manchester in 1878 were John Grayson and Thomas Howson when they played for £300. This was thirty-seven and a half times what the winner of the Open Championship golf picked up that year at Prestwick GC and was probably the biggest knur and spell purse ever played for.

Earlier than all the players mentioned so far, in the 1820s and 1830s, famous Yorkshire cricketer Tom Marsden was playing for large sums of money against Joseph Lax. Before Marsden and Lax were on the scene, Bancroft and Winterbottom played for £100 at Doncaster racecourse which resulted in Bancroft being immortalised in Enoch Ratcliff's famous *Trip Match* poem. These were not the only ones playing for big money in the 1820s and 1830s. James Binns of Keighley played Barker of Adwalton in 1824 for £40 on Baildon Moor. Both players lived about ten miles away from the playing location. Robert Lee of Woodhouse was playing for forty sovereigns in 1831. A sovereign was a gold coin with a nominal value of one pound.(twenty shillings). As opposed to a guinea which had been introduced in 1663. Between 1717 and 1816 the value of the guinea was fixed at twenty-one shillings. Then, between 1839 and the early 1860s, the most notable player was probably Matthew Thompson from Barnsley who was still appearing in fifty pounds a side challenge matches in 1869. A few other names playing in big money matches in the 1830s included Michael Garforth, William Wharton, John Jubb, Squire Jagger, George Dyson, Joseph Thackray and John Ganger.

All the way through the 1800s and up until WW2 there was no shortage of big money challenge matches occurring throughout the north of England. Many hundreds of players would often play for sums between 50 - £300. Thousands of other lesser players also played for smaller wagers e.g. £5 – £20 range, or for even smaller monetary prizes or other prizes such as a copper kettle which were given at local pub handicap / sweepstake events. These lesser events were taking place simultaneously at small towns, villages, and hamlets all over the north of England. Just one tiny handicap event could attract dozens of entries which often necessitated a series of elimination heats which could stretch out over several weekends. I don't know if the big money knur and spell players were staking their own cash or if rich men were backing them, as mostly happened in many of the early golfing wagers. But for sure some of the big knur and spell prize money played for would have been enough to buy several houses in those early days.

When comparing all the great knur and spell players of the past it isn't a completely straightforward task because many players were just specialists at one format of the game. Some just focussed on long knock competitions. Others were better in handicap events where they were no doubt skilful at manipulating the myriad of handicapping variables, which were very much more diverse and complex than golfing handicaps. Some were experts at hitting from the spring-loaded spell. Others were experts at hitting from the gallows (pin). Some had a strong preference for wooden or stag knurs whereas others flourished with the ceramic pot knurs. Many were not especially long hitters, but they were very consistent. One player used to lay bets that he could hit the flying knur from the spell and never have an air shot in one hundred consecutive rises. In over forty years of playing competitive knur and spell, the story goes that no one ever saw Jim Crawshaw fail to connect with a flying knur. These consistent players were more successful at the 'aggregate score' format of the game, where the distance hit with every rise was measured and counted. I suppose that it was like some golfers are better at match play than they are at stroke play. What made Jim Crawshaw special was that he was proficient at all formats of the game. The other thing which made Jim special, and many of the other knur and spell champions too, was that they didn't try to protect their legendary status by refusing to accept challenge matches. When we read about the early golfing legends, such as Allan Robertson, this was a very common practice in golfing circles. In the 1840s and 1850s Robertson was regarded as the best golfer in Scotland. He retained this reputation until he died in 1859. But he didn't play many individual challenge matches during that period and opted to play mostly four-ball matches in which he partnered his chief singles rival, Old Tom Morris. In other words he was a canny old Scot!

On the other hand, Jim Crawshaw, and all the other knur and spell champions, regularly put their reputations on the line by playing many matches every year when they were at the peak of their powers. They didn't play the old smoke and mirrors trick which the golfers often played! In fact in their search for big money challenge matches they often took big risks by enticing the opponents to accept the challenge by offering them very big yardage starts. i.e. imposing very big handicaps on themselves. Also they didn't wait for someone to challenge them. Often they were the ones initiating the challenge. What is more, they often issued the challenge publicly by advertising in *Bell's Life* or other local newspapers. These could be specific challenges targeted at individual opponents, or they could be more general challenges aimed at playing against 'any man in England'. They were also prepared to travel quite extensively to fulfill a challenge. Even from the late 1830s, in an era when travel wasn't easy, Barnsley based player Matthew Thompson would often play in Leeds, Bradford, Halifax, Sheffield, Manchester, Wakefield, Baildon, Dewsbury, Doncaster etc, as well in lots of small villages or remote moorland locations. Many of the top players were doing the same thing.

Another similarity to golf throughout the 1800s and the early 1900s, was the number of brothers and the number of fathers / sons who played knur and spell. This wasn't as apparent in knur and spell after WW2, although it was still common in golf.

In the above section, I have singled out a few knur and spell champions, but in doing so I am acutely aware that I have probably done a great disservice to a very long list of knur and spell players from the 1800s by not giving them a mention. There were hundreds if not thousands of very good players in that era. Many of these players were capable of attracting large crowds of fee-paying spectators and many of them had long and distinguished playing careers over many decades. Maybe the period between 1800 and 1850 was the peak period for knor and spell playing. There were so many players in those days who were regularly playing big money challenge matches. Contests for thirty, forty, fifty or even one hundred pounds were 'a dime a dozen'. The following list is just a tiny fraction of the names which were regularly appearing in the newspapers where significant amounts of money were involved.

William Sutcliffe, Henry Mollart, George Dimelow, Jonas Balm, James Binns, William Wheater, John Metcalf, Robert Rawnsley, Jimmy Bedford, Cain Fozzard, Sutcliffe Laycock, Abraham Priestley, James Denton, John Lister, Thomas Greenwood, Will Judd, Elijah Tankard, William Wheater, John Butterworth, Willie Lamb, John Speight, Joshua Kendal, Benjamin Foster, George Cherry, Thomas Pollard, Marmaduke Houldsworth, Charles Scargill, Daniel Gunson, Thomas Foster, George Wadsworth, Emmanuel Blamires, Benjamin Wainwright, John Willie Dixon, Robert Lee, Thomas Jackson, John Ward, Ned Homer, Joshua Rhodes, Joss Butler, George Leach, Jacob Ellis, Ben Walker, James Maltby, Henry Hitchen, Robert Greenwood, Joseph Coward, Harrison Coates, John Rider, Job Farsley, William Dyson, Joseph Dawson, Henry Greenwood, James Hollins, John Dixon, James Barker, Thomas Calvert, Asa Shackleton, Joseph Leach, Jabez Parker, Jonas Farrah, Andrew Shepherd, George Dyson, Richard Gaunt, Dick Galloway, Fred Speight, George Farnsworth, Isaac Atkinson, Elijah Waller, Kit Halstead, Tom Ladd, Hiram Butterworth, John Pickup, Charles Ogden, Henry Oxspring, Joseph Thackray, John Jagger, Joseph Boocock, Bill Waterhouse, John Ganger, William Dobson, Hiram Hodgson, Ned Pearson, Jesse Bentley, William Wharton, Jeremiah Holme, George Drabble, Michael Garforth, Robert Shackleton, Samuel Longbottom, Joseph Hicks, William Royd, Benjamin Tyas, Watson Bullock, George Barber, Job Senior, Aaron Farrar, John Hebblethwaite, Sam Moss, Herbert Smith, Richard Pearson, Squire Jagger, John Sykes, Tom Rawnsley, Henry Newell, Joseph Cook, David Smalley, Waddy Bolton, George Sheldon, Harry Kellet, Tom Pearson, Richard Wildon, Frank Wild, Walker Wainwright, Joshua Butt, Dick Hemmingway, Paul Bretherick, Joseph Fleetwood, John Starkey, William Horrocks, Edward Hanson, David Baines, Edward Sharpe, Amos Dixon, Joseph Travis, Oliver Child, Fred Moore, Job Cockcroft, Barker Halstead, Tom Blackburn, Joseph Driver, Billy Anness, Roland Aspinall, Bert Walton, Harry Benson, Robert Spencer, Holgate Birtwistle, Jimmy Laycock, Herbert Bateson, Reuben Bannister, Fred Hargreaves, Harry Stainsby, Jack Ellis, Harry Buchanan, Seth Townsend, Joseph Fox, Smith Jepson, George Foster, Philip Rushton, Bob West, Willie Lamb, Joseph

Wood, Enoch Clayton, Barker Halstead, Amos Cook, John Brown and John Jubb.

There undoubtedly will be lots of important players missing from this list. Some of these players could also have been unofficial World or All England champions. Certainly, there would be many County champions amongst them. There were no official knur and spell records to source the information from. Information which has been mentioned has been gleaned from old newspaper reports which were often sketchy and inaccurate because many reporters had no idea what knur and spell was all about.

No doubt every one of these players, and many more like them, had great stories to tell. When Joseph Leach of Baildon died in 1902 at age fifty-six he was said to have been an All-England knur and spell champion for many years. Another famous surname around the Colne and Trawden knur and spell scene over a very long period was Travis. Joseph Travis lived in the small hamlet of Cottontree which is part of Trawden village. He was born in 1868 and was already playing in local knur and spell handicaps by 1886. In 1890 he won a match at Lower Hartley near Todmorden shooting eleven score (220 yards). He was still competing in handicap events in 1942 at age seventy-four and still racking up competitive numbers allowing for his handicap which enabled him to at least win some of his heats. Joe was a clogger and was also a pummel head and stick maker. In 1938, according to the *Nelson Leader* newspaper 26 August, at seventy years old, Joe was second in a handicap event and his son John was third in the same event! Incidentally, when I was a young boy in the late 1940s I remember that there was a small clogger's shop on the corner of Clogg Heads which leads around to the old Chelsea area of Trawden village. My mum had all my school clogs made there. This shop, one of three or four such shops in the village in those days, was run by a man called Travis, who was probably Joe or his son John...probably the latter. I never saw Joe's name in any of the big money events played outside of the Colne area. He was obviously someone who preferred to stay in his own backyard, or close to it, and someone who mostly played for the love of the sport. However, with at least fifty-six years of actual competition playing he probably had more longevity in the sport that any of the aforementioned 'Colne Giants'. So too did eighty-seven years old Amos Shepherd from Thurgoland near Penistone and eighty-four years old Jim Howson from Stairfoot near Barnsley. As reported in the *Bradford Observer* 8 May 1950, the evergreen Amos, who had worked over sixty years in the coal mines, lost his knur and spell challenge match to the younger man on this occasion. The 1800s were the glory days of knur and spell. What I was able to personally witness in the late 1950s and 1960s was only part of the long lingering but futile effort to survive.

There are many rich sources of knur and spell information which I have been unable to examine. Not the least of these will be the *Annals of Barnsley and its Environs* by John Hugh Burland which is a series of five books (over one and a half million words) and which contain many knur and spell references. Burland was born in Barnsley in 1819. His work covers the period 1744 – 1864 and is held in the Barnsley Library Services at Barnsley Museum. Annals also exist for many other towns and cities in both Lancashire and Yorkshire.

Chapter 7

Great golf matches, knur and spell, rabbits and lawnmowers

In Scotland, most of the reports on big money golf matches in the early days (1600s and 1700s) involved either royalty, noble aristocrats or wealthy landowners. Most of the members at Scottish clubs and at Blackheath GC would have operated betting books within their club, but these generally would have been relatively much smaller bets. Indeed, from the *Blackheath Chronicles*, it was clear that bets between members generally revolved around a few bottles of claret. This booze was always kept at the club and was consumed by the members. Even though they appeared to be an extremely boozy lot, the money lost on bets generally did not appear to be disproportionate to incomes.

As the transition from retained club maker to club professional took place, big challenge matches between club professionals started to appear in the newspapers. Amongst the first Scottish professionals to start playing the big challenge matches would have been Allan Robertson. Newspaper reports of these started to appear from the mid-1840s until his death in 1859. But he had only a handful of challengers and the so-called 'Great Golf Matches' were few and far between. Until he died Robertson was regarded as the best golfer in Scotland. The only Scottish newspaper reports of big money golf matches in the 1700s always seemed to involve titled and privileged people and generally not the golf equipment artisans. The story about Robertson being the best golfer in Scotland was probably something of a con. Many times, when he was challenged, he declined to play. He especially avoided matches against Old Tom Morris and preferred to only play with him as a partner in doubles matches when his chances of winning would have been greatly enhanced.

When Robertson died, a tournament was held to find his successor, and the Open Championship was born in 1860. Less than ten players entered and more than half of these were just making up the numbers. From 1860 onwards, big money golf challenge matches between the professionals became more frequent. However, at least for the next twenty-five years these big matches involved very few actual players and very few venues where they were played.

The combatants came from just a few Scottish families. Names which have since become synonymous with the history of golf such as Morris, Park, Dunn, Strath, Anderson, Fernie, Auchterlonie, Campbell etc. Even in 1885, twenty-five years after the first Open Championship, it was still being dominated by a few Scottish families. Playing in the event that year there were four Simpsons, three Morrises, three Andersons, three Auchterlonies, three Parks, three Fernies, two Sayers, two Paxtons, two Kirkaldies and two Campbells. It was well into the 1890s before English names started to appear in the top ten.

In the last two decades of the 1800s, after the rule change which involved separating the greens from the tee-up areas, more Scottish golf clubs were springing up and there was a massive explosion of new golf clubs in England and around the world. All these clubs were starting to employ club professionals and the big money challenge matches began to also proliferate, especially between English and Scottish club pros in the early 1900s.

However, when it came to big money challenge matches, if we exclude a handful of matches between royalty, noblemen and very wealthy landowners, golf was well behind knur and spell in this aspect of the two games. Reports of many big money knur and spell challenges appeared in English newspapers from the early 1800s and had probably been occurring even earlier than that. Besides which, the knur and spell challenge matches involved dozens if not hundreds of different players and a similar number of different venues where the matches took place. The remarkable thing with the knur and spell challenges was that they were happening with the cloth cap and clog brigade. i.e. a sector of the community which one would have thought would find great difficulty in raising high stake money. This could be anything from £10 to £200 per man, the high end of which would be enough to buy several houses in those days.

Knur and spell probably took its big challenge match mentality from what had been happening with cricket from the late 1600s / early 1700s. Golf was about one hundred and fifty years behind cricket in this regard and fifty to one hundred years behind knur and spell. Not only did both cricket and knur and spell attract big money challenge matches between ordinary working-class people long before golf got in on the act, but they also attracted large crowds of spectators who were prepared to pay entrance fees to come and watch while they boozed and gambled at the same time. Knur and spell in England would often get a crowd of up to ten thousand spectators many decades before the first truly English golf club even existed. This is quite amazing when we consider that many of the contests were held in remote moorland locations to try to avoid interruption by the police. In 1871 spectators at a knur and spell match in Leeds were charged four pence admission which with a ten thousand strong crowd would rake in about £167. Pub landlords were the chief promoters of knur and spell matches. The gate money take at these events would be swamped by the quantity of booze they sold during and after the match and by the amount of dosh which changed hands from the gambling side of things.

But let's get back to the story. Why do I think that knur and spell may have been a forerunner to the game of golf? Firstly, along with *hornussen*, *jeu de crosse* and maybe *rebatta* in Italy, it is probably more like golf than any of the games which have been put forward elsewhere. The ball used (the knur) and the club used (the pummel) are more like the equipment used in golf than any of the other games. The grip used by players looks very much like a regular baseball grip which some players use today. The swing used is more or less identical to an old-style golf swing, and, just like early golf, there is no green and no hole. The winner is the one who hits the knur (or series of knurs) the furthest. In some contests the match was decided by the longest single hit. In other events, the total distance accumulated from a pre-agreed number of strikes (rises) won the day. In some competitions the two formats were run simultaneously. i.e. the main match was an 'aggregate score' event, but a separate prize was also awarded for the longest knock. I don't know exactly when the word 'rise' found its way into knur and spell terminology signifying a hit, a strike, or a stroke. However, it has been used for at least the last two hundred years. It may not even refer to what the knur does after it has been hit (?). It could just refer to when the knur has been launched into the air from the spell before it is hit by the pummel. Knur and spell was not the only pub sport which used the word 'rise' in its terminology. The old sport of pidgeon shooting, which was around from at least 1750, and saw massive wagers as high as two thousand pounds in the early 1800s, also commonly used this word. i.e. The distance from the shooter to where the birds were released was referred to as a twenty-five-yard rise or a thirty-yard rise. If two birds were released simultaneously this was called a 'double rise'.

Knur and spell could be between two individuals or between two teams of any number of players or even multiple players all contesting as individuals. Often a team from one village pub would play a team from another village pub. Sometimes it may have been a team from a particular textile factory (or mine) playing another factory (or mine) team. The ground where they played was marked by pegs in twenty-yard increments. Each twenty yards being one score. Thus, if someone hit the knur two hundred and forty yards that was recorded as twelve score. In other words, it is just about identical to a modern day long-driving golf competition. Reports I have seen said that the knur and spell boys used a chain for measuring the twenty-yard increments. Several reports I saw mentioned that the chain they used was a Gunter's chain. However, I very much doubt this because a Gunter's chain was sixty-six feet in length (twenty-two yards). Gunter invented his chain in 1620. It was used all around the world by surveyors as a land measuring device. The chain had one hundred individual links which were each 7.92 inches long. The links were normally arranged in groups of ten which were marked by brass rings. So, it would not have been suitable to measure twenty-yard increments unless they had modified it by a special mark just part way down one of the links. What it was useful for though was measuring the length of a cricket pitch. To this very day a cricket pitch is still exactly one Gunter chain in length. The knur and spell boys may of course have used a specially purpose-made twenty-yard chain, but it wouldn't have been a standard Gunter's chain.

Let's not also forget that for about the first two hundred years, golf in Scotland did not involve the use of a hole or a flag or a green...even though they still called it golf! It was well into the 1600s before anyone ever mentioned a hole! It was 1743 before the word 'putt' first appeared in the literature and long after that before flag poles and flags appeared. Even, in the 1850s when David Robertson played Captain Kirk at Homebush, Sydney, Australia, I am not sure if they used mundane things like holes and flags. They just went from 'St James's Church to Lyons Terrace and back twice.'

When *The Australasian* newspaper golf writer Harry Culliton discussed Alexander Arthur Reid's letter to the newspaper on March 8, 1930, he also added a personal piece to the article describing how in the 1890s he and a friend had gone to some paddocks one day in Kew 'to play golf'. They just picked out a rough course in the morning and played a game in the afternoon. There was no golf course there at the time...just rough paddocks. There were no greens, no holes etc. They would have just hit from one tree to another, across to another tree, then to a gate post and so on. In this form of playing golf it really didn't matter that they were fixing the distance and counting the strokes rather than fixing the strokes and counting the distance. When no small target like a hole was involved, the player who won would always be the one who could hit the ball the furthest. Effectively they were just playing a form of long hitting, akin to knur and spell. There is every chance that the canny Scots started to use a hole and a flag just to differentiate themselves from knur and spell!

It is very interesting that golf historians still hold up the Robertson and Kirk game as an example of early golf having been played in Australia, even though it wasn't proper golf at all as we know it today. Yet, whenever knur and spell is mentioned, which is very rarely indeed, they shoot it down as not being relevant because it doesn't involve a flag and a hole. I'm not really sure just how that works? Actually, I do know how it works, but I am too diplomatic to expound!

An excellent source of examples of this form of golf are the *Blackheath GC minutes* prior to 1897. In the 1800s the club maintained a 'betting book' and details of all kinds of weird bets are given. Many of these bets had nothing to do with getting the ball into a hole! A typical bet was shown for October 1822. 'Captain Finlayson says he will give two gallons (of claret) to the club if Mr Cunningham drives from the middle hole to Hunter's or Laing's hole, hole high, in three strokes. Mr C teeing his ball each time, taking six balls on the day he selects.' The Blackheath GC did have holes at this time and sometimes the bets involved how many strokes taken to hole out. But frequently the bets had nothing to do with holing out. They just involved distance covered in the least number of strokes.

The reason why this kind of play was popular in those days is very simple to explain. For the first four hundred years of its existence golf was played on land where the grass was kept 'short' by rabbits and flocks of sheep eating it. There were no beautifully manicured greens like the ones we see today. Little cutting by man was done and even this had to be done by scything. For a long time, many centuries in fact, even the holes they used were very rough and crude affairs. So, putting out was a big lottery on the very poor and bumpy 'greens'. Discerning golfers who liked to punt on the game would quickly recognise this. Hence in many cases they would just reduce their games to a long driving contest even though holes existed. Things only started to improve slowly from the mid-1800s after a man called Edwin Budding from Gloucestershire in England invented the first hand pushed mowing machine in 1830. His first machine became commercially available from Ransomes in 1832 and by 1850 over fifteen hundred improvements to their twenty-one-inch mower had been made. Ransomes introduced horse drawn mowers for larger grass areas in about 1870 but this was already many years behind their competitors. According to *The Municipal Park Design and Development* (1840-1880) by Hazel Conway, Manchester Council in Lancashire had ordered two horse drawn thirty-inch mowers in 1857 from B Samuelson of Banbury. The mowers cost eleven pounds ten shillings each, horses not included, and they got a five per cent discount for ordering two. The mowers were not for use on golf courses because there were no proper golf courses in Manchester at that time. They were bought to mow the big areas of grass in Queen's Park and Philip's Park. After the onset of the Industrial Revolution there was an explosion in the construction of public recreational parks and gardens throughout many of England's big cities between 1840 – 1880. Although it was only after 1830 that lawn mowers began to be used, we do know that garden rollers had been around at least fifty years before that. Even in 1782, adverts for garden rollers appeared in the *Newcastle Chronicle*. Not sure if any of these rollers were used on golf courses in those days, or only on country mansion lawns. Probably not!

It is perhaps a little surprising to learn that the man who is regarded by many to have been England's 'greatest ever gardener', Lancelot 'Capability' Brown (1716 – 1783), did all his great work long before the advent of the lawn mower. Brown hailed from a small hamlet close to Morpeth in Northumberland. He laid out about one hundred and seventy large parks and ornamental gardens all across England for rich aristocratic families during his illustrious career, plus the odd one or two in Ireland, Wales and even Germany.

When I say 'no proper golf courses in Manchester' I should not forget that from about 1818 a few wealthy Manchester businessmen were playing golf on Kersal Moor, Salford. The early club called Manchester GC, and later called Old Manchester GC, was very exclusive and limited to just twelve members, most of whom were ex-pat Scots. According to the *Manchester Courier and Lancashire General Advertiser* 30 September 1837, the club had been instituted as early as 1814 by William Mitchell from Holt Town. They appeared to fire up in 1818 and by 1820 they already had a clubhouse. However, they shared Kersal Moor with the general public. According to reports they did not have proper fairways and no greens, so they wouldn't have had any use for big horse drawn mowing machines. Interesting though that both Queen's Park and Philip's Park are both only a few miles away from Kersal Moor. Holt Town is just a short walk away from the City of Manchester Stadium which became the new home for Manchester City FC when they left their Maine Road ground in 2003. One of the best places to see some of these early lawnmowers and grass cutting gear is the British Lawnmower Museum in Southport which is located just a stone's throw away from the Royal Birkdale GC.

This Manchester GC was in fact the second oldest club in the world to ever start up outside of Scotland after the Blackheath GC. For most of its early life they played on a five-hole course. The course and club disappeared in the 1880s, but the golf society just went into abeyance. They re-surfaced in the 1890s under the new name of the Old Manchester GC with a twelve-hole course and new pavilion at nearby Broughton Park. In the early 1900s they moved to a nine-hole course at Vine Street near Kersal Moor where they stayed until the early 1960s when they folded again. Again, the society itself went into abeyance. Since then they have not had their own course or club house, but they still get together a few times each year to play other courses. In 2018 they celebrated their two hundredth birthday and the City of Salford allowed them to play using old hickory golf clubs on a temporary three-hole course rigged up on Kersal Moor specially for the occasion.

Kersal Moor (Salford) had been a famous sporting place long before the Old Manchester golfers turned up. Archery had been practised there for centuries. Horse racing started there in 1687 and continued until the Jacobite Rising in 1746 when the track was moved to another location not too far away. According to *Bell's Life* in 1841 running races were held on Kersal Moor. Another very significant thing in British history was associated with that area. In 1913 there was a fire in the Old Manchester GC club house. It turned out that suffragettes had set fire to the club house and also painted 'Votes for Women' slogans on the thirteenth green. Emmeline Pankhurst, who was one of the leaders of the activist movement, lived in Seedley, Salford, about three miles from Vine Street where OMGC were located. Seventy-five years earlier, in 1838, Kersal Moor had also been the site of a huge mass political meeting which saw the birth of a working-class movement known as Chartism which pushed strongly for 'One man, one vote'. This movement eventually gave birth to the UK Labour Party. For several decades after 1838 the Liberal Party steadfastly resisted any change. Just like the Australian Liberals resisted for years the 2018 / 2019 Royal Commission into the banking scandal. It was only after the Liberal PM Lord Palmerston died in 1865 that the Liberals through Liberal PM Benjamin Disraeli eventually, and reluctantly, agreed to change in a vain attempt to cling on to power. The Reform Act of 1867 was the first step towards manhood suffrage. Before this act came into force only one million out of seven million men in England and Wales had any voting rights in elections. Of course, no women had the vote in 1867, so that meant that only around seven per cent of the total adult population in England could vote. Around the same time (in 1854) a very similar thing happened in

Australia. The Ballarat miners in the Eureka Stockade stood up for their rights against a very intransigent government. They lost the battle, but the unexpected result of their efforts was the birth of Australian democracy which we all enjoy today.

After the 1914 -1918 war there was an acute food shortage in England. Ten acres of the OMGC course were ploughed and sown by the Salford Corporation Cultivation of Lands Committee for provision of foodstuffs. I never saw any reports about knur and spell being played on Kersal Moor but that doesn't mean that it never happened. It was certainly played at many places such as Old Trafford and Harpurhey which are both less than five miles from Salford. It was also played at Swinton, which is only about three miles away from Kersal, and at Heywood which is about seven miles away.

We have to be careful not to confuse this 1818 Old Manchester GC with the current Manchester GC which is located in the Manchester suburb of Middleton. Even though Manchester was the second biggest city in England outside of London in 1900, this surviving Manchester GC was only started in 1882 with just eight ex-pat Scottish members. The Greater Manchester population in 1901 was well over two million. It began life as a very small nine-hole course played at Manley Park in Whalley Range which is a short walk away from the current Old Trafford soccer and cricket grounds. It had no clubhouse. At that time there would have been thousands more knur and spell players in the Manchester area than there were golfers! And of course if we totalled the membership of this club and the club at Kersal it wouldn't even add up to the number of knur and spell players turning up in those days to play in one single small village event...and there would have been hundreds of knur and spell events happening at villages all over Lancashire at that time. In 1898 this Manchester GC moved a short distance to a site in Old Trafford before moving to Middleton in 1912. Between 1890 and 1900 about ten golf clubs started up in the Manchester area. Most of the other clubs in this area started up after 1900 including Denton GC (1909) which runs alongside the A57 main road to Sheffield, and where I played occasionally when I worked in the town in the late 1960s. Approximately twenty golfers, nearly all ex-pat Scots, in Greater Manchester in 1882 from over two million people demonstrates quite nicely what a non-entity golf was in those days.

At the time of Budding's invention of the push-mower only Blackheath and Manchester GCs existed in England. Even as late as 1897 in the BHGC minutes there is no mention in the expenditure items of any club money being spent on mowing equipment. They do however show money spent on retainers for golf club makers from the late 1700s (about ten pounds per year). Also, in 1787, they paid William Holt (the captain's man) one shilling per week to take care of the five holes which existed at that time. By 1801 they employed a club maker called Donaldson to do both jobs. He was paid about ten pounds per year to be the club maker and an extra three pounds five shillings and six pence to make the holes, paint flag poles and repair flags. The use of flags and flag poles must have only started very late 1700s (at least as far as BHGC was concerned). In a 1778 painting of one of their club captains, the hole was shown as being marked only by a sprig of whin from a gorse bush.

Whether any of the Scottish golf courses were quick to take up the new mowing invention is not known. But I suspect that they probably didn't do it until well after the guttie ball came on the scene in about 1850. In *The Book of Golf and Golfers* in 1899 by Horace Hutchinson there is a chapter dedicated to the design and maintenance of greens which was written by someone from Sutton & Sons, an English company specialising in grass seeds. They covered the proper treatment and laying out of greens on different soils. At the time they were generally recommending different mixtures of red fescue, finer species of Agrostis, Poa Pratensis and dwarf perennial rye grass. Fertilisers suggested were nitrogen, phosphoric acid, potash and lime. Farmyard manure was still used by many golf courses in place of man-made fertilisers...even on greens. Regular mowing and rolling was certainly advised, but no mention of aeration. Motor mowers had still not been invented at that time. It is doubtful that they could cut the grass down to the tenth of an inch height which they often need today in order to get the green speed required in modern tournaments. No stimpmeters in those days. They had been invented in the 1930s but didn't come into regular use on golf courses until the 1970s. However, it is obvious that hand pushed mowers were well and truly in vogue by the end of the 1800s for use on greens and horse drawn larger mowers for use on fairways and rough areas. Certainly by the mid-1890s Ransome's small hand pushed mowers were being advertised in the *Golf Far and Sure* magazine and were said to be in use at a fair number of golf courses across England and Scotland.

One possible reason for the delay in the uptake of this new grass-cutting technology is obviously financial. In 1830 many of the Scottish clubs were struggling to survive. They were too busy selling all their assets and not in a position to fork out money on new ones. Another possible reason may date back to the first rules of golf drawn up in 1744 by Ye Honourable Company of Edinburgh Golfers. The very first rule they listed may help explain quite a few things. i.e. After holing out on a green the player should tee up for the next hole no further than one club length from the last hole! Just imagine the kind of chaos this would cause. Firstly, it would mean that any players behind would have to wait until everyone had teed off before they could play their approach shots to the green. In the old days this would not have been a major issue because there were relatively few players. Secondly, we must remember that wooden (and certainly not plastic) tees had not yet been invented and players had to tee up on a pile of sand. I am not sure if teeing up was compulsory in those days. Today, many players do not tee up if they are playing with an iron, particularly on short holes. Most teeing areas are like demolition sites with divot marks everywhere. They would be even worse if the tee boxes were not moved up and down regularly. With all this action taking place within one club length of the hole on bumpy greens which were not closely mown, it must have been like putting out on a bomb site with divot marks and sand all over the place! No wonder those Blackheath GC chappies often just bet on distance and not on strokes taken!

Between 1744 and 1875 there were two or three attempts to improve matters by gradually increasing the distance from the flag where teeing had to be done. However, it wasn't until about 1875 when Old Tom Morris at St Andrews decided that enough was enough. He made the bold move to completely separate the tee-up area from the greens. Possibly they had mechanical mowers before that date, but if not, the start of a very big change would probably have occurred from that time onwards.

If we look closely at the *Blackheath GC Chronicles*, and specifically at *The Laws of Golf* revisions at the end of the Chronicles, we can clearly see the evolution of the teeing area and putting green throughout the 1800s. From the first rule in 1744 which stipulated 'one club length', it was a very slow process of change. In 1828 the BHGC committee changed it to not exceeding four club lengths and not nearer than two club lengths. They kept it the same in 1844. In 1860 it became not nearer than four club lengths and not further than six. In 1868 it was not nearer than six and no further than nine. They kept it the same in 1874. Eventually, in 1879 they followed the St Andrews example and split the greens from the tees, when their local law stated that 'The ball must be teed within, but not more than one yard behind, the line marked by the professional'.

Maybe not all golf clubs separated the teeing areas from the greens at that time. According to the golf rule section in *Cassell's Book of Sports and Pastimes* dated 1891, the place of teeing was said to be 'no nearer the hole than eight nor further than twelve club lengths, except where special ground has been marked by the links keeper, which shall be considered the teeing ground.' So even in 1891 maybe the separation of teeing area from green was still an optional thing which was in a transition period? All the golf drawings in the *Cassell's 1891 book* still showed the caddies hand-carrying all the golf clubs loosely without any golf bags.

The other thing which must have contributed greatly to the obvious reluctance to putting out in many of the bets laid, was the condition of the ball itself. The old featherie balls were just segments of leather stitched together like an old 'casey' football and stuffed full of feathers. It would have been impossible to make such balls perfectly round, even when new. After they had been hit a few times they would have quickly gone further out of shape, especially if the ground was a bit wet. So, when we have very bumpy putting surfaces combined with balls which had lots of flat spots, it is easy to see that putting would have been very much a lottery. In fact, it would have made a great Fred Karno or Marty Feldman sketch! (The Marty Feldman golf sketch on *YouTube* is a must watch).

Of course, in their medal competitions at Blackheath GC they did putt out and count the total number of strokes. However, to illustrate the lottery of putting out in those days on *scheisenhausen* putting areas (it would be romantic to call these areas greens) we just need to look again at the *Blackheath golf club* minutes. In an 1823 Medal event played over three rounds on a five-hole course by a measly eight competitors, the scoring range was from 105 to 143 strokes. The average score was 117.4 which equated to 7.83 strokes per hole. In 1843, in another Medal competition played over twenty-one holes, the range was 175 to 272 strokes with an average of 210.64 or 10.03 per hole. But how many strokes were they taking to arrive at the 'green'? Well, according to their minutes even in 1813, a good drive with a featherie ball and a long-nosed club was said to have been five hundred feet (approximately one hundred and sixty-seven yards). This was the best drive in ten hits by one of their top players. It was not a typical drive by the average player. By the early 1840s, outstanding players like Allan Robertson at St Andrews had recorded a long drive of two hundred and fifty yards. But even allowing a much shorter hit than this it would mean that most 'greens' could be reached in three or four hits. In 1843 the seven holes at Blackheath GC had the following yardages.

Hole #1	170 yards
Hole# 2	335 yards
Hole# 3	380 yards
Hole# 4	540 yards
Hole# 5	500 yards
Hole# 6	230 yards
Hole# 7	410 yards

There was no mention of 'par' hole ratings in 1844. That didn't come until much later, maybe around 1870.

Their top players should have been able to reach the greens or be very close to the green in a total of twenty-five shots or maybe just one or two more than this. Over three rounds (twenty-one holes) the good players would take no more than eighty shots to reach the greens. But they were taking one hundred and seventy-five shots overall. This meant that they were taking ninety-five putts across twenty-one holes i.e. averaging four to five putts per green. It is therefore quite understandable why they would often just bet on shots taken to reach the green and not always on total shots to hole out. Of course, it was a different game again for the less skilful players. Even if we allowed them one hundred to one hundred and twenty strokes to reach twenty-one greens, it still means they needed a further seven or eight putts per green to hole out!

After the guttie ball was introduced things improved quite quickly. Even by 1857 there was an article in the *Fife Herald* about golf balls which referred to featheries as a thing of the past and 'an awful time to look back on'. In *Bell's Life* dated 19 April 1863, twenty members competed for the BHGC Spring Medal over three seven-hole rounds. The winner shot one hundred and twenty-seven and the last to finish shot one hundred and seventy-five. Two cards were not handed in which probably meant that they would have been even worse than one hundred and seventy-five. The average hole length for the course was three hundred and sixty-six yards which meant that the best players should have been reaching the greens in about sixty strokes. Thus, they would still have been averaging more than three putts per green and the lesser players would have been averaging more than four puts per green. Of course, greens and teeing areas had still not been separated at that stage.

This form of 'golf' is much more like the game of knur and spell than it is like the modern game of golf. i.e. In the game which Robertson and Kirk played they controlled the distance covered and counted the number of strokes taken. Whereas in knur and spell they fixed the number of strokes taken (which they called rises) and counted the distance covered. In both cases the accuracy element of the modern golf game was missing.

As we all know, the putting lottery didn't last forever. We can easily plot the big improvements in the Blackheath GC medal scores from 1844 onwards when they changed their course from five to seven holes. Medal competitions were played over three rounds (twenty-one holes) and by the mid-1850s at least twenty-two strokes had been taken off the three round scores. The replacement of the featherie balls by guttie balls had an immediate and profound impact giving more than a one stroke per hole reduction. By the mid-1880s there was a further sixteen stroke reduction in the three round scores which undoubtedly came about after the separation of the teeing area from the putting green in 1879. Then between 1880 and 1897 there was a further seven to ten shot improvement which can probably be attributed to a combination of things (big evolution in green design and grass technology, mowing machines etc, continual improvement in ball technology, big change in golf iron club technology away from the long nose wooden clubs and of course many more golf professionals who were constantly raising the bar for playing).

If we look at some of the scores reported in newspapers at the Manchester GC in the 1830s, 1840s and 1850s we can regularly see scores of eighty or ninety for ten-hole medal competitions with the highest score of one hundred and sixty for ten holes recorded by a gentleman called Malcolm Ross who had been a club member for forty years. I suspect that putting conditions on Kersal Moor were even worse than those at Greenwich Park, Blackheath!

Chapter 8

Spells, pins, pummels and Grammar School boys

There were two main versions of Knur and spell. The one which predominated in Lancashire used a small gallows type apparatus to tee up the ball which was suspended using a string noose arrangement. Thus, in this form of the game the player was hitting a stationary ball. The gallows frame was made of wood, but I never discovered which type of wood they used. In Lancashire, the gallows frame was often called a 'pin'. The horizontal arm from which the string was suspended was adjustable so that the player could set the ball at his preferred height from the ground.

Great care was always taken when setting up the gallows. A plumb line was used to ensure that the upright piece was exactly vertical, and a spirit level was used on the arm to ensure that this was exactly horizontal. The string had a kind of loop or noose at the end which was used to cradle the knur. It did indeed look like a miniature version of a hangman's gibbet! Often, a measuring stick was also used to make sure that the knur was always suspended at the same height every time. Sometimes, in very windy conditions, the noose end of the string was itself attached to another piece of string which was then pegged to the ground to prevent the knur from blowing around. Often this form of knur and spell, for obvious reasons, was referred to as knur and pin or knur and sling. Sometimes it was called 'pin tipping'. The positioning of the pin on the competition ground, and its setting up, was a long winded and finicky process, much of which I suspect was something which didn't necessarily help the player to make a good strike and was just something which added to the 'theatricals' and mystique of the game.

While over in Yorkshire, centred around the Barnsley and Sheffield areas, a spring device attached to a piece of wood which launched the ball into the air was used. This device was called a spell. The base to this device was often made of oak wood but other types of wood may also have been suitable. At least one maker of this equipment used an iron base for the device. In this form of the game the player obviously hit a moving ball. During the 1800s the spell developed into a very elaborate device with a fancy spring mechanism and was something of a work of art. The spring had a cup attached to it, about two inches from the loose end, where the knur was placed prior to activating the spring. I never actually saw a close-up of exactly just how the spring worked. I am pretty sure that it wasn't a coiled (helical) spring. It would have been a strip of springy metal. i.e. the kind of metal used these days for pallet strapping or maybe even the metal used for a flexible band-saw blade with the teeth ground off. Probably the proper description would be a leaf spring. Just one strip working in isolation rather than several strips of different lengths bolted together as used in the old vehicle suspension systems on cars. I think there was a sort of thumb-screw arrangement used for adjusting the amount of power required from the spring when it was activated. The run of the mill spell had cast iron fittings. But some of the super stars of the game had spells with fancy brass fittings on a mahogany base. A typical spell was about thirty-three inches (eighty-two centimetres) long and about five of six inches wide. It had spiked legs at each corner which were driven into the ground to stop the device moving when in play. It was designed to launch the ball into the air at the same height and same speed every time it was used. To check this, they activated the spring mechanism several times without trying to hit the knur and they made sure that when the knur fell to the ground it landed in the same place every time. Prior to hitting the knur, the top players often used to chalk their pummel heads just like a snooker or billiards player chalking his cue. For hundreds of years prior to the 1800s the spell was just a very simple arrangement like the one used in the ancient English game of trap-ball. Essentially it was just a short plank of wood on a fulcrum with a ball shaped depression carved in the plank to hold the knur. In many parts of Yorkshire this was simply known as a 'wooden kicker' and the pummels were often called gel-sticks. When the player 'tipped' this primitive kind of spell there was no consistency in the height of the launched knur. It depended on how much force the player used to start the process. Indeed, because of this early mechanism for launching the knur, the game of knur and spell itself was often just referred to as 'tipping'. In a Battle of the Roses between Lancashire and Yorkshire the player could choose which method of teeing up he preferred. Not all Lancashire players used the gallows. Some preferred to use the spell because they were hitting a moving knur. And not all Yorkshire players hit from the spell. Some opted to use the gallows or the pin as it was more often called. Even in an all Yorkshire or an all-Lancashire contest, either pin or spell could regularly be found. There was a preference for the spell in Yorkshire and for the pin in Lancashire, but nothing was cast in stone.

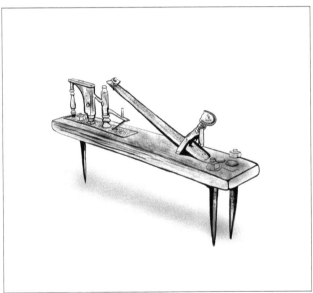

Typical 1800s spell used mostly in Yorkshire but not exclusively

The spells were not manufactured by any large commercial operations. As far as I know they were always made by a cottage industry. That didn't mean the spells were just Mickey Mouse contraptions. Some of them were quite elaborate and some of them even had patent protection. e.g. A new patent was granted to Mr G Humphrey of Sheffield in 1887 for 'an apparatus for playing knur and spell'.

Depending on which method the player used (spell or gallows), the swing used was somewhat different. With the spell, the knur was projected up into the air and a bit forward. Many of the players I have seen using the spell seemed to stride forward during the swing in order to connect with the knur. It often looked a bit like a Happy Gilmour swing or maybe the famous Gary Player 'walk'. With the gallows, where the knur was stationary, the swing was a much more conventional golf swing. With the better players the feet didn't significantly move during the swing. At least one player I read about actually drove pegs into the ground on the outside of each shoe (or clog) to prevent the feet from straying.

Having played golf myself for over sixty years, or at least something that purports to be golf, and having also attempted knur and spell when I was a teenager, I can say for sure that the knur and spell swing was much more difficult to perform than a golf swing. This is because the knur was either hit out of mid-air if using the spell or was hit from a very elevated stationary position if using the pin. The wooden knurs were a bit smaller in size than golf balls, but the ceramic (pot) and stag knurs were significantly smaller than golf balls.

The difficulty of hitting a much-elevated ball was clearly demonstrated to me only a few years ago when I attended the Abu Dhabi National Golf tournament in the United Arab Emirates. Many of the top PGA professionals, including Irishman Rory McIlroy and American Phil Mickleson, were playing in the event which was ultimately won by German Martin Kaymer. In full view of the very impressive clubhouse frontage, which is designed to look like a giant falcon, all the pros were warming up. Nearby, a young English professional, whose name escapes me, was giving a demonstration of trick shots. One of the tricks he performed was hitting golf balls which had been teed up on bamboo canes between chest and waist height. He blasted ball after ball close to three hundred yards using his driver. Sometimes using both hands, sometimes using just his left hand or just his right hand and sometimes playing left-handed but using a right-handed club turned over. Sometimes just stood balanced on his left leg and sometimes just stood on his right leg. He even hit the ball over three hundred yards without even looking at the ball while he was still looking (and talking) directly at his audience. He also smacked five balls in a row way over two hundred yards from a kneeling position. After this amazing demonstration he invited good amateur golfers from the crowd to step up and have a go at the bamboo cane trick. About half a dozen single figure handicap players came forward. Needless to say that I was NOT one of the volunteers because I already knew just how difficult the task was. They each had four of five attempts at hitting from the canes. Not one of these low handicap players even made ball contact with any of their efforts! A few days later I did manage to wangle a round on the Abu Dhabi National course playing with son-in-law Mark and his friend 'Old Git' Stuart. It was a beautiful course which surprisingly, in the middle of the desert, still had very respectable fairways, but somehow I always seemed to be playing off sand!

Naturally, just like golf, there was a massive difference in knur and spell swings between top exponents of the game and the average Joe Hacker. When I sit at Wattle Park GC enjoying my post round coffee, near the first tee, it is often like watching a Ronnie Corbett comedy sketch with lots of air swings and balls going in every conceivable direction. When we look at the historical knur and spell swings on the internet videos it is no different. However, if we look at the old photos of former world knur and spell champion Len Kershaw, who as far as I know always played off the pin, we can see that he played with great poise and invariably completed his swing in a well-balanced position. What is more, to my untrained eye, his finishing position looked remarkably similar to how todays good golf professionals finish. If ever there was game where the top exponents deserved to be called 'esotericists', then knur and spell must surely have been that game! Len Kershaw is probably still the reigning world champion because there probably hasn't been another world championship since he won his last title!

This major difference in the game between spell users and gallows users was a constant bone of contention. The Yorkshire players always accused the Lancashire players of having a big advantage because they were always hitting a stationary knur. The Lancashire players always retorted that it was the Yorkshire players who had the advantage because they were always hitting a moving knur which already had some momentum. The striking point of the knur by the spell users was obviously always in front of where the knur was at the start of the process, maybe at least one yard, so this was also another advantage. In a match of say thirty rises, where the aggregate distance of all thirty rises was recorded, the spell user gained an overall thirty yards. Matches between two evenly matched opponents could sometimes be won by less than ten yards over thirty rises. So a thirty yard 'free' gain was not insignificant.

Despite the controversy between spell and pin users, neither method was exclusively used in either Yorkshire or Lancashire. Extensive research revealed that there were many events played in Yorkshire where both players were Yorkshiremen, but they still opted to use the pin. This was particularly true in the 1900s when use of the spell seemed to decline. In the 1950s I only ever saw the gallows (pin) being used in the Colne area.

Most pot knurs were about one inch in diameter and weighed half an ounce. This compared with golf balls at either 1.62 or 1.68-inch diameter and weighing about three times as much as a knur. If anyone is interested to read more detail about how knur and spell is played or more detail about the equipment used and how the club (pummel) is made there is plenty of information on *Google* including a few good videos. The Cowling website is maybe the best summary of the game. There is a video on *YouTube* entitled *Ower Bit Bog Oil*. Some imagination will be needed to understand the local dialect used throughout the video. For example, the title of the video when translated literally means 'Over by the Bog Hole'. In the context of the knur and spell match it means that the knur has been hit towards a boggy part of the field where they are playing.ie. an area of wet spongy ground where the flying knur could easily penetrate the surface and be lost. Cowling is a small village just a few miles away from Colne. There is also a book penned by Stuart Greenfield and Paul Breeze called *Colne Giants* which gives much information and stories about the game. Stuart Greenfield and Len Kershaw, both former world champions from Colne, also feature in another great video dated 22 February 2014, entitled *How Lancashire Kept the Cup*. This video gives many details on how their pummels were constructed and how knur and spell champions approached the game. Around 2014 / 2015 there was also some knur and spell played in village gala days in a few Yorkshire villages (Cowling, Bradfield, Silsden etc.) more or less as a novelty attraction, but it didn't generate sufficient interest to spark a revival.

The players set up their gallows or spell side by side on the field of play separated by a suitable distance. This was usually about fifteen feet apart but could be less if there were many competitors in the event, especially if it was a narrow field. Obviously, players had their preferred setting-up place. Just like golfers change their position on the tee depending on the hole configuration and depending on their own particular swing and ball flight shape. They would also have their own ideas of where the best position may be to stand the best chance of being able to take advantage of any tail wind etc. To prevent any arguments about setting-up positions they drew lots to decide their places. Once this place had been allotted, they were generally fixed in this place for the duration of the event.

Although the gallows (pin) or the spell were the two chief alternative methods used to play the game, occasionally a third method was agreed between combatants. This was where neither the gallows or the spell were used at all and both players agreed to 'play by hand'. In these challenge matches both players would hold the knur in one hand and the pummel in the other hand. They would throw the knur into the air and then proceed to thwack it all in one movement. They usually had the choice of whether to hit one-handed or with both hands on the pummel. This variant was not very common, but it did crop up occasionally in newspaper reports in the 1800s. A variant of this third method was where the knur was balanced on the pummel head before being tossed into the air and hit all in the same movement. Yet another game involving a wooden knur was described in the *Sporting Life* newspaper 10 March 1883. This was where three Bradford men had a contest to see who could throw the knur the furthest by hand without hitting it with a pummel. The winner picked up the thirty pounds stake money!

I have no idea when or why the two methods, spell or gallows, evolved. I suspect that the spell is the older of the two and probably evolved from the simple plank on a fulcrum used in the ancient game of trap-ball dating back to the 1100 / 1200s.

In the same way that over many years there have been umpteen different ways to spell the word 'golf', over the centuries, and in different areas, knur and spell (or closely related games) also went under many other names (see more on this later). These included trap-ball, tipcat, bat and trap, trip-stick, nipsy, buck and stick, cat-stick, tripp, kibble and nurspel, spell and bullet, tipping, bad-stick, trib and knur, potty knocking, knur and pin, trippet, buck and trap, pottyrise, gell sticks, knur and sling, dog-stick, peggy, kibble and knor, hippal-stick, northern spell, norspell, nor-spell, dab and trigger, trap and knur, dab-an-thricker, dab N' Nor, billets etc. Knur and spell itself often appeared in umpteen different spellings which included knurr and spell, knor and spell, knorr and spell, Knar and spell, Kner and spell, nurr and spell, nurspell and dandy, nur and spell, spell and nurr, spell and nor, spell and ore, spell and knur, dab and spell, and knur spell etc. As mentioned in the Kendal *Boke of Recorde* in 1657 it may have also been called 'kattstick and bullvett'. The *Kendal Mercury* 18 February 1858 was still reporting on Shrove Tuesday knur and spell events. In the *Westmorland Gazette* (Kendal) 15 October 1853, it mentioned 'the playing in the streets of Kattstick and Bullyett, the former of which, under the name of spell and nurr, still maintains its ground in the neighbourhood, though wisely enough banished from our streets.' Often in the newspapers a knur and spell contest was just reported as 'a knur match', a 'tipping match', 'a knur striking match', 'a trip match', 'a buck match', 'drive knor' or simply 'playing at knur' or 'nurr-playing'. The interesting thing is that no matter the date of the newspaper reports, knur and spell was always described as an ancient game or a game emanating from time immemorial. E.g. The *Leeds Intelligencer* 20 August 1829, writing about a knur and spell game said 'a very excellent and well contested match, at this ancient game, was played on Woodhouse Moor...'

The club they hit the ball with also had different names in different regions of England such as pummel, kibble, knur-stick, buckhead, trip-stick, pommel, bat-stick, trevit-stick, tribbit, gelstick, nurr stick, buckstick, trippit, and primstick.

I only ever saw one reference to the game being called 'gell and spell' and that was in the 1794 diary of Abraham Shackleton which is held by the *West Yorkshire Archive Service* in Bradford. The short entry on 19 January 1794 just mentions that he 'went out to play at gell and spell, Keighley'. I suspect that the word 'gell' in this case is referring to the pummel as a 'gelstick'. I think he may also have been the same Abraham Shackleton who for many years kept a series of weather diaries for the area which are now held at Cliffe Castle in Keighley.

According to the *Sportsman, London* newspaper dated 10 December 1867, in a game played at Barnsley, the pummel was also called a bob-stick. No, it was never called a giggling pin...that is something completely different! Many of the 'junior' closely related versions of knur and spell, such as trap-ball, bat and trap, and tipcat, were very old games which pre-dated golf and which were played all over England and not just in the Danelaw area. Even in 2021 bat and trap is still played in Canterbury in Kent and a few other places in the south of England. This is probably the game which dates to the 1200s and features in one of the stained-glass windows in Canterbury Cathedral.

It is possible that this Barnsley reference to 'bob-stick' was referring to the game of nipsy and not knur and spell. This game was also very popular in the Barnsley and Wakefield areas in addition to knur and spell. It was sort of a junior version of knur and spell which was still played primarily by miners. The implement used was significantly shorter than a knur and spell pummel. The nipsy stick I have in my study is about seventy-one centimetres long (twenty-eight inches) and is carved in one piece from a miner's hickory pickaxe handle. My understanding is that all nipsy sticks were carved from a single piece of wood and did not have detachable heads like knur and spell pummels. However, just as the knur and spell players did, the nipsy players also had their own 'black magic' techniques for compressing the head to increase the density of the wood in that area in order to give it better longevity and improved performance off the club face...albeit that they didn't use multiple wood types in the construction of the head as happened with knur and spell sticks. The head part on my nipsy stick is about eleven centimetres long and between five and seven centimetres wide. This stick came with a carved wooden knur which sinks quickly in water. I don't have any provenance for it, but my guess is late 1800s or early 1900s. Later than this, nipsy players were probably using ceramic pot knurs similar to the knur and spell boys. It could even be that the nipsy boys didn't always use a spherical shaped missile. They could have used a more oval shaped one like the one used in the game of billets. Generally the nipsy players only used one hand when striking the knur. According to the *Sheffield Daily Telegraph* April 1950, the world nipsy champion that year was a sixty-two-years-old miner called Ted Hammond from the small village of Ryhill in Yorkshire. He beat fifty-three-years-old Dick Beedon from Riccall, another small village about nine miles south of York. Beedon had held the unofficial world nipsy championship for twenty years at that stage. It looks like nipsy, same as knur and spell, was mostly being kept alive by the old-timers! The report also mentioned that nipsy had evolved from the more ancient game of knur and spell. Ryhill is also where some very good friends of ours live, Mike and Joyce Shaw. Fifty odd years ago Mike and I studied polymers together at the same Manchester college. Riccall is close to the River Ouse. In the 1950s a heap of old skeletons were found there which historians believe probably date to 1066 when the Vikings under King Harald Hardrada were defeated at the nearby Stamford Bridge by the English King Harold Godwinson who later that year bit the dust at the Battle of Hastings.

Nipsy stick and knur

The pummel used in knur and spell had two main components...a shaft and a head. Prior to the mid-1800s the shaft was made of ash, lancewood, hazel wood, greenheart, or hornbeam. These very early knur and spell shafts would probably have been very roughly carved from tree branches. (see Baildon Hall Club photos) In the 1688 Kincaid diaries he said that the golf shaft must be hazel. I don't know if golf copied knur and spell or vice versa. Probably from about the mid-1800s onwards hickory was also used after this wood became the preferred material for golf club shafts. One of the reported sources for use in knur and spell shafts was to beg, steal or borrow a railway shunter's pole. These were generally about sixty-six inches long, made from hickory, and were ideal for tapering down into a knur and spell shaft. The tapering was often done with a piece of sharp glass. Another wood source for shafts was to use a tapered down old billiard cue. The best billiard cues are made from ash. Some of the cheaper ones use maple wood. The pummel heads were always a more complicated structure and were a composite of two or three different woods glued together. Just like early golf clubs the base wood for the backing on most pummel heads was beechwood. But over the years many kinds of wood were used for the pummel faces. These included boxwood, apple, plum, holly, sycamore, and bird's eye maple. Top knur and spell players had their own favourite combinations. In many challenge matches between 1850 and the early 1860s, hazel heads and holly knurs were specified. Also, they often had several different pummel head constructions which were used to choose from depending on the wind conditions during a match. Golf club makers started to use American persimmon wood for their woods from about 1900 until the late 1980s but as far as I know the knur and spell guys never switched to persimmon. I also know that the guys who made the pummel heads had some very interesting home-made technology for effectively increasing the density of some of the woods they used. In layman's language they had a crude technique for compressing the wood which after several repetitions gave them a significant density and hardness increase. This was usually followed by some kind of heat treatment. Bitumen was used to help secure the head to the shaft and linen thread used by the old cobblers to stitch leather soles on to uppers was used to bind the head end of the tapered shaft in a simple splicing arrangement. I did see several adverts in the *Sheffield Daily Telegraph* dated 1858 where they specified pot knurs and three-inch-wide heads. The efficiency of attaching the heads to the shaft often left something to be desired. There are many old newspaper reports where heads flew off the shaft when striking the knur and hit a spectator or a fellow competitor, on several occasions leading to fatalities! As regards the weight of a pummel, this could vary quite a lot depending on the length of the shaft etc. I have seen pummel weights mentioned in the five or six-ounce range (140g -170 gms) but I don't know if this was typical. From the *Colne Giant* details given below I suspect that these were only the pummel head weights. Modern large head titanium golf drivers are around three hundred grammes, but the old hickory and persimmon drivers were around fourteen ounces (390 - 400gms). Lead weighting was very commonly used in the old wooden drivers. Still in 2019, some golfers like to even change the weight distribution on their metal headed drivers by using small pieces of lead sheeting and double-sided adhesive tape. As far as I know lead weighting was never used on pummel heads in knur and spell, but I could be wrong.

In late 2019 I was very lucky to meet with Alistair MacDonald during a regular meeting of the Trawden Arms 'History Group'. I had been welcomed into this group by a fellow Trawden School chum of mine called Stuart 'Knocker' Heap. Stuart is a few years younger than me. He got his nickname from his prodigious footballing skills which he revealed at a very early age. He also gave me a hiding on the squash court when I was in my fifties!

It turned out that Alistair, through his wife's side of the family, still had an old set of knur and spell equipment which they kept as a sort of family heirloom. This 'tackle' had been used from the mid to late 1950s to the early 1990s by Ted Griffiths who had worked as a civil servant in Colne. Ted had played under the alias of 'The Colne Giant'. Although he never won a world championship, he was a top player of his day and did win many long knock events. He was one of the feature players in the book about knur and spell called '*Colne Giants*' and also appeared on the front cover of the original edition.

Alistair very kindly loaned this equipment to me for a few weeks during my Trawden visit in November / December 2019 and allowed me to take photographs etc. (see photos opposite). The gear was kept in an old hessian sack tied at the top with string. It consisted of four complete pummels, two loose replacement pummel heads and a gallows (pin) arrangement for teeing up. The four shafts on the completed pummels measured 42.25 in, 42.5 in, 42.25 in and 42.00 in. The heads were from 3.00 – 3.125 inches high and 2.25 inches wide and were made using two different wood types glued together. In all cases the thickness of the hard wood face was about 2 cms and the thickness of the backing wood was about 3 cms. So the total

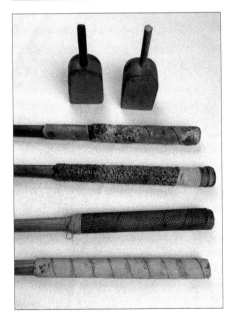

Typical knur and spell equipment being used in 1950 – 1990 period

lengths of all the complete pummels were from 45 – 45.7 inches long. This is very similar to the average modern driver length. These were probably average pummel lengths. I have seen reports of 48-inch shafts being used and also of much shorter shafts being used.

The total weights of the pummels were 318 gm, 360 gm, 402 gm and 350 gm. Weights of the two loose pummel heads were 160 gm and 162 gm respectively. This meant that the actually shaft weights were approximately 157 gm, 199 gm, 241 gm and 189 gm which indicated that on average there was a bit more weight in the shaft than in the head. These total weights are not too far away from the old driver weights of that period.

I don't know if the wooden shafts were ash or hickory. All the shafts were quite flexible, but some were whippier than others. All the shafts were tapered. Shaft diameters at the head-end ranged from 1.18 cm to 1.24 cm. At the grip-end they ranged from 2.48 cm to 3.02 cm (excluding the grip thickness). The loose heads both had some dowel rod inserted in to the head which was fixed by a combination of gluing and pinning. In every case about 2.4 inches of dowelling protruded from the head but it was difficult to see exactly how far into the head the dowelling went. In some heads the dowelling had been pinned by a small 3- 4 mm diameter dowel through the pommel face at a depth of about 1.25 cms from the top of the head. On one head the dowelling had been given a flat face which would match up with another flat face on the shaft end prior to being spliced using some bitumen and then thread binding. On the finished pummels Ted Griffiths had then added some black polyvinyl chloride (PVC) electrical tape to further strengthen the joint. By the late 1950s pvc tape would have been available, but of course this would not have been around when knur and spell was at its peak in the 1800s. All the pummel heads had been finished with a nice wood stain and obviously a great deal of care had been taken in making them. Some of the pummel heads had Ted Griffith's initials carved on them, 'E.G'.

The grips on the finished pummels were all in the 8 – 10 inches range. One was a towelling or cord fabric type of material, but the others were all synthetic constructions typical of the period with pimples similar to ones used on cheap table tennis bats.

As far as I know all the pummels were made by guys in the village in their garages or garden sheds. However, adverts for supply of pummels and other pieces of knur and spell equipment were sometimes seen in sporting newspapers. For example, in the *Sporting Chronicle, Manchester* dated 20 March 1907, Messrs Farrar & Greenwood were advertising 'Badstick Heads' for knur and spell players, with price enquiries to be made to the Fieldhurst Tavern, Cornholme, Todmorden. I don't think pummels generally were ever called badsticks, so I can only surmise that in this case it must have been a tradename for their pummel heads. i.e. an early version Big Bertha!

The pin or gallows in Ted's sack was a very simple construction with a spiked metal end for fixing into the ground. I don't know what kind of wood it was made from. Nor did I take measurements. However, some of the photos of the gallows were taken with pommels in the same picture.

The measurements of these pommels are known so it would be easy to ascertain the measurements for the gallows if required. Usually the gallows would be erected using a plumbline and a spirit level, but these items were not present in the sack.

Danny Hey, a good friend of my nephew Steve, very kindly took some great photos of all the gear using his 'Rolls Royce' camera. Of course, these were typical of the pummels being made and used in the second half of the twentieth century. If we look at the 1862 print of the champion Yorkshire player Kirk Stables which is available on-line, we can see that the pummel which Kirk played with was remarkably similar to the ones Ted Griffiths played with over one hundred years later. The head shape and size appeared to be almost identical. Maybe the shaft Kirk played with was slightly thicker. Ash versus hickory? We also need to look closely at the photos taken of the equipment found in Baildon Hall to get an idea of what knur and spell sticks looked like in the early 1600s.

The Kirk Stables print appeared in the *Illustrated Sporting News and Theatrical and Musical Review* dated September 10, 1862. This sporting magazine had only been founded in March 1862 by a London printer and ran until 1870. The Kirk Stables print was in one of the early editions and maybe served to confirm just how important knur and spell was as a game in that era. The prints were actually made using a wood engraving technique which in turn had probably been based on an early photograph. Apart from being used in the magazine, these prints could also be bought separately by anyone who wanted a picture of their sporting hero to hang on their bedroom wall at home or to adorn the walls of their local pub.

From a cost point of view knur and spell was always a much cheaper game to play than golf. According to *Routledges Every Boy's Annual* dated 1871 it was also played in schools at that time. In that same publication it mentioned that best quality spells used in top matches could be bought for one guinea i.e. twenty-one shillings or just over one-pound sterling. These would have been the ones with an oak or mahogany base and brass fittings. In the *Morpeth Herald*, 20 September 1879, a spring spell was offered as first prize in a knur and spell handicap at Bedlington, north of Newcastle in Northumberland and not far from the border with Scotland.

This spell had a lock catch and all the latest improvements and was valued at one pound ten shillings (thirty shillings). Lower quality spells as used in schools would cost much less.

As we can see from an article in the *Blackburn Standard* dated 21 September 1895, knur and spell wasn't just played in ordinary schools. It was also played in Grammar Schools where the supposedly brighter students attended. In this article an old BGS boy, the Reverend John Bidgood Bennett, who had attended Blackburn Grammar School, was reminiscing about his time spent there from 1845 to 1855. He said that knur and spell was probably his favourite past-time. Apparently, the pupils with rich parents had beautiful lignum vitae knurs, a fancy spring mechanism spell and a high-quality pummel. The poorer students had more rudimentary equipment. Blackburn is in north-east Lancashire. No doubt, once he had decided on his chosen career as a vicar, Mr Bidgood would probably have been obliged to abandon his teenage love for knur and spell. Most churches and chapels chastised knur and spell players because of their strong links to gambling and boozing.

Another example of knur and spell at school appeared in *The Guisborian* dated April 1933. This was the school magazine for Guisborough Grammar School in the North Riding of Yorkshire. This school had been founded in 1561 as a free school for the sons of local farmers and tradesmen. In 1933 one of their old pupils was talking about school experiences in 1860 and talked about having played knur and spell. Australians may be interested to learn that Guisborough is less than ten miles away from Marton-in-Cleveland, where Captain Cook was born and raised. It is also just a few miles away from the North Yorkshire Moors where knur and spell playing was rampant.

Yet another grammar school where knur and spell was played was Heath GS in Halifax which is one of the oldest institutions in that town. Not quite as old as Guisborough GC but certainly dates to Queen Elizabeth I's era and the 1590s. This school survived more than four hundred years until 1985 when it was merged with another school and renamed Crossley Heath school (Thatcher years!). In one of their school magazines they mentioned having a knur and spell club at the school well into the 1900s. For hundreds of years Halifax and all the surrounding area had been a hot bed for knur and spell playing. This school retains archival documents as far back as the 1590s. Examination of these may well reveal exactly when they first played knur and spell. At the time they played knur and spell in the 1900s the game was already almost extinct. So I can only imagine that this club was a throw-back to a time when knur and spell playing at the school was more popular. i.e. a sort of old school tradition being maintained. Not on the school curriculum, but still retained as an option for aficionados or for reasons of tradition.

One of the reports of knur and spell played at grammar schools mentioned that just about every young boy in those days (in the north of England) had his own knur and spell equipment. Just as these days every young boy has his own football and cricket bat! The fact that knur and spell was played in grammar schools in the mid-1800s is quite interesting. Pupils who attended grammar schools in those days were often the sons and daughters of relatively privileged people. Many of the grammar schools were free but you still had to pass an entrance examination in order to win a scholarship to attend there. How I ever managed to win a scholarship is a complete mystery. We never had any books at home when I was a kid, and we didn't have a public library in the village. The only thing I ever had a chance to read were comics (*Dandy*, *Beano* and *Topper*). And that was only because I had a part-time job delivering newspapers. My heroes were *Desperate Dan* and *Dennis the Menace*! I was already going to Colne Grammar School before we had our own twelve-inch black and white TV! I suspect that grammar schools would not have been playing knur and spell in the mid-1800s if it had been called poor man's golf at that time. Such a description would not have aligned with the grammar school image. The 'poor man's golf ' tag must have come much later. Of course, knur and spell was not played at Colne Grammar School in the 1950s when I was there. The game was already on its last legs by then. In my time at CGS I represented the school at rugby (union), cricket, football (soccer), cross country running, javelin throwing and chess. The only thing I missed out on was swimming. I was just about as much use as tits on a fish when it came to swimming!

The other important confirmation that many young boys played knur and spell, albeit a macabre one, was the regularity of newspaper reports throughout the 1800s of both serious injuries and deaths amongst the young players. Several fatalities were caused by errant flying knurs or by pummel heads detaching from the shafts during the striking action. Equally tragic were the number of drowning deaths being reported. The *Gloucester Herald* 11 February 1865 reported that two Bradford boys had drowned when they hit their knur on to the thin ice of a mill dam. The *Yorkshire Post and Leeds Intelligencer* 28 March 1873 reported that an eleven-year-old boy had drowned in the River Wearne trying to retrieve an errant knur. The *Barnsley Chronicle* 22 June 1861 mentioned that a farmer was facing court for encouraging his dog to attack some boys who were playing knur and spell in one of his fields. There were also dozens of other reports where young boys were reprimanded for playing knur and spell on the Sabbath.

In Dewsbury and Batley best quality pummels (including shaft and head) cost five shillings. In Durham separate pummel heads sold for six pence each and the player himself attached the head to the shaft using wax cord or thread. Box-wood knurs also sold for six-pence each. This compares with about five shillings for a featherie ball in the 1850s and about one shilling for a guttie ball after 1860. Thus, a featherie was at least ten times more expensive than a wooden knur and a guttie was twice as expensive. Ceramic knurs were much cheaper than wooden knurs because they were mass produced and not hand made. Even in 1908 the *Burnley Express* on 12 March ran an advert for a company called the Couldwell Supply Co, Rotherham offering half-ounce pot knurs at only two shillings per gross, with a minimum order quantity of a five-gross lot. This equates to about six knurs for one penny. The same company were advertising in the *Barnsley Chronicle* in August 1907, even cheaper, at one shilling and six pence per gross (ten gross lot) or one shilling and nine pence (five gross lot). Regent Pottery of Hanley in Staffordshire advertised in the Sheffield Evening Telegraph June and August 1917 at 15 shillings per 1000 knurs. This was in the middle of the First World war, so obviously some of the old codgers, who were too old to fight, were still bashing the little pills around. This makes the ceramic knurs about thirty-six times cheaper than the wooden knurs and three hundred and sixty times cheaper than featheries. Considering that a wooden or ceramic knur would also be much more durable than a featherie ball (at a guess ten times more durable and maybe more), it is not difficult to understand why knur and spell playing far outstripped golf in the early days.

I have seen reports that wooden golf balls were used before the hairy and featherie golf balls. But I have never seen a wooden golf ball (apart from the ones used during the second world war) and most serious golfing authorities doubt whether wooden golf balls were ever used. However, I strongly suspect that they would have been used. There are two reasons for my thoughts. Firstly, from a very early date (before golf started) wooden knurs were used to play trap-ball and probably knur and spell. Golfers at the time would have been well aware of the existence of these wooden knurs which were omnipresent in all the northern counties of England and very close to Scotland. It would have been very easy to make a slightly larger version of the wooden knur. Or for an ad hoc game they could have even played golf with a knur and spell ball of which there would have been many thousands in circulation at any given time! As far as I know there were no commercial operations making and selling these wooden knurs. But there was a widespread cottage industry of guys making knurs just to make a few extra bob each week.

An even more important reason would have been the price. We are told that golf in Scotland was accessible to all classes from the earliest days. However, there is no way in the world that an ordinary working man in Scotland could afford to buy either featherie or the imported Dutch balls before that. The initial cost of buying these balls would have been prohibitive and the constant need to re-stock because of lost or damaged balls even more prohibitive. A wooden ball would have been a tiny fraction of the price to buy and would have endured much longer providing they were not lost in play. In fact, golfers could have done the same as some knur and spell players did and carve their own wooden balls for no cost at all. I cannot think of any other reason how an ordinary working man in that era could have afforded to play golf. Either the working Scot played with wooden balls or else it is a complete myth that working men in Scotland played golf at all until well after the guttie ball was invented. Both these ideas are at odds with the conventional stories spewed out by golf historians.

The probable answer to my dilemma came after I read IMC Macintyre's paper entitled *Edinburgh Surgery and the History of Golf.* In that paper

Macintyre suggests that in the fourteenth and fifteenth centuries two variants of the game of golf appear to have developed in parallel. There was a short game played in churchyards by ordinary people. There was also a longer game played on the links by the aristocrats. That would certainly make a lot of sense. The short game would have used the cheaper wooden golf balls and the long game the very expensive leather golf balls. This explanation also ties in with things I have read about knur and spell also being played in churchyards in England from the earliest days. I imagine that the sticks which the ordinary people used would have also been different from the purpose-made clubs used by the rich. The poor people would have used self-made clubs carved from a single piece of wood. Probably like an inverted walking stick. These would have been the so-called Sabbath sticks which poor people used to hit wooden balls with when on their way to church. Of course, they were all coming from different directions when on their way from home to the church, so they wouldn't have been playing proper golf. i.e. no holes as target. Effectively they would have been playing the Scottish version of knur and spell.

A newspaper article on 13 April 1613 from Aberdeen tends to support McIntyre's idea. Two players by the same name, John Allan, were fined three pounds for 'setting ane goiff ball in the kirk yeard (church) and striking the same against the kirk'. Neither player was a rich man. One was a bookbinder, and the other was a cutler. The balls they used were probably wooden and wouldn't travel too far. It is inconceivable that a poor man would direct an expensive leather ball into a church wall which would completely knacker the ball. Obviously flags and holes didn't figure in this particular activity. Sounds like they were playing the Scottish version of knur and spell. And the chances are that this game preceded golf in Scotland!

If McIntyre's explanation is correct, then the obvious question which must be asked is the following. Which came first, the short game or the long game? Well, the sheer number of poor people would outnumber the rich people by at least fifty times, so I know where my money would be! A similar thing probably happened with knur and spell. The short version of knur and spell was trap-ball which has been dated back to at least the 1100 and 1200s. The equipment used for trap-ball was cheaper and less sophisticated that the knur and spell equipment.

If wooden balls were used to play golf in the very early days, it was certainly not the only time in history when this happened. During the Second World War there was a massive natural rubber shortage around the world because the Japanese had taken control of all the rubber plantations in Malaysia. Golfers in South Africa who couldn't get 'normal' golf balls started to play with wooden golf balls. Wooden golf balls were even mooted in the United States and according to the *Sunday Post* 25 June 1944, an English company also put a wooden golf ball on the market. The ball looked like a normal ball and weighed the same, but it obviously performed quite differently. Driving distance was only about one hundred and thirty yards and it was very harsh on wooden clubs. Clearly it was never intended to replace traditional balls, but some golfers were happy to use them as a stopgap measure rather than no golf at all. I do have some photos of these war-time wooden balls which were kindly sent to me in 2019 by my great friend Yorkshireman Mike Shaw, who spent all his working life with Dunlop golf balls. He still has a couple of these wooden golf balls in his study.

The shortage of natural rubber to make golf balls with was never going to cause the world any great hardship. However, natural rubber was also required for more important things like tyres. This forced the Americans into developing large scale synthetic alternatives. They came up with a rubber called GRS (Government Rubber Styrene) which eventually became known as SBR (Styrene Butadiene Rubber). In 2018 every car tyre in the world is still made with this kind of rubber. To give credit to where it is due we should point out that, like many other things, the basic groundwork for these synthetic rubbers had not been done by the Americans. Even in the early 1900s both German and Russian scientists had done much of the basic research on polymerisation using a variety of different monomers.

Natural rubber wasn't the only thing in short supply during World War II. There was a big shortage of iron and steel which were needed to make war ships, tanks, guns, ammunition etc. This resulted in a nation-wide appeal for scrap metal, both in the UK and America, which could be melted down and re-cycled. Ordinary families even cut down the iron railing fences around their homes in order to contribute. The stubs where the iron railing was cut from the low wall in front of my mum's little terraced house in Trawden can still be seen. In Jack Greenwood's book, *A Trawdeners's View*, there is a photo of mum's house taken in 1904 where the railing is still intact. In 1940 the R & A at St Andrews had a big appeal for old iron-headed golf clubs and old steel shafts to support the war effort. Many of the beautiful old hand-made golf clubs may have disappeared in the process. Could be one of the main reasons why old clubs are relatively hard to find these days.

For anyone wishing to actually see some of the old knur and spell equipment (pummels, knurs, spells, and pins etc) or photographs and drawings of the sport, there are plenty of examples which have been preserved in museums and by historical societies all over the north of England. The following list mentions just a tiny fragment of what is available.

A very good one is at the Bowes Museum at Barnard Castle in county Durham. Not far away from that is the Beamish Museum near Chester-le-Street. The Tolson Museums in Kirklees Leeds and at Ravensknowle Hall in Huddersfield, the Bolling Hall Museum at Bradford, York Castle Museum, Skipton Museum, Abbey House Museum, Kirkstall in Leeds, the Dales Countryside Museum in Hawes, and the Clitheroe Museum in Lancashire are just a few of the many others. Leeds University has a very good photographic archive and also the Ecclesfield District Archives. So does the University of Reading in their Archive and Museum Database. Barnsley Museum's film archive is worth seeing and the Denby Dale and Kirkburton Archive Collection. The Borthwick Institute Archives at York also has some interesting information. Baildon Hall Club has some very old knur and spell equipment on display. Hull Museum Publications has some interesting items. Another, which is not all that far away from Barnard Castle, is the Swaledale Museum at Reeth in the North Yorkshire Dales. That part of Yorkshire was famous for lead mining which had first been carried out in that area back in Roman times. It flourished from about 1675 until the 1860s in places around Reeth including Grinton, Blakethwaite, Gunnerside, Arkengarthdale, Richmond, Crackpot, Keld, Oxnop, Heahaugh, Muker, Hurst, Kearton, Fremington, Langthwaite etc. The Old Working Smithy Museum at Gunnerside also has some knur and spell equipment on display. The Killhope Museum near Cowshill also has some knur and spell equipment. This is in the lead and silver mining region of the North Pennines around Nenthead, Alston and Allenheads. Alston is less than thirty miles from Carlisle and obviously not far from the Scottish border. The Cawthorne Jubilee Museum near Barnsley was opened in 1889. Information on knur and spell can also be found in the National Coal Mining Museum at Overton near Wakefield and in the Hartlepool Museum.

Another place well worth a visit is the Folk Museum at Shibden Hall in Halifax. Apart from a very nice display of old knur and spell equipment, Shibden Hall is famous for being the family home of the famous diarist Anne Lister who died there in 1840. Lister was a celebrated lesbian who was colloquially known as 'Gentleman Jack'. One of her relationships was blessed at a church in York and she is noted for effectively being part of Britain's first ever lesbian 'marriage' in 1834, even though it wasn't legal in those days. Not far away from Shibden Hall is the Heptonstall Museum at Hebden Bridge which also has a knur and spell display. The building occupied by this museum was once the home of Heptonstall Grammar School which had been built in 1642.

There are many places in that region where the Vikings settled, and knur and spell was found all across the country from Sunderland in the east to Cockermouth in the west. Knur and spell wasn't just played by coal miners. It was also played by lead miners, tin and silver miners, jet miners, ganister miners, fluorite and barytes miners, ironstone miners, stone miners (quarrymen), as well as seniors and minors. I am afraid that all this was a bit too early for bitcoin miners! Ganister is a high quartz content sandstone used to make refractory silica firebricks used in steel and other furnaces. It was mined in the 1800s around the Worrall area near Sheffield in places such as Deepcar, Bolsterstone, Oughtibridge and Stocksbridge, all of which were very big knur and spell playing places.

Another place to see some nice photos of old knur and spell equipment is to peruse some of the auction house catalogues. These regularly have spells, pummels, and knurs up for auction, although pins / gallows are rarely seen. Often the basic dimensions of the spells and pummels etc will also be given.

Chapter 9

Kings, queens, aristocrats and other bludgers

When the Duke of York (later King James II of England) played golf at Leith Links in 1681 / 1682, the cost of his golf balls and equipment were recorded in his secretary's pocketbook which is held in the *National Library of Scotland*. His secretary was Sir John Werden who was baron of the exchequer for Cheshire in 1664 and a Member of Parliament in London for many years. The Duke spent six pounds, nine shillings and two pence. This included three pounds for twelve dozen balls at five pence each and almost three pounds ten shillings for the clubs. What we must remember is that these would have been English pounds. At that time one English pound was worth twelve Scottish pounds. So that means one ball cost five Scottish shillings. From the *Scottish Mining website* we can see that the average Scottish wage in 1679 was between seven and eight Scottish shillings per week. This means that your average working man in Scotland in around 1680 could afford to buy six 'featherie' golf balls per month IF he spent zero on his rent, clothes, and food! Buckley's chance baby!

I wonder what the Duke planned to do with the one hundred and forty-four golf balls he bought? No matter how bad a golfer he may have been surely there was no way he could lose or damage that many balls in one round of golf? More than likely he took the unused balls back to London with him and played at Blackheath? I suppose that the fact that he bought so many balls would suggest that he was buying the clubs and balls outright and not just hiring them.

The game of golf which the Duke of York played was reported as being the first ever international match. The Duke was forty-nine years old at the time. He teamed up with a local Scot called John Patterson against two English noblemen in the Dukes entourage. It seems that the two English nobles were claiming that golf originated in England. The Duke disagreed, and the match was to decide the issue with the customary big wager at stake. How a golf match could decide that issue is a complete mystery...but that is another matter. The Duke and Patterson won the match and Patterson was able to buy a house with his share of the winnings. The Duke presented Patterson with a plaque to commemorate their victory. Patterson 's house no longer exists in Canongate Edinburgh, but the plaque can still be seen on a nearby property.

What we have to remember is that the first so called international golf match was said to have taken place in the 1681-to-1682-time frame. Whereas the clubs which Werden paid for in his pocketbook notes were in February 1679. So there was at least a three-to-four-year period here where James could have played quite a lot of golf.

The Duke of York was crowned King James II in 1685, but his reigned was short-lived. There was the Glorious Revolution in 1688 which led to James doing a runner to France early in 1689. Effectively he abdicated, but if he hadn't, he would have been topped. As with most of the issues over the centuries, religion was behind all his problems. James was pro-Catholic which Parliament didn't like, especially when he produced a Catholic heir which by then would have been an absolute no-no. The outcome for the 1688 issues was the Bill of Rights in 1689 which is still in force in 2019. St Cloud GC in Paris was still not in existence in 1689 so James's golfing days probably ended abruptly.

Many critics have said that there was no golf club in England at that time. The first English golf club to start up was Blackheath in the 1700s. So where did the English noblemen get the idea in 1682 that golf started in England? It could have been from James **VI/I** and his Scottish entourage playing ad hoc 'golf' at Greenwich Park near Blackheath in the early 1600s, more than a century before any club was formed there. Or James's teenage son, Prince Henry, playing near Richmond Palace around the same time. They may even have heard about George Villiers, the Duke of Buckingham, playing golf against Sir Robert Deale in 1624 on Therfield Heath near Royston in Hertfordshire. Royston is about fourteen miles south of Cambridge and forty-seven miles north of London. In fact, the gurus at the *Scottish Golf History* (SGH) site have proudly pronounced that George Villiers was indeed the first Englishman to play golf and that Sir Robert was 'a second' English golfer to play. I am not sure just how that works. If this was the first game of golf played by both men, I would have thought that jointly they could BOTH lay claims to being the FIRST English golfers to play the game. I can only suppose that they (SGH) must have inside information which tells them that George teed off first!

The English noblemen playing at Leith Links in 1682 may not have been the first Englishmen to play golf. Although I have been unable to find the transcript, I did read somewhere that King Henry **VIII's** first wife, Catherine, in a letter written to Cardinal Wolsey in 1513, talked about golf becoming quite fashionable in England. This was many decades before Mary Queen of Scots picked up her niblick. As far as I am aware , neither King Henry **VIII** nor his Queen consort Catherine ever travelled to Scotland, so she wouldn't have seen it played there. In fact 1513 was the year when England gave Scotland their biggest ever hiding on the battlefield at Flodden in Northumberland. Henry **VIII** was across the English Channel at the time fighting the French, but the English still managed to hammer the Scots even with their 'reserve team'. I wonder if the English noblemen at Leith, a hundred and sixty nine years later, had heard about the Queen Catherine letter? I wonder if Catherine had seen or heard about knur and spell being played in England and confused the two games? I wonder if the Scottish *debacle* at Flodden, and Catherine's letter, had really been the embryo for the Scottish denial of knur and spell?

It must be observed at this point that SGH has a track record of rating one golfer as first and the other golfer as second when in fact they both played in the same match. They also announced that King James **IV** was the world's first known golfer to play in 1504 when he beat Patrick Hepburn, the 1ST Earl of Bothwell...location unknown but thought likely to have been at St Andrews. At least in this case there is evidence that King James owned some golf clubs before 1504 when he bought them in 1502 from a Perth bowmaker. So, it is highly likely that he played golf somewhere from at least 1502, albeit not a proven fact. I personally know people who own some golf clubs but have never actually played the game! In the case of Hepburn, we don't know if he had some clubs before 1504, but other aspects of his life suggest that he may also have played before 1504. He was born in mid-Lothian very close to both Leith links and Musselburgh where early golf is known to have flourished. When he played in 1504, he was already forty-nine years old, and the king was about thirty-one. I would suggest that it is highly unlikely that Hepburn was playing his first game of golf at that age. I doubt that anyone would be so brash as to put up a wager to beat someone at golf if they had never played the game before, especially someone who was knocking on fifty years of age. Remembering that life expectancy in the 1500 / 1600s was only about thirty-five. So, in 1504 Hepburn had already reached a very good age and was well past his use-by date. Without further proof, perhaps it is only safe to say that King James **IV** and Patrick Hepburn were jointly the world's first ever known golfers? At least on this occasion Hepburn, unlike Sir Robert Deale, had the good grace to allow the man higher up the pecking order to win!

The reliable information source which SGH uncovered on the Villiers matches gives details of three separate occasions between October 1624 and January 1625 when George played golf. On all three occasions his expense account shows that he spent money on both clubs (battes) and balles. Buying a few golf balls each time I can understand, but why would he buy clubs each time he played over just a short three-month period? Maybe he chucked a tantrum and broke a club every time he missed an easy putt? Or maybe the clubs were just hired? To me this seems quite likely when we also know from the information source that the money for both clubs and balls was paid to the 'Gofball keeper by George Villiers's financial controller, Sir Sackville Crowe.

George was very matey with King James **I** of England who had a royal lodge and hunting ground in Royston. James had also been King of Scotland since he was born in 1566. Until he was old enough Scotland was effectively ruled by regents for quite a long period. In his boyhood he learned to play golf on one of the islands in the middle of the River Tay, Perth (Even today there is a King James **VI** GC on Moncrieff Island in the Tay River which was laid out by Tom Morris in 1897. It is affectionately known as the 'King Jimmy'). He had already assumed the King of Scotland duties by the time Queen Elisabeth **I** died in 1602. After her death he went to London to also become King James **I** of England. He spent most of his life in England after that until his death in 1625 and only went back to Scotland once, in 1617, which was his fiftieth anniversary year as king of the Scots. Villiers went with him. It was a three-month trip from 13 May to 4 August 1617. They travelled with a very large entourage and the trip involved a two-year logistical pre-planning exercise to ensure that they were all wined, dined and entertained at every stage of the long journey.

Although James was already about fifty years old, he and Villiers may have played golf on this trip. Certainly they went to all the likely golf playing places such as Edinburgh, Leith, Stirling and St Andrews. In 1996, an article entitled *The Scottish Progress of James VI, 1617* by William and Peter McNeil was published in *The Scottish Historical Review XXV,1: No.199 April 1996, 38-51*. This article, which I have not been able to access, was an account of this three-month trip and may well reveal details of any possible golf played.

All this piece of English history would have been quite different if Queen Elisabeth I had married and had children. When James took over as king of England in 1603 he was only 'heir presumptive' and not 'heir apparent'. The Scots and English were still at loggerheads with each other for at least another hundred years, until the Act of Union in 1707. During this period, golf in England was limited to just a handful of nobs playing on Greenwich Park or at Therfield Heath, while knur and spell had already spread all across the north of England.

James divided his time in England between London, Theobald Palace in Cheshunt, and Royston. In London he had several palaces at his disposal. Two of these were Greenwich Palace and Eltham Palace. Greenwich and Eltham are both just south of the River Thames and are only four miles apart. About mid-way between Greenwich and Eltham is Blackheath. There is plenty of anecdotal evidence that King James I of England and his Scottish entourage played golf in Greenwich Park just to the south of where Greenwich Palace was located in the early 1600s not long after he had arrived in England. Greenwich Park was a big area of about two hundred acres i.e. one to two miles in length. Blackheath GC, which for a long time was entirely made up of ex-pat Scots working in London, started with a five-hole course in the 1700s laid out around the south end of Greenwich Park. It is very likely that this club, which was the first golf club to start in England, evolved from the golf played by King James **I** and his courtiers. However, their early club records were apparently lost in a fire, so we may never know the true story. In the 1840s they expanded to a seven-hole course and in 1923 they moved about three miles further out to Eltham because there was no room to grow into an eighteen-hole course at Blackheath. The current Blackheath GC is very close to Eltham Palace.

Despite having these great facilities and others so close to London, King James spent a disproportionate amount of his time at Royston which was only twenty-seven miles away from his palace at Theobalds where he eventually died. Here he could get away from the smelly London atmosphere, the hurly burly of Westminster and also away from 'her indoors'. At his Royston hunting lodge, which was completed in about 1607, he had a significant staff. These included Sir Martin Hume, Master of Harriers, who was paid an annual salary of two hundred pounds and was also in charge of four horses and a footman. Then there was Richard Westley who was Keeper of the Game. He had to preserve the game against poachers within a sixteen-mile radius of Royston. Three huntsmen were each paid three pounds per month plus an allowance of about sixty-six pounds to feed 'twenty couples' of hounds. There was a massive dog kennel and yard at Royston! For times when he wasn't hunting, James also employed a Cock Master called George Comer (please don't laugh) who oversaw the Royal Cockpit. Cock fighting was a very big sport in those days. He also had a Keeper of the Gardens, Keeper of the Robes, and personal secretaries to keep him up to date on any developments at Westminster. It is also highly likely that he had a Keeper of the Raptors because he was very fond of falconry which he practised on every possible occasion. Many of the royal staff were housed in the area of Royston which is now called Kneesworth Street. One very important appointment not mentioned so far was the vermin catcher. His job was to destroy all foxes, badgers, wildcats, otters, hedgehogs and all crows, rooks, choughs, kites, buzzards, cormorants, ospreys, and other ravenous foul! What an ornithologist's delight Hertfordshire must have been in those days before Jimmy came on the scene! As a blue heritage plaque titled 'King's Paradise' describes, which can still be seen in modern-day Royston, King James also had a private bowling alley in the town for himself and his courtiers to amuse themselves on.

Royston is only twenty-four miles away from the village of Newmarket in Suffolk. King James also spent much time there involved in horse racing. Newmarket went on to become famous as the home of British thoroughbred racehorses. Charles **II**, King James's grandson, was even more into horse racing and had a residence at Newmarket. He would have been there around the time when the first of the original 'foundation sires', Byerley Turk, arrived on the scene. This was an Arabian stallion brought in specially to breed with English mares. Between 1680 and 1753 there were three Arab stallions brought in for this purpose. The other two were Darley Arabian and Godolphin Arabian. Every thoroughbred horse born since that date can trace its lineage back to one of these three sires.

The point about this story is that if King James had a 'Keeper of the cocks', a 'Keeper of game', a 'keeper of the hounds', a 'Keeper of the Garden', a 'Keeper of the Raptors', a 'keeper of ye bowling alley' etc, he probably also had a 'Keeper of ye gof clubes and balles'! We already know that the king had commanded that all the territory within a sixteen-mile radius of Royston be protected as his royal hunting grounds. The village of Therfield is only about three miles from Royston. Therfield Heath, where they played golf, is only about half a mile away from Royston. Both are comfortably within the hunting ground protection zone. Other towns in Hertfordshire also had royal hunting protection zones around them. Places such as Hitchin, Barnet, Hadley, South Mimms and Totteridge were all within easy reach from Theobalds Palace.

It sounds to me like King James had his own private golf course in Royston for him and his family and close friends to play on. Just like the current royals have private family golf courses at both Windsor Castle (from 1901) and at Balmoral (from 1920s). We must remember that in those days very few people were playing golf. Golf clubs were all hand-made and each club took several days to make. It is highly unlikely that the 'Gofball keeper' kept a stock of ready-made clubs for sale just in case some random nobleman popped in looking to buy some. He was perhaps more likely to keep some hire-out clubs.

The record also shows that George lost the two pounds wager against Sir Robert. This may suggest that Sir Robert was a more accomplished golfer than George and may have been a more experienced player. Maybe

Sir Robert had played previously and was really the first ever English golfer in his own right? But I don't think so. In any case, a lowly 'Sir' beating the only Duke in England at that time! Whatever must he have been thinking about? He could have been locked up in the Tower of London for doing that!

King James befriended twenty-two years old George Villiers in about 1615 when he was about forty-nine years old. James died in 1625, so he would probably have been too old and sick to play with Villiers in October 1624. However, he probably played with Villiers sometime in the years between 1615 and 1624. It has been documented that King James was just about still capable of riding his horse to go stag hunting in 1622 and also to indulge in another favourite sport, falconry. Although reports said that he did fall off the horse a few times, it may suggest that if he was still fit enough to ride horses, he would also have been fit enough to still play golf. However, I also saw contradictory stories that by 1619 James was so sick that he had to be carried about in a chair or litter. So, he sounds as if he was borderline at that stage. However, he did make the long arduous trip back to Scotland in 1617 with Villiers which suggests that at least in that year he was relatively OK.

When James became King of England in 1603, he inherited a £400,000 royal household debt courtesy of Queen Elisabeth I. This had increased to £600,000 by 1606 and had blown out to £900,000 by 1618 because of James's extravagant spending and total lack of financial acumen. However, all was not lost. Help was at hand from Sir Lionel Cranfield who had risen from poverty to become a wealthy merchant financier. Cranfield was the ultimate wheeler and dealer who had his finger in lots of pies. He was knighted in 1614 and he was an MP from then until 1622. He had entered Royal service in 1605. He was also Surveyor-General of Customs from 1613-1619. This was a newly created post which Cranfield himself had suggested to the Earl of Northampton in 1612. In 1617 he carried out a commercial reform of the Kings Household. In 1621 he was appointed Lord Treasurer and in 1622 he was made the 1st Earl of Middlesex. Between 1618-1621 Cranfield was able to get the royal household budget moving in the right direction.

One of the first things which Cranfield did was to notice from James's expense accounts that a significant amount of money was being spent on expensive imported golf balls from Holland. He would also have been aware of this importation from his job in the Customs department. Cranfield also involved himself in licensing and patent matters where he could make some nice income. No doubt the monopoly from King James to a local Scottish ball maker in 1618 to make featherie golf balls would have been done at Cranfield's instigation (see story on this later). In the big scheme of things, imported golf balls would have been a trivial item for Cranfield to worry about compared all the big-ticket commodity items coming into the country such as wine and tobacco. In those days they could probably have crammed all the golfers in Scotland into a few Mini Coopers! (the last time I looked at the Guinness World Record book it was twenty-seven people into one Mini) However, if he could earn some brownie points by helping to better control the King's personal budget it was worth doing. There was plenty of largesse to be had in King James's time!

This story is a very good indication that James was still playing golf in 1618. Otherwise why would he have been buying so many golf balls that it worried his new finance minister when he did the royal household review? We know from an abundance of sources that James only once returned to Scotland after he had moved south in 1603. So where was he playing all this golf to need lots of golf balls? On his own course at Royston would be a good bet. And who was he playing with?

Well. After catching James's eye in 1614, Villiers shot up the ranks very rapidly indeed. In 1614 he got a job as Royal-Cup bearer to King James which probably meant that he could serve the king his pint of frothy. He was knighted in 1615 as a Gentleman of the Bedchamber (again please don't laugh because I didn't make that up!). In 1616 he had a triple whammy when he was appointed as King's Master of the Horse, made a Viscount and a Knight of the Garter. In 1617 he was made an Earl. In 1618 he became the Marquess of Buckingham and by 1619 he was also Admiral of the Fleet (maybe he had experience sailing a tinny on the River Lea near Theobalds?) He became Duke of Buckingham in 1623 and at the time was the only Duke in England. He must have done a fantastic job when he was Gentleman of the Bedchamber! My guess is that he would probably have played golf with James at Royston, and maybe in Scotland, between 1615 and 1619.

As far as I can ascertain, George Villiers never occupied the much sought-after position of Groom of the Stool during his meteoric rise to fame and power. Whoever held this position had the very important job of assisting the king whenever he went for a crap. English kings had employed someone to wipe their backsides at least from King Henry **VIII's** reign in the 1500s and this glorious privilege was not discontinued until King Edward **VII** ascended the throne (no pun intended) in 1901. I initially thought the word 'stool' in the title Groom of the Stool referred to the king's faeces, but this is not the case. It was actually the name of the luxuriously padded portaloo which was carried about wherever the king went. There was no way he was going to dive behind the bushes if he was caught short when out hunting or playing golf at Therfield! From about 1660 the Gentlemen of the Bed Chamber got even luckier when they were also recruited to wipe their bosses' bums as the two roles were combined.

One mystery we must address is, IF 'ye gofballe and clube keeper' on Therfield Heath was indeed employed by King James, why would a blue-eyed boy like Villiers have to pay money to play? Perhaps the new austerity measures which were imposed on the Royal Household by Sir Lionel Cranfield from 1618 were still in play and King James had to be at least seen to be trying to curb his expenses? (Very likely!) In this respect we must acknowledge that King James probably created a precedent for today's royal family. They must also be feeling the pinch because, relatively recently, they now allow 'outsiders' to play on their private royal golf courses at both Windsor Castle and Balmoral, including a few corporate days. Needless to say that playing opportunities for 'outsiders' are quite restricted and tightly controlled.

The other even more obvious reason Villiers would have to pay is to remember that although King James was king of England, he was a Scot. There is probably no other nationality in the world with a more justified reputation of being tight with their money than the Scots. Maybe one but I can't mention the name because I would be accused of being racist! Make that two, because Yorkshiremen are not far behind the Scots! Although he was a spendthrift when using other people's money, James's innate Scottish penny-pinching qualities would certainly have come to the fore. He was probably the only golfer at Royston who could spot a bawbie (a Scottish sixpence) on the ground from a hundred yards away!

This idea that James had his own private golf course is still pure conjecture. To my knowledge, no proof (or primary evidence as the golf historian gurus like to call it) for this has yet come to light. However, the fact that golf was played at Therfield Heath in 1624 can be substantiated. And the fact that King James's very close friend for the last ten years of his life, George Villiers, played there in late 1624 and again in early 1625 can also be substantiated. I struggle to think of any other scenario which could explain the known facts. I have difficulty believing that the 'keeper of the gof clubs and balles' could have been an entrepreneurial village blacksmith who thought he could boost his earnings by starting up a golf course. However, if the course and the equipment were not owned by King James and were indeed run by an enterprising village pub owner, then it would certainly explain why Villiers had to cough up money to play.

On further reflection, and after more research, I have to admit that the cross relationship between George Villers, Sir Lionel Cranfield and King James was even more incestuous than I could have imagined. And when I said earlier that Cranfield was a 'wheeler and dealer' with fingers in lots of pies, this was probably a massive understatement. See his biography in *The History of Parliament, British Political, Social and Local History* website for a very detailed account of his shenanigans. Very early on in the piece Cranfield had identified Villers as a man to tuck in behind on their common journey up the creepologist's ladder. Not only did they do business together which mutually feathered each other's nests, but in about 1620 Cranfield married Anne Brett who was Villiers's cousin. In the end this proved to be Cranfield's downfall. In 1624 Cranfield tried to oust Villiers from his prime position as King James's 'blue-eyed' boy and replace him by his own brother-in-law, Arthur Brett. The coup was a dismal failure as both Villiers and King James strongly resisted most of Cranfield's budget measures. One for you, two for me etc. Cranfield himself was impeached for corruption and subsequently fell from grace very quickly, even though he was pardoned by King Charles **I** in 1625 after James had died. All this was happening around the time when Villiers and Deale, and maybe Jimmy himself, were playing golf at Therfield, so I think to myself what a wonderful world! Luckily for us the absolutism practised by James **I** didn't see out the 1600s. The Glorious Revolution and the Bill of Rights came in 1688 / 1689, since when we have been a constitutional monarchy. Monarchy or Republic? Well, a republic allowed a superstar like Donald Trump to run amok for four years. Even a deeply flawed monarchy may not look so bad. Maybe we need a new system that hasn't even been thought of yet? But if we think we are perfect, and never look for it, we will never find it! The Australian Liberal Party has about 80,000 members and the Labour Party about 60,000 members. Why do we tolerate between 0.2% and 0.3% of our population dictating what we all do? It's only 0.0003% if we just count the ones working in parliament! And I use the word 'working' very loosely!

In King James's time the population of Royston would have struggled to be a few hundred. In 1801, one hundred and seventy-five years after he died, less than one thousand people lived there. Apart from the expense account records, the other possible indication that golf was played in the area is that a local landmark, just about one mile from Royston centre, is called Goffers Knoll. The interesting thing is that this knoll is situated just east of Royston, whereas Therfield Heath is situated just west of Royston. i.e. they could be about one to two miles apart. The knoll is elevated and Therfield Heath is even higher with magnificent all-round views especially into Cambridgeshire. I have never been there, but my guess is that Goffers Knoll could be seen from the Heath in 1624 looking back across Royston town. The Cambridgeshire District Council *Historic Environment Setting's Assessment* carried out on the land at Muncey's farm near Royston in 2014, tends to support this idea. I must admit that all spellings I have seen of Goffers Knoll did not use an apostrophe as in Goffer's. Therefore, it may be that Goffers Knoll had nothing to do with golfers at all and was just named after some intrepid explorer or archaeologist called Goffers. There are some very ancient barrow burial mounds on both Goffers Knoll and also on Therfield Heath. I don't when the knoll was first called Goffers. However, it does appear on an old 1801 map of Royston which I have seen.

So at least it was there long before the Cambridge University guys started to play golf on Therfield Heath. Having said that, if we look at a modern-day map of Blackheath, we can see that running south from the junction of Chesterfield Walk, Charlton Way and Shooter's Hill road, we can also see a Goffers Road (also without any apostrophe). If we then compare that with the old course map shown in the *Blackheath Chronicles*, we can see the same road which runs right through the playing area of the old Blackheath seven-hole course. This map doesn't mention Goffers Road by name, but it does show the Whitfield Mount landmark which one of the holes went straight over in 1844. To me this suggests that in both cases 'Goffers' refers to 'Golfers' and not to some old dude called Goffers (after all it is Goffers and not Gaffers!). Although, just to complicate things, there have been suggestions that there could be a burial barrow at Whitfield's Mount like the one at Goffers Knoll! I wonder if Villiers *et al* were tonking featheries around Therfield Heath and the plebs were having a bash on the other side of town at Goffers Knoll with wooden balls? Stranger things have happened!

It is difficult to know exactly when the word 'golf' became the universally accepted spelling for this sport. The strange thing is that in one of the very earliest records where this sport was mentioned in 1457, it talked about King James **II** banning 'ye golf' on Sundays. Shortly after that in 1460 a poem written by Gilbert de Hay also used the word 'golf'. Between then and now (2018), we have seen umpteen different spellings used. These include goff, goffe, gowf, gowffe, gowff, golf, gof, golff, gouf, gouff, goufe, goulf, gouffe, goif, gauff, golph, goiff and golve. There are probably others I have missed. However, somewhere along the line we went full circle and returned to the first ever recorded spelling. Many of the British newspapers (English and Scottish) were already regularly using the word 'golf' throughout the 1700s...but not always. Adverts for silver arrow and silver club competitions, regularly played in the Edinburgh area from about 1744, generally used the word 'golf'. Goif and goiff are Gaelic words, so places where they would be used and found are probably restricted at least to places north of the Firth of Forth. References to goiff dated 1538, 1545 and 1613 have been found in the Aberdeen area, but by 1781 Aberdeen

GC themselves were talking only golf. Most of the places I have seen the words 'goff' or 'goffers', or combinations such as 'gofballes' or 'gofclubes', seem to be in England. The goffe spelling appeared in the Royal Warrant Association Records from the early 1660s. Many of them date to the early 1600s such as Prince Frederick Henry playing during his tuition days around the 1608-1612 period and the Villiers/Deal match in 1624. However, on page two of the *Blackheath Chronicles* there is a photo of a silver club with silver balls affixed by the captains of the club over a one-hundred-year period. The inscription on this club says 'August 16, 1766, the gift of Mr Henry Foot to the Honourable Company of Goffers at Blackheath'. Later in the *Chronicles* there is mention of an advert they put in *The Public Advertiser*, 2 April 1788, 'GOFF CLUB', Assembly House, Blackheath. Two years later, in 1790, there is painting of club captain William Innes where the artist's dedication says, 'to the Society of Goffers at Blackheath'. So, the oldest club in England were using the word 'goff' and its derivatives at least up to the end of the eighteenth century. Since both goff and goffer go back to the early 1600s, this suggests to me that Blackheath GC's history may well go back much further than 1766. If they had truly only started up around 1766, I feel that they would be talking about golf and not using an archaic word like goff. Another hint that Blackheath could be much older than 1766 can also be gleaned from page forty-four of their *Chronicles*. There they have a photo of some old golf clubs which were said to be representative of the type of clubs used at the very beginning of the 1800s. I understand that these clubs are in the BHGC artefact display cabinet. Attached to a very long iron (several inches longer than a modern-day driver) there is one ball claimed to be one hundred and seventy-nine years old. This means it could possibly date back to the 1620s. I don't know if they have any provenance on this ball, but if they do it would slot their history well back into the 1600s. If not as a formal club then certainly as a group who played together in that era. The fact that they say the ball is one hundred and seventy-nine years old suggests that they must have some information about it. I don't think dates were ever stamped on balls. This is such a precise age to claim for anything. Normally with something old like this they may say 'about fifty-years old' or 'about one-hundred years old' or they may give a range of years. Even if the ball was attached to the club at a later date and the one hundred- and seventy-nine-years dates back from 1897 when the *Chronicles* were published, it still dates back to 1718.

Incidentally, this photo of these early 1800s golf clubs at Blackheath is very interesting for another reason. There are twelve clubs in the photo and ten of them are iron clubs. Only two are wooden headed clubs. This seems quite strange when we consider that only featherie golf balls would have been available in the early 1800s and iron clubs had the reputation of not being kind to leather balls! I had always been under the impression that wooden clubs would have mostly been used in those days to minimise ball damage. However, it is apparent from many of the bets detailed in the BHGC minutes dating back to the late 1700s, that iron clubs were being used much more regularly than I had previously been led to believe. What we must remember on this BHGC photo is that cameras had not been invented in the early 1800s, so this image must have been taken much later, maybe when the *Chronicles* were written in the 1890s. So it is possible that 'younger' clubs could have *snuck* into the display cabinet at that time.

So far, I have only seen one regular reference to the word 'golve' and one to the word 'golph'. The former was often used in the Kincaid diaries dated 1687/1688. Kincaid lived and played in the Edinburgh and Leith area. This is where all the Flemish people went to back in King David's time. Golve sounds to me like the Dutch word kolven. Golph was used in 1758 by the Rev Alexander Carlyle when he was talking about his golfing experiences at Molesey Hurst.

The use of all these variants of the word golf is maybe not all that difficult to explain. When golf started around 1450 more than ninety percent of the population were illiterate. People would just try to spell the word as the spoken word sounded i.e. phonetically. However, problem with this is that people in different areas of England and Scotland spoke hundreds of different dialects. Even in 2018, if a Lancashire lad like me went to the Newcastle area and tried to understand someone speaking in 'broad Geordie', I would struggle. In truth, it was much worse than that. I can recall that even in the small Lancashire village where I was raised, I would sometimes listen to some of the old men coming out of the pub speaking old Lanky dialect, and I had no idea what they were talking about! Additionally, different regions often used different words for the same thing. As explained elsewhere in this story, the same thing happened with knur and spell. Sometimes it was called something which didn't even look remotely like knur and spell e.g. dab and trigger. When daily newspapers came on the scene in the early 1700s things started to change quickly. By the end of the 1700s there were more literate people than illiterate people. There was an even bigger change in the 1800s during the Industrial Revolution.

If we are looking at foreign languages which contain the word golf, we do need to be a bit careful. For example, the English word for a stretch of sea with a deep inlet and a narrow mouth is a gulf. However, the German word for gulf is *golf* and the German for golf is *das golfspeil*. However, just to trick us the Germans do have the Volkswagen Golf. The French word for gulf is *golfe* and the Spanish / Italian word is *golfo*. However, the Portuguese word for golf is *golfe* and the Spanish / French / Italian word for golf is *golf*. Confused? It just means that if we see only a short phrase in isolation and the context is not perfectly clear, as for instance a line from a poem, then please *vaya con pies de plomo*.

If George Villiers was indeed a regular player at Royston from 1615 to 1624, his time was running out. He may have continued playing with James's son Charles **I** after the king died, but only for a short time because Villiers was assassinated in 1628 when he was only thirty-six years old. Charles **I** also came to a sticky end when he was executed for high treason in early 1649. He backed the wrong side in the Roundheads and Cavaliers debacle! Soon after that the palace at Theobalds where King James died was demolished. They lived in very dangerous times in those days! Just to clarify, the Roundheads and Cavaliers debacle had nothing to do with circumcision! It was all about Oliver Cromwell and King Charles knocking the crap out of each other during the English Civil War of 1641 – 1652. This war had started following the Grand Remonstrance in December 1641 when a list of grievances was presented to King Charles in the English Parliament. The movement had been led by John Pym who was a staunch Puritan and fiercely anti-Catholic. Charles had a catholic wife, so he was obviously between a rock and a hard place!

After being in exile in Holland for a number of years, Charles I's son, Charles **II**, was eventually restored to the English throne in 1661. Oliver Cromwell had died in 1658. His body was exhumed and was chopped up and different parts were exhibited publicly in various places around England. During Cromwell's time in charge, the Parliament had actually declared England to be a Republic.

One of the first things which Cromwell did in 1649 when he took over was to abolish the system of Royal Warrants whereby suppliers of goods and services to royalty were granted the right to use this fact when they advertised their wares. Soon after Charles **II** was re-instated he reversed this decision. We know from the Royal Warrant Holders Association records that 'a Sword and a Goffe-club maker' had been granted warrants by Charles **II**, who himself was a keen golfer. Another thing the Puritans and Cromwell did was to ban Christmas celebrations.

We should certainly not dismiss the years between 1604 and 1615 without further examination. Particularly the period from 1607 to 1615 before George Villiers arrived on the scene. In 1607 King James had fallen in love with twenty-years old Robert Carr who, surprise, surprise, had also been a Gentleman of the Bed Chamber. By 1608, at age twenty-one, Carr had his own personal quarters in Royston courtesy of the king. Apparently King James **I** was teaching Latin to the young Robert...*Benedictus*! By 1610 / 1611 he had been made Viscount Rochester and in 1613 he was elevated to Earl of Somerset and later the same year was made Treasurer of Scotland. Although I know of no evidence that Carr ever played golf, we do know that James and Carr were more or less inseparable from 1607 to 1615. At that time James was still only about forty-one and was more than likely playing golf more regularly. So, I reckon there is a good chance that James and Carr played golf at Royston before Villiers turned up to spoil the party. Maybe something will eventually turn up on this? Prior to teaming up with James, Carr had spent some time in Scotland as a page boy to the Earl of Dunbar who was also Earl of Lothian. During this period, when he also visited Edinburgh regularly, he may have had some exposure to golf.

One thing we can say with absolute certainty is that King James must have been a man of great energy. Apart from his passion for golf, cockfighting, bowling, falconry, horse racing and hunting etc and his rumoured dalliances with various Gentlemen of the Bedchamber, he didn't neglect his conjugal duties. After he married Anne of Denmark, they had three children who survived to adulthood. Anne also had at least three miscarriages plus another four children who died when still infants. As King of England he also had to keep abreast of what was happening at Westminster. Of course, this helped him to dodge being assassinated by Guy Fawkes *et al* in the famous Gun Powder plot of November 1605. He is also credited with commissioning the translation of the Holy Bible from Latin into English. I don't know where James found the time and energy for all this activity. Maybe he had a good milkman called Ernie?

Returning to the 1682 game at Leith Links, yet another possibility is that the noblemen who played with the Duke of York confused golf with knur and spell or trap-ball or both. To the uninitiated, who knew little or nothing about either game, at first sight they would seem to be very similar games. Yes, they may have seen some guys hitting balls about randomly on Greenwich Hill at Blackheath or they may have heard about the Therfield Heath and Richmond activities. But, as far as we know, those were the only places in England where golf may have been seen during the 1600s. On the other hand, knur and spell was ubiquitous throughout the northern counties of England. There were hundreds or even thousands of different towns, villages, and hamlets where it would have been seen. Unfortunately, we don't know the names of the two noblemen or where they hailed from. If they were from Yorkshire, Lancashire, Durham, Lincolnshire, Cumbria, Northumberland, Cheshire, Derbyshire, Staffordshire, Shropshire, Nottinghamshire or even Worcestershire, it may help the case. Particularly if they also had any involvement with County Courts where they may have heard about knur and spell being played illegally on Sundays in that period. An attempt to identify the two noblemen is made in a later chapter...see The Old Troon Clubs chapter.

The other unfortunate thing is that knur and spell was, as far as I know, never played by royalty or any of the aristocracy, so it never attracted the same publicity which golf did.

It is maybe worth pointing out at this stage that the part of England which we now know as Hertfordshire, where Royston, Cheshunt and Therfield Heath are all located, was founded after the Saxon - Viking wars of the ninth century. Alfred the Great and the Danish King Guthrum the Old made a treaty after the Battle of Ethandun in 878. In it they agreed to split that area of England down the middle. The eastern half went into the Danelaw and the west half into Mercia. Basically, the boundary ran along the line of the River Lea and then along the famous Watling Street which had been constructed by the Romans. Although the Danes controlled that area for a while they didn't settle, and the Saxons continued to live there. Although it was part of the Danelaw there was no evidence of knur and spell. Royston, Cheshunt and Therfield would have all been part of the Danelaw at one stage. It is maybe interesting to know that Therfield Heath is one of the very few places in England where the very rare Pasqueflower can be found. This deep purple flower blooms at Easter time. Legend has it that this flower only ever appears in places where dead Vikings were buried.

Chapter 10

Dead Poet's Society
and paintings

To get another perspective on this situation we need to look at the famous diary of Samuel Pepys. He was born in 1633, the same year as the Duke of York, and he kept his diary from 1660-1669. The diary is over one million words long and it gives what is often regarded as the best insight into English life and events during that period. On May 8, 1668 he wrote 'The Duke of York himself said of his playing at trap-ball is true'. We can also look at Sir Walter Scott's historical novel *Peveril of the Peak* which was based on things happening in about 1678. Scott was a novelist and poet who was born in Edinburgh in 1771. He lived much of his life in mid-Lothian and the Scottish border country and very close to where golf started. His novel also makes a direct reference to trap-ball. Now this is very interesting because trap-ball is the little brother of knur and spell. The most prominent chronicler of the 1100s, William Fitzstephen, also wrote about this game. It was a short form of knur and spell which was often played by children. It was also played by adults in pub environments where space was restricted. If they didn't have a three-hundred-yard-long field near the pub, they would often play trap-ball which was played with implements which were designed to launch the ball much shorter distances. I understand that in trap-ball the hitting implement is much shorter than in knur and spell and the player hits one-handed (more like the more modern game of nipsy). If the Duke of York knew about trap-ball, he would certainly have known all about knur and spell. It would appear that when he played the golf game at Leith with the two English noblemen, he was pulling their plonkers and obviously got a kick from taking money off them.

Another famous English poet and clergyman, John Langhorne, was born in Winton, Cumbria, in 1735. Not far from Penrith and not far from the Scottish border. He did his early schooling in Winton and then Appleby Grammar School where the headmaster was the famous Latin Scholar, Richard Yates. Appleby-in-Westmorland is about forty-two miles from the Scottish border. In 1748, at age thirteen, Langhorne was already reading and translating ancient Greek. After Langhorne's death, an article by a biographer in the *Penrith Observer* quoted Yates as saying, 'Langhorne he found a promising pupil, who worked all day long, not as one of his biographers says playing football, spell and nor or Scottish Raid in playtime'. Spell and nor of course is another way of saying knur and spell. Yet another strong indication that knur and spell was already very widespread in England long before golf really took off in Scotland.

Probably even more famous than any of these writers was John Bunyan (1628 – 1688). His most celebrated work, *The Pilgrim's Progress*, first published in 1678, has never been out of print over the last three hundred and forty years! Although it may be difficult to prove, many people believe that more copies of this book have been sold than any other book in history, apart from the Bible. In one of the more recent biographies about Bunyan's life by Kevin Belmonte, reference was made to both tipcat and spell and nor being played during his early life. Apparently, in his youth Bunyan loved to play at cat and dog which was often abbreviated to 'cat'. Bunyan has been credited with the comment that the game of cat is more like a type of knur and spell than cricket. This is yet another good indication that both knur and spell and cricket were around in the early 1600s.

Knurr and spell has also been referred to in a document which details the memories of a famous son of Halifax in Yorkshire called Joseph Crabtree. Apparently, he went to school in Rishworth near Sowerby in 1766. In these memory documents he talked about 'the rough games of football and knurr and spell' and also commented that the girls joined in. About a century earlier, another of the Krabtree family, Henry, also went to school in Sowerby. He went on to write a country almanack called *Merlinus Rusticus* in 1685. This may also talk about knurr and spell but to date I have not located a copy. Another famous pupil at the Sowerby school with Henry was John Tillotson. He went on to become an Archbishop of Canterbury. After his primary schooling in Sowerby, John did his secondary schooling eighteen miles away at Colne Grammar School, where yours truly attended in the 1950s.

In 1887 a London born author and poet wrote a long short story about knurr and spell in the form of a series of chapters included in a charity book called *Voluntaries for an East London Hospital.* He was Walter Herries Pollock (1850 -1926). The story was a humorous discussion between two friends about the game of knurr and spell. This book also appeared in *Bernard Shaw's Book Reviews* which were originally published in the *Pall Mall Gazette* from 1885 – 1888. Voluntary Hospitals had been started in about 1740 to provide medical care for the poor people in society. There were five such hospitals founded in London alone which included all the famous research and teaching hospitals such as Guys Hospital. These hospitals existed mostly on voluntary contributions until 1948 when the Labour Party under Welshman Aneurin Bevan founded the National Health Service. William Ernest Henley, who most people will recall wrote the *Invictus* poem which Nelson Mandela later made famous, also contributed a series of poems to the 1887 *Voluntaries* book.

Yet another famous English writer whose works I have not had a chance to explore in any detail for possible mention of knur and spell is Arthur Ransome. He is probably most famous for his children's books series 'Swallows and Amazons' and the 2016 movie film of the same name. Arthur was born in Leeds in 1884 which was one of the main Yorkshire centres for knur and spell playing. He died in 1967 and is buried at the tiny village of Rusland in the Lake District where knur and spell was also played. As a child he spent many summer holidays just a few miles away from Rusland at another small village called Nibthwaite on Coniston Water. Knur and spell was played there too. It would not surprise me if knur and spell popped up somewhere in some of his works because in almost every Cumbrian village at that time knur and spell was often played on annual village sports days which involved the whole communities. If he didn't play the game himself he would certainly have known all about it. Another major sport at all the Cumbrian village sports days was wrestling. Many of the knur and spell players were also good wrestlers. There is a dedicated Arthur Ransome room at the Kendal Museum of Lakeland Life.

Rusland and Nibthwaite were both part of Lancashire up until 1974 when the county boundaries changed. They are both only a few miles away from Lake Windermere where I holidayed as a young teenager in the 1950s as a member of Colne Lad's Club under the leadership of Bernard Gregson. I spent many happy hours at Colne Lad's Club in my early teens playing table tennis and snooker, probably at a time when I should have been at home doing school homework! What's that I hear about a misspent youth? Over the last forty odd years however, this early table tennis practice has served me well in many battles against *meu gran amic Catalan* from Breda, Salvador Torras. The club had been founded in 1937 by Colne Rotary Club. This was probably my earliest exposure to the good work done by Rotary clubs. Little did I know then that fifty years later I would serve as a Rotarian eleven thousand miles away in Melbourne, Australia!

We stayed at Hammerbank near Troutbeck Bridge, which had been built as a private residence in the 1850s. It had since been bought and donated by Earl Peel in 1938 to the Lancashire Association of Boy's Clubs as a holiday adventure centre. Later in the 1900s it was re-named Windermere Manor and now serves as a specialised hotel for blind and partially sighted people. Memories of my time there are very sketchy. However, one lasting memory which stayed with me was rowing across Lake Windermere to Belle Grange Bay and back in a very much overcrowded rowing boat. Windermere, which is the biggest natural lake in England, at that point is just under one mile across. None of us had lifejackets and with the overcrowding the boat sat very low in the water. Since I was not a very strong swimmer, and with choppy conditions, I was terrified that we may capsize into water that was about sixty-seven metres deep and very cold. Luckily, we made it back safely, and I am still here to tell the tale. None of the activities at Hammerbank included knur and spell playing although this game was still drawing large crowds of spectators into the Rusland Valley in the 1930s.

Long before Arthur Ransome, English poet William Wordsworth (I wandered lonely as a cloud), was also firmly ensconced in the same knur and spell playing territory. He was born in Cockermouth in Cumbria in 1770 and died in Rydal near Ambleside on Lake Windermere in 1850. Everywhere he went in the Lake District during that time he would have come across knur and spell being played. The same can be said of several of Wordsworth's contemporaries, particularly Samuel Taylor Coleridge and Robert Southey who together with Wordsworth were known as the Lake Poets in the early 1800s. Coleridge also gets mentioned in a later chapter under the heading 'Why?'.

Another writer from the 1600s was White Kennett (1660-1728) who was an English Bishop who specialised in ancient history, especially the period from the end of the Roman Empire in 410 AD to the fall of Constantinople in 1452 AD. At one point in his career he was Bishop of Peterborough which was in the Danelaw area and knur and spell may have been played there. In an unpublished glossary about antiquated northern sayings and expressions, *Etymological Collections of English Words and Provincial Expressions,* he talked about 'to play at knur and knor', 'knur-sticks and knurl-sticks' and 'a little round chessball'. I don't know what a 'chessball' was. Maybe it was called this because chess pieces and knurs were both made from boxwood. Even when he wrote this Glossary, Kennett often quoted other earlier publications as references to support his list. This strongly suggests that knur playing in England was in existence in England at least when golf started around 1450, and probably even earlier.

Although many of these old poets and writers or their biographers have mentioned knur and spell in their poems and essays, I was very surprised that I could not find a whole poem written about the game. Particularly when we consider that there have been lots of poems written about both golf and cricket. For something that appeared to me to have been a very big part of the fabric of society in northern England for hundreds of years, it seemed to be a glaring omission. Therefore to hopefully offset this apparent paucity, and to guarantee the avoidance of self-written doggerel, I asked a good friend of mine if he could create some suitable verse. Timothy St Julien Barber is an Englishman living in Melbourne. He has been writing poems and stories for sixty odd years and is a person of letters *par excellence*. The following poem is called *Beneath Time's Passing Bell* and it brilliantly brings to life this ancient game which was ubiquitous throughout the Danelaw for many centuries.

Where are they now the lads and men
Who played at knur and spell?
They've spun off into history
On time's spinning carousel.

Their names are barely memories,
Faint lines upon a page
But once their fame was greatly praised
And sung from age to age.

Off on stark and lonely moorland,
Removed from prying eyes,
The game of knur and spell was played
'Neath wild and open skies.

'Midst ling and tussock grass and whin,
Where still the curlew cries,
The arcane game of knur and spell
Was fought for, rise by rise.

And hidden, too, from Church and Crown,
From the swift arm of the law,
The sheriff and the constable
And the cruel inquisitor.

The game was outlawed by the Crown
And King James *Book of Sports* :
To upset James the first could see
One hanged by all reports...

Or clamped within the pillory,
Or locked up in the stocks,
Or whipped and tortured, thrown in goal
Behind strong walls and locks.

A wooden ball hung from a string
And driven with a club...
The games were advertised in code
In tavern, inn and pub.

And folk would come from miles away
To lay their money down
And rally at the meeting place
Beyond the bounds of town.

The ground was cleared and levelled out
Around the pin or spell;
The player, called a laiker, pegged
His stance with pins as well.

And all the while the publicans
Would ply the crowd with ale
That they'd brought in by the dray load
Over hill and over dale.

The great crowd quaffed vast seas of ale
Then, stirred to fever pitch,
Placed huge bets on their champion
To win and make them rich.

The knur was placed upon the spell
Or hung upon the pin,
The laiker stepped up to his mark
And prayed his knock would win.

He carefully set his heel and toe
According to his mark
To swing his stick, his pummel, through
A horizontal arc.

The crowd went silent on the field,
You couldn't hear a sound,
As the laiker made to drive the knur
Across the open ground.

The spell was sprung, the pummel swung,
The knur flew through the air...
The ref'rees chained each knock in yards
For the watchers standing there.

Then some would cheer, and some would curse
Or simply hang their head,
Whilst some, on hearing who had won,
Would wish that they were dead.

How could so innocent a game
Arouse such wrath, such ire,
Be viewed by Church and Crown alike
As worthy of hellfire?

The Crown, the Church, the Inns of Court,
Were staunchly Puritanic
And gambling and drunkenness
Were held to be satanic.

And yet, despite the deadly risk,
Folk flocked from far and near,
On foot, by horse, by coach and four-
Their zeal surpassed their fear!

The origins of knur and spell
Are lost far back in time;
They p'raps go back to Viking Days
When the Norse were in their prime.

In the counties of North England,
The Danelaw as it's known,
The game of knur and spell took hold
And could not be overthrown.

The working men of Lancashire
And Yorkshire somehow made
The game of knur and spell their own-
That Cap and Clog Brigade.

They'd turn up in their thousands
To bet and drink and play-
The game was still illegal but
They turned up anyway!

The laikers oft' used alias names
To trick and foil the Law
And knur and spell swelled to a tide
That no one could ignore.

More popular by far than golf,
More rewarding than hard graft,
The doughty cap and clog brigade
Made knur and spell their craft.

But time is unpredictable,
It's famine, feast or drought...
The game of knur and spell declined
And slowly faded out.

So, where are they now the lads and men
Who once played knur and spell?
They've vanished like the game itself
Beneath time's passing bell.

A.M.D.G.
T. St. Julien Barber
28 August 2020

The poem's title, in just four simple words, very cleverly manages to link the earliest days of knur and spell with its final demise in the late 1900s, by using the 'Passing Bell' or 'Death Knell' tradition which started in King Henry **VIII**'s / Queen Elizabeth **I**/s era. These days few mortals are honoured with a church death knell. The best that most of us can hope for, to announce our departure, is a few kind lines in a newspaper obituary column. The last time I can remember a very slow, single, haunting bell peal was at the time of Lady Diana Spencer's funeral in 1997. The tintinnabulation during that sad day is ineradicably etched in my memory. English poet John Donne (1573 – 1631) first coined the phrase 'for whom the bell tolls', which Ernest Hemingway later 'borrowed' in 1940 as the title of his bestselling novel of the same name. Needless to say all this 'knelling' activity coincided with the early development days of knur and spell. The full John Donne quotation is even more profound.

> 'Each man's death diminishes me,
> For I am involved in mankind.
> Therefore, send not to know
> For whom the bell tolls,
> It tolls for thee.'

Would that more people in 2020 could think on that!

All this talk about bells also reminds me of Edgar Allan Poe's famous poem, *The Bells*, where he makes onomatopoeic use of the word 'bells'.

As may be expected, no sooner had I written the last few paragraphs about knur and spell / poetry when Murphy's Law reared its head, and I finally came across the elusive poem I had been searching for. It was a poem called *The Trip Match* written by a Yorkshireman called Enoch Ratcliff in the 1820s. It is not a general poem about the game, but one about a specific match played in that era. The poem immortalises a man called Bancroft from Stannington who beat a man called Winterbottom from Sheffield on Doncaster Racecourse playing for £100 in the Yorkshire Championship. The venue for this match is interesting. Both Stannington and Sheffield are about twenty-five miles away from Doncaster. Riding in a stagecoach, or maybe on horseback, this would have been a fair old trek in the 1820s.

According to the *Sheffield Register* 1787, Watson's stagecoach fare for that trip was five shillings and sixpence. This would not have been an insignificant cost for the loser to pay who came away empty-handed. By a strange coincidence, when I first started travelling to college in Manchester from Colne in 1959, the return fare on the X43 double-decker bus which ran (and still runs today) hourly from Skipton to Manchester (stopping at Colne) was also five shillings and sixpence. If anyone wishes to read *The Trip Match* poem in its entirety, it can be found in *The Songs of Joseph Mather : to which are added Memoir of Mather and Miscellaneous Songs related to Sheffield with Introductory Notes* by John Wilson dated 1862. In April 1827 Winterbottom was at it again when he played the famous Yorkshire cricketer, Tom Marsden, for ten pounds a side. He lost this match too!

Although most of the poets mentioned hitherto are well and truly in the past, this does not preclude modern wordsmiths from referring to old games in their works. One such scribe was born in Leeds in 1937, the same year that Colner Billy Baxter won the World Knur and spell Championship at the Alma Inn in Laneshawbridge. His name was Tony Harrison, and he was educated at Leeds University in the heart of knur and spell playing country. In his *School of Eloquence and Other Poems* published in 1981, his poem *The Rhubarbarians* refers to the Luddites in the Industrial Revolution of the 1800s as ' shadows in the moonlight playing knur and spell'.

Even more acclaimed was another Yorkshireman called Ted Hughes. He was born in the Calder Valley near Mytholmroyd in 1930 and spent his teenage years at Mexborough Grammar School. In 1984 he was made Poet Laureate and held this post until he died in 1998. As such he was a member of the Royal Household and was paid a small salary accordingly, a tradition which had been started in about 1616 by our old friend King James I shortly before he published his famous Book of Sports. Hopefully, Ted was partial to a glass or two of sherry! All his young life before university Ted Hughes lived in big knur and spell playing places. I don't know if Ted ever wrote about knur and spell in all his massive body of work, but we do know from one of his biographers that he played knur and spell as a boy.

Not only poets wrote about knur and spell. Short story writers and novelists such as George Oliver Onions did the same. Oliver Onions was born in the knur and spell heartland of Bradford in 1873 and died in 1961. Several of his stories and novels refer to knur and spell.

A more contemporary writer is Jane Sanderson who spent her early years in the small Yorkshire mining village of Hoyland near Barnsley. Following a career in journalism, Jane then turned to BBC Radio producing before publishing her first historical fiction novel, *Netherwood*, in 2011. Hoyland is only about five miles away from Darfield and even closer to Wombwell. Midway between Darfield and Wombwell we find Netherwood Country Park which is bisected by the River Dove. On the banks of this river a big country mansion called Netherwood Hall had been built in around 1710 on a site where an old manor house dating to the 1400s had previously stood. After various different owners, this mansion was finally demolished in 1963. This could well be where the inspiration for the *Netherwood* novel came from. The novel is set in the early 1900s and has much in it about a big challenge knur and spell match between two fictitious mining villages. At that point in history knur and spell had already been played in every single surrounding village and hamlet around Wombwell, Darfield and Hoyland for several hundred years!

Apart from the apparent lack of knur and spell poems, there seems to be an even bigger famine when it comes to knur and spell paintings. In fact to date I haven't found one single knur and spell painting. This is a ludicrous situation when compared to what happened with golf, bearing in mind that for a long-time knur and spell was much more popular than golf.

The nearest I have come to a knur and spell painting was the drawing by George Walker which was engraved and converted to an aquatint print by the Havell family and published in 1814 in a book called *The Costume of Yorkshire*. Walker was born in the knur and spell heartland of Leeds in 1781. He probably did this work sometime between 1800 and 1814. i.e. over two hundred years ago.

It is also worth noting that even this drawing may not be an accurate depiction of knur and spell. When Walker did this picture he was really trying to make a statement about the clothes which his subjects were wearing. He may not have paid too much attention to trying to ensure that the knur and spell elements shown were accurate. I am not even convinced that the clothes he has wrapped his subjects in were really the type of garments being worn by the common working people in many of the different 'occupational' scenes throughout his book. He may have had some other agenda, like dressing them how he would have like to see them being dressed!

Prints from engravings were also available for some of the early knur and spell superstars such as Kirk Stables from the early 1860s onwards. Not long after that, old photographs of knur and spell players and of knur and spell matches and knur and spell crowds regularly appeared. From time-to-time drawings of knur and spell equipment also appeared in some publications. I am still trying to find an actual painting! Surely from the many thousands of knur and spell players who enjoyed this game, over many centuries, a painting must exist somewhere?

Chapter 11

Trapball, kilts, a surgeon's son and lots of meanderings

Whether or not the match which the Duke of York and John Patterson played at Leith was the first 'international' golf match has been questioned by Dutch sports historian Geert Nijs. Firstly, he doubts whether John Patterson could have been a good golfer because he was a cobbler. Well, cobblers worked with leather and did lots of stitching. It is well documented that many cobblers also made featherie golf balls. Even in 1554 cordiners (new shoemakers) and cobblers (old shoe repairers) were mentioned in a legal dispute at Leith as also making leather stitched golf balls. It is also well documented that golf ball makers and golf club makers were often themselves very adept at playing golf. All the historically big names in golf such as Tom Morris, Allan Robertson and Willie Park came to be great golfers via the equipment side of golf. We don't know for sure, but it seems highly likely that Patterson also made golf balls. Mr Nijs also questioned whether a Duke who later became king would play with a man from the lower classes such as John Patterson. The Duke was not a stupid man. He wanted to win the bet, so he probably asked around the town who was a good golfer and Patterson's name came forward. It mattered not one iota that Patterson was a humble man. Winning the big bet was much more important than that! Secondly, he doubts whether the Duke himself would have been a good golfer because there was no golf played in England at that time. He talks about the Duke playing hand-tennis which would hardly help him to play golf. Nijs has obviously never heard of trap-ball which has been well documented in many sources and which the Duke was apparently very fond of playing. He has probably never heard of knur and spell either. Trap-ball was a short form ball and stick game which was played in England long before colf or kolf were played in Holland. Knur and spell was a long form version of trap-ball and is also a very ancient game perhaps dating back to Viking days. Both these stick and ball games were extensively played in England when the Duke was around and indeed long before that! Both games required exceptionally good hand-eye co-ordination in order to play well. Anyone who could play trap-ball or knur and spell well would almost certainly also be able to play golf well.

Apart from doubting both Patterson's and the Duke's skill level, Nijs also then quotes a 1668 Dutch painting which he claims to show a colf game between someone in a kilt (assumed to be a Scotsman) on the ice somewhere in Holland. He asserts that this, and not the Duke of York's match, was the first international match. How he has arrived at this as being a 'colf' match is a mystery. It is played on ice. There are people everywhere in the painting all within a very short distance of each other. If anyone had attempted to play a normal golf type shot under those circumstances, there would have been dead bodies lying about everywhere. It is much more likely that they were playing the short form of kolf using very short distance push strokes.

Now I am not an expert on kilts, but I do know that the kilt was a Celtic thing and not exclusively a Scottish thing. Kilts are worn in Scotland, Wales, Ireland, Isle of Man, Cornwall, Brittany in France and even Galicia in Spain which had ruled the Netherlands for about one hundred years just before this painting was done. The tam o' shanter style cap worn by the player could indicate a Scot but not necessarily so. This shape of head gear was commonly worn throughout northern Europe from the 1500s. If Geert Nijs can somehow tell that this was definitely a Scot playing whatever the game is, he is a better man than I am, Gunga Din! Maybe Mr Nijs is a world expert on tartan design and can even tell us which highland clan the player belonged to? I suppose it is also pure conjecture that the people in the painting were playing a match and not just a few random guys practising their game? Whatever the game is.

What is possibly another very old game which could be a forerunner to knur and spell is the game of billets. This game was also very common in Lancashire and Yorkshire. It involves a stick about the length of a golf stick made from holly. It has a grip like a golf grip. The head was a cylindrical shape about four inches long and usually made from hornbeam. There was a groove cut near the end of the head and at the start of a game, a short stubby and slightly curved piece of cylindrical wood called a billet was balanced in this groove. This billet was made from boxwood. When the player was ready he just threw the billet into the air in front of him using his stick and then just whacked it as far as he could, all in the same movement. The longest hit won the game. In other words, like trap-ball, nipsy and peggy, it was just another miniature form of knur and spell which could be played in more restricted areas than a large knur and spell field. In the 1600s and 1700s there were pubs in both Lancashire and Yorkshire called 'The Crooked Billet'. In fact, there are still many existing pubs throughout England called the Crooked Billet especially in the Home Counties and London area. Many of the Crooked Billet pubs were located around village greens where the game of billets would have been played. There is a Crooked Billet on the edge of Wimbledon Common and also one on Hook Common in Hampshire. The word billet is known to have its origins dating back to Anglo-Norman French, so this game could very easily pre-date golf in Scotland. Many people think this game was originally played by the Saxons who were in England before the Vikings arrived.

Of course, one didn't necessarily have to be a rich man oneself to play with proper golf clubs and leather balls. It worked just as well if one had a rich daddy. Such a lucky boy was Thomas Kincaid The Younger who was a medical student in Edinburgh about 1687. He was the son of a successful surgeon and apothecary working in Edinburgh. The interesting thing about this wee Scottish laddie is that he kept a very detailed set of notes between 1687 and 1688 which are currently preserved in the *National Library of Scotland*. These notes give much information on golf excursions he made with friends to play both at Leith Links and at Bruntsfield Links. Thomas recorded details about how much they paid for a coach ride from Edinburgh to and from the Leith Links. Also, how much he paid for golf balls, club repairs and how much they spent on entertainment after the game on food and drinks. On one occasion he spent fourteen shillings to buy three golf balls. The return coach and horses trip cost ten shillings. On another occasion he spent fourteen shillings on collips which made him very sick. Not sure what collips are. I thought they may be scallops but it could refer to a kind of meat stew. There was never a fee listed to play golf. Presumably, anyone could go on to Leith Links in those days and play for nothing just like they could at St Andrews. Despite this it was not uncommon for him to spend thirty or forty shillings during a golfing day out which was equivalent to about five weeks wages for the ordinary working man in Leith in that period.

The other thing Thomas Kincaid The Younger left us with, which is also held in the *National Library of Scotland*, is the first documented instruction on how to swing a golf club. His descriptions of how the various parts of the body should move during a golf swing and where the power of the golf swing comes from are classic. Of course, his description would also apply equally well to the knur and spell swing!

There were also similar games played elsewhere in Europe going back centuries which should also be given consideration. These include the game of *fiolet* which was played in the north west of Italy near the region of Valle d'Aosta. Also, *la rebatta* which was played in the same region and a game called *jeu de la tappet* which was played in the Picardy region of Northern France.

Some of these games were miniature versions of the long driving form of the game. Just like today we have golf, miniature golf, driving ranges, long driving competitions, world putting championships and pitch/putt courses. The very old game of trap-ball which is a short-form version of knur and spell is shown in drawings in the William Fitzstephen chronicles dating back to the 1100s. Although this game was played all over England and not only in the Danelaw.

When you talk to your Japanese friends who live in Tokyo, they still talk about going out to play golf. Even though the only place they have ever been to is one of the ginormous multi-level driving ranges where they queue up for hours just for the privilege.

We also have golfers who don't play tournaments at all but make a living just going around the world doing trick shots. Just like early Australian star golfer Joe Kirkwood did when he teamed up with Walter Hagen in the 1920s and 1930s.

In the late 1800s and early 1900s clock golf was very popular and as recently as 2016 equipment for this game could still be purchased.

There are approximately thirty-two thousand golf courses in the world and every one of them is different. The Rules of Golf as laid down by the R&A or the USGA may be omnipresent but infinite variation in the playing experience is always the order of the day. And that is before we even start to consider all the different competition playing formats such as stroke-play, match-play, par, bogey, four-ball, foursomes, Ambrose, Stableford, bisque par, skins, eclectic etc.

Although there was extensive Viking presence in Scotland during the 793 AD – 1066 AD period, I found no evidence which confirms that Knur and Spell was originally a Viking game or that the Scots even knew about it when they took up playing golf around 1450. There is, however, mountains of evidence that the Scots knew all about knur and spell long before the golf explosion which occurred in the second half of the nineteenth century. Attempts to find out if Knur and spell was ever played in parts of Scandinavia prior to the Viking invasion have so far been fruitless. Nevertheless, I still like to romanticize about the idea that maybe modern-day golf did develop from an old Viking game! After all, I do have a Viking surname and a granddaughter called Freja named after a Viking goddess! That said, I suppose I should keep an open mind. Instead of golf emanating from knur and spell maybe it was the other way around? Or maybe the two games developed side by side along similar timelines? The reason why this latter suggestion may be a strong possibility is that when golf started in Scotland it was a rich man's sport. The first golfer in Scotland in 1502 was King James **IV** and one of the first in England was Henry, Prince of Wales, the son of King James **VI**, who used to play in the early 1600s with his courtiers on what later became Blackheath GC. Even in Scotland golf remained as just a rich man's sport for a long time, even though courses like St Andrews were public golf courses. This was mainly because of the high cost of golf balls. The old featherie balls, which were predominant until the guttie ball was introduced in 1847/1848, were handmade and the cost of these balls was well out of the range of the ordinary working man. It wasn't just the initial high cost of buying the featherie balls. An even bigger stumbling block was the relative fragility of the ball itself. Even in dry weather they were very easily damaged during play. If it rained, they fell in a heap very quickly. Couple these two factors with the knowledge that the fancy mowing machines which we use today did not exist. Course maintenance was not like it is today. In those days, the rough was 'very rough', so apart from damaged balls it was much easier to lose them too. The expensive featherie balls would definitely need to be replaced far more frequently than modern balls do. This all started to change after 1850 when the guttie ball appeared, and golf in Scotland gradually became popular with the middle classes. In 2016 there are still five hundred and fifty golf courses in Scotland for a population of just over five million people. That is almost sixty per cent more golf courses per capita than Australia! And we think that we have a lot of golf courses!

This wasn't the case in England where golf remained mostly a pastime for the wealthy and was very much a status symbol well into the twentieth century. Even in 2016 there are many golf clubs in England where working-class people would still be looked down on and not be welcome. I suspect the same applies in Australia. It wasn't until well after World War **II** that public and municipal golf courses in England started to proliferate that ordinary working-class people could afford to think about playing golf. Once golf courses did become more accessible to the masses, it didn't take long in Northern England for the playing of knur and spell, colloquially known as poor man's golf, to peter out. Although there were a few attempts to revive interest. The last serious attempt was in 1991 when Lancashire won the Pennine Cup against Yorkshire at the village of Bradshaw near Halifax, West Yorkshire. Len Kershaw won that day and Stuart Greenfield, who had won the world championship in 1971, was second. The Hargreaves Arms over Monkroyd in Laneshawbridge organised a few minor long knock competitions after that, but it was still the same old players, Greenfield, Kershaw, et al, who were turning up to play. They were all getting very long in the tooth by then and no young blood could be enticed into the game. The light probably finally went out on knur and spell in 1995. Stuart Greenfield, who was already in his sixties, still managed to finish runner-up that day to Frank Lenthal, a long-time adversary from Yorkshire.

Chapter 12

Golf starts in Baildon (Yorkshire) almost three hundred years after knur and spell

According to their website, the Royal North Devon golf club at Westward Ho claims to be the oldest club in England when it was founded in 1864. It was the club which the famous John Henry Taylor was associated with when he was winning five British Opens in the late 1800s and early 1900s. However, what is also claimed to be the first golf club established in England, Blackheath GC, was founded in the early 1600s. But that may not have been the date when an actual course was played on. Probably at first, they were just playing on open heath land. The date of 1745 is often mentioned as the date the club was formed, but tangible evidence at Blackheath only dates back to 1766. I suppose that Royal North Devon's claim to be the oldest is because they are still playing on the same site where they started in 1864. Blackheath GC moved about three miles from Greenwich Hill to their current Eltham site in 1923. So, I suppose that Royal North Devon is the oldest surviving course in England and Blackheath is the oldest club. Of course, the Old Manchester GC at Kersal was about fifty years older than Royal North Devon but their course and club house did not survive. However, as a society of golfers playing at other courses they did survive, and they are still listed accordingly in the latest *R & A Handbook*.

In 1553, almost two hundred years before Blackheath GC was formed, a man called Robert Baildon built Baildon Hall in West Yorkshire. Baildon is a small town (population 15,000) about twenty miles from where I was born and raised and is even nearer to the earlier mentioned village of Cowling. The hall had been built on the site of a medieval manor which dated back to the 1200s. The Baildon family can at least trace their history back to Hugh de Baildon who died in 1220 and was probably born about 1150 or 1160. He may or may not have had any connection to the original medieval manor. Some of the 1200s structure still survives and is part of the south wing of the current hall.

Imagine my delight when I discovered that in the 1980s, when they were doing restoration work on the south wing of Baildon Hall, they found some knur and spell equipment ensconced behind an old wall. Along with the old knur stick they also found a knur and an old knife which had probably been used to hand carve knurs with and maybe also whittle the stick. This knur stick at about three feet or ninety-one to ninety-two centimetres long, was somewhat shorter than the pummel lengths being used in the 1800s and 1900s. However, this is maybe not surprising when we consider that the average height of a man in the late 1500s and early 1600s was probably a few inches shorter than in the 1900s.

Wattle / daub plaster fragment showing 1618 inscription at Baildon Hall
(Photo: Barry Wilkinson)

During the restoration work they also found a piece of plaster which was marked 1618 and had the initial 'W'. The plaster was on a part of the old Hall which had been constructed with the ancient wattle and daub technique. Apart from the date and the initial there could also be seen two interesting designs scratched into the plaster (see photo opposite). These are probably experimental designs made by one of the craftsmen who eventually worked on the ornate ceilings throughout the manor house. The design on the right-hand side appears to have featured a quincunx theme as indicated by the five dots. The wattle and daub technique for constructing house walls has been used in various parts of the world for at least six thousand years. In England the method certainly preceded the Romans. It was extremely popular in the Tudor Period (1485-1603) when the south wing of Baildon Hall is known to have been built.

The owner at that time was William Baildon. Both the equipment and the piece of plaster can be seen in display cabinets at the Baildon Hall Club which is now a private members dining club. William Baildon had been born in 1562 and died in 1627. He could easily have been playing knur and spell from 1575 onwards or even a few years earlier. William Baildon (1562-1627) also had a son called William Baildon who was born in 1588 and died just before his father in 1627. This William obviously never inherited the Hall from his father. However, he could have been the one playing knur and spell around 1618 when the equipment may have been hidden. Reason to think this is because William Baildon (1562-1627) is known to have been going blind in 1618 and was totally blind by 1625. So he would probably not have been playing knur and spell in 1618. On the other hand his son William would have been about thirty years old at that point and would have probably been at his peak. The other thing which may be relevant is that William Baildon (1562-1627) was an amateur antiquary and is believed to have supplied information on the history of Baildon and surrounding area to Roger Dodsworth (1585-1654) who was a lifelong antiquary who collected notes for his unpublished *History of Yorkshire* over many decades. Dodsworth was born in the knur and spell playing stronghold of Helmsley on the North Yorkshire moors. When he died his large collection of manuscript notes ended up in the Bodleian

Library at Oxford University. Maybe this unpublished history could contain some information on knur and spell?

Methinks that stuffing old knur and spell equipment behind a wall in the South Wing of Baildon Hall for future generations to find is something that an antiquary may have been inclined to do? Baildon Hall Club also have an article dated 1685 which talks about knur and spell being played in Sheffield at that time. Just like some of the early 'golf', two men were fined for playing trippit (knur and spell) in the churchyard and for abusing the vicar's wife who must have been admonishing them. According to a booklet called *Baildon Hall, a History of a Yorkshire Manor* written by club member and former club president Barbara Boyes, this reference was obtained from various documents held at the *Borthwick Institute* in York.

William Baildon (1588 – 1627), who died before his father, also had a son called Francis (1627 – 1669). Francis married his wife Jane in around 1650 and probably did some renovations after they married. Jane lived until about 1691. Whether it was Francis or one of the Williams who had hidden the knur and spell equipment behind the wall is not known definitively. However whoever it was, it was probably put there during the 1600s. From all accounts Francis was a bigger layabout than his dad or his grandad had been. My money would be on one of the Williams or even both of them.

The equipment had probably been hidden there at a time when knur and spell was banned by the government from being played. King James **I** of England, who at the time was also King James **VI** of Scotland, had issued a declaration in 1617 in the form of a *Book of Sports*. Its official title was *The King's Declaration of Lawful Sports*. Initially it was just intended for the county of Lancashire but in 1618 it was applied to all England. This declaration listed sports which COULD be played on a Sabbath. Cricket, football, and knur and spell were not listed and hence were banned. To be fair to King James, he himself was not keen to interfere in the leisure time of the English people. He had only intervened with this declaration after the Puritan magistrates in Lancashire had banned the playing of ALL sports on Sundays. They had done this as part of a power battle they had been having as a splinter group in the English Church. Although the Protestants were by now in charge of the English Church, the Puritans believed that there were still far too many Catholic legacies remaining. The House of

Commons had earlier passed bills in 1606 and 1614 in favour of banning Sunday sport but these had not received approval from either King James or from the House of Lords. The Baildon family were known to be staunch royalists. In fact Robert Baildon, before he re-built the Hall in 1553, had been Groom of the King's Chamber and Wardrobe in 1526 to none other than King Henry **VIII**. Earlier, in 1520, Robert had also been a Groom of the Chamber to Queen Catherine of Aragon. This was at the famous 'Field of the Cloth of Gold' meeting between King Henry **VIII** and King Francis **I** of France held at Balinghem, a tiny village near Calais. Around that time Catherine had mentioned ' being busy at golfe' in a letter she had written to Cardinal Wolsey. Maybe she had heard about knur and spell from Robert, or he had heard about golfe from her? So William Baildon would no doubt have been bending over backwards to comply with any edict from King James! The Baildons were not an aristocratic family. They were one notch below in the pecking order at the gentry level but would certainly have aspired to migrate upwards. Apart from the *Book of Sports*, 1618 had other historical significance. That year Sir Walter Raleigh was beheaded at Westminster.

It was very magnanimous for King James to intervene in this way. However, there was one minor problem. In 1618 about seventy per cent of the male population in England were still illiterate. The man in the street would have no means to buy a *Book of Sports* and he would not be able to read it anyway. The church would probably have been the main outlet for this book and their scholars would have been among the few who could read it. How they interpreted the book to their parishioners, when they were the ones trying to ban all sports in the first place, could, I imagine, be open to some high degree of scepticism.

According to the *Whitby Sessions of the North Riding Record Society* dated 27 April 1624 a man called Milnes of Aislaby village was before the court for playing knur and spell on Easter Day during the time of the afternoon service. Aislaby is very close to many knur and spell playing villages of the North Yorkshire Moors such as Danby, Ainthorpe, Leaholm etc. It is also close to both Whitby and Scarborough where knur and spell was also played. In the same record a Thirsk man was summoned for the same offence. In the 1638 summer meeting of York Quarter Sessions several people were tried for playing unlawful games. In 1633 King Charles **I** had re-issued the *Book of Sports* with strong support of William Laud the Archbishop of Canterbury. Fortunately, the government found the law very hard to enforce. Archbishop Laud fell out of favour in 1640 and the *Book of Sports* was publicly burned in 1643, just two years before Laud was executed. Thirsk is also on the North Yorkshire Moors and is just a few miles away from Helmsley where we know that knur and spell was played in the 1700s. Thirsk is also where famous veterinarian James Alfred Wight, better known by his James Herriot penname and his *All Creatures Great and Small* book and TV series, lived and practised for about fifty years.

However, this may not have been the real reason for the abandonment of the law. The English Civil Wars (1642-1651) between the Roundheads (Parliamentarians) and Cavaliers (Royalists) had just begun which resulted in James **I**'s son, Charles **I** being executed and his son, Charles **II** being exiled. At a national level, the end of the wars resulted in a win for the Roundheads and the rise of Oliver Cromwell. After these wars, never again did the English monarchy have the final say in how England was governed. It also ended the monopoly of the Church of England. At the grass roots level, in the counties, there was also a power struggle going on. The commercial oligarchs of the developing industrial towns of Yorkshire such as Halifax, Leeds, and Sheffield, were having their own battle against the manorial courts of the old English feudal system. Up to that point the lords of the manor had been able to dish out extreme punishments such as stocks, public whippings and even gibbet beheadings for what we would regard these days as very petty crimes. Their powers too were diminished after the Civil Wars.

Charles **II** did in fact make a comeback after nine years in exile when Cromwell died in 1658. Charles was re-instated as king. According to legal documents his period of rule was backdated to 1649 and he kept the top job until he died in 1685. Oliver Cromwell could well be the reason why the British Monarchy has survived as long as it has. Cromwell ruled England more or less like a dictator under Puritanical influence. The English people didn't like it, and they have preferred to maintain the monarchy ever since, despite all its shortcomings and the greater frequency of *anni horribiles*.

Charles **II** was probably the best loved of all British monarchs. The fact that he had dozens of mistresses and sired at least twelve illegitimate children only seemed to endear him to the people. He made the current royal mob look like a bunch of choirboys! In fact one specific law under Oliver Cromwell could have been the chief reason why the people wanted the monarchy back. This was the law which stated that acts of adultery were punishable by death. If Cromwell had survived and retained power with that law in place, England's population would have plummeted and the royal family in particular may have been obliterated! It may be worth mentioning that Charles **II** was not the star royal performer when it came to sowing his wild oats. Henry **I**, one of William the Conqueror's sons, was believed to have been the begetter of at least twenty-four illegitimate offspring! (nine sons and fifteen daughters).

There probably wasn't too much knur and spell playing going on during this Civil War period. In total about two hundred thousand people throughout England died in these wars (soldiers plus civilians). Several of the main battles were fought in what had been the Danelaw area. In fact, some of Oliver Cromwell's troops (Roundheads) were billeted at Baildon Hall during the struggles. A battle between the Roundheads and Cavaliers was also fought on the site of the current Colne Cemetery in July 1643. Colne, Trawden and Laneshawbridge were all located in Blackburn shire and fought on the side of the Parliamentarians (Roundheads) against the Royalists. Colne Cemetery is also the final resting place of Wallace Hartley. He was the Colne born band leader on the ill-fated Titanic luxury passenger liner which had an argument with an iceberg in 1912 on its maiden voyage.

Whether the knur and spell equipment at Baildon Manor had been there since 1618 (which is most likely) or when the house was built in 1553 or when the south wing was originally built in the 1200s is not known. If it was there from 1618, it could line up more or less exactly with the arrival of golf in England if we are to believe the stories of early golf at Blackheath. It also links in nicely with the golf played at Therfield Heath. If it had been there since the house was built, that goes back to when golf started in Scotland. And if it had been there since the south wing was built, that pre-dates golf either in England or Scotland and lines up with *kolf* in Holland! Whatever the case, this is a good indication that at the very least knur and spell developed in tandem with golf and may even have pre-dated golf in Scotland.

Certainly as far as golf played at Baildon is concerned, the knur and spell boys on Baildon Moor were probably close on three hundred years ahead of the golfers. Baildon GC, which currently plays on Baildon Moor, was established under another name in the early 1890s. Old Tom Morris himself was involved at some point in its design. Just for the record, Baildon Hall Club is less than one mile away from Baildon GC.

If the equipment found in Baildon Hall belonged to William Baildon himself it may also raise a question mark about just when knur and spell became known as 'poor man's golf' and who first coined the phrase. Obviously, the owner of a big manor house, the lord of the manor, could never be classed as being poor! We cannot completely rule out the possibility that the equipment had belonged to servants working in the manor house. However, if William Baildon had confiscated this sports gear from his staff, I would imagine that he would just have thrown it away rather than hide it behind a wall.

The 'poor man's golf' question also arose after reading the *History of Topography of the Townships of Little Timble, Great Timble and the Hamlet of Snowden in the West Riding of the County of York* by William Grainge. All these places are in the same general geographical area as Baildon and close to both Ilkley and Otley. In this book Grainge talks about knur and spell being an old Saxon game (i.e. pre-Viking) and relates a story about a knur and spell team match played at Fewston Bents in the 1770s between Jonathan Robinson / David Spence and two unnamed opponents. Fewston is a small village which is less than sixteen miles away from Baildon. Jonathan was part of a family of master builders and was also a landowning farmer and linen weaver. His family had owned Swinsty Hall in the Parish of Fewston since the late 1500s or early 1600s. He was baptized at Fewston in 1758. He married in 1779 and had five children. The Robinson family continued to hold sway at Swinsty Hall into the 1800s. A photograph of Swinsty Hall in William Grainge's book published in 1895 shows how grand this place was. Today Swinsty Hall is a heritage listed building and as far as I know is still owned by the current England football manager, Gareth Southgate. David Spence was a highly successful village tailor. Neither of them would be classed as poor. It seems that at least in the 1600s and 1700s in Yorkshire, knur and spell was played by well-heeled people as well as poor people. Well-heeled in this instance would not include royalty or the aristocracy. It would only refer to self-made men who had started off from relatively humble beginnings. If knur and spell had indeed been an old Saxon game, maybe golf started off as 'rich man's knur and spell?' Jonathan Robinson was said to be a very imposing man with great athletic abilities. He was over six-foot tall which for that era was quite tall. He was apparently also a star at playing knur and spell. In his match with Spence they were reported to require over fourteen score (two hundred and eighty yards) with his last rise to beat their opponents but did it with ease.

Another interesting revelation for me in the Grainge book is that in about 1640 the Robinson family had dealings with the Cunliffe family of Wycoller. This tiny hamlet in Lancashire, which is about thirty miles away from Fewston, is only about one mile from the village of Trawden where I was raised and is mentioned several times elsewhere in this book. The ruins of the Cunliffe manor house can still be seen there.

Around the time that Robinson and Spence were playing knur and spell in Fewston Bents, another group of chappies were also playing in the Dewsbury area of Yorkshire. This was revealed by a story which appeared in the *Leeds Times* dated 19 May 1838. During the Dewsbury Fair of that year, five old school mates met by pure accident at a butcher's stall in the marketplace. The five were described as farmers and retired gentlemen. They had apparently not seen each other since their schoolboy days. They reminisced about how many years had passed since they played football and knur and spell together. When they added up their ages, the five men had a combined age of four hundred years. Thus, they had an average age of eighty years which would have been close to double normal life expectancy for that era. They would have all been born around 1758-1760 and would have been playing together as schoolboys in the 1770 - 1780 period. Dewsbury is over thirty miles away from both Fewston and Sheffield confirming that knur and spell was already widespread in the 1700s.

I was unable to discover who first came up with the name of poor man's golf as a way of referring to knur and spell. I first saw reference to it in the late 1890s newspapers. Most of the articles which used it were in the 1900s and were in English newspapers and not Scottish ones. I suspect that the saying probably came from one of the early English golf journalists, but this is a pure guess. The *Tamworth Herald* 19 March 1910 was writing about 'The popularity of Plebeian Pastimes', of which knur and spell was listed as one. At the same time in the *Lowestoft Herald* knur and spell played by Barnsley miners was described to readers as a kind of Plebeian golf. In what may have been the first golf magazine, *GOLF A Weekly Record of 'ye Royal and Ancient' Game,* there was the occasional mention of knur and spell, but I never found any reference there to poor man's golf. The first issue of this classic magazine appeared on 19 September 1890. I have also seen reference to a *Knur and Spell Chronicle,* but no details could be found. In the 1830s there was a penny weekly newspaper published in London called *Poor Man's Guardian* (PMG). Possibly the idea of Poor Man's Golf (PMG) came from this, but I doubt it because I suspect this was too early.

Although written references to knur and spell playing in the 1600s and 1700s do exist, they don't appear to be very numerous. This may be because daily newspapers didn't arrive until the early 1700s and even then sporting coverage was not extensive. After 1800 coverage began to gain momentum, and this was happening well before *Bell's Life and Sporting Chronicle* started in 1822. From a study of the places where knur and spell was being played during the first quarter century of the 1800s, it was very evident that the game was already extremely widespread and well established in Lancashire, Yorkshire, Lincolnshire, Derbyshire, Cumbria, Westmorland, Northumberland, County Durham, Staffordshire, Cheshire and Nottinghamshire. What's more, this spread had occurred long before the railway network began to mushroom in the 1850s. Travelling around the country in the late 1700s and early 1800s was no picnic. Roads were poor and there was no railway. Journeying by horse or stagecoach was slow and very uncomfortable. Despite these difficulties players still moved about quite a bit. They were not just playing other men in their own village. According to the *Leeds Mercury* September 1824, a man from Keighley played a man from Adwalton on Baildon Moor for forty pounds. Both these towns are about eleven miles from the Moor. However, the lure of being able to win what amounted to several times the annual wage of a labourer just for one knur and spell match was obviously a big incentive. In 1842 a player from Heckmondwike in West Yorkshire played a man from Newcastle in Northumberland. These two towns are over one hundred miles apart. In *Bell's Life* 20 January 1856 it reported that a man from Leeds was to play a man from Walsall. Again two towns over one hundred miles apart. The same newspaper in 1859 mentioned that a Baildon man was to play at Old Trafford in Manchester...over fifty miles apart.

As the railway network expanded travel began to get easier. When the world championship at Abbey Hey, Manchester was played in 1878, the two combatants came from Grenoside in Sheffield and Chapeltown in Leeds. Both these places are over thirty miles from Manchester. However, both Leeds and Sheffield had direct rail links to Manchester by then. In fact on the day of the championship, the Manchester, Sheffield and Lincolnshire Railway Company were offering cheap afternoon excursion fares, stopping at Fairfield Station which was only one mile away from Abbey Hey Park.

Although the provenance of the Baildon Hall knur and spell equipment probably needs more work to be done, it is highly likely that this is the oldest example of knur and spell equipment still in existence anywhere in the world. It is certainly the oldest I know about having worked on this subject for several years. If it really was hidden behind the wall in the south wing of the manor house in 1618, as seems a good probability, it is very unlikely that it was new equipment just produced on that day for the purpose of establishing a 'time capsule'. It is more likely that it had already been used to play with and was hurriedly hidden there after King James's *Book of Sports* had been published banning the sport.

This equipment is still on display in a cabinet at Baildon Hall. In March 2021 I was very kindly provided with some photos (see overleaf) of the display by Baildon Hall club president Oswyn Parry and former club president Barbara Boyes. These photos confirm very conclusively that the knur stick was already a very well used stick at the time it was hidden behind the wall. The knur stick is riddled with woodworm from head to grip. The binding which is used to attach the spliced head to the shaft is daggy and falling off. The shaft itself is very bent and is very amateurishly fashioned from a tree branch and unlike 1850s and 1950s shafts which may mostly have been made from old billiard cues or old railway shunters poles

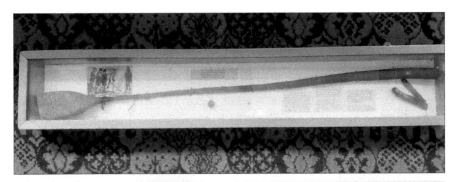

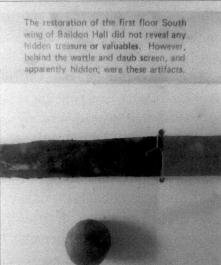

The restoration of the first floor South wing of Baildon Hall did not reveal any hidden treasure or valuables. However, behind the wattle and daub screen, and apparently hidden, were these artifacts.

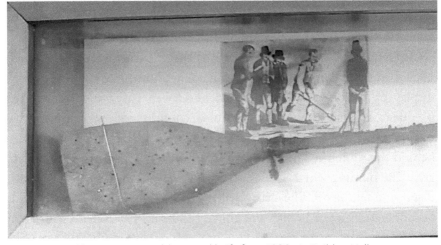

Very rare pummel, knur and knife from 1600s in Baildon Hall

and consequently are much straighter. The head shape is very similar to the 1850s and 1950s shapes although it was not possible to discern whether or not this early pummel had a dual wood construction with a hard wood face. However, my impression is that it is just a simple one-piece head which has not been compressed to increase its density. The photos also strongly indicate that the old knur is probably made from staghorn knur and not wood. The knur is very small and is slightly creamy in colour. It has regular sized drill marks, which probably indicate lead filling, as opposed to the irregular size borer holes.

In earlier correspondence Barbara Boyes of the club had given me a description of the equipment. She had to do this through the display cabinet glass front because she was unable to open the sealed cabinet. Her rough estimate of the knur size was only about fifteen millimetres diameter. This may not be an accurate measurement, but nevertheless it is very small and much smaller than the wooden knurs, whether they be holly, boxwood or lignum vitae. It is also smaller than the ceramic knurs which followed. I have never previously seen a stag knur or even a photograph of one. However, different reports I have seen in various articles have suggested that staghorn knurs were always smaller than wooden knurs. The fact that there was a knife found with the equipment suggests that the knur was carved. The old Baildon knur was also much smoother than the carved wooden knurs. The size, the colour and the smoother surface strongly suggest to me that the old Baildon knur is made from staghorn. But until we have a chance to examine it under a microscope, and maybe also do a couple of analytical tests and possibly an X-ray, this will remain just a guess. I have always imagined that staghorn knurs were probably used before wooden ones, but I have never seen any proof of this. The Baildon knur may support this idea since this it is probably at least a 1600s knur and maybe even earlier. The only drawback to this idea is that Baildon is close to fifty miles from Sheffield which was quite a long way in the 1600s and 1700s. Availability of imported staghorn as a raw material for making knurs may have been restricted mostly to the cutlery making industry in Sheffield and surrounding areas.

The old knife which was found with the ball and stick is also very interesting. From the position it is shown in the photo It appears to be something like a folding single blade pocket knife, but the tip is not pointed.

It is very round. The blade edge of the knife is quite damaged through extensive use. It was clearly an old knife at the time it was hidden. Pocket knives in the Sheffield area first started to appear in the 1600s. I wonder if this knife could be a very early Barlow knife? The history on these kind of knives is nebulous. The year 1670 , and the name Obadiah Barlow, is sometimes mentioned as the first appearance date, but this may not be accurate. In reality it may be earlier than this. The Company of Cutlers in Hallamshire had been formed in 1624 and Sheffield already boasted the biggest knife making industry outside of London at that time. Knife making in Sheffield existed at least from 1297 and by 1379 about twenty-five per cent of the town's population were metal workers. This old knife which is on display at Baildon Hall club does have some lettering on the blade, but it is difficult to decipher through the glass case. Registered Cutler's marks were first set up by Cutler's Juries in the 1500s, so close examination may enable a more accurate dating. I am definitely not a knife expert, but this knife looks to me to be very old. The blade surface is totally blackened. On further inspection, through the cabinet glass, part of the blade may also be broken away from the handle. This makes me wonder whether it really was a folding type of knife where the blade fits inside the handle or if it is a fixed blade knife. The butt or pummel of the knife reminds me of a miniature *cervelliere* which was a sort of iron skull cap worn by the Crusaders to give them some head protection. It appears to be a very cheap and basic knife. The handle seems to be crudely fashioned and is a much deeper yellow colour than the knur. I suspect that the handle would be made from animal bone rather than staghorn, but I am only guessing. If the knife and the other equipment really were hidden there in 1618, as suggested by the date mark scratched on the wattle and daub, they could all be very early 1600s or even late 1500s. It would be very interesting to have this knife more closely examined by an old knife specialist.

One thing about this equipment is very clear. With such a basic and relatively short pummel construction and with such a tiny knur, the distance hit with this gear would have been much shorter than the distances recorded in the 1700s, 1800s and 1900s. It could well have been the kind of paraphernalia which the plebs used to play games in and around church yards, similar to many early golf reports in Scotland. i.e. no hole or flag involved and just a church door or a gravestone as a crude target.

But how does this Baildon Hall knur and spell equipment stack up age-wise against the oldest known golf sticks still in existence? i.e. the ones known as the Old Troon golf clubs? The last I heard of this old collection it was still being held at the British Golf Museum in St Andrews.

Chapter 13

The Old Troon clubs

The Old Troon clubs had been found in a sealed cupboard of a house in Hull in Yorkshire in the 1890s. The find included eight old clubs and an old newspaper dated 1741. The house had previously been owned and lived in for a long time by the Maister family, a very rich merchant family. It had been destroyed by fire at one stage and re-built. So this may rule out the Maister family having had these clubs for a long time prior to 1741. But not necessarily so because the family also had several other properties across the Hull and Holderness region and the clubs may have been held at any one of these properties prior to the fire. During much of the 1600s and 1700s the city of Hull was essentially controlled by a relatively small number of shipping merchant magnates, including the Maisters, in an oligarchic manner. The Maisters were not part of the aristocracy *per se*, but nevertheless they considered themselves to be classed as gentry. i.e. the class level just below the nobility.

Since the emergence of these old golf clubs in the 1890s much work has been done by many people to discover the original source of these clubs. Who made them? Where were they made? Who were they made for? How did they come to be in Hull? All the clubs had the same markings which included a royal crest, a thistle, and some initials. One theory has attempted to link the clubs to King James I of England and maybe to his third son Charles I. If this proves to be the case it would put both the Old Troon clubs and the Baildon Hall knur and spell equipment into exactly the same time frame. Another theory has suggested that the clubs are at least one hundred years after James I and that the markings on the clubs are more an example of Jacobite symbolism. The Jacobite movement was mostly in the first half of the 1700s. If the latter was verified then the Baildon knur and spell equipment could be significantly older than the Old Troon clubs. What we do know from several independent reports, is that the Old Troon clubs are in very good nick. They haven't been played with much. What we also know is that no one has yet come up with an answer which satisfies all the pundits. So I may as well throw my twopenneth into the ring!

The Jacobite movement was active from about 1688 to the 1750s. Effectively it ended in 1746 when Charles Edward Stuart (aka Bonnie Prince Charlie) was beaten at the Battle of Culloden near Inverness in Scotland. The Jacobites were Scottish Highlanders, but they also had some English, Irish and French supporters. Their aim was to overthrow the Hanoverian monarchy and return the Stuarts back into power. They were very active in and around the birthplace of golf. Before the Battle of Culloden the Jacobites had taken both Edinburgh and Perth with little sign of resistance in September 1745. Then in January 1746 they also won a battle at Prestonpans near Musselburgh. This all happened only a very short time after the first golf club, the Honourable company of Edinburgh Golfers, had been formed at Leith Links in 1744.

That same year, 1744, the first ever rules of golf had been drawn up by an Edinburgh surgeon called John Rattray. This gentleman would have been a freemason because the whole club were freemasons in those days. Rattray was also a staunch Jacobite supporter and in 1746 he was the field surgeon at the battle of Culloden where he had to take care of the bonnie prince himself. Unfortunately for him, the Jacobites were thrashed, and Rattray was quickly arrested and was in grave danger of being beheaded on a charge of treason. However, through his golf club connections he had many friends in high places and they were able to extricate him from the mire and save his neck. Rattray was a fair golfer and went on to win three silver arrow golf prizes with the Honourable Company.

I don't know if the Maister family in Hull were Jacobite supporters or freemasons or both. I suspect that at least they were not Jacobite supporters because the town of Hull as a whole were strong supporters of William and Mary after the Revolution. But any supporters had to be very careful. They couldn't openly have meetings with other Jacobites, or risk being accused of treason. Just owning some golf clubs with Jacobite symbols on them would have been quite dangerous even if you were not a Jacobite yourself or a Jacobite supporter and enough to arouse suspicion. Because of this, a whole series of code words, symbols and rituals were developed to avoid being caught. The symbols on the Old Troon clubs may well be an example of this symbolism. And which part of the community would be best equipped to carry on this kind of behaviour? Maybe the freemasons who were already well practised in the art of subterfuge. The fact that the Old Troon clubs in Hull were found locked away in a cupboard, out of sight, and not displayed on someone's wall, was probably because they were frightened of being accused of being a Jacobite supporter. During the uprising Edinburgh, Perth and Prestonpans, in the very heart of golf's birthplace, were all taken by the Jacobites without much of a fight. This strongly suggests to me that John Rattray was not the only Jacobite in the Leith golfing fraternity. I suspect that Scottish golfers generally would have had to keep a low profile during the Jacobite movement days.

I have also seen quite a lot of commentary about the Old Troon clubs as to whether or not they were a 'set'. Well, back in the hickory shafted days I wonder whether too many people worried about matching sets. I well remember Australian professional golfer Jack Harris telling me about his time as a junior professional in the 1930s at Yarra Yarra GC in the prestigious Melbourne sand belt. One of Jack's routine jobs was to clean and store member's clubs. One of their members was called Willie Hope. He had emigrated from the UK and won the Australian Amateur Championship at Royal Melbourne GC in 1933. Even in the late 1930's Willie still played with hickory clubs. One thing which always stuck in Jack's mind was that virtually every club in Willie's bag was from a different club-maker. Jack told me that this was often the case with hickory clubs. He rarely, if ever, saw matching sets of hickory golf clubs. That doesn't mean that matching sets didn't exist. But it perhaps means that they were not very common.

Naturally, most of the provenance work to date has focussed on trying to decipher the aforementioned golf club markings. And several very plausible ideas have been put forward to support the theories. Maybe additional information could be discovered by working back from the discovery point? Why were the old golf clubs in Hull around 1741 in the first place when obviously no golf was played in Hull or Yorkshire at that time, or even in England, apart from Blackheath or maybe Royston. Both of which were many hard days ride away from Hull.

We know that the owner of the house in Hull in the 1890s had no interest in golf himself. But did the Maister family have a golf interest in the 1600s and 1700s? The Maister family had arrived into the Hull area in the second half of the 1500s and are believed to have come from Kent. They created a trading dynasty which lasted well over two hundred years and well past the time of the Jacobite Uprising in 1745. It is highly unlikely that the Maisters themselves would have commissioned the Old Troon clubs to be made. Blackheath was the only place they could have played and that was miles away. However, we can't totally dismiss the possibility that the Maisters had these clubs made. There was a thriving coastal shipping trade in those days out of the port of Hull. They would regularly ship south to London and also ship north to the port of Leith in Scotland. It is not such a ridiculous idea that the Maisters could have been in Leith and seen lots of people playing there on the links and decided that they would like to have a go at this. Let's not forget that in those days 'playing at golf' did not always involve playing with a hole and a flag. There are plenty of examples where people just went into any old paddock or any bit of rough heathland, maybe aiming at trees or gateposts as targets or just seeing who could hit furthest. The Maisters had country estates in Holderness outside of Hull and they would have had plenty of spare land just to bash balls up and down. However, the symbols on the clubs would need some vivid imagination to support this idea.

If the Old Troon clubs did indeed come from a royal connection, then we need to try to pinpoint which was the most likely source. i.e. What were the most likely places where the Maisters and royalty could interact? Or alternatively which highfliers did the Maisters interact with who may have been an indirect link with royalty? The best succinct summary of the Maister family history is the *Hull Webs History of Hull*. There is also much information about the Maisters in *The History of Parliament, British Political, Social and Local History*.

The first Maister who may have had the chance to associate with royalty was probably William Maister who was born in 1597. He was a young man who was likely to have been active in the business maybe from about 1620 onwards. So he would be operating just about from the time when King

James **I** of England was giving up the ghost. He died in 1664 so he would also have been around when King Charles **I** was frequenting the links, but only in his last three or four years. However, William was very much in the business building phase during those years. He was based in Hull and not London, and his company had still not achieved the grand status they eventually reached. I would be very surprised if the Troon clubs had come from any contact this William had with either King James **I** or with his son King Charles **I**. Particularly when we consider that the Siege of Hull took place in 1642 which would not have endeared King Charles **I** to the businessmen of that city. England was on the brink of a Civil War and Hull, governed by Sir Thomas Hotham, was anti-royalist and supported the Parliamentarians in the struggle. But of course it can't be completely ruled out because Charles **I** had made an earlier visit to Hull in 1639 and been well received on that occasion. By May 1646 he had already surrendered and by January 1649 he had been beheaded. Charles **I** may have played some golf at Therfield Heath, but according to most reports he didn't spend anywhere near as much time in Royston as James **I** had.

William (1597) had a son called Henry (1632-1699). Henry would have probably been too young to have had a chance to interact with Charles **I** but he didn't die until 1699 so he would have overlapped with both Charles **II** and James **II**. However, he too was busy building the business and didn't have the parliamentary connections that subsequent Maisters had. It is unlikely that he was the Maister who acquired the Old Troon clubs.

The next Maister who had the chance to brown nose was also called William Maister who was born in 1662 and died in 1716. He was the son of Henry (1632). With the arrival of this gentleman on the scene, the chances of acquiring 'royal golf clubs' by the Maister family increased very dramatically. During his time in charge the Maister family had already developed into a very powerful and eminent organisation. William was very good friends with John Holles, the Duke of Newcastle, who was governor of Hull, and had many other friends in high places. William became Whig MP for Hull in 1700 and kept this job over eight parliaments. During this period he would obviously have spent much time in London and have had ample opportunity to fraternise with both the aristocracy and royalty. This William Maister had married the widow of George Dickinson in 1697. George was the customs collector for both Hull and Plymouth ports and had extensive properties in both Hull and Holderness. Through this marriage William Maister acquired two properties in High Street from the Dickinson family and also a Winestead property. No doubt one of these High Street properties was the one which burned down in 1743. It had obviously been built prior to 1697. If William Maister and Sir John Werden had a direct relationship prior to 1697, this union would probably have strengthened it. If they didn't have direct contact before 1697, then this event may have facilitated the establishment of such a link. The two members of the royalty who were around between 1662 and 1716 who were known to have played at least some golf were King Charles II and King James II (previously the Duke of York). Maister House in High Street, Hull is still standing in 2020. Since 1966 it has been listed as a National Trust building and at the time it was the only property in Hull on the list... maybe it still is?

Charles II was born in 1630. After his dad was arrested in May 1646 he went into exile in France with his mother. He was only sixteen years old at this time and probably had not had a chance to play much golf by then... if indeed any at all. After Oliver Cromwell died Charles II was restored to the English throne in 1660 at the age of thirty. By 1661 he had already re-instated a Royal Warrant grant to a goffe-club maker which had earlier been cancelled by Cromwell. If he didn't already have any clubs he may have got some new ones at that time. Maybe we can find out from the Royal Warrant Association to which golf club maker the grant was issued. This could maybe give some very valuable clues. I suspect that the warrant would have been granted to a Scottish bower / golf club maker because there wouldn't have been any golf artisans in England in 1660. Maybe the Mayne family were still the favoured royal golf club makers at that time? Probably Charles II didn't play too much golf, if any, in Scotland. Although he had been crowned King of Scotland in 1651 at Scone which is only two or three miles north of Perth, it was well documented that he didn't like Scotland and hardly ever went there. Nor could I find any record of Charles **II** playing golf at Therfield Heath although he did go there occasionally. His true passion was horse racing, and he frequently went to Newmarket which is twenty-four miles from Royston and where there was also a royal palace. It is not clear whether the golf setup at Therfield was still operating in Charles **II**'s time. After the execution of his father in 1649 the Royston royal setup appeared to quickly fall into a state of poor repair and chunks of the complex were taken over by lots of different people. (See *Royston: British History Online* for a very good account of Royston's early history and also for a good account of how the royal buildings were broken up into different parcels.) Other than that he seemed to spend most of his time in London except when he evacuated to Salisbury in Wiltshire in July 1665 to get away from the Great Plague which was devastating the city. He returned in February 1666 when he helped to fight the Great Fire of London in September that year. Actually when we look at Charles **II**'s personal life, with all his great number of mistresses and illegitimate children, it is difficult to see when he would have had time to play any golf at all! No wonder his nickname was 'The Merry Monarch'. So where did he play his golf? Blackheath or Greenwich Park? Charles **II** died in 1685 at age fifty-four. William Maister would have been about twenty-three in that year. Could he have somehow got hold of Charles **II**'s golf clubs when he died? Probably not, but possible.

King James **II** (1633 – 1701) was also known to be a very keen golfer and trap-ball player when he was the Duke of York. However in 1648 at age fourteen he also fled England during the Civil War and was exiled in France until the restoration to the throne of his brother in 1660. Before becoming king for a short time (1685 – 1688) we know that he played some golf at Leith Links in Scotland when he was the Duke of York in the 1679-1682 period. He had probably only started to play golf after 1660. Therfield Heath had probably ceased operation then, so apart from when he visited Scotland I don't know where he would have played in England unless it was at Greenwich. I suspect that he may not have played much golf between 1660 and 1675. After the Restoration he had been made the Lord High Admiral in command of the Royal Navy. In 1664 he had taken New Amsterdam in the USA from the Dutch and it was later re-named

New York in his honour. He was involved in the Second Anglo-Dutch War (1665-1667), the Third Anglo-Dutch War (1672-1674), the Great Fire of London (1666) and also went through the Great Plague (1665). He was deposed from the throne in 1688. Could twenty-six years old William Maister have snaffled James's clubs before he was forced back into exile. Again, probably unlikely, but quite possibly he got them some years after the Revolution. James **II** turned out to be the last Catholic monarch of England.

The last William Maister had a son called Henry who was born in 1699 and died in December 1744. Henry was also MP for Hull between 1735 and 1741. So he would also have had the Westminster connections which his father had, but probably for a shorter period. Henry was the Maister who was actually living in the house in Hull where the Troon clubs were found at the time of the old newspaper which was found in the cupboard with the clubs (1741). According to his biography Henry lost his wife and two children in a fire when the house burned down in 1743. If this was true, how come the clubs (and the newspaper) were not destroyed in the fire? They may have been placed in the cupboard after the fire when the house had been re-built. In which case the 1741 newspaper, which would have been two or three years old at the time of the re-build, could have just been an old newspaper they lined the cupboard with. However, I suspect that not many people keep newspapers for two years. Reports did say that the original house was 'dramatically damaged by fire'. Maybe the sealed cupboard was still intact. The house was re-built in 1744. Henry died in 1744 before the re-build had been completed. The construction was completed by his brother Nathaniel and another brother. Maybe they did not have to completely bulldoze the site and some of the original structure was still standing. Afterall, this building was very substantial. It was not a wood and paper mâché structure like many of today's modern edifices. Of course we can't rule out that these clubs may have been stored at one of the many other Maister properties in the wider Hull area prior to the fire. What I haven't been able to discover is exactly when the original house, before the fire, had been built, but it was probably before 1697. So the only thing we can be absolutely sure about in all this story is that the 1741 newspaper could NOT have been put in the cupboard prior to 1741. It could only have been put there in 1741 or any time after that. We can't even be sure that the newspaper and the old clubs were put in the cupboard at the same time. And we don't know if the newspaper was just incidental shelf lining or was it an entire folded up newspaper which had purposely been put there as a date marking. There is even an outside possibility that the clubs were put in the cupboard during the time when George Dickinson owned the house, prior to 1697, and that the newspaper found its way in there at a later date and was something of a red herring. However, if the clubs, and 1741 newspaper, had already been in the cupboard before the fire, and had somehow survived the fire, it seems strange that they would completely re-build the house and leave the cupboard and its contents as they were before the fire. There are still many unanswered questions arising from this avenue of investigation.

During Henry's time there were two royals on the scene who played golf as far as I know. And they were not really on the scene. Firstly there was James **II**'s son, James Francis Edward Stuart (1688-1766), also known as the Old Pretender. He was brought up in St Germain-en-Laye in Paris and later found refuge in Rome supported by Pope Clement **XI** and later by Pope Innocent **XIII**. James Francis had hopes of regaining the throne after Queen Anne died in 1714, but his last serious attempt fizzled out in 1715. Then there was his son, Bonnie Prince Charlie (aka Charles Edward Stuart or the Young Pretender), the grandson of James **II**. Charlie had been born in exile in Rome in 1720 and apart from when he attempted the Jacobite Uprising in 1745 he spent all his life in Rome. (is *up*rising another example of tautology? I imagine that if you are rising there is no other way you can go but up?) He died there in exile in 1788. His father James Francis had also died there in 1766. There are several reliable eyewitness accounts of Charlie playing golf in Rome at the Villa Borghese between 1738 - 1740. However, the Maisters probably had the Troon clubs several years before the 1745 uprising. So it is very unlikely that the Troon clubs had belonged to Bonnie Prince Charlie or to his father James Francis. But again it cannot be completely ruled out.

I should point out the *Scottish Golf History* website seem to be in favour of the Old Troon clubs belonging to Bonnie Prince Charlie. They base this view on the fact that some eminent golf club design expert has declared that the shape of the wooden clubs in the Troon collection closely resembles some prize silver clubs known to have been made in 1740s. At the same time they think that the iron clubs in the Troon collection are most likely from the 1600s. It all sounds very airy-fairy to me. The Bonnie Prince only came to Britain once in his lifetime. He landed at the small island of Eriskay in the Outer Hebrides on July 23 1745...no golf courses there in 1745. He was thrashed less than nine months later at the Battle of Culloden near Inverness on 16 April 1746. During the intervening time he had fought several battles apart from Culloden and also marched his forces from Eriskay to Derby in England and then back to Culloden. A round trip of over one thousand miles! If they were lucky, armies moved at about ten miles per day. So I imagine that more than half of his time in Britain would have been spent marching, retreating, recovering and actually fighting battles. After the 16 April 1745 he spent about five months in the Western Highlands evading capture before finally escaping to France. I suspect that the chance of him having some golf clubs with him on this trip, let alone actually playing with them, would have been very slim! Apart from this there didn't seem to be any remotely feasible explanation in this theory as to how the Troon clubs ended up with the Maisters in Hull. I suppose that on his way back to France, Charlie must have detoured up the Humber for a nice pint of beer at Ye Olde Black Boy or Ye Olde White Harte.

When Henry Maister (1699 – 1744) died he left three sons...Henry (born 1730), William (born 1731) and Arthur (born 1737). All these were underage when the house fire happened in 1743 and probably would have were not involved in what happened with the Old Troon clubs. Apart from which none of them subsequently had a serious interest in either in running the business properly or in public service. Consequently, by the time Henry (1730) died in 1812 the Maister company was in serious decline. This probably means that the two Maisters most likely to have 'collected' the Old Troon clubs are William (born 1662) or Henry (born 1699). William would appear to have had many more opportunities than Henry to fraternise with any of the likely 'disposers' of the old clubs. But proof? There ain't none! So far!

I wonder if any of the young Maisters ever did the Grand Tour of Europe which was traditional between 1660 and 1840 for young gentlemen from well to do families. This Tour was seen as part of their worldly education and always included Rome on the itinerary. In fact one of the eyewitnesses of Charlie playing golf in Rome, nineteen-years old Lord Elcho (David Wemyss), was on a Grand Tour in 1740 when he met the Bonnie Prince in Italy. Wemyss was both a well-known Jacobite supporter and a freemason. After the Jacobites had been routed, he spent the rest of his life exiled in France and Switzerland. Maybe Lord Elcho played golf in Italy with the Bonnie Prince / James Frances Stuart and brought some clubs back to Scotland when he returned. Maybe they were even Elcho's own clubs which he had decorated with Jacobite symbols? I don't know if Lord Elcho played golf but certainly golf had been played on the links at Wemyss on the Fife coast a long time before the golf club there was founded in 1857. There is a strong possibility that he was a golfer, but very unlikely that he had owned the Old Troon clubs.

I find it highly unlikely that the Bonnie Prince himself would have brought some golf clubs with him from Italy when he arrived in the Outer Hebrides in July 1745 to start his campaign to win back the English throne. After the failed uprising, the Bonnie Prince went back into exile and lived for another forty-two years. No doubt he would have been fit enough to play plenty more golf. So to my mind it is very unlikely that the Old Troon clubs were his. This theory also doesn't explain why there appeared to be effectively three 'sets' of three (assuming one lost or broken iron club).

The fact that Bonnie Prince Charlie played golf at all is fascinating. He had been born in Italy and spent all his life there. He definitely hadn't been brought up in Scotland playing golf. He only went to Scotland briefly during the failed attempt at the Uprising in 1745. So we can only assume that he learnt to play golf in Italy from his dad...who had forty-six years to teach him. However, his dad, James Francis Stuart, also lived in exile all his life and also spent no time in Scotland. So he himself only had thirteen years to learn to play golf before his dad, James **II**, died. James Francis must have learned to play golf in St Germain. And that may mean that King James **II**'s clubs had not been disposed of by Werden, Graham or Ashton after the Revolution. Or he had asked one of his Scottish contacts to send him or bring him some more clubs to Paris after he settled there. This would not have been a big problem. James **II** had regular Scottish visitors in St Germain while he lived there. And the same applied to James Francis and Bonnie Prince Charlie when they were living in Italy. The plot thickens!

One of the 'Scottish' visitors to Rome from 1773 – 1777, although I don't know if he met with the Stuarts or not, was Robert Home the portrait and landscape painter. He was there to study art under a Swiss neo-classical artist called Angelica Kauffman. Robert Home was born in Hull around 1752. His father was Robert Boyne Home who was an army surgeon who had moved about quite a bit. Robert Boyne Home was born in Scotland (1713) and died in Hull (1786). He had lived in York at one time and was earlier associated with Greenlaw Castle in Berwickshire in the Scottish Borders, the area where many of the Home family came from, and also with Canongate in Edinburgh where the Patterson / Duke of York house mentioned in the first international match story was located. Perhaps when he was in Hull he may have had opportunities to come across the Maisters who were very prominent citizens of that city. Eventually Robert Home the painter ended up as a successful artist in India and he died there in 1834. The time when Robert Home was studying in Italy would have coincided with the time that Bonnie Prince Charlie may have been getting rid of his golf clubs. James Frances Edward Stuart, his father, had died in 1766. By 1773 – 1777 the Bonnie Prince himself would have been fifty-three to fifty-eight and may have stopped playing golf. Could Home have acquired the Stuart clubs during this fairly lengthy sojourn in Rome? He didn't go to live in India until 1791 so he could have passed on the clubs to the Maisters sometime during the intervening fourteen years. But of course that would mean that the clubs could not have been put in the High Street cupboard in the 1740s and would make the 1741 newspaper a red herring. Robert Home the artist had four brothers and four sisters and most of them appear to have been born in the York / Hull area between 1748 and 1756. Eight years would give the Robert Boyne Home family plenty of opportunity to come across the Maisters in the higher level of Hull society. The Maisters were well into commissioning family portraits to hang up in their swanky residences, so there could even be a chance that young Robert painted some of them. Another one from left field, but may be worth a quick look? If anything had transpired between the Maisters and the Homes during that period the incumbent at Maister House would have been Colonel Henry Maister who was there from about 1760 to early 1800s.

Robert Home the artist was not the same Reverend Robert Home who was implicated in the Alexander Carlyle / John Home golf club from 1757 which eventually found its way to Blackheath GC. This Robert Home was minister at Polwarth in Scotland. His sister Joan married John Home the Molesey Hurst golfer .i.e. John Home and the Reverend Robert Home were brothers-in-law (see this story in later chapter). All these Homes came from within a very small area in the Border Region of Scotland so I guess that they would have all been related in some way or other. Many of the Homes had quite big families and there seems to have been significant inter-marrying going on. Of course it's all perfectly legal in the UK, where even first cousins are allowed to shack up. Robert Home the painter had a son who was also called Robert.

At this stage, it seems to me that the two firm favourites to have been the original owners of the Troon clubs are Charles **II** or James **II**. That is IF the clubs had indeed belonged to royalty and not just to some avid Jacobite supporter who had a lot of Jacobite symbols stamped on them. But the timing of the actual acquisition could still be problematical. It was 1700 before William Maister became active in Parliament. Charles **II** had already been dead about sixteen years at that point and James **II** had been in exile about thirteen years. From a pure timing point of view, the Bonnie Prince theory would fit best, but for reasons explained this seems unlikely.

At this point it may be worth looking at the royalty who came after James **II**. We had William and Mary, Anne, and a succession of four Georges. Queen Anne who died in 1714 was the last Stewart monarch. As far as I know none of the succeeding royals during the Hanoverian period of the 1700s or even very early 1800s had any interest in golf whatsoever. Could it be that one of these was doing a spring clean and decided to throw out a few old clubs?

Possible, but again unlikely.

If I was a betting man, which I am not, my best guess would be that the Old Troon clubs had belonged to James **II**, formerly the Duke of York who is said to have played in the first ever international golf match. I suspect that when he was deposed in the Glorious Revolution of 1688 he would have had no time to hang about looking for his golf clubs. Saving his backside would have been higher on his list of priorities. He lived the rest of his life in Saint-Germain-en-Laye, a Paris suburb which is less that ten miles away from Neuilly-Sur-Seine where I used to visit regularly in the early 1970s on carbon black business at an office on Avenue Charles-de-Gaulle. It is only eight miles from St Cloud GC, but that was not yet in existence. Even if his original golf clubs had been disposed of following the Revolution that would not mean that he couldn't play golf again while he was in St Germain. He would have had plenty of old Scottish supporters coming to see him there who could quite easily have brought him some new clubs.

If the Old Troon clubs had belonged to James **II**, maybe even back in the time when he was Duke of York, what explanation can we dream up as to how the clubs ended up with the Maisters? And how can we account for the effectively three 'sets' of three? (I am not sold on the idea that the duplicate clubs were just spares in case of breakage.) Well, this is where we have to bring Sir Jonto himself into the equation. Back in February 1679, when the Duke of York was forty-six years old, he played golf at Leith links. On that occasion his private secretary, John Werden (1640-1716), was with him, and forked out a significant amount of cash for both golf clubs and lots of golf balls. This was recorded in detail in Werden's pocketbook which is currently held in the *National Library of Scotland*. Unfortunately, I don't think the pocketbook mentioned how many golf clubs had been bought or any details of the clubs themselves. The Duke of York went back to Scotland several times after that before he was crowned King James in 1685 and probably John Werden accompanied him each time. In fact Werden was secretary to the Duke of York from 1673 – 1685. This may be significant. Golf clubs all with the same symbols on would not have been available to buy off the rack. They would have been made to order. The Duke made many visits. He could have ordered the clubs on one visit and collected them on a subsequent visit or maybe had them delivered to him. On one subsequent occasion the Duke played with a local golfing artisan called Patterson against two English noblemen in a match which has since been acclaimed as the first ever international golf match. I have seen both 1681 and 1682 mentioned as dates for when this match took place. I suspect that Patterson would have had his own equipment. It is not clear whether the Duke brought his own equipment with him or whether he and the two noblemen needed to buy more equipment. It is hard to imagine that the noblemen would have had their own gear because there were no golf courses in England at that time where they could play. Only Blackheath GC MAY have existed in England at that time (or at least as a golfing society playing on the heath) and they only had ex-pat Scottish members. Could it be that the Duke bought himself and the two noblemen some clubs? (three spoons, three play clubs, plus three irons) This is maybe not such a daft idea because the cost of the clubs and balls was chicken feed compared to the size of the wager which had been made when we recall that Patterson built himself a very nice substantial house with his share of the winnings. The cost of the clubs and balls would have been mere 'incidentals' and would not have even scratched the surface of the size of the overall wager. They would also have spent several times the cost of the clubs and balls on dinner after the match. Maybe, in his capacity as private secretary, after the game Werden also had to attend to the luggage travel, storage and safe keeping of the equipment when they returned to London? Whatever the case, Sir John certainly knew all about the existence of these particular golf clubs. After the Duke of York had become king James **II**, Werden was also Surveyor-General to Queen Mary of Modena (James's wife) in the two years prior to the Revolution (1687 / 1688).

Maybe the Maisters didn't have any direct contact with the Duke or afterwards when he was King James, but they probably did have plenty of opportunity to spend time with Sir John Werden. The Maisters spent much time in Sweden where they sourced vast quantities of iron ore and timber which they imported through the port of Hull. In fact the Maisters had someone from the family permanently based in Sweden. Werden spent significant time in Sweden as a special envoy (1670-1672). During that time he would have had ample opportunity to mingle with major English companies trading with Sweden such as the Maisters. The Maisters also spent a lot of time in both London and Amsterdam dealing with banks and financial institutions to arrange Bills of Exchange and shipping insurance for all their extensive trading activities which were not restricted to Sweden. Werden had two separate stints working in Amsterdam and maybe would have also had a good chance to meet the Maisters there. But more importantly, Werden spent significant time in the House of Commons as MP for Reigate. He spent even longer, and perhaps more significantly, as commissioner for customs (1685-1694) and (1703-1715). As a major importer the Maisters would have more or less lived in the customs department, greasing the palms of officials to facilitate a smooth passage of their goods through all the port bureaucracy! To say nothing about lobbying the MP in Parliament for lower import duties! Their opportunities to come into direct contact with John Werden were almost limitless over a long period. By the time James had become king in 1685 he was already into his fifties and maybe wasn't fit enough to play much more golf. It would not surprise me if the majority of his golf was played between 1675 and 1685, but certainly after 1670 because of all his war activities in the 1660s. From 1700 William Maister was MP for Hull and spent a lot of time in London. James had gone into exile in 1689 and probably never had time to worry about golf clubs. It seems to me that between 1690 and 1716, when both William Maister and Sir John Werden died, there could be a good chance that the clubs swapped hands in that period. William Maister had a big reputation for continuing to conduct Maister business while he was attending Parliament. Although most of us will think it is impossible, conflict of interest in Parliament was even more rife in those days than it is today! The Jacobite connection is certainly there with Sir John Werden. In 1683 it was recorded that he had employed John Ashton, a future Jacobite plotter. Throughout his career there had been several occasions when Werden was accused of corruption by his political opponents. His customs commissioner post would have certainly tested his integrity in those days! However, we need to also be aware that as far as King James himself was concerned, the position of commissioner of customs was something he would keep a very careful eye on because he had a vested interest. Without any approval from Parliament, James had levied all kinds of customs duties on imported goods, and this was a major source of his personal income. If the 1679-1682 clubs had indeed been in Werden's safe keeping, he may well have been comfortable disposing of them after James had fled to France.

As it happens, John Ashton turns out to be maybe almost as big a prime suspect to be the 'club disposer' as Werden himself. Maybe even more so. While James was on the throne from 1685 – 1688, Ashton was clerk of the closet to King James's wife, Mary of Modena. After the Revolution in 1688 he worked tirelessly on behalf of the exiled couple trying to sort out their affairs after they had escaped to France. This devotion eventually cost him his life when he was hanged for treason at Tyburn in January 1691. Perhaps in the two-to-three-year window after the Revolution, Ashton may have disposed of the clubs or may have been instrumental in helping Werden to acquire the clubs. They may have even been partners in crime. Maybe there is correspondence between the Maisters, Werden and Ashton held in the Maister letter collection at Leeds University?

The relationship between the Werden family and James **II** actually went back long before Sir Jonto got involved. i.e. when James was just a humble Duke of York. After the Restoration, John Werden's father, Robert (1622-1690), had brown nosed himself into all kinds of wonderful situations. As early as 1642, Robert's own father, John, had used his influence to get Robert the position of colonel in the army under Sir John Byron. Robert then quickly demonstrated that he was a chip off the old block and by 1662 he was Groom of the Duke of York's Bedchamber (here we go again!). In 1665 he was a lieutenant in the Duke of York's guards. By 1667 he was a major and by 1672 a lieutenant colonel. He was MP for Chester between 1673-1679 and again from 1684-1685. In 1678 he was 'brigadier of the horse' and in 1679 he was comptroller of the Duke of York's household. In 1685 he was made 'brigadier of all our forces' and later the same year was appointed major general. Rumour has it that when he was a boy his dad had bought him a set of toy wooden soldiers, so he was well qualified to lead England's defence forces! And naturally he would go on to ensure that his son John would also land himself into a sinecure position where he could continue the family's royal bum sniffing tradition more or less unabated. John Werden was already fifty years old by the time his father Robert died. So Robert lived long enough to continue helping his son's cause well into old age. Robert had obviously read the James **I** / George Villiers rule book from back to front several times. He had learned the lessons very well and had passed on all the lurks to his son! Despite all these favours from James, Robert Werden displayed no loyalty. When the Revolution came in 1688 he abandoned ship and was again rewarded by Queen Mary **II** who gave him the treasury post in her government. But this only lasted a short time as Robert Werden died in 1690. Tragically Mary herself died of smallpox in 1694 at age thirty-two, but not before the relationship between the parliament and the monarchy had been forever changed when the *Bill of Rights* was passed in 1689. John Werden lived another twenty-six years after his dad died during which time he would have had plenty of time to fix up a nice deal with William Maister for some pre-loved golf clubs. Probably between 1700 and 1716, but possibly before then.

Now here is a mad idea which has just flitted through my mind. Let us meander back to the well documented first international golf match in 1681 or 1682 between the Duke of York, Patterson and two English noblemen. Unless I have missed it, no one has yet identified the two mystery English noblemen. Since this is obviously an important missing piece of the jigsaw, it needs to be addressed. What if those two esteemed gentlemen had been John Werden and John Ashton? We already know that John Werden was probably in Leith at the time of the famous golf match. We also know by the self-declaration paper by John Ashton at his treason trial in 1691 that he had been receiving favours from James for the past sixteen years i.e. since at least 1675, and that Ashton had been appointed by Werden. There was already a cosy relationship established between the three of them. Maybe not a *ménage à trois* as such, but more of a platonic friendship between three golfing, gambling and claret swilling buddies. Now wouldn't that be interesting?

Another candidate to have been one of the mystery noblemen playing in the Leith game was Richard Graham, 1st Viscount Preston (1648-1695). He had been a strong supporter of James when he was Duke of York. He had been made a peer of Scotland in early 1681 and was in the Scottish Parliament early August 1681. He was also with the Duke of York in both Edinburgh (July 1681) and Leith (late August 1681). He was also with John Ashton, after the Revolution, when they were both arrested trying to charter a boat to take them to France to deliver incriminating documents to the exiled King James. They were both charged with treason, but Graham was finally given a pardon by Queen Mary after he had dobbed in all his co-conspirators. After his pardon he kept his head down and lived the rest of his life out at Nunnington, close to the North Yorkshire moors and in the heart of the Helmsley and Malton knur and spell country. The Papers of Richard Graham (1st Viscount Preston) were bought at auction in 1986 by the *British Library 96 Euston Road, London.* Could be some very interesting things in these papers. Nunnington Hall is part of the National Trust and is open to the public for visits.

Richard Graham's pedigree followed a long and similar path to the Werden family. He had been made a member of the Privy Council in 1685. Then when Charles **II** died in 1685 he was made chancellor to Catherine of Braganza the queen-dowager (Charles's widow). By 1687 he was Lord Lieutenant of Cumberland and Westmorland and in 1688 he was one of a council of five appointed by King James **II**. As with the Werden's, the family boot licking went much further back than that. Graham's grandad had been 'Master of the Horse' in 1624 to none other than the champion bum kisser of all time, Georgie Villiers, the 1st Duke of Buckingham. The very same Georgie who had been playing golf at Therfield Heath, Royston in 1624 with Sir Robert Deale. They had all come up through the same 'Jobs for the Boys' school!

But wait, there's more! The nepotism certainly didn't end there. Richard Graham (Viscount Preston) had a brother called James Graham (1650-1730). Jimbo made an excellent Master of the Buckhounds. He was also

Keeper of the Privy Purse to the Duchess of York from about 1677 and also to the Duke of York himself by 1679 and after James was made king from 1685 – 1688. As such he was a very prominent member of the royal household. In December 1688 when James **II** fled to France via Rochester, James Graham didn't go with the king to France, but his son did. James Graham stayed behind to take care of the king's financial affairs. As such he would have been another prime candidate for the 'golf club disposer job.' In this regard he would obviously have been working very closely with John Ashton. After the Revolution he was also arrested with his brother Richard and accused of high treason. Both of them managed to talk their way out of it. So now we have four likely suspects to choose from who could be the English noblemen playing golf at Leith in the first international match. i.e. Richard Graham, James Graham, John Aston and John Werden. They were all close to each other. Between the four of them I suspect that they would have been extremely well placed to have been 'disposers' of the royal golf clubs. They were all close to the Duke of York, later King James, and his wife. Werden had plenty of opportunity to interact with the Maisters over a long period. Both Werden and James Graham could have mixed in Westminster after 1700 with William Maister. The Graham family lived at Levens Hall near Kendal in Cumbria where knur and spell was played even in the 1600s and which is still in existence in 2020. It would have been quite easy for the Grahams to confuse knur and spell with golf! Note that the title of Viscount Preston did not apply to the town of Preston in Lancashire. It was for the village of Preston in Haddingtonshire, East Lothian just a few miles away from Musselburgh GC and right in the centre in those days of where golf was firing up.

It gets even worse! Richard Graham (Viscount Preston) had a cousin who was also called Richard Graham. He was a solicitor who had chambers in Clifford's Inn in 1663. He had also been brought to the attention of the Duke of York by Lawrence Hyde, the Duke's brother-in-law. Richard Graham the solicitor was a Gentleman of the Privy Chamber (1682-85) and assistant solicitor to the treasury (1685-89). After the Revolution he tried to do a runner to the continent but was arrested and dumped in the Tower of London. He was eventually released, but the stress had been too much, and he died in December 1691. The Werdens, Grahams and Ashton between them definitely had the field covered!

So far it has been difficult to establish whether or not Werden, Ashton and the Grahams were in Leith when the first international match was on. However, there is a place where this information may possibly be found. On 5 May 1682, the Duke of York, when he decided to go to Leith to play golf, opted to sail from Sheerness (or Margate) to the port of Leith instead of being bumped around for several weeks in a stagecoach. As may be expected for a man of his calibre, he didn't penny pinch on this trip. He sailed aboard a sixty-gun warship called the *HMS Gloucester* which had been the first vessel in the British Navy to be named after an eponymous port in the 1650s. This arsenal was comprised of demi-cannons, culverins and demi-culverins. This boat was 117 feet long with a 755 tonnage. Its crew was 210 - 340 excluding guests and civilians. Of course he couldn't go on such an important trip without all his entourage, so he took a whole flotilla of ships along with him to include all the sycophantical hangers-on. Among this vast armada were included ships called, *Happy Return*, *Ruby*, *Pearl* and *Dartmouth*. All these ships were frigates which were also equipped with significant firepower. Anyone would have thought that the Duke was embarking on a naval war campaign and not just going to Leith for a game of golf! He was able to incur all this vast expense even though at this stage he was still only a humble duke and not yet a king. His elder brother Charles was still on the throne. Unfortunately, the warship James was sailing in hit a sandbank close to Yarmouth and ran aground. A large number of the people on board lost their lives in this disastrous shipwreck. Maybe James even had his clubs on board with him and they went down with the ship as he scrambled to get ashore safely. But James himself did survive and nothing would deter him from getting his game of golf. He jumped on one of the other ships in the fleet and finally arrived in Leith on May 7 (he must have had a strong tail wind). After partnering Patterson and cleaning up his mates in the famous golf match, assuming that this was indeed the trip when the famous match took place, he left Leith again on May 15 and arrived back in the big smoke on May 27. No mention can be found of Werden, Ashton or Graham in any of the shipwreck incident writeups, so probably they were not part of the king's very close confidants on board the *Gloucester*. However, maybe they were passengers on one of the many other ships in the fleet which didn't run aground. In February 1679 we know from one of John Werden's notebooks, in which he did a sketch of the Leith skyline from on board ship, that he had arrived there on HMS Mary which was a 66-foot royal yacht built in 1677 with 166 tonnage. It had a normal ship's complement of thirty people excluding guests and carried eight three-pound guns. HMS Mary was in naval service for well over one hundred years. Maybe this vessel was also in the 1682 flotilla? Perhaps a search of any surviving ship manifestos could confirm this...or otherwise. Coincidentally, the first captain of HMS Mary was in charge of HMS Gloucester in 1682 when it ran aground off Yarmouth, for which he was subsequently court martialled. The Duke's entourage was very large. Just on the *Gloucester* the number of fatalities had been one hundred and thirty which included several notable aristocrats. There must have been hundreds of people in the full fleet. This May visit to Scotland was the second trip he had made that year. Only a few weeks earlier he had been in Leith at the end of February 1682. He left Leith on board the vessel *Duke of Albany* on March 6 bound for Yarmouth and *en route* to join his brother King Charles II in Newmarket. Maybe the international match had taken place during this earlier visit.

It must be noted that the *Scottish Golf History* website gives the date of the first international match as 1681. I am not clear how they arrived at this date. As far as I know there are no dates on the plaque or the coat of arms which can still be seen in Canongate where Patterson built a house with his share of the winnings. Either way, 1681 or 1682, it would not change the main thrust of my mad idea...and we still need to establish how the Old Troon Clubs came to be possessed by the Maisters, whoever originally owned those clubs. In other words even if James went to Leith in 1681 as well as twice in 1682, he probably still took John Werden, Viscount Preston (Richard Graham), James Graham and possibly John Ashton with him on the boy's weekend jaunt. It should go without saying that the 'club disposer(s)' and the 'English noblemen at Leith links' do not need to be inextricably linked. Even if none of the four gentlemen mentioned actually participated in the first international golf match, that does not preclude them from being involved in the club disposal process. Alternatively, they could have played in the international match and still not have been involved in the club disposal process.

While we are talking about Werden, Ashton and the Grahams as being potential candidates to have been among the noblemen playing against the Duke of York in the first ever international golf match, we must not forget that the mystery noblemen had apparently claimed that golf was invented in England. Where and how did they reach that conclusion in the first place? Well, Werden was very active around Cheshire where knur and spell was played. Richard Graham hailed from Cumbria where we know knur and spell was rampant in the 1600s. John Ashton's family came from Liverpool which is not far from Cheshire and also close to many Lancashire knur and spell playing areas. There is every chance that they would all have known something about knur and spell and may well have confused the two ball and stick games.

I would certainly date these Duke of York clubs in the 1679 – 1682 period. During that time the English Parliament had been doing their utmost to pass laws which blocked James's succession to the throne in the event that something happened to his brother King Charles **II**. They were worried about having a Catholic heir to the throne after his marriage to Mary of Modena. During this period he spent much time away from London in either Belgium or Edinburgh. In November 1679 he had become King Charles's Viceroy in Scotland. This three-year period is probably the time when James would have had most time and most opportunity to acquire golf clubs and to play golf. Between 1679 and 1682 he spent all but seven months in Edinburgh. It was known as the Exclusion Crisis period, but no new blocking laws were ever passed. He would have had stacks of time to play golf and also to have golf clubs made. Of all the royals between 1600 and 1745 he would by far have been the one who played most golf. Just as the current Duke of York, Andrew, is the most prolific modern English royal golf player.

If, and it still is a big IF, the Old Troon clubs had indeed belonged to the Duke of York before he became King James **II**, we can then set about the task of discovering where were they made and who made them. Where is probably fairly easy. It is almost certain that they were made in Scotland and equally likely that they were made in Edinburgh where James spent a great deal of time. There are two clues in Sir John Werden's pocketbook about a possible maker. Firstly, in February 1679, the money for the clubs and balls were paid to a gentleman called John Douglas. In the pocketbook entry it doesn't specifically say that Douglas was a golf-club or ball maker, but it would seem to make some sense that he probably was. Back in the 1400s, 1500s, 1600s and most of the 1700s, it was probably the case that all or most the golf club makers were also bow makers for archery. i.e. (bowers). I have not been able to establish that John Douglas was a bower and club maker. Maybe an examination of the *Burgh Records* held in the *National Records of Scotland* could throw some light on this. Secondly, in the Werden pocketbook entry under the above-mentioned ball and club listing, there is something else written which I have been unable to completely decipher from Werden's handwritten notes. However, part of this additional entry does appear to refer to a 'Mr Mayne'. Another word of this undecipherable scribble looks to me like 'Rules'. Maybe that this was the first time the Duke and his mates had ever played golf? It has been well recorded in many places e.g. Samuel Pepys Diaries etc , that the Duke was a very keen trap-ball player back in England. This stick and ball game also required very good hand / eye coordination, so the transition to golf would not have been all that difficult. Now if my old eyes have not deceived me, that could be quite significant. It is well documented that the first set of golf clubs had been supplied to James **VI/I** in the very early 1600s by William Mayne who was both a bower and a golf club maker. William died in 1612 but his dynasty probably continued long after his death through his son and other family connections who were trained as bowers. Robert Mayne was still training people in 1640 and people he had trained, and who they in turn had trained, were still active in this business at the end of the 1600s. Maybe John Douglas was a golf club maker who had been trained in a setup which had evolved from the Mayne dynasty? Or alternatively, if he was just a golf club seller concentrating on the marketing of the products, he could have still had family connections to the remnants of the Mayne organisation. Again the *Burgh Records* may reveal more detailed information on this.

A Scottish painter called Allan Stewart (1865-1951), who was more famous for his depictions of military scenes, did a painting in 1919 of the first International golf match. In his blurb about the figures in his painting he talks about Patterson and the Duke of York, but like everyone else he apparently didn't know the names of the two English noblemen, even though they are shown in the painting. My feeling is that these noblemen may not have been very eminent members of the aristocracy, otherwise they would surely have been named. If Werden, Ashton and the Grahams were part of the entourage maybe they would have been a bit down the pecking order? It is interesting to note that when Allan Stewart died in 1951, his final resting place was in Dalry church yard in Ayrshire, the Scottish home of knur and spell!

I would be very surprised indeed if the clubs had belonged to James **I** or even to his son Charles **I**. However, having said that, please allow me to throw up yet another mad idea which is completely 'out of left field'. What I have read about the Old Troon clubs in Ian Crowe's *A Theory of Provenance* is that they are not a set, even though they are all liberally marked with identical symbols which suggests that they were all made by the same person. The *Scottish Golf History* website states that because of the markings this shows that they were made at the same time. I am not sure how they can make that statement with any degree of positivity. Probably same era, but I don't think we can completely rule out that they may have been made at different times. There are eight clubs in total, six woods and two irons. The woods in particular are interesting because there appears to be three pairs of two...three play clubs and three spoons. In his writeup Mr Crowe asks the question 'Could it be that the clubs were used by three players who also shared the irons?'

This immediately made me think back about something which has been bugging me for quite a while. i.e. When George Villiers played golf at Therfield Heath in the October 1624 to January 1625 period, his expense accounts showed that he forked out cash on three separate occasions for both balls and golf clubs. He did this over a very short time frame... four months. As I have discussed elsewhere in this book, my conclusion about this was that he was probably hiring the clubs and not buying them outright. I don't think there would have been a club maker at Therfield Heath who had readymade clubs available off the shelf to purchase. I also concluded that the course they played on at Therfield must have been King James I's private course. If my conclusions on this are correct, there could have been several golf clubs available for hire which were managed by 'ye goffe balle and club keeper'. It may be significant that he referred to a 'Gofball KEEPER' and not to a 'Gofball SELLER'. Could it be that the Therfield Heath clubs somehow found their way to the Maisters after James, George, Charles *et al* had all kicked the bucket? And what if they were NOT hire clubs and George Villers had actually bought them? This could possibly explain why there were three pairs of the same wooden clubs and may also account for why they all had all those symbols plastered all over them. One curious thing about the three different occasions when Villiers played at Royston was that the amount of money he coughed up for 'battes and balles' varied on each visit...one pound eleven shillings / one pound five shillings / ten shillings. Maybe on the second and third games he had some balls left over from the previous visit and had to buy fewer balls each time? I have concluded that 'ye gofball keeper' was probably an employee of King James. However, there is no proof for this. He could have been a Royston entrepreneur trying to make a quid. Afterall, Royston in those days had an abundance of public houses and inns, many of which were coaching houses. We know throughout history that publicans were not backwards in coming forwards when it came to dreaming up money making schemes. Royston was on the main road out of London for any stagecoaches travelling north. There would have been a constant flow of wealthy people passing through who may have been seeking some leisure activity. Royston may have been a good place to start such an enterprise. The centre of Royston is where two very old roads intersect. i.e. the east-west Ickneild Way and the Roman north-south Ermine Street. In fact one of the modern-day main attractions of the town, the Royston Cave, is located beneath this intersection. This cave had been discovered in 1742, which is just about the same time that the old Troon golf clubs could have been hidden in the Maister cupboard in Hull. The cave has some very interesting wall carvings which some historians (but not all) believe may be connected to the Knights Templar. The other thing which is still bugging me is that on the other side of Royston town to Therfield Heath there is a place known as Goffers Knoll. I would love to know how this hill got its name, because it appears to be a different place to where Villiers *et al* played golf.

Mr Crowe also commented that 'It is also notable that there is no putter'. To me this is not such a big mystery. Because of 'the first rule of golf' drafted in 1744, the area where putting was done was always a complete rubbish tip until Old Tom started to separate 'greens' from tee-up areas in the late 1800s. Up to that point putting was a complete lottery and just about any club would suffice. One could have used one's appendage to putt with and still putted just as well (or as badly) ! Allan Robertson often used to play in challenge matches using the same club to both drive and putt with. When Old Tom won the Open at Prestwick in 1864 he also used the same club to drive and putt with (Have a look at the Hugh Philp-made driver-putter in the British Golf Museum at St Andrews). So maybe the Troon clubs had belonged to James **I** after all. Maybe not his own personal clubs, but just some hire-out clubs from Therfield?

On further reflection about the types of clubs which are in the Old Troon collection, I was reminded about the letter from a man called Alexander Monro to a friend of his called John Mackenzie which was written 27 April 1691. This is reasonably close to the date when the Duke of York would have been buying his clubs. Monro at the time was Regent of St Andrews University and Mackenzie was a lawyer living in Delvine which is close to the River Tay and about sixteen miles north of Perth. The handwritten letter is held in the *National Library of Scotland*. Both these men would have been pretty wealthy. The Mackenzie family had a big estate in Delvine and still do. In this letter Monro was describing some golf clubs which he was sending to his friend as a gift. He described the clubs as a 'ane Sett of Golfe-clubs consisting of three' which included 'an play club, ane scraper and ane tin fac'd club'. This sounds to me to be just about one third of what the Old Troon clubs were. It also sounds to me like this is what you would give to someone who was just starting to play the game i.e. a 'starter set.' In a postscript to his letter Monro also explained the markings on the clubs. These included the initials of the maker, GM, who was obviously an artisan working in St Andrews at that time. It also included the clubs owners initials, JMK, for John Mackenzie. I suspect that golf clubs in those days would have all been bespoke (i.e. made to order), and not available off the shelf. More than likely they would have had some shafts and various types of club heads in stock which still had to be assembled and customised. But I don't know if this is true or not. Reading this letter also makes me feel that maybe there was one club missing from the Old Troon clubs. i.e. originally there could have been three play clubs, three spoons and three scrapers. Let us remember two things. The old wooden shafted clubs were quite fragile compared to modern clubs. They were often damaged or even broken in regular play. They were not kept in nice golf bags like we have now. They were always carried loose. If not stored properly they were quite prone to warpage and maybe drying out which made them break more easily. In a photograph I have seen of the Old Troon clubs at least one of them was bent like a cucumber and most of them had at least some permanent bend in them. I don't know if they are still like that because I know that it is possible to straighten them out a bit. It is very conceivable that one of the scrapers had been damaged or broken in play or even lost (because they were kept loose) before they arrived at the Maisters. Again, I don't know for sure, but I would think that when the Old Troon clubs were first found in Hull they would have been stored loose in the cupboard. Could it be that when the Duke of York played at Leith he had bought 'ane Sett' for himself and 'ane Sett' for each of the two noblemen? All the 'Setts' were not identical. The two surviving iron clubs at least are different. I have to add at this stage that in various different articles I have noted that there seems to be different opinions about exactly what a 'scraper' golf club was. In quite a few writeups they talk about a scraper being some kind of a wood similar to a two or three wood. However, in *The Category of 'Golf' in a New Historical Thesaurus of Scots* from the University of Glasgow, they list a scraper as an iron club like a niblick or bunker club. The latter description, and even the name of the club itself, suggest to me that it was an iron club and not a wood. Lots of holes can be poked in this theory as it can with all the other postulations on this subject which I have read. It is yet another mad idea!

I don't know exactly how long the Therfield / Royston golf set up survived after Charles **I** was executed in 1649. Theobalds Palace, which was not far away, had already been demolished by 1650. The Royston palace buildings were quickly falling into a bad state of repair. So trying to work out how the Maisters may have got hold of these clubs is still fraught with difficulty. Royston is one hundred and fifty miles away from Hull. Stagecoaches travelled at about five miles per hour. Another wild thought is that Royston was a regular coaching stop on the main road between London and York. The Maister company was a very big trading house. They conducted many of their deals in London and on occasion probably needed to bunker down in Royston for an overnight stay? As the Royston royal residence eventually lapsed into a state of disuse, maybe some old clubs came up for auction.

There is a great deal of written information about the Maister family history available. This includes a collection of letters which are held in the special collections Department at Leeds University. I don't suppose that these letters would show any direct reference to the Old Troon clubs. However, maybe a study of the correspondence would reveal whether or not the Maister family were Jacobites or even Jacobite sympathisers. Such a study may also turn up names of correspondents which may suggest possible links to the Old Troon clubs. The Westminster connection of the two Maisters who served as MP for Hull may well prove to be the most likely manner in which the old clubs ended up with the Maisters.

Despite all the various possibilities discussed, what we should not lose sight of is the fact that during the 1600s and 1700s, there were no other golf courses in England apart from Therfield Heath and Blackheath. So options in England were very limited. Therfield was probably just James **I**'s own private course. Blackheath was exclusively ex-pat Scots in those days. They were all freemasons and many of them were probably Jacobite supporters as well. Although there is anecdotal evidence that a society of golfers played at Blackheath from 1608, actual written records prior to 1787 have not survived. Maybe there was deliberate destruction of the early records during the Jacobite days to avoid being implicated? They do have some artefact evidence which dates to 1766 and maybe even earlier. So at least on available evidence Blackheath can probably be ruled out as being a possible source of the Old Troon clubs.

When we read the *Blackheath Chronicles* club minutes we see that the first mention of a club maker there was in 1788 when a man called Donaldson was paid ten pounds ten shillings i.e. ten guineas. He was still there in 1801 and was then paid an annual allowance of fifteen guineas plus three pounds five shillings and sixpence for making the holes and repairing the flags. This annual fee must have been a retainer. He presumably would have charged for any new clubs he made or any repairs. He died in March 1815 and the BHGC paid eight pounds eleven shillings and sixpence for his funeral costs. Thus he stayed at the club at least twenty-seven years and must have made and repaired quite a lot of golf clubs in that time. But it was all probably a bit too late to have included the Old Troon clubs in his portfolio!

This Donaldson was probably Andrew Donaldson who had previously been a bower and club-maker at Bruntsfield near Edinburgh. He had left Scotland in 1782 under some sort of a cloud and had been planning to join the army. How long he stayed in the army or whether or not he went to Blackheath earlier than 1788 is not yet known. However, after arriving at BHGC he stayed there until he kicked the bucket, so it appears that BHGC must have been quite happy with his golf club making and repairing services, otherwise they would have booted him out long before 1815. It may be safe to say at this point that Donaldson was the first golf professional to work in England, albeit that he was a Scot, and that Blackheath GC was essentially a Scottish club. We must also be aware that the job description of 'professional' had not yet been coined. In the late 1700s and early 1800s Donaldson (1788 – 1815) was only ever referred to as a 'club-maker' and 'hole-maker' by Blackheath GC. The first time they called their club-makers 'professionals' was when Willie and Jamie Dunn were there from 1851 to 1865. Before the Dunn brothers arrived on the scene, BHGC had at least four more club makers...Ballantyne (1815 – 1817), Cockburn (1817 – 1822), Poke (1822 – 1823) and Sharpe (1823

-1834.) Probably one or two more are missing from this list after Sharpe died. From 1865 when the Dunn's left until 1895 they had a procession of professionals which included Charles Hunter, Bob Kirk, Thomas Manzie, C Thomson, W. Anderson and George Brews. It is possible that in Scotland some of the artisans, such as Allan Robertson and Willie Park Sr, were called 'professionals' in the early 1840s and prior to 1851. But I am unsure about this. They may still have just been called club and ball makers and BHGC may have been the first club anywhere in the world to use the term 'professional'. Of course Robertson et al were obviously doing the same kind of work as the Dunn brothers. I have seen stories about Allan Robertson from the 1840s where he is referred to a 'professional', but I don't know if these stories were written after 1851. The same doubt can also be applied to BHGC and the Dunn brothers because their *Chronicles* were only written in the late 1890s. So is possible that the 'professional' description applied to the Dunn brothers was also added later. It is only a question of when the terminology was first used. Maybe the only definitive first use of the word 'professional' was at the time of the first Open Championship at Prestwick in 1860? There had been a 'goffe-club and balle keeper' at Therfield Heath, Royston in 1624 / 1625 but we don't know his name and we don't know if he made those clubs or just looked after some clubs and balls which King James **I** had brought from Scotland.

I can't imagine that a private individual, outside of the royal family, would have been brave or stupid enough to have commissioned the Old Troon golf clubs to be made which were plastered with so many such blatantly obvious Jacobite markings, unless they were made when James **I** or Charles **I** were around (It would have been perfectly acceptable in their days to have these kind of markings on golf clubs). And even then it seems very unlikely that a private individual would have so many copies of each stamping made on each club. Nor would they have been likely to order multiple versions of the same club. Not only were there very few golf clubs or golf societies playing in England in the 1600 and 1700s, but obviously there were very few actual golfers too and even fewer golf club artisans who could actually make the clubs. That leaves us with the final conclusion that these clubs were probably made in Scotland and probably belonged to one of the aforementioned royal family. Unless of course one of the Maisters sailed from Hull to Leith one day on business and witnessed all the many golf societies playing on Leith links and decided that it would be nice to have some golf clubs...even if they didn't play golf and also had nowhere to play! Who knows? Maybe one day we will know the truth!

Over the years there have been several theories put forward about the provenance of the Old Troon clubs and I have probably read all of them. They all go into great detail about what the symbols on the clubs mean and also into great detail about how the approximate manufacturing date can be pinpointed by the actual shape / design of the clubs. All these theories have much to commend them. However, I have still not seen anything which offers even a remotely plausible explanation as to how the clubs ended up with the Maisters. Very few ideas for how the Maisters got these clubs have been put forward, and the ones which have been propounded all seem extremely far-fetched to me. My personal feeling is that the Old Troon clubs had belonged to the Duke of York and that they had ended up in Hull through interaction between Sir John Werden and William Maister. I suspect that the disposal process had probably been facilitated by either John Ashton, Viscount Preston or James Graham (or all of them), but Sir John Werden is my favourite to have been the key link man with the Maisters. Unfortunately, there is nothing concrete to prove this idea...only strong circumstantial evidence.

Interpretation of the symbols on the Old Troon golf clubs is something which eventually seems to be at odds with many of the theories propounded. These symbols could mean all manner of different things. Do they relate to any of the Stewart royal family? Do they refer to the maker of the clubs? Do they refer to some private owner who just happens to have the initials 'IC' or 'JC'? Or was someone having a bit of fun and decided that even Jesus Christ (JC) couldn't hit a decent golf shot with clubs like these?

The consensus of opinion seems to be that 'IC' is in Latin and refers to Iacobus and Carolus (James and Charles). So far so good. That could apply over a long period provided that no one worries about who proceeds who. For me it is hard to swallow the idea that a private owner or even a golf club maker would plaster the clubs with so many crowns and thistles. And how many times does he have to be reminded about his own name? Having said that I could be convinced that a one-eyed royals supporter may relish having clubs covered in such an outward show of devotion. Just as today collectors of royal memorabilia still buy mugs, plates, towels etc. covered in royal wedding or coronation blurb.

Someone has pointed out that identical decoration has been seen on sporting memorabilia etc from the late 1600s. I don't know if the order of the letters on the clubs needs to have any succession meaning. Could it be James **I** / Charles **I** (father/son) or James **II** / Charles **I** (son/father) or James Francis / Bonnie Prince Charlie (father/son) or even James **II** / Charles **II** (brother / brother)? Neither James Frances nor Bonnie Prince Charlie ever became king, although they did set up court while they were in exile and even went through the charade of conferring various ceremonial positions to their loyal supporters. Could it be possible that the original insignia which William Mayne stamped on the very first clubs for James **I** when he was appointed royal-club maker in 1603 has since been perpetuated throughout the 1600s on any clubs which the Mayne family has made for any subsequent Stewart royals?

Let us for a moment try to put ourselves in the Maisters' shoes when they bought or somehow acquired these old clubs. I can't imagine that they would buy the clubs at a pub in the port of Hull from a Scottish ship's captain called Jock Campbell (JC) who lived in the Gorbals district of Glasgow! The Maisters almost certainly didn't play golf themselves. There was nowhere to play in Hull or for that matter nowhere to play anywhere in the whole county of Yorkshire. Although we can't completely rule out the possibility that they used the golf clubs for amusement by hitting up and down paddocks on their Winestead country estate in Holderness without using holes and flags. I can't envisage them buying any old nondescript golf clubs from any old Joe Hacker. I could only see them buying the clubs if there was some historical significance attached or if they had belonged to some notable or important person, such as royalty etc. And even then I imagine that they would need to reassure themselves about the provenance of the clubs. So the person (or persons) they got the clubs from would need to be someone they trusted and someone that they could easily link to the clubs original owner. At this stage Werden *et al* still seem to be the only players in the game who tick all the boxes.

If my conclusion is correct and the Old Troon clubs really had belonged to the Duke of York, then this would probably make the old Baildon Hall knur and spell equipment more than sixty years older than the Old Troon clubs! If, on the other hand, they dated to around the 1741 newspaper in the Maister cupboard, or even later than that, it would make the Baildon knur-stick more than one hundred years older than the Old Troon clubs. Maybe golf really was rich man's knur and spell? Zip-a-dee-doodah, zip-a-dee-ay, my, oh, my, what a wonderful day... where's *James Baskett's* bloody bluebird when we need it? Probably perched on top of a sprig of whin on the old Blackheath golf course at Greenwich...whistling Dixie!

What we do know with absolute certainty is that knur and spell, poor man's golf, was extensively played in the east riding of Yorkshire at least one hundred years before any golf was played there and probably much longer than that. Places such as Hull, Hedon, Preston, Southcoates, Beverley, Tadcaster, Sculcoates, York, Holderness (Patrington, Ottringham), Pocklington, Seaton Ross etc were all playing knur and spell from the late 1700s / early 1800s and probably earlier than that. In fact there is even a chance that the Maister family played knur and spell. In addition to their property interests in the city area of Hull they also had extensive land and property holdings in the Holderness area, especially in the villages of Patrington and Winestead which are only one or two miles apart. It is well recorded that knur and spell, known there as dab and trigger, was played in Patrington, Ottringham, and many other villages around Holderness. Hull GC first started up with a nine-hole course in Anlaby Road around October 1904. They didn't move to their current site in Kirk Ella until 1924. Kirk Ella is a very old village dating to the eleventh century. It is about five miles west of Hull and is a very desirable residential area. More or less equivalent to the Toorak of Hull. Hull GC these days has a very posh clubhouse which includes Kirk Ella

Hall which was built around 1778 as a private residence for the wealthy Kirkby family. Earlier golf clubs in East Yorkshire had been founded between 1889 and 1898 at Brough, Beverley and Hornsea, but all these clubs were long after knur and spell in the area.

Chapter 14

Every man and his dog, but don't use your own name

When gleaning information about knur and spell players from over an approximate two-hundred-and-fifty-year period, it was apparent that they came from a very wide range of occupations. Yes, it is true that miners and textile workers (weavers, tape sizers, beamers, twisters, spinners, bobbin turners etc) featured very strongly. However, knur and spell players could also be farmers, builders, dry-stone wallers, steel workers, blacksmiths, cobblers, pub owners, postmen, saw-grinders, tailors, iron mongers, potters, bookmakers, glass blowers, quarrymen, cord cutters, gamekeepers, shepherds, inn keepers, warehousemen, electricians, road builders, carpenters, stone dressers, chemical workers, tilers, professional footballers, butchers, soldiers, fork makers, train drivers, wool-sorters, cattle men, auctioneers, professional cricketers, milkmen, carpet-makers, musicians, horse shoe nail makers, machine tenters, chimney sweeps, shop keepers, joiners, policemen, cordwainers, cutlery workers, puddlers, gardeners, wood merchants, teachers, gelderds, factory owners, fishermen, wheelwrights, blast furnace operators, mechanics, shipyard workers, schoolboys, bakers, engineering workers, moulders, ostlers, filesmiths, grocers, bricklayers, doctors, plumbers, mechanics, stone masons, tradesmen, peruke makers, civil servants, traffic wardens, cloggers, slaters, skinners, carriers, village postmasters, clothiers, green grocers, cabmen, jobbers, poachers, scientists, writers, leather tanners, dyers, crane drivers, showmen, mill directors, farm bailiffs, overlookers, stone dressers, plasterers, wool-combers, farriers, railway shunters etc. Pretty much everyone apart from the nobility and golfers!

Since coal miners and textile workers were both prolific knur and spell players, it is easy to see why the tiny village of Trawden in Lancashire where

I was raised was active in this sport and in many of the other pub sports mentioned throughout this book. Written evidence of coal mining in Trawden as early as late 1200s and early 1300s exists and locally mined coal was still being sold in Trawden during the late 1800s. Similar documentation exists for the textile industry in Trawden. Hundreds of years before the Industrial Revolution started and textile production became mechanised, hand-loom weavers were scattered throughout all the various hamlets which made up Trawden Forest (Beardshaw, Winewall, Cottontree, Wycoller etc). In fact long before Trawden actually got the name it has today, in the 1200s and 1300s it was known as Trochdene or Trouden.

John Kay invented his flying shuttle in 1733, James Hargreaves his spinning jenny in 1764 and Richard Arkwright had opened his first water-powered textile mill in the 1770s. However, the cottage industry of hand-loom weavers in Trawden, and probably other places, struggled on at least until 1840 and maybe a bit later. This is despite the fact that from about 1840 there were at least eight and maybe ten cotton mills built and operated in the Trawden Forest area. This is quite amazing considering Trawden's small population. By the 1960s most of these cotton mills had been and gone.

The other thing which was very apparent was that many of the regular big-money knur and spell players gave themselves an alias. Maybe that was deliberately done to make it more difficult for the police to track them down when illegal gambling or illegal liquor supply were being conducted. Some typical cognomens were Derbo, Cocky, Long Dick, Targer, Whistle, Clogs, Butch, Snap, Milk Boy, Robson, Brassey, Marlow, Curbey, Tinnier, Child's Lad, Ginger, Craven, Shipley Bill, Coddy, Gaffer, Jumping Jack, Rough, Patent Plough, Soldier Johnny, Driver, Young George, Clayton's Novice, Tarvey, Bill at St George, Japple, Young Yook, Twitch, Jackson's Lad, Pinchem Bill, Bob at Jumps, Old Roper, John o' Mount, Mally Will, Jack o' Harry's, Rosin, Happy Newsome, Old Paul, Fatty, Pep, Striker Bill, Magic, John o' Polly's, Gerse, Billy Milker, Jack at Back, Bough, Pistol, Shiveram, Dyson's Lad, Kit, Old Blanch, Swaddy, a Knight of the Inner, Bang-Down, Mucky Jack, Gawkey, Hustler Bland, Bob o' Tums, Snarlo, Bill at Mute, Strong, Trott, Shepherd, Throstle, Boss, Waxy, Tidy, Duke, Humpy, Taylor's Novice, Collie, the Moor-end Stag, Derry Duce, Tiger,

Sandy, the Colne Giant, Pooley, Limbs, Applechops, Nigger, Snacky, Todd's Lad, the Dancing Master, Punch, Tucker, Old Yank, Smasher, Cowling's Lad, Bill at Mount, Jacky Dagger, The Inimitable, Young Rob, Chalkface, Jem o' Jemmy, Cutty, Old Ned, Clogger, Jakey o' Saras, Little Tack, Buck, Little Tommy, Rangler, Jack Holly, Tommy Todd, Old Nutty, Pin, Dosey, Whimpenny Swallow, Nobby, Gullett, Bushman, Tom o' Gents, Chisels, Jas, Doss, Jas, Crow, Whist, Crutchy, Faulty, Choppy, Shiner, Jimmy o' Dicks, Rubber, Gosh, Tidley, the Yorkshire Lad, Slater, the Crookesmoor Nonpareil, Swallow, Moffitt, Bill Jacking, Smokey, Boy Harry, Fred o't Delves, Cobbler, Muff, Uncle Butch, Tato, Weasel, Spank, Baisty, Joiner Jack, Craig of Stone Chair, Hunk, Tim o' Bathy's, Jokes, Horsforth Lad, Tall Boy, Young Farrah, Bolton, Nimble Graham, Yock, Six-foot Nelson, Heptonstall Bill, Senior, Tinker, Young Atha, Jacky o' Sam's, Calah, Nook, Warren, Harley, Old Williams, Ronah, The Veteran, Young Cahill, Herb, Ben o' David's, Mousey, Mister Jimmy, Jockey, Philadelphia, Sycie, Dram's Lad, Sweep, The unknown, Benny, Squire, Gibson's Novice, Bill o' Dick's, Old Man, Crop, Manny, The Tough One, Kid, Cricket, Caleb, Agg, Whiston, Young Derbo, Fat, Bob o' Jeff's, Bobbie, Old Pat, Billy Mash, Seth, Jacky o' Jackie's, Dash, Bob o' th' Juntas, Push, Pet, Tug, Smith's Novice, Scranny, etc. I am definitely not an onomatologist, so please don't ask me to come up with a list of derivations.

It wasn't just the knur and spell players who often gave themselves an alias. Similar lists could also be compiled for all the other games which were associated with pubs and gambling over many centuries. i.e. quoits, prize fighting / bare knuckle fighting, cock fighting, wrestling, arrow throwing, road bowling, pedestrianism (running and walking), rabbit coursing, pidgeon / sparrow / starling shooting etc. In fact anything where prize money and big gambling were involved. The most common cognomen for runners was 'stag'. We had the London Stag, the Hampstead Stag, the Little Stag, the Moor-end Stag, the Park Stag, the Leicester Stag, the Suffolk Stag, the Wild Stag, the Bald-Faced Stag, the Mountain Stag, the Stalybridge Stag, the Burton Stag etc.

Those of you with eagle eyes will have noted that knur and spell did have its very own 'Tiger' who played about one hundred and thirty years before we got a 'Tiger' playing golf. Not only that, but the Tiger in 1868 was also a 'TW'. His surname was Watson and he hailed from Castleford in Yorkshire!

That year must have been a good one for Tigers. There was also a Tiger in the first cricket team ever to tour England from Australia in 1868. His traditional name was Bonnibarngeet (see more about this tour later).

Of course, bye names were still in common use in Trawden when I was a young boy in the 1940s and early 1950s, especially for the older villagers. One of the few I can remember was an old guy called Herbert o' Fushes. I think his correct family name was Rushton, but I don't know what o' Fushes actually meant.

The above list of knur and spell alias names has well over one hundred names on it, but it only represents one per cent or even half a percent of all the names I came across in the big money games of knur and spell. Which means that there were thousands of big money players. However, the vast majority of people playing knur and spell did not play in the big money matches. They just played in the low-level handicap events or village sports days or quite often just for bragging rights amongst mates. These events maybe gave out small monetary prizes or more often they played for a prize such as a copper kettle. Often there could be fifty to a hundred entrants in a handicap event and most of them never got a mention in the newspapers. They were just anonymous players unless they came in the top three or if a novice player beat one of the established stars in one of the early heats. On any given day there could be handicap competitions taking place all over the north of England. In and all-around big towns such as Leeds, Barnsley, Halifax, Bradford, Hull, York, Manchester and Sheffield, but also in small hamlets and villages miles from anywhere. There is no question whatsoever that throughout the 1800s knur and spell was a considerably more popular game than golf in England and much more widely played. Not only that, but during the 1800s knur and spell in England was also much bigger than golf in Scotland! *Och, yer bum's oot the windae!*

Chapter 15

Pub sports rule…cockfighting, bear-baiting, prizefighting and arrow-throwing

Although there appears to be no evidence that any royalty or noblemen ever played knur and spell, there is plenty of evidence that they did play or involve themselves in many other pub sports. James **I** of England played golf, bowling, hunting and cockfighting. All these sports were closely tied to pubs in his day. James **II** of England played lots of trap-ball, at least when he was the Duke of York. Trap-ball was essentially a pub game and a short version of knur and spell. Cockfighting was an enormous pub 'sport' which was conducted all over England. This sport was far older than golf or most of the other sports mentioned in this story. As soon as daily newspapers came on the scene in the early 1700s, they were bombarded with cockfighting events. Many of the cocks which fought were owned by aristocrats and the wagers which they made were generally much bigger than either the golf or the knur and spell wagers. According to the *Stamford Mercury* 5 June 1718, Lord Granbee and Matthew Lidster Esq each had thirty-five cocks fighting for forty guineas. The *Betting Household Act 1853* banned cockfighting in England, but it was not banned in Scotland until 1895. Just before the 1853 ban came into force, Lord Derby had been an owner of cocks fighting in the last legal fight which took place in London. The 1853 Act was able to close down cockfighting pits at public houses, but it didn't stop cockfighting. They went 'underground' and one hundred and forty odd years later in 1995 we still saw reports in British newspapers alleging illegal cockfighting events despite the best efforts of the RSPCA. Of course, they are never advertised and are always arranged by bush telegraph and are usually held in remote farming locations.

For hundreds of years prevention of animal cruelty was not high on the agenda in England. From the 1300s to the late 1700s or even early 1800s, animal baiting (bulls, bear, badgers etc) using pepper and teams of dogs (e.g. Old English Bulldogs) was a major source of 'entertainment' for all sections of the population including the aristocracy and the man in the street. These events were most often held in front of a pub or at least very close to a pub. Pub landlords were mostly the promoters of such 'desirable spectacles'. The infamous Bear Garden in London had an onsite pub built into the complex where patrons could continue to eat and drink while they watched chained up bears being ripped to shreds by packs of dogs! These barbarous sports didn't completely disappear until the *Cruelty to Animals Act* was finally passed in 1835.

Royalty and noblemen didn't just get involved with bearbaiting, cockfighting and trap-ball at pubs. Their involvement in cricket was probably far greater than both these sports combined. According to the *Derby Mercury* 31 July 1735, a cricket match was to be played at Bromley in Kent between the Prince of Wales's and Earl of Middlesex's teams. The *Newcastle Courant* 23 July 1737 reported that his Royal Highness the Prince of Wales and ten Gentlemen played a match at cricket at Kew, for a considerable sum against his Grace the Duke of Marlborough and ten other noblemen and Gentlemen. The *Caledonian Mercury* 7 July 1740 told us that his Royal Highness the Duke of Cumberland has made a match at cricket to play on Hounslow Heath. In the *Kentish Gazette* dated 28 August 1779 we heard that a match of cricket for five hundred guineas a side had been made by the Duke of Dorset, Lord Tankerville and Sir Horace Man of Hampshire, with two men given, against all England. Rest assured that a match involving over one thousand pounds in the 1700s was very big *moolah* indeed. One hundred and seventy-five years later when Australian golfer Peter Thomson won his first British Open in 1954, he picked up just seven hundred and fifty pounds.

Royalty and the aristocracy also got involved in prize fighting which was a big sport all over England in the 1600s, 1700s and 1800s. Of course they were not there to participate. They just attended for the spectacle and for purposes of gambling. Many of these pugilistic events were held at public houses where knur and spell matches were also being promoted. In fact one of the most famous knur and spell players in the late 1850s and early 1860s, a Yorkshireman called Kirk Stables, was also a prize fighter. Kirk would have been a bare knuckles fighter. The Marquess of Queensberry Rules, which included the use of boxing gloves to protect the hands, did not come into force until 1867.

The point about mentioning things like cockfighting and cricket is that royalty and aristocrats attended these events at pubs. Often they could be the same pubs which were also holding knur and spell events. So, they were probably at least well aware of the existence of knur and spell. The kind of pubs the upper crust would normally have frequented would not be the ale houses and tippling places used by the working poor. They would have been the coaching houses where they made overnight stops on long journeys like the one mentioned later on the North Yorkshire Moors at Ainthorpe near Whitby. Stagecoaches and coaching houses were probably in the decline by 1850 because the railway system had mushroomed. The stagecoaches which were still used were mostly for short trips and not cross-country trips.

Whether or not members of the aristocracy ever played at knur and spell has yet to be demonstrated. However, we do know that knur and spell was sometimes played on their land. One such example of this was reported in *Bell's Life*, 1838, when knur and spell playing took place at Wentworth Park near Rotherham. This is a 180-acre park surrounded by a large fifteen-thousand-acre family estate where Wentworth Woodhouse is located. In 1838 it was the family seat of the 5th Earl Fitzwilliam. Before the Earls Fitzwilliam inherited the estate in the 1700s, several prime ministers had lived there. It had been built in the Jacobean era (early 1600s) during the reign of King James I and is probably the largest private residence in the UK. Earl Fitzwilliam also had substantial land holdings (eighty thousand acres) in North Yorkshire, in and around the town of Malton. This is close to both the picturesque Howardian Hills and the North Yorkshire Moors National Park. According to the *Sheffield Daily Telegraph* 30 November 1864, he was still giving permission for the Malton annual knur and spell handicap to be held on his land. Wentworth Park and Malton are seventy-one miles apart. Malton is also just six miles away from the amazing Castle Howard stately home. Less than five miles south of Malton are the tiny villages of Birdsall and Langton. According to the *Yorkshire Post and Leeds*

Intelligencer 16 December 1871, Lord Middleton of Birdsall House and Mrs Norcliffe of Langton Hall both gave permission for the plebs to hold their Malton Open Rabbit Coursing Meeting on their land. So the landed gentry were not just supporting knur and spell. They were facilitating other pub organised events too. Fans of Gentleman Jack of Shibden Hall will no doubt be aware that Isabella Norcliffe was one of her many lovers as revealed in the famous *Anne Lister Diaries*.

Not all the aristocracy were as accommodating as Earl Fitzwilliam and Lord Middleton however when it came to allowing sport to be played on their land. According to the *Sheffield Daily Telegraph* 12 October 1911, Lord Allendale of Bretton Hall near Wakefield had taken champion knur and spell player Joe Machen to court for trespassing on his land to play a knur and spell match. Bretton Hall was built in about 1720 and was located in a two-hundred-acre estate overlooking the River Dearne. Machen was fined twenty shillings for this indiscretion.

Readers may have noticed that brief mention was made earlier about the sport of 'arrow- throwing'. This sport was very popular in Yorkshire in the second half of the nineteenth century and early part of the twentieth century. In can also still be found in England in 2019. It is different from the pub game of darts which is often colloquially known as a game of arrows. Arrowing-throwing has been carried out since at least the time of the Norman Conquest in 1066. In Yorkshire, many of the pubs which promoted knur and spell contests also held arrow throwing events. e.g. the Cardigan Grounds in Leeds, the Quarry Gap Grounds in Bradford, and the New Belle Vue Grounds in Halifax all hosted arrow throwing. Indeed, some of the knur and spell players also threw arrows. One of these was Adam Fozzard who was born in Ardsley in 1871. At one time he was landlord of the White Horse Inn at West Ardsley near Wakefield. Another knur and spell player, who was also a regular arrow thrower in the 1880s, was a gentleman called Muff Quarmby. Now there's a name to conjure with!

Basically the players used an arrow similar to the ones normally propelled by a bow, but they threw it by hand. The throw was assisted by some string attached to both hand and arrow which enabled a sort of 'sling' throw. Akin to the sling which David used to slay the Philistine giant, Goliath, in the *Bible's Book of Samuel* story. The string had to be longer than the arrow itself. One end was knotted and lodged in a groove or slit which was cut into the arrow shaft near to the flights. The other end was wrapped around the throwing hand which gripped the arrow near to the arrow tip end. It was essential that the string be wrapped just once around the shaft prior to throwing. It was also important that the string be kept taut until the point of release and that a full follow through be completed. The string around the shaft imparts spin to the arrow which stabilizes its flight and is the reason why good distance can be achieved. The arrow was thus thrown like a javelin with an outstretched arm. Once the arrow was up and flying the string remained in the throwing hand. I suspect that the arrows used were all self-made. The contest was usually held in a field behind the pub. Just like knur and spell it was a case of who could throw the arrow the furthest and there was no target involved. Players would each have a pre-agreed number of throws e.g. thirty, and again like knur and spell there were two formats. They could play where the single longest throw could win, or they could play where the aggregate score for all thirty throws was counted. The contest could be between just two players or between two teams of players. Stake money of one hundred pounds or more could be involved and big gambling was ever present. Distance covered was measured in scores same as knur and spell. A handicap system whereby one less skilled player could be given a few scores start by his opponent was also used. Of course the distance an arrow could be thrown by this method was much less than a knur could be hit. Even so, throws over one hundred yards are common. Almost certainly the archers and the arrow throwers understood the principles of applying spin to a projectile long before the golfers worked it out for golf balls, even if they didn't know the actual physics involved. The gun shooters also worked out the importance of spin to their projectile long before the golfers had a clue. They knew that with their smooth bore muskets etc that the distance and accuracy of their shot was poor. So they invented 'rifling' of their gun bores with a grooved pattern from at least the 1500s onwards in order to apply spin to their ammunition.

Arrow-throwing appears to have been played only in Yorkshire and mostly in a very small area of Yorkshire. In fact, the vast majority of contests found were in Leeds or Bradford or in towns / villages which are all within about fifteen miles of one of those two cities. Places such as Halifax, Wakefield, Huddersfield, and Keighley. However, within the area encompassed by the places mentioned, arrow throwing was extremely popular and was played in dozens if not hundreds of small villages and hamlets. Today the area described is highly populated with two or three million people. Obviously in the 1800s there would not have been so many people there, but relatively speaking it would still have been a busy place as the Industrial Revolution was in full swing. One of the star arrow-throwers was a man called Thomas Baxter from the Bradford suburb of Bowling. He played in the 1860s. In 1863 he was advertising to play any man in the world for twenty-five pounds a side and giving any opponent fifteen score (three hundred yards) start over thirty throws. i.e. ten yards start each throw.

Outside of that area, I did read that a Burnley man called Dick Holt was once hailed as a world champion arrow-thrower. The arrows he threw were thirty-two inches long. Burnley is in East Lancashire but only about twenty miles away from the Yorkshire town of Halifax where arrow-throwing was very popular. However, I strongly suspect that Dick Holt may have been a Yorkshireman who just happened to reside in Burnley. He may well have done all his arrow-throwing in Yorkshire even though he lived in Burnley. Although this game was only ever played at places all within twenty or thirty miles away from where I was born, I never saw this game being played, nor had I ever even heard of it. Although it was often played alongside knur and spell matches it was never as popular as knur and spell. Nor does it appear to have spread all across the former Danelaw counties as knur and spell did. The wager size for arrow throwing was never as high as the big knur and spell matches, but it was often still more than a year's wage.

Of course, in those days there was no choice in Yorkshire between knur and spell or golf because the latter did not yet exist in that county. Blackheath GC was probably going when Robinson and Spence played but that is located many miles away in the London area. Several days hard coach and horses ride over bumpy unmade roads in those days! I suspect that golf at Therfield was not surviving by then. In any case it is also many miles away from Yorkshire. The first golf course to start up in Yorkshire itself was Cleveland GC in 1887. Knur and spell had been thriving in Yorkshire for at least two hundred and fifty years at that stage. So, I suspect that the term 'poor man's golf' or even 'collier's golf' was a relatively modern description added to knur and spell. I wonder if it may have even been a patronising term dreamt up by the snobbish English golfing community. More than likely!

Chapter 16

Vikings and Anglo-Saxons

My personal inclinations are to rule out knur and spell being an Anglo-Saxon game. The reasons for this are straight forward. The Anglo-Saxons arrived in Britain long before the Vikings. They came just after the Romans had left England in about 410 AD. They never went in numbers to Scotland, Wales, or Ireland. They only ever settled in England. However, they did wander all over England and they did have a presence in Yorkshire where the density of knur and spell playing was highest. However, the densest population of Anglo-Saxons was definitely in the southern counties of England and very little knur and spell was played in these counties. The so called 'Anglo-Saxons' were not one single mob. They were three distinct peoples who came from Germany, Denmark and the Netherlands. The Saxons mostly settled in Essex, Middlesex and Sussex. The Jutes mostly stayed around Kent and the Angles went to East Anglia and Northumbria. When knur and spell was found in the south of England it was usually being played by itinerant Yorkshiremen. Whatever the case, knur and spell appears to have been played in just about every place where the Danish Vikings settled throughout the entire Danelaw area.

Another reason I tend to rule out the Anglo-Saxons dates to when the kingdom of Northumbria was much bigger in area than it is today. i.e. back to the days when all southern Scotland around Edinburgh and the Lothians was part of England. In those days Northumbria was split into two separate kingdoms; Bernicia and Deira. For much of the time when the Angles were in charge, these two kingdoms were regularly fighting each other. Even the Jutes, Angles and Saxons were regularly squabbling with each other. They also had to frequently contend with the marauding Scots. After the Vikings had established the Danelaw area, the Angles in the north part of Northumbria were still around in that area. However, by the time the Vikings arrived into Northumbria this kingdom had seriously declined in importance compared with the kingdoms in the south of England. There were not so many Viking settlements established north of the River Tyne i.e. north of Newcastle and Northumbria. This may well account for why the density of knur and spell playing is low when we go north of the Tyne. There was some knur and spell played in places like Bedlington, East Sleekburn, West Moor, and Morpeth, but nothing like the very high density played in Newcastle, Durham, and all Danelaw places south of there.

Yet another strong reason to rule out the Saxons is to look at the Birmingham area of England. The Birmingham metropolitan area in the West Midlands is the second biggest metropolitan area in England after London with a population of three to four million. This area was never ruled by the Vikings. The Great Heathen Army of Norsemen went very close to the area when they trudged up Watling Street, the old Roman Road stretching from just north of London up to Merseyside. They went through places such as Fazeley near Tamworth in Staffordshire and then Repton in Derbyshire both counties where knur and spell was found. However, the Vikings never established settlements in the West Midlands area, so it remained just outside the Danelaw and dominated by the Anglo-Saxons. Consequently, virtually no knur and spell or very little knur and spell was ever played there despite the big population. I only ever found two references to knur and spell played in that area. According to *Bell's Life* in 1870 there was a match played in Moseley which was a trendy village just a few miles from Birmingham city centre. It was also played at Walsall, which is about ten miles north of Birmingham. These days Walsall is part of the West Midlands but in the 1800s it was part of Staffordshire. About thirteen miles due east of Walsall is the little village of Tettenhall. The Vikings never settled here but they did suffer a heavy defeat there in 910 AD at the hands of the Saxon kingdoms of Mercia and Wessex. Tettenhall is also famous for 'Tettenhall Dick'. Contrary to what some of you may think this is not the name of a medieval porn star. It is actually a variety of pear used for centuries in the production of an alcoholic drink called perry. It is made using a fermentation process similar to how cider is made from apples. Knur and spell was definitely played just a bit further north in Derbyshire, mostly in the eastern half of the Peak District not far from

Sheffield. This coincides almost exactly with locations where place names of Scandinavian origin are found.

After the Vikings had established the Danelaw, the Anglo-Saxons did not disappear from England. They continued to occupy most of England south of Watling Street (Wessex etc) and also had a presence north of the River Tyne. Their influence in these areas did not fully end until William the Conqueror defeated King Harold, the last Saxon king of England, in 1066.

In most writeups by learned historians about Anglo-Saxon culture, and especially about the likely games they played, there is little mention of ball games. They would have known about the Romans and their paganica / harpastum leather balls, but they don't appear to have taken a liking to this particular leisure activity. Although there has been some suggestion that they played the game of billets, gambling games with dice and various board games seem to have been their forte. None of this can be said with any great certainty because the Anglo-Saxons themselves were not geniuses with the pen and ink. Much of what we know about Anglo-Saxon history came to us through the writings of the Venerable Bede (672 – 735 AD) and most of this was compiled several hundred years after the event so will obviously be fraught with inconsistencies and inaccuracies. We should therefore still keep an open mind when it comes to Anglo-Saxons and knur and spell.

Chapter 17

Blame it all on the Roman Emperor Constantine

King James **I** of England was not by any means the first English or even Scottish monarch to interfere in the playing of games on Sundays. Various monarchs had been doing similar things over the previous two centuries. Henry **VIII** had at least two attempts at this, one of which was his list of unlawful games given in the 33ʳᵈ Statute dated 1541. Edward **II** (1314), Edward **III** (1349), Richard **II** (1389), Henry **IV** (1401) and Edward **IV** (1473) all had a go at banning various sports. Almost certainly, in all cases, the monarchs were being pressured by the church to ban the playing of sport on Sundays. And the pressure didn't stop after the Book of Sports in 1618. All the way through to the late 1800s ordinary people were hassled by the church. In 1685 in Sheffield, two men were given a bollocking for playing the banned game of Tripp (knur and spell) in a churchyard and verbally abusing the vicar's wife who must have been admonishing them. About one hundred years later in the same city, according to the *Sheffield Local Register* 12 February 1790, 'Nine men put in stocks for tippling in a public-house during Divine service, and two boys made to do penance in church for playing at trip during divine service, by standing in the midst of the church with their trip-sticks erect'. In the *Lancaster Gazette* 5 April 1806, a verdict of accidental death was recorded when a head flew off a knur and spell stick during a 'spell and nor match' and hit someone at Witherslack in Westmorland. Also, according to the *Lancaster Gazette*, 3 February 1810 a youth was taken to the vestry of Blackburn Parish church by the local constable for playing knur and spell on Sunday during service time. In the *Stamford Mercury*, 23 March 1821 sixteen boys were fined for playing nor-spell on Sunday at Waddington. Waddington is about four miles due south of Lincoln city centre. In the *Durham Chronicle,* 9

October 1824, two men were fined 3s 4d each for profaning the Sabbath by playing at Buck-stick during time of divine service at West Rainton, north of Durham. Likewise, on 20 October 1827, two players were committed to the house of correction for one week for playing at 'spell-ore' on the Sabbath in the parish of Giles , Durham. St Giles church in Durham had been built in 1112. The *Preston Chronicle*, 14 April 1832, reported that a man had been sent to prison for trial because he played spell and nor on Sunday. The *Lancaster Gazette* 9 February 1833 talked about scenes of drunkenness with knur and spell being played outside a church in Bolton on the Sabbath. The *Hull Packet*, 28 February 1832, reported that a boy had been convicted of playing dab and trigger on Sunday near Sculcoates. The *Preston Chronicle*, 2 May 1840, told us that many lads had been summoned to the Town Hall to be charged with playing spell and norr, cricket and other games on Sunday last, during divine service. The *Durham Chronicle*, 26 January 1844, reported that a man had been charged with trespassing in a farmer's field on the Lord's Day, playing at spell and knor. The *Westmorland Gazette,* 20 December 1851, reported on two youths before the court for playing knor and spell on Sunday and for causing damage to a farmer's field at Collinfield near Kendal. The *Kendal Mercury*, 3 September 1864 talked about several men who had been placed in front of the pulpit of their church, where they were compelled to stand until the end of the service, holding their spells and knurs, cat-sticks, balls etc. The *Stamford Mercury* 8 February 1867 also reported that six boys in the Lincolnshire village of Waddington had been locked in the stocks for playing nor-spell on Sunday. The *Newcastle Courant* 22, January 1882, reported that two boys had been fined for playing knur and spell on Town moor, Newcastle on Sunday.

The use of public stocks as a means of humiliating and punishing people in public spaces by locking them in by their feet, had been around in England since the *Statute of Labourers* in 1351. Every town and village in England had some stocks. Although they have never been officially abolished, the last time they were actually used in England was about 1872. So the above-mentioned Waddington example of 1867 may have been one of the last cases. In some other countries around the world, stocks are still used. Even in 2020, some residents of the town of Chinú, Colombia in South

America, who had broken Covid-19 quarantine rules, were castigated by this method. Chinú is about three- or four-hours' drive south of Cartagena where I visited a few times in the 1970s with my old mate Guillermo Mesa (I called him Bill Table) to see his carbon black manufacturing plant. The stocks in my hometown of Colne were fairly unique. They were designed to hold three people and were also fitted with four iron wheels so that they could easily be moved around the town. Until the late 1900s they were kept in front of St Bartholomew's Church. These days I think they are kept in Colne Heritage Centre.

All the above instances involved admonishment for simply playing the game on Sundays. If illegal gambling or illegal liquor supply were also involved, which almost inevitably was the case, then it was a much more serious situation. Even as late as 1875 the *Manchester Evening News* was reporting a case in Leeds where a knur and spell promoter was fined one hundred pounds plus costs for allowing illegal betting at one of his events. If he couldn't pay, the alternative was six months in jail with hard labour!

If we want to know more about how it first came about that playing games, or doing other things on Sundays, was frowned upon by the church, we need to travel back in time much further than any of the above-mentioned monarchs to when the Romans were calling the shots. It all started in the year 321 AD when Roman Emperor Constantine decreed that working on Sundays was banned. Prior to that, Saturday had been the day of rest.

Constantine had spent quite a bit of time in England, in York, and also fighting the Scots north of Hadrian's Wall. He was also the same guy who changed the name of the Turkish city we now know as Istanbul, from its earlier name of Byzantium to Constantinople. It is very interesting that when Constantine issued this decree he was probably not a religious man. For some reason he had legalised Christianity in 313 AD, but he himself did not convert to Christianity until he was on his death bed in 337 AD. After that it was open slather. Give'em an inch and they take a mile!

The Catholic religion was dominant in Europe, including England, until King Henry **VIII** fell out with the Pope in the 1500s. However, as England moved away from Catholicism, they couldn't agree exactly what the replacement religion should look like. Over the next few hundred years splinter groups sprung up everywhere. Thus we got the Protestants, Anglicans, Puritans, Presbyterians, Baptists, Methodists, Wesleyans, Inghamites, Congregationalists, Nestorians, Calvinists, Moravians, Pentacostalists, Quakers, Episcopalian, Independents, Unitarianism, Sandemanians / Glasites and Papists. The latter were what the non-Catholics called Catholics. i.e. Popery, which in the early days was a pejorative term. As if all these non-Catholic splinter groups was not enough, the Catholic church itself had all manner of different orders such as Jesuits, Dominicans, Benedictines, Trappistines, Carmelites, Bethlehem Brothers, Cistercians, Order of St Augustine etc. Thus the big 'religious mess' we find ourselves in today is hardly surprising!

In the early days of both golf and knur and spell, back in Charles **II**'s reign, public anti-Catholic sentiment was very strong, and paranoia was rife. We just need to consider the infamous Titus Oates led Popish Plot conspiracy episode in 1678 to get a feel of how this manifested itself. In this instance the Jesuits in particular were falsely accused of planning to assassinate Charles **II** and were persecuted accordingly. While all this was happening, Charles's brother James, the Duke of York, himself a Catholic, was happily playing golf on Leith Links in Edinburgh. Also by this time, knur and spell in Baildon was probably in business again since the Book of Sports had long ago been destroyed in a big bonfire!

The very first religion which ever appeared in Trawden, the north east Lancashire village where I was raised, was the Quaker religion. The Religious Society of Friends (Quakers) had been founded in 1652 by George Fox after he had supposedly experienced a 'vision' on Pendle Hill in Lancashire just about eight miles from my birthplace. Long before the seventeenth century was out, there was already a Quaker community established in Trawden. Quakers flourished in Trawden for the next two hundred years, but they had fizzled out before the end of the 1800s. Evidence of their presence in Trawden can still be seen going over Mire Ridge at the old Quaker Burial ground which was established in 1658 near old Trawden Hall. From about the 1850s this very small cemetery was used by non-conformists. In 1922 one of Colne's most famous sons, Sir William Pickles Hartley, was laid to rest there. After finishing his education at Colne Grammar School,

William Hartley established one of England's biggest jam making empires. He was also a very prolific philanthropist. One of the many gifts he made to his birthplace town was Hartley Hospital near Laneshawbridge where my father Jack passed away in 1973. Son Jonathan and I visited this old cemetery in 2017. One of Hartley's very old giant cast iron jam making pans is permanently on display in Rock Lane Trawden, just around the corner from the Trawden Cenotaph and from my mum's house.

Another early church in Trawden was the Inghamite chapel in the tiny hamlet of Winewall which founded in 1752. This was one of the earliest churches started by Yorkshireman Benjamin Ingham after he had broken away from both the Church of England and the Moravian Church (Unitas Fratum). The latter had descended from the Bohemian Brethren form the 1400s. Ingham had earlier belonged to the 'Holy Club' at Oxford University alongside John Wesley et al. Winewall Inghamites closed several years ago. The only two Inghamite churches still open in England in 2020 are just a few miles away in Salterforth and Wheatley Lane. Winewall, Salterforth and Wheatley Lane were all knur and spell playing places. Moravian churches are still scattered across England. There is one in Dukinfield in Greater Manchester where I worked for five years prior to emigrating to Australia in 1983. It has been there since 1755. Knur and spell was played in Dukinfield too.

Moreover, it wasn't just playing games or gambling and drinking on Sundays that many of these groups were against. They were against any work being done on Sundays and against any shops or trading. In the 1800s the most vociferous group in England was probably the Lord's Day Observance Society (now operating in 2019 under a different name) which was founded by Anglicans in 1831. Over the years this group were against all kinds of things happening on Sundays. They wanted to ban Sunday newspapers, stop train travel and many other things too numerous to mention.

The *Sunday Trading Act* 1994 in England relaxed regulations considerably. However, Sunday bans had been difficult to enforce, and long before 1994 there had been a high degree of tolerance with Sunday activity.

In most countries in Europe, it was the Catholics who were most aggressive in this area. In England, although about sixty-per cent of the population are Christians, the Catholics only accounted for about eight per cent of the population, so they were not in control. It is quite different in many other European countries. In Poland, for instance, more than ninety per cent of the population are Catholics and in Italy about seventy-five per cent. They have much more success in those countries when trying to enforce the Pope's edicts. Other religions in England are still at a very low level, so their influence on this matter is also quite low. About five per cent of the people follow Islam, one point five per cent are Hindus and all other religions are less than one per cent. About twenty-five per cent of the English class themselves as non-religious. The split of religions in the UK is changing fairly quickly. By 2050 the percentage of both Muslims and Buddhists is expected to more than double. We can only hope that in future the Pope and his boys get their act together. We certainly don't want them wasting their time trying to bring paedophile priests to justice. They should be concentrating on the real sinners, the mums and dads who have the temerity to work on Sundays to try to put some food on the table for their kids!

Actually, all this anti-booze stance by the churches was somewhat hypocritical. For hundreds of years churches had used beer selling as a way for them to raise funds to help the poor and needy in society. These were referred to as 'help-ales' or 'church-ales'. However, when the Puritans came along in the late 1500s and 1600s, all this was frowned upon. Needless to say, Friar Tuck and his mates didn't give a monkeys about the Puritans. Monks had been brewing beers since the 400s. At its peak there were hundreds of monasteries across Europe involved in this business. They did it in a very scientific way and produced some very strong, high alcohol content beers. Not only did they sell beers to customers and travelling pilgrims, but they also consumed copious quantities themselves, as well as using the profits to help the poor and needy. Even today the monks are still up to their old antics. There are fourteen recognized Trappist monk monasteries around the world still with brewing operations. These can be found in Belgium, Netherlands, Austria, England, France, Spain, Italy, and the USA.

Although it has mostly been the monks who got stuck into the grog, the nuns didn't want to completely miss out on all the fun. Over the year several nuns have also brewed beers. One of the most famous, who may still be making her favourite tipple, was sister Doris at Mallersdorf Abbey in Bavaria. Nuns have been brewing at this convent since the late 1800s. The same site had been used by Benedictine monks for brewing since the 1100s. I am not really sure just how the monks and nuns rationalised beer brewing (and drinking) as part of their ascetism. But that is another story!

Chapter 18

More Romans, Dutch balls, a very special Derbyshireman and the bard

Just as a matter of interest, the date of 1618 has other historical golfing significance. It is the date when the 'featherie' golf ball was first invented which was a little leather case ball stuffed with compressed feathers. Little leather balls had been used in Scotland long before that date. From 1486 to 1618 they had been imported from Holland where they had been a biproduct of the Dutch Agricultural Revolution. The Dutch themselves probably got the idea from the Romans who had a hair-filled leather ball with which they used to play a game they called *harpastum*. King James, or more precisely his minister of finance, had become concerned about just how much money was being spent importing the balls from Holland, so he ordered that they be made locally in Scotland. In 1618 James **VI** granted a twenty-one-year patent to Messrs Melville and Berwick to manufacture golf balls in Scotland. However, there was one minor problem. The Dutch leather balls were stuffed with cow hair and so that the king's patent could not be challenged they presumably could not copy the Dutch balls exactly. The Scots had to make a significant design change and came up with the idea of stuffing the balls with feathers instead of cow hair. It is also probable that the Dutch themselves had patent protection on their cow hair golf balls. This is not such a major design change as it sounds. Both cow hair and bird feathers are chemically similar. Both belong to the keratin family. The Spanish, Italians (Venetians) and Dutch were all much more advanced than the English or Scots in those days in the evolution of patent protection. From 1589 'patents for inventions' were granted in the States General of the United Provinces of the Netherlands and were recorded in the 'deed of books' in Holland. Around that time King James was in the habit of granting 'letters patent' but these were often regarded by the public as an abuse of power by the Crown to help prop up favoured monopolies rather than to give protection to inventors for their new discoveries.

There is yet another very interesting fact about the year 1618 AD. It was the year that the first Dutch newspaper was published. If there was any patent dispute about golf balls going on between Scotland and Holland, something about it may turn up in these early issues which can already be found on-line. Unfortunately, *Ik spreek geen Nederlands*. For the next two-hundred and thirty years these 'featherie' balls held the roost until they were eventually knocked off their perch by the guttie ball which started to come in around 1850 or a few years earlier. OMG, the puns get worse!

The town of Baildon, mentioned earlier in relation to 1618, is surrounded by extensive moorland where the game of knur and spell was played. The *Leeds Intelligencer* 15 July 1824 reported on a match on Baildon Moor between two combatants for forty guineas a side. Baildon GC is on the edge of this moorland and was only founded in 1896. Knur and spell had pre-dated golf in Baildon by at least two hundred and seventy-eight years! Baildon Moor itself has far more history than this. In fact, as shown by a series of cup and ring marks on ancient granite rocks, it is known that there was Bronze Age activity going back to around 2000 BC. Australian readers with good memories will recall that Baildon GC is where Trawden-born Sam Walsh played his early golf. Sam lost to the great Ossie Pickworth in the 1948 Victorian PGA championship final at Commonwealth GC in Melbourne. Ossie is still the only man in history to win three consecutive Australian Opens. It would have been four if he hadn't started to lairise in the final round at the Australian GC, Kensington in 1949 when he was five shots ahead of Eric Cremin with only nine holes to play. Apart from Jack Harris, Ossie is also the only other man in history to have won three consecutive Victorian PGA championships.

Another interesting find was reported by the University of Sheffield in 2009. For some time before that they had been doing an archaeological dig on the ruins of an old Medieval manor house in Sheffield called Manor Lodge. This place had originally been built around 1525 and used as a medieval hunting lodge by the earls of Shrewsbury. It was mostly demolished in 1708 apart from a few old ruins and from that time an old pottery kiln was active on the site. During the dig they found some old ceramic knurs which were dated back to the early 1700s.

There is plenty about the game of knur and spell mentioned in newspapers of the 1800s and 1900s. However, it is more difficult to find written evidence about knur and spell going back to the 1700s, 1600s, 1500s or earlier. Before the 1700s there were no daily newspapers. They started to appear in the 1700s, but their sporting coverage was not extensive. A few odd reports can be found on golf in Scotland but nothing for golf in England. I never found any knur and spell reference in the newspapers from the 1700s, but trap-ball did appear throughout that century, as did football, stool-ball, and cricket. From the few reports found it was clear that playing sports was frowned upon. In the *Norfolk Chronicle* dated 9 July 1785, it talked about idle and disorderly persons playing at trap-ball and other games.

However, I did come across an article which mentioned the *Songs of Joseph Mather*. This gentleman was born in the small village of Chelmorton near Buxton in 1737. Buxton is in the Peak District of Derbyshire. It is about thirteen miles away from Baslow where we know knur and spell was played and about twenty-five miles from the knur and spell mecca of Sheffield. He moved to Sheffield in 1751 where he was apprenticed for eight years to a filesmith working in the cutlery industry. It was a very poorly paid job (one penny per month wage with an extra penny at Easter, Christmas, Shrove Tuesday and Whitsuntide), so he began writing ballads and broadsheets to supplement his income which he sold in the street for a penny or a halfpenny. Even in 1801 the Indenture of Apprenticeship in the Sheffield cutlery industry was still over a seven-year period and apart from the actual work duties other interesting things were also stipulated. e.g. No going to taverns or alehouses. No fornication or getting married. No playing of unlawful games (like knur and spell).

After he had served his apprenticeship he performed his ballads in the local pubs. He was like the Bob Dylan or the Sixto Rodriguez of the 1700s. His ballads were all satirical, giving social commentary of what everyday life was like for the ordinary working classes in those days. He loved to have a go at the bosses and anyone else in authority. In fact he was a Jacobin (not to be confused with Jacobite).This was a radical political group which had formed in the late 1700s inspired by Robespierre and the French Revolution. He lived in the insalubrious part of town known as Cack Alley which linked Lambert Street and West Bar in modern-day Sheffield. Sounds a bit like what Australians would refer to as Shit Creek! He could read but he couldn't write. He had friends who could write who used to scribe all his ballads. He was very familiar with the Bible and in one of his broadsheets he observed that the working-class people were more inclined in the 1700s to go and play football or knur and spell than they were to go to church. He even referred to knur and spell as a 'fine old Yorkshire game' which suggests that it had been played for quite some time before the 1700s. Mather also wrote a song in the 1700s called *The Trip Match* in which he wrote 'Last Easter Sunday, with bat, stick and trip, to Pitsmoor Firs I did eagerly trip'. This was more than likely a reference to a knur and spell match. Pitsmoor was a small village near Sheffield in those days. It has long since been swallowed up by the urban sprawl.

In the early to mid-1700s knur and spell playing was very popular among the working classes. This was because many of them were under-employed and consequently had plenty of leisure time. Knur and spell playing was something which kept them occupied and didn't cost much to play. When the Industrial Revolution started in the late 1700s this started to change as people found it easier to find full-time employment.

There is much about Joseph Mather to be found in the Sheffield Central Library. Joseph Mather died in 1804 aged sixty-seven. This was a fine old age to live for someone working in the Sheffield cutlery industry. In March 1857, an article in the *British Medical Journal* reported that average life expectancy for knife and file grinders was only about forty years, ranging from twenty-five to fifty-seven years. A few years before Mather died, a gentleman called Joseph Strutt wrote a book called *Sports and Pastimes of the People of England* published in 1801. This gives quite a bit of information about knur and spell and also talks about it being an old game, which again supports the idea that it went back further than the 1700s. Also, in the early 1700s John Wesley started the Wesleyan chapel movement. It was noted from the records of the Norfolk Street Wesleyan chapel in Sheffield from that period, that the workers in the cutlery industry were prone to heavy drinking and gambling linked to both football and the 'old game of knur and spell'. Nearly four hundred years later and things haven't changed very much. Compare the beer swilling and gambling culture associated with the relatively modern game of AFL in Australia! The drinking will be at least on a par and the gambling now will be much worse with instant touch-button phone access via dozens of betting 'apps' (applications) which can be downloaded from licensed bookmakers such as Ladbrokes, sportsbet, neds, bet365, betfair etc.

An interesting thing about Joseph Mather is that he used to get his broadsheets printed by a gentleman called James Montgomerie. James was a newspaper proprietor in Sheffield. Although he lived and worked for most of his life in Sheffield or other Yorkshire towns, he originally hailed from the town of Irvine in Ayrshire, Scotland. This is very close to where the Open golf championship was conceived at Prestwick. It is even closer to Dalry where we know knur and spell was played in the mid-1800s. Montgomerie died in Sheffield and to this day remains one of Sheffield's most respected citizens. Montgomerie had a religious upbringing. He was outspoken on humanitarian issues and often championed the causes of the ordinary people. From the broadsheets which he printed for Joseph Mather he would have been well aware of the propensity of the Sheffield working classes to play knur and spell on Sundays rather than go to church. Today we can still see a statue of James Montgomerie in front of Sheffield Cathedral. There should also be one of Joseph Mather and his donkey which he used to ride through the streets of Sheffield, seated backwards, peddling his broadsheet ballads.

The *Songs of Joseph Mather* were never published as a collection until 1862 when along came John Wilson with a great appraisal of the poems together with lots of explanatory notes etc. This publication gives a great insight of what life was like in Sheffield during the 1700s. Maybe the thing which stands out most is just how big a problem the drinking culture was in those days. There were almost four hundred pubs and alehouses in Sheffield at that time. Apart from beer and ale, the 1700s were notorious for the amount of spirits and liquor which was consumed. In 1743 the six million population in England and Wales gulped down about nineteen million gallons. By 1843, six years into Queen Victoria's reign, the sixteen million population were far more temperate. They only consumed about eight million gallons of the hard stuff! i.e. Three gallons each per year down to half a gallon each! It was not unusual in the 1700s for pubs to have boards outside openly encouraging hedonistic debauchery. For example there was one board which said, 'You can get drunk for a penny, dead drunk for two pence, and have clean straw for nothing!' In other words, you could sleep it off in the stables! Joseph Mather captured this in a ballad which he wrote, part of which said...

> 'then those that were able, retired to the stable, and slept
> with their nose in each other's backside.'

Obviously a group scatology session!

Maybe something similar was happening when Hilaire Beloc wrote 'and the tedding and the spreading of the straw for a bedding' in his famous *Tarantella* poem which he wrote a while after a night in a tavern at Canfranc in the Aragon Valley when crossing the Pyrenees in the early 1900s with a young lady from Scotland. Maybe he was trying to get to Roncesvalles on the French Camino and had missed the little yellow arrow?

By the first half of the 1800s it was a fairly common custom for beer and gin to be drunk mixed together in one drink. This drink was known as a 'dog's nose' which consisted of a generous tot of gin topped up in a pint glass with a dark beer or a stout beer such as Guinness which had been founded in Dublin in 1759. The resultant drink looked black in appearance like a dog's nose. It was apparently a favourite tipple of Charles Dickens (1812-1870). Maybe *Great Expectations* is what the Sheffield proletariat had after swilling down a few 'dog's nose' drinks!

By sheer coincidence, another Englishman who went on to have an enormous world influence, was also born in 1737 in the village of Thetford in Norfolk. He also came from a modest family and started work as an apprentice corset maker. His name was Thomas Paine. Like Joseph Mather he also had strong views about the inequities in society and became a prolific pamphleteer. After the December 1773 Boston Tea Party he went to America in 1774 where he didn't like what the government in London were doing to keep the people in the new colonies downtrodden. The American War of Independence began in April 1775. In 1776 Paine published a pamphlet there entitled *Common Sense* which was widely read in America and which supported full independence for the new colony. Later he also published *The American Crisis (1776- 1783)*. Both these documents had great influence on people like Benjamin Franklin, Thomas Jefferson, Abraham Lincoln, John Adams, George Washington and many others. He went back to England in 1787 and in 1791 he went to France from where he was actively involved in the French Revolution and also launched his famous treatise *Rights of Man* which had a go at the English monarchy and at the aristocracy in general. Indirectly all these happenings had a very big impact on the early years of Australia's history. Transportation to America was stopped and was re-directed to Australia (more on this later).

As we may imagine, Thomas Paine was a great hero in the eyes of Joseph Mather who himself was a Jacobin and quite an outspoken activist. In the early 1790s when Paine was being hounded by all the enemies he had made in England amongst the rich landed classes, Mather wrote and performed a poem called *God Save Great Thomas Paine*. When he performed this poem in his local Sheffield pubs he sang it to the tune of the current British national anthem. While all this singing and activism was going on, the plebs of Sheffield continued to booze, fornicate, gamble and play lots of knur and spell! Not necessarily in that order!

The Court Session Records provide much information for what was happening in the 1600s and will also be available for earlier centuries.

An interesting source of social comment is also provided by the works of Billy Spokeshave (aka William Shakespeare) who died in 1616 just before the *Book of Sports* was published. Billy was extremely prolific and wrote all his plays, poems, and sonnets between 1590 and 1613. He lived all his early life in Stratford-on Avon but did all his literary work in London. Neither of these were places where Knur and spell was played. However, the famous bard clearly showed from his writings that he was well versed in what was going on throughout England and even in the rest of Europe for that matter. He was particularly fond of Yorkshire where knur and spell was a very prominent sport. Yorkshire is mentioned many times in

Shakespeare's works, the first complete edition of which was published in 1623. I read somewhere that in one play or poem he talks about 'knur sticks' but I was unable to find the exact reference. Elsewhere I found references to him talking about football, tennis, quoits and also over fifty different other sports. Quoits is a game that throughout the centuries was often mentioned in the same sentence as knur and spell and is probably the older of the two games. He also refers to the 'playing of illegal games' so he was obviously well aware of the King Henry **VIII** Statute. It is perhaps interesting that even though Shakespeare referred to many sports in his writings, golf was not included in those sports.

For those who think I am being disrespectful to the famous bard by calling him Billy Spokeshave, let me offer this weak explanation. During my teenage years when I had to slog through *Julius Caesar* during English literature classes, this was the name by which he was affectionately known to myself and all my school pals. We didn't know it at the time, but I since learned that over the years there has been over eighty different spellings of this famous surname. So, yet another version is probably not going to make much difference. And sixty years later I still remember to beware the Ides and embrace the tides...as well as to mistrust men with a 'lean and hungry look.'

Shakespeare wasn't the only English literature subject which was given the insolent classroom schoolboy treatment. We had plenty of others too. One I have fond memories of was Matthew Arnold's epic poem, *Sohrab and Rustum*, which we always referred to as *Sore Arse and Rusty Bum*.

Chapter 19

Knur and spell, the Danelaw, Manchester United FC, slaves and potteries

At the end of the day, it is very difficult to know if knur and spell pre-dates the playing of golf in Scotland. But it almost certainly pre-dated most of the actual golf clubs in Scotland. However, when it comes to golf played in England that is a different story. Reasonably good evidence exists that knur and spell was at least played in England at the same time as golf began there and probably even earlier. Certainly, knur and spell pre-dates every single golf club in England. Why it spread much faster than golf across the northern counties of England and not across the whole of England is difficult to explain because trap-ball (a junior version of knur and spell) was played all over England from very early times (1100s and 1200s). Maybe because there were more open moors where they could play, away from built-up areas, could be the main reason. Probably most of the equipment used to play knur and spell was cheap and self-made, whereas golf clubs were made by professionals (blacksmiths or bowmakers etc). Golf too probably started that way but once they had the idea to form golf clubs and build golf courses, it became a much more expensive proposition.

The two main northern counties where knur and spell was played were Lancashire and Yorkshire. Documentary evidence takes knur and spell back in those counties to at least the 1700s and with the Baildon Hall find probably back to the early 1600s. Whereas the first ever golf club in Lancashire is said to be the West Lancashire GC founded in 1873 and the first in Yorkshire was the Cleveland GC founded in 1887. Royal Liverpool GC at Hoylake was founded in 1869 and was also in Lancashire at the time of founding. It has since been re-zoned as Lancashire's boundaries have shrunk. The previously mentioned Old Manchester GC founded in 1818, which still has club members but no course and no club house, probably needs to be somewhere in the mix. Also founded in 1869 was Alnmouth GC in Northumberland. The Colne GC, where I first got hooked as a caddie, was founded in 1901. The British golf legends Harry Vardon and John Henry Taylor had played an exhibition match at Colne GC in 1911. Both players beat the course record 73 on that day with Vardon creating a new record of 67.

Knur and spell had been played for at least two hundred years before organised golf clubs in northern England started to appear. However, it wasn't a structured sport. There were no formal clubs as such, and matches were usually arranged around pubs and drinking/gambling. Most of the time it was a question of challenge matches being arranged for an agreed stake money from each side. Such a challenge could be between two individuals or it could be between two teams. It didn't have a governing body. It wasn't played on designated pieces of land designed for the purpose. Any old field or stretch of moorland could be used, so long as it was long enough (at least three hundred yards) and providing the grass was short enough so that they didn't lose the knur too easily. The more isolated the field or stretch of moorland the better because that made it easier to conduct the illegal gambling and boozing part of the deal with less chance of being caught by the long arm of the law. Lancashire and Yorkshire are both geographically quite close to Scotland, maybe about one hundred miles away. County Durham, Westmorland, Cumbria, and Northumbria where knur and spell was played in the mining communities are even closer to Scotland. It is very possible, and indeed highly likely, that the Scots knew all about knur and spell from the Northern English. (Or the Northern English knew about golf from the Scots.) One thing is for sure. Yorkshire, Lancashire, Cumbria, Westmorland, Durham, and Northumberland are all much nearer to Scotland than Holland is, and you don't need to cross over water to get there.

The only thing which still puzzles me is the following. If knur and spell didn't develop until the 1400 or 1500s or even later, I don't know why they would have chosen a Viking sounding name several hundred years after the Vikings had been kicked out of Britain. Maybe it was because the switch from Roman to Anglo-Saxon, from Anglo-Saxon to Viking, from Viking to Norman and so on, was never a clean break. The transition from one to the other would take place over many generations. When the Viking army and government left England in the 1040s that doesn't mean that all Vikings would leave the country. Many would have been born in England and inter-married with Anglo-Saxons. Not forgetting that the Anglo-Saxons themselves came from the European continent in the first place - mostly from Germany, Holland, and parts of Northern Denmark. All of them left a legacy of their individual cultures which lasts even to this day. The last Anglo-Saxon kings of England were in fact Edward the Confessor, who reigned from 1042 – 1066, and King Harold **II**, who had a very short time in power before he was defeated at the Battle of Hastings later in 1066 by William the Conqueror.

On reflection, I must conclude that the highest concentration of place names where knur and spell was played was in Yorkshire. There were quite a few, such as Colne, which were in East Lancashire or in South East Lancashire, but only a handful of miles across the border from Yorkshire. There was also mention of Lincolnshire, County Durham, Westmorland, and Northumbria, but all these places are relatively close to the border with Yorkshire. I didn't find any reference to knur and spell being played in West Lancashire (i.e. along the Irish Sea / Fylde coasts) which had been invaded by the Norwegian Vikings and not the Danes. However, there is newspaper evidence, *North West Evening Mail*, that big crowds were attracted to knur and spell matches in the Rusland Valley in the 1930s. The Rusland Valley is in the Lake District area of England. It is fairly remote and sparsely populated. These days it is part of Cumbria which borders on Scotland. In the old days, prior to 1974 when the county borders were changed, it was part of Northern Lancashire which was detached from the rest of Lancashire. Knur and spell in this part of Lancashire was not restricted to the Rusland Valley. According to many articles found in *Soulby's Ulverston Advertiser and General Intelligencer* newspaper dating back to the 1800-1850 period, knur and spell was widely played throughout the Furness and Cartmel Peninsulas, the Lake District and Cumbria. Places such as Hawcoat and Newbarns (suburbs of Barrow-in Furness), Ulverston, Pennington, Newland, Dalton-in-Furness, Greenodd, Bouth, Lowick Bridge, Rusland,

Kirkby-in-Furness, Hullater, Ulpha, Walney, Little Urswick, Lindal in Furness, Marton, Cartmel, Spark Bridge, Sandside, Beetham, Witherslack, Oxen Park, Backbarrow, Ireleth, Staveley, Far Sawrey, Natland, Middleton, Much Urswick, Jerry Beck, Haverthwaite, Kirkby Lonsdale, Sellat Mill, Nibthwaite, Browedge, Rosside, Collinfield, Oxenholme, Helm Hill, Longlands, Hutton, Crooklands, Killington, Windermere, Ambleside, Grizedale, Ullswater, Milnthorpe, Bowness, Asby, Crake Valley, Near Sawrey, Grayrigg, Holmescales, Winton, Sedbergh, Askam, Penny Bridge, Arrad Foot, Stainton with Adgarley, Levens, Appleby, Penrith and Kendal. Most of these were tiny villages or hamlets with only a few hundred people or less. Kendal is only fifty-five miles and Penrith only thirty miles from the Scottish border. What we must remember is that through the years and in different counties, knur and spell has been known by different names. In the *Lancaster Gazette* 5 April 1806, I discovered that 'spell and nor' was played at Witherslack in, what was then, part of Westmorland (now in Cumbria). Witherslack is a miniscule hamlet in the middle of nowhere! In the *Carlisle Patriot* 22 August 1818, 'spell ore' was played at Beetham in Westmorland. In the same year and same county, there was a court case reported in the *Westmorland Gazette* from Appleby Assizes relating to illegal 'spell ore' playing. Appleby is only about forty miles from the Scottish border. Knur and spell was also played at Cockermouth and Longlands which are only thirty-five and twenty-eight miles respectively from the Scottish border. Mid-way between Lancaster and Kendal is the tiny hamlet of Arkholme where knur and spell was played in the 1850s. This place is unique for an unusual reason. It is one of only two 'Happy Villages' in Lancashire. i.e. villages where all the men sent to fight in WWI returned home safely. Arkholme sent fifty-nine men and Nether Kellet sent twenty-one men. Strangely enough both these villages repeated this happy experience in WW2.

In 1891, the small village of Milnthorpe, about eight miles south of Kendal, had a population of around one thousand people. In the 1840s and 1850s, spell and knor was regularly played near at least four pubs in that village i.e. United Friends Tavern, Bull's Head Inn, Coach and Horses Tavern and Station Inn. Entrants at any one of these events would be several times the number of golfers who played in the first British Open golf tournament in 1860. The Bull's Head and the Coach and Horses still survive in 2020.

Indeed, I believe that the vast majority of places where knur and spell was played would have been part of the area known in the Viking Age as The Danelaw. The Danelaw was essentially the part of England which was north of a line drawn between London and Chester which was governed by the Danish Vikings. That line was marked by Watling Street which was an old Roman road between the two cities. There is no doubt that throughout what had earlier been known as The Danelaw area, knur and spell was extremely widespread. It was played in many hundreds of towns, villages and even hamlets. Many of the villages and hamlets where it was played never became big enough to justify having their own golf course. In fact, many of the hamlets where it was played only consisted of a few dozen houses and were so small that they were never even big enough to have their own church. But they probably had a pub! In a newspaper cutting dated 14 February 1901 there was a report on a match which took place at Much Urswick (now called Great Urswick). Apparently, the village champion had lots of mates who spent much of their spare time making knurs for him.

Although the Lancashire epicentre for knur and spell was probably Colne, the game was found much further west and much further north than that. In the *History of Leagram* by John Weld it talks about farming families in villages around the Forest of Bowland and Ribble Valley area getting together in the late 1700s and early 1800s to play knur and spell. In places such as Leagram, Clayton-le-Dale, Wilpshire, Whitebirk, Goosnargh, Longridge, Whittingham, Grimsargh, Inglewhite, and Ribchester which are all north of Preston and north-west of Clitheroe where knur and spell was also played.

Although many hundreds of the places where I found reference to knur and spell being played were small towns, villages or hamlets, the game wasn't just restricted to country areas. I found a newspaper article from 1844 (*Manchester Courier*, 6 December) where the local council of the suburb of Harpurhey were announcing plans for a new public park which included facilities for 'cricket, knur and spell, and football.' This was very interesting because Harpurhey is only three miles away from Manchester city centre which was in those days located in South East Lancashire. It was also interesting because at that time knur and spell was obviously considered to be a major sport played by the working-class people on a par with cricket and football. Apart from very small concerns at Blackheath in London and Old Manchester GC, golf in England wasn't even on the radar screen in 1844. Harpurhey is also only about three miles away from Kersal Moor where the Old Manchester GC played in those days. Interesting also that the golf boys didn't get a look-in at the new park development plans? Even closer to the city centre than Harpurhey is the Deansgate area of Manchester where knur and spell events were arranged in 1866.

Knur and spell was also played at Newton Heath which is only one mile away from Harpurhey and is where I started my polymer studies in 1959. And of course, any sports history buff worth his salt will know that Newton Heath is also the place where the world's most famous sporting club was born. This club, the brainchild of a Liverpudlian, started off life as Newton Heath LYR Football Club (Lancashire & Yorkshire Railway) in 1878 and originally played in green and gold colours. Maybe they harboured secret aspirations to be Aussies? They became the mighty reds of Manchester United in 1902. Almost certainly the top knur and spell players in those days would have earned more money than Manchester United football players. Just imagine that! Manchester United didn't move to Old Trafford until about 1909. At least fifty years before that move knur and spell had been played at Old Trafford. In *Bell's Life in London and Sporting Chronicle* 23 December 1860 a man called Parker played a Blackburnian at Old Trafford using wooden heads and wooden knurs. Interesting that Old Trafford was said to be 'near' Manchester at that time even though it is only two miles from the city centre.

Having given United a plug, I had better not leave out Manchester City FC. They were formed as St Marks FC in 1880 at West Gorton which is also just a few miles south east of the city centre. Gorton, which is a Viking derived name following a battle between the Danes and the Saxons, was also famous in the past because it was the home of Belle Vue Gardens. This was a big entertainment complex which also had a zoo attached. Almost thirty years before Manchester City FC were formed, I found newspaper articles for knur and spell being played at Belle Vue in 1851.

As the city of Manchester expanded it didn't take long before all that area had been swallowed up by the city. The place where they played knur and spell in the 1850s and 1860s would probably not have been exactly where the MUFC stadium is currently located. Just eight hundred metres away is the Old Trafford Cricket ground which started in 1857 as the Manchester Cricket Club and later became the home of Lancashire cricket. I also doubt whether knur and spell would have been played at the Old Trafford Cricket Ground because it would not have been long enough to cope with the distances that wooden knurs were being hit (up to three hundred and seventy-two yards). It could possibly be that knur and spell was played in the old Royal Botanical Gardens which was opened as early as 1831. This was a twelve-acre site which had belonged to Sir Humphrey de Trafford. The gardens had been opened by the Manchester Botanical and Horticultural Society and the site had been chosen by John Dalton who was a giant of atomic theory in the late 1700s / early 1800s. I later studied polymer chemistry and polymer physics at John Dalton College in Manchester after it had been opened by Labour Prime Minister Harold Wilson in 1964. Incidentally, John Dalton was born in 1766 near Cockermouth in Cumbria where knur and spell was also played.

In 1856 or 1857 there was a massive art exhibition held at the Old Trafford Botanical Gardens site. Even to this day it has been the biggest art exhibition held anywhere in the world. However, I suspect that the most likely scenario is that knur and spell was probably played in a field adjoining one or more of the old pubs which existed in Old Trafford at the time. One likely place was the Bishop Blaize pub which was later re-named as the Talbot. Another was the Trafford Hotel which was run in those days by a Mr Lambert. Both these pubs are situated on or close to Chester Road and are about mid-way between the football ground and the cricket ground. They are also close to where the Botanical Gardens would have been. Lambert also had a thirty-six-acre farm nearby where in 1850 he was also holding steeplechase and pigeon shooting events. Whatever the case, one of the main drivers which helped to make Old Trafford the great sporting hub we see today was the cricket-ground railway station which was opened in 1862. Known for many years as 'Warwick Road Station' it was the first station of its kind in England. Apart from knur and spell, cricket and horse racing, another big sport throughout the 1800s which the working classes participated in was pedestrianism. Effectively this was long distance walking, often up to one thousand miles. It was enjoyed all over the Manchester area and not just at Old Trafford. In fact, it was a nationwide activity which often involved very heavy gambling. Just like knur and spell, cricket, horse racing and cockfighting, the wagers placed were often much higher than what was happening in golf. After the first World War, part of the Royal Botanical Gardens was developed into the White City Stadium which hosted greyhound racing, motor-cycle dirt track riding and stock car racing. It was all demolished in the late 1900s and converted into a big shopping precinct.

Many other sporting activities also flourished at Old Trafford in the mid-1800s and virtually all of them were promoted by pub landlords in fields attached to their pubs. Apart from the sports mentioned so far there were professional quoits matches, prize fighting, polo matches and even a champion team of American baseball players played there in 1874. Probably the biggest sport of all between 1840 and 1870 was professional athletics which mostly involved both running and walking events. Pubs all over the wider Manchester area, including Old Trafford, had running and walking tracks attached to them.

At the previously mentioned Newton Heath where MUFC was born, there were two famous grounds. The Copenhagen Grounds belonged to the Shears Inn pub. This ground opened in 1857 and had a six-hundred-yard track with a two hundred and thirty-five yard straight for sprinters. There was also the Royal Oak pub grounds which opened a six hundred and fifty-one-yard cinder track in 1864.

Perhaps an even more important pub venue, and one that is very relevant to both my wife Kathleen and me, was the Snipe Inn in Manchester Road, Audenshaw. This pub had built what was probably the earliest athletics track attached to a Manchester area pub by about 1840. By the 1860s they had a six hundred or seven hundred yards cinder track with a three hundred yards straight. In those days Manchester was part of south east Lancashire. Audenshaw borders on Denton where Kathleen was born and lived until she emigrated to Australia. As a teenager she had to pass through Audenshaw each day to attend Ashton-under-Lyne Grammar

School. In the mid to late 1960s I lived in Denton and played rugby in Audenshaw. I played for Old Aldwinians RUFC which was Audenshaw Grammar School Old Boys and had the honour of being the very first non-Audenshaw GS pupil ever to play for the club (having been a Colne GS old boy). Their most notable player had been Eric Evans MBE who played for England from 1948 to 1958 and captained them for his last two seasons. Eric was President of Old Aldwinians from 1960 – 1966 and it was during this period when I joined the club, having previously played several seasons as scrumhalf with Colne & Nelson RUFC. The Snipe Inn was one of our favourite after-match watering holes along with the nearby Old Pack Horse Inn near Guide Bridge station in Audenshaw. Today the Snipe Inn still survives, but sadly the Old Pack Horse bit the dust in February 2020. Maybe as a casualty of Covid.

Although the Snipe Inn hosted quite a few knur and spell matches, this was a very minor part of what they did. The previously mentioned athletics activities, known incidentally in those days as pedestrianism, was one of their major 'outside pub' attractions. Challengers came there from all over Britain to compete in walking, running, and jumping events. In 1914 there was a seventy-five-yard handicap sprint event which attracted one hundred and twenty-five entrants including two guys from Australia. According to the *Sporting Life* newspaper dated 8 October 1862, Hiram Yeadon from Leeds competed in a 'standing spring jump' contest at the Snipe Inn against Joseph knight for twenty pounds. Around that date Hiram also regularly competed in knur and spell matches, rabbit coursing and dog racing events all over Yorkshire. The same Hiram Yeadon had also been involved in a very serious altercation involving Wesleyan Chapel reforms in the mid-1850s and had been injured during an incident with a blunderbuss.

However, athletics, knur and spell and dog racing were only one of the many things they did at the Snipe. Between 1837 and 1937, when most of the land behind the pub was sold off to developers, they were entrepreneurs extraordinaire. They hosted sparrow and pidgeon shooting matches, rabbit coursing, dog racing, bicycle racing, horse racing, wrestling / boxing matches, trotting races, quoits matches, bowling matches, angling competitions and in 1928 only the second ever motor bike speedway racing event in England was held there.

They also had a Pleasure Ground behind the pub which had its own lake where the fishing events were held and its own bowling green. Brass bands played regularly in this area which also had a large separate building which served as a dance hall with music provided by Droylsden Old Band. This building also held a Rhubarb Show in 1863 where prizes were also given for other garden products such as 'heaviest stick of celery'. The Pleasure Grounds also boasted a hot house, a vinery, and a horse racing and trotting track.

The land behind the pub must have been quite extensive because in 1864 they were also advertising good pastureland for cows and horses. In 1899 they were holding monthly horse sales there. In 1914, one of their racehorses, a mare called Lady R, which had been put out to pasture a few years earlier, was buried in the Snipe Beer Garden.

All the above-mentioned things were in addition to normal 'inside pub' activities and usual community responsibilities for that era such as holding public auctions and coroner inquests etc.

A very interesting feature of all these mid-1800s pub activities was that competition entrants or paying spectators could make payment using postage stamps as currency in lieu of cash. The first postage stamp in the world, the famous Penny Black, had only arrived on the scene in 1840, which was the same year the Snipe athletics track opened. Evidently the entrepreneurial pub landlords were quick off the mark when it came to adopting new technology. According to *Bell's Life* the Snipe were still accepting stamps as cash in 1862. Of course by the time Kathleen and I were operating in the Denton / Audenshaw area in the 1950s to 1960s all these attractions, along with the now very rare Penny Black stamps, had long since disappeared. But the Snipe Inn itself was still standing and we did enjoy the odd beer there occasionally.

While all this pub activity was happening at pubs all around the Manchester area, a similar thing was also happening at pubs in all the large industrial towns of Yorkshire. All these places had large population growth in the 1800s and this gave rise to a big expansion in the number of pubs. For example, in the 1820s Bradford had about eighty pubs, but by 1875 this had increased to around one hundred and forty.

While the Snipe, Copenhagen and Royal Oak Grounds were some of the bigger venues in the Manchester area, hundreds of other smaller pubs were also getting in on the act. In Yorkshire some of the larger venues included the Quarry Gap Grounds in Bradford, the Cardigan Arms Grounds in Leeds, the Queen's Grounds in Barnsley, Halifax Racecourse and Doncaster Racecourse which also hosted all kinds of sporting activities. But again, hundreds if not thousands of other smaller Yorkshire pubs, and pubs in all the former Danelaw counties, were doing likewise.

The 1860s probably saw the peak of the professional athletics with very big purse money on offer, high numbers of spectators, and massive gambling. However, professional athletics was short-lived. Mostly because it had a very bad reputation for match fixing and other corrupt activities which often gave rise to violent disputes. It declined rapidly after 1870 and from that time onwards amateur athletic clubs started to appear. It didn't take long for these guys to get organised and by 1880 the Amateur Athletic Association of England was founded (AAA's). Not too long after that the first athletic club in Victoria Australia fired up when the Melbourne Harriers formed in 1890.

Some of the runners also fancied their chances at knur and spell. According to *Bell's Life* in 1842, one such runner was Henry Molyneux who ran under the alias of the Moor-end Stag. He was challenged by Thomas Greenwood that year to both run and play knur and spell at Heaton Norris near Stockport in Cheshire. They also had a return match at both sports in the same year at Mount Skip, Wadsworth near Halifax.

Another Manchester suburb where I found knur and spell had been played was Denton which is just five miles from the city centre and where I worked for much of the 1960s. I was employed by a company called Rotunda which was part of the giant BICC electric cable making group. One of the best things I worked on there was my involvement in the formulation of a high voltage cable repair tape based on polyisobutylene which is a saturated polymer with no weak double bonds. Because of this it had exceptional thermal ageing properties. The unique properties of this tape were that it would stretch several hundred percent and then self-lock. It would also self-amalgamate under water. It was an ideal tape for high voltage cable repair under adverse field conditions where it could be used in a non-crosslinked configuration. For many years it was probably the company's bestselling and most profitable product. The other more important thing about Rotunda is that it was where I first met the 'divine package', her indoors. Undoubtedly the luckiest day of my life!

Denton borders on Gorton and is close to Abbey Hey, Audenshaw, Chadderton, Hollingworth, Broadbottom, Openshaw, Dukinfield, Haughton Green, Stalybridge, Hyde and Levenshulme which were all knur and spell playing suburbs. All these places in the Manchester suburbs (apart from Old Trafford) are on the east side of Manchester. They are located on or close to the main cross-Pennine roads which lead to the big Yorkshire knur and spell centres of Sheffield and Barnsley both of which are a little over thirty miles away. The knur and spell world championship in 1878 was held at Abbey Hey which is four miles from Manchester city centre. The winner picked up three hundred pounds. The Open Championship golf winner in 1878 at Prestwick GC picked up just eight pounds! Abbey Hey is very close to Belle Vue, Gorton where Manchester City FC kicked off. It is highly likely that knur and spell didn't survive too long in all these inner-city areas. Knur and spell didn't have its own grounds. And it was quite a dangerous game to be played where it shared public spaces with other activities. There were many newspaper reports about people being struck by flying knurs or by heads coming off pummel sticks.

Manchester had a long history going back to when it was a military camp for the Romans. After that it was basically Anglo-Saxon under the rule of the Kingdom of Northumbria and in the year 870 it was sacked by the Danish Vikings. The 1800s, when knur and spell and all the other mentioned sports were booming in the Manchester area, it was all fuelled by the booming cotton industry. In fact during that period Manchester even had its own nickname...Cottonopolis!

If it is not just a big coincidence that Knur and spell was just played in the Danelaw area of England, then all this strongly suggests that knur and spell was played in England long before golf was played in Scotland. This is because the Danelaw period started and finished a long time before the Scots started playing golf in the 1400s.

We should remember however, that although Yorkshire, East Lancashire, Lincolnshire, Durham, Cumberland, and Westmorland were the chief areas of the former Danelaw where knur and spell was played, probably none of these existed by those names in the Viking days. In fact, the whole of the north part of England was known as the Kingdom of Northumbria in those days. Places such as Bedlington, East Sleekburn, Morpeth and West Moor in Northumbria where knur and spell was definitely played are all north of the Tyne River and in fact are all north of Hadrian's Wall. Knur and spell was played in this region which is only forty or fifty miles from the Scottish border and maybe one hundred miles from Leith. The first time the word Yorkshire appeared in the *Anglo-Saxon Chronicle* was in 1065. It was 1182 before the Lancashire name turned up. The Vikings had been and gone by that time.

During the Viking days there were three pockets of land north of the Tyne River which were bought by the Bishop of Durham and thus became part of Durham County, even though they were on the opposite side of the River Tyne to Durham. For hundreds of years starting from the early 900s, Bedlington was capital of a small area called Bedlingtonshire which included East Sleekburn and bordered on Morpeth. They were all associated with mining and knur and spell. This small enclave existed until 1844 when Bedlingtonshire became part of Northumberland. This may possibly explain why knur and spell was found in this area because there were many knur and spell places in County Durham south of the Tyne. i.e. Places such as Durham, Chester-le-Street, Barnard Castle, Bishop Auckland, Darlington, Hartlepool, Middleton-in-Teesdale, Ferryhill, Bishopwearmouth, Mickleton, Bowbank, Copley, Stockton-on-Tees, Seaton Carew, Bearpark, South Church, Norton, Shiney Row, Houghton-le-Spring, Carrville, Newbottle, Philadelphia, New Lambton, and a myriad of other smaller places far too numerous to mention.

The other two small enclaves were Norhamshire on the River Tweed and right on the Scottish border and Islandshire which covered Lindisfarne where the first Viking raiders landed. Both these enclaves were very small and didn't have significant coal mining interests.

Just for completeness there was another very tiny Durham enclave in North Yorkshire and much further south than Durham. This was

Craikshire which centred around Crayke Castle and just two miles east of Easingwold. I didn't find any knur and spell there but in every direction it was surrounded by old knur and spell playing places.

West Moor, which was also a mining place, was not in Bedlingtonshire. It is about eight or nine miles south of Bedlington but still a few miles north of Newcastle. Australian trivia buffs will be aware that West Moor and Killingworth is where arguably the greatest invention of the Industrial Revolution came from. This is where coal miner George Stephenson invented the world's first ever steam driven locomotive in 1814. He lived in West Moor for several years when he worked at Killingworth Colliery. George's parents were both illiterate. He himself did not start to learn to either read or write before he was eighteen in 1799. When George was doing all his best work, knur and spell was booming in all the places he lived. Later in his life he settled at Tapton near Chesterfield in Derbyshire. This is very close to all the knur and spell hub around Sheffield and Chesterfield. Being a coal miner and being surrounded throughout his life by knur and spell it would be surprising if at some point he did not play this game.

Knur and spell does not seem to have been played much in the southern counties of the Danelaw area (e.g. Essex, Suffolk, Cambridgeshire, Norfolk, Huntingdonshire, Bedfordshire, Hertfordshire, Northamptonshire, or Leicestershire). However, all these were very small size counties compared to Yorkshire which was bigger in area than the next two counties combined. It is also true that far fewer Vikings elected to establish settlements in these smaller counties than the ones who went to Yorkshire. In any case, those next two counties included Lincolnshire which was the second biggest area in the Danelaw, and knur and spell was certainly played in that county. There were literally hundreds and hundreds of towns, villages, hamlets and even cities across the whole of Northern England where knur and spell flourished. In fact, in the former Danelaw area there are at the very least three thousand different place names. It was very popular in the mining regions but by no means restricted to these areas. What we must consider is that for each of the hundreds and hundreds of places where knur and spell was played, and maybe even several thousand places, we are not talking about just one knur and spell player coming from each of those places. We are talking about dozens of players from each of those places and probably hundreds of players from some of the bigger places. Which means that at its peak in the 1800s there were many thousands of knur and spell players in England.

It is true that there were some Viking settlements in most of the southern Danelaw counties. However, most of these counties were close to the Kingdom of Mercia border. There was continual fighting between the Vikings and the Mercians which would not have been conducive to game playing.

East Anglia in particular is a sizeable area which was at one time part of the Danelaw where knur and spell appears to have been absent. There could be several reasons for this. Firstly, East Anglia was always a very strong Anglo-Saxon area. King Wuffa was the head honcho back in the 500s. Even though it was conquered by the Danes and became part of the Danelaw in 869 AD it didn't stay that way for long. It was re-conquered by Edward the Elder and became part of the Kingdom of England in 918. East Anglia was probably the first place in the world where English (i.e. Old English) was spoken.

When the Danes were there it was always sparsely populated. A big part of East Anglia back in those days, all around The Wash area, was under water or at least very marshy. The Fens were not drained until the 1600s with technology from the Dutch. This included much of Norfolk, some of south Lincolnshire, part of Cambridgeshire and part of Suffolk. This was obviously not suitable terrain for playing knur and spell.

Having said that, I did come across an old wooden spell being offered at auction in June 2017 by Holts Auctioneers of Wolferton, a tiny hamlet in the royal Sandringham estate in north Norfolk. If they had acquired this item locally it could perhaps suggest that some knur and spell was played in Norfolk. In any case Wolferton is only about fifteen miles from the border with Lincolnshire, where we know knur and spell was definitely played.

Although knur and spell was present in Lincolnshire, which was also part of the Danelaw, it did not appear to have been as widespread as perhaps may have been predicted. Lincolnshire, and especially the Lincolnshire Wolds, was extensively settled by the Vikings. However, if we look at places which are found on or close to the one hundred- and forty-seven-mile-long Viking Way, which starts in Rutland and ends near the River

Humber in north Lincolnshire, we can indeed find places such as Lincoln city, Waddington, Grantham, Stixwould, Gainsborough, Stamford, Stow and Skellingthorpe where knur and spell activity was found. However, I was expecting to find much more evidence in the Lincolnshire Wolds itself where there are dozens of tiny Viking settlements. Maybe the famous English Poet Laureate, Alfred Lord Tennyson, wrote about knur and spell? He was born at the small village of Somersby in 1809 and spent much time in this county.

It is possible that the reason for lack of evidence is because knur and spell was known by quite a few other names in that region. I may just have not entered the right words into the search engine. For example, across the other side of the Humber in Hull and the Holderness region, which is close to Lincolnshire, knur and spell was known as dab and trigger. In Lincolnshire it was often called kibble and nerspell. There may be other names which I am completely unaware of.

The other more likely explanation is the low overall population and low population density factors. After Yorkshire, Lincolnshire is the second biggest county area wise in England. However even in 2019, Lincolnshire's population is only fifteen per cent the size of Yorkshire's. And the distribution of those fifteen per cent is interesting too. There are about eleven hundred different towns, villages, and hamlets in Lincolnshire, but only three of them with any size. i.e. Lincoln (100,000), Grimsby (88,000) and Scunthorpe (80,000) which are all very small compared to the large urban areas in Yorkshire. In 1850 Lincolnshire's population was only about 407,000 versus 755,000 today. It never had the big, densely populated, industrial towns and cities which Yorkshire and Lancashire had. It could be possible that a certain critical mass was necessary before extensive game playing started to evolve.

Leicestershire and Rutland were also part of the Danelaw, but where to date no knur and spell playing activity was found even though there are quite a few places with Viking names. Both these counties have low population, especially Rutland which has the lowest population of any English county (only 17,000 in 1801). In that same year Leicestershire only had just over half the population of Lincolnshire. In addition to this, both these counties were in the very south of the Danelaw and bordering with the Kingdom of Mercia with whom there was continual conflict.

The two biggest knur and spell playing counties were Yorkshire and Lancashire with about 370 and 420 people per square kilometre respectively. Compare this with Northumberland, which mostly stretches from Newcastle up to the Scottish border, where we only find about 62 people per square kilometre and consequently less knur and spell playing.

Much of the general coverage in non-sporting newspapers of the 1800s and 1900s tended to describe knur and spell as a mystical game of little consequence which was esoteric to Yorkshire. However, this gives a completely inaccurate picture. It does not take long when trawling through old newspapers going back to the late 1700s and throughout the 1800s, to discover that during that period knur and spell was a very much bigger game than golf. It was played over a very much larger area than golf was played and in many more individual places. It also had far more participants than golf in the UK and this probably didn't change until after World War I, despite the massive explosion in golf from the late 1800s. In 1850 there were an estimated total of fifty or sixty golfers playing in England at two clubs. A single knur and spell handicap in 1850 at some remote village at the back of beyond could easily attract more players than that. Multiply that by several thousand and we can get an idea of just how much bigger knur and spell was than golf.

Furthermore, this picture can be gleaned even though for most of its existence, much of the knurr and spell was played surreptitiously. The police were continually arresting people for playing on Sundays during church service times. They also fiercely hounded players and spectators alike on any day of the week if they got a smell of any illegal gambling or illegal liquor supply. The latter were an integral part of the knur and spell scene, so they often played in remote moorland venues and the 'doggers-out' were an important part of the promoter's setup arrangements. For many of the knur and spell gatherings there would have been a deliberate attempt not to advertise the event in advance so as not to give the police a head start. When matches were advertised, they often went into the newspapers on the day of the event or the day before the event, to give the police less time to get organised. The adverts were generally very short and kept deliberately confusing for anyone who wasn't familiar with the game. For this reason, it always remained a 'mystical' game for English people outside of the northern knur and spell playing counties. This mysticism can easily be seen by reading old articles on knur and spell published by southern based newspapers. They didn't know what knur and spell was and they were constantly trying to solve the mystery! Because the people in the south of England were generally ignorant about the niceties of knur and spell they often used to make fun of the game when they wrote about it. No doubt this was done to try to disguise the fact that they knew nothing about the game and to add some padding in order to bulk up the article. Articles on knur and spell were also appearing in newspapers and magazines all across the USA in the 1850 – 1900 period. But they had no idea what knur and spell was all about either! I suspect that even within the northern former Danelaw counties of England detailed knowledge of exactly how knur and spell was played was not known by the wider community outside of the knur and spell playing cohort. It was never shown on TV, it was a sport which didn't lend itself to outside radio broadcasts, there were no books on the subject, videos / YouTube did not exist, and newspaper reports were generally very short and not readily understandable to the general populace. Everyone in the Danelaw would know of its existence but few would be able to explain its finer points. Even though I have researched this game for several years, I am sure that a die-hard knur and spell player would argue, and probably justifiably, that I still don't really know all that much about it.

One place I found reference to knur and spell being played which appeared to break the pattern, was Bromsgrove just north of Worcester. In the *Worcester Chronicle*, September 1847 there was a report about a woman being hit on the head by a flying knur at Bromsgrove. This was way south of the Danelaw area which existed at the time of the Norman Conquest. However, I later discovered that in the very early Viking days, this part of England was also part of the original Danelaw area. It was the eastern part of the Kingdom of Mercia and had been re-conquered in 920 AD by Edward the Elder who was the son of King Alfred the Great. Another unexpected place where knur and spell was played is Newport in Shropshire. However, this was a similar story to the Bromsgrove one. It had been part of the original Danelaw area but only for a short time until the Danes were driven out and it reverted to the Kingdom of Mercia.

The Vikings had also been in other Midland counties including Nottinghamshire and Staffordshire and at least some knur and spell was played in both these counties. Knur and spell was played at Tickhill on the South Yorkshire / Nottinghamshire border and at Somercotes near the Derbyshire / Nottinghamshire border. Somercotes was the centre of the east Derbyshire coal mining area. It is about sixteen miles south of Chesterfield, only seventeen miles north of Nottingham and fifteen miles north of Derby. Knur and spell was also played south of Chesterfield at Boythorpe. Knur and spell was played at the Rifle Volunteer Inn, Somercotes in the late 1800s. It was also played at Sutton-in-Ashfield and Babbington which are both in the Nottinghamshire coal mining area and less than ten miles from Somercotes. This place is an interesting one because from its name we can tell that it was an old Saxon settlement. Just two miles away there is Kirby-in-Ashfield which was an old Danish Viking settlement. In the part of Nottinghamshire north of Sherwood Forest, which was part of the Danelaw, there are many old Viking settlements such as Scrooby, Serlby, Thoresby, Bilby etc all of which are just a few miles from both Tickhill and Sutton. Apart from a small area in the south, Nottinghamshire mostly has borders with and is almost completely surrounded by South Yorkshire, Derbyshire and Lincolnshire which are all knur and spell playing counties. So, it wouldn't surprise me if knur and spell had been played there too. Although almost every single one of the hundreds and hundreds of places where knur and spell was regularly played were inside the Danelaw area, there were a few Danelaw places where knur and spell did not seem to be present. I suspect that these places were where the Vikings went, and maybe had short stays, but didn't settle.

The only reasons I could think of why this should be the case are as follows. The Vikings were not a single nationality. There were Norwegians, Danes, and Swedes. When the Great Heathen Army arrived in 865 / 870 AD they consisted of all three types of Vikings. They landed in the South of England and more or less followed the old Roman Road of Watling Street as they moved north, plundering as they went. Watling Street went through or close to several places in the East Midlands such as Tamworth, Repton etc and the Vikings did leave some evidence of their presence in these places. Even as late as the 1980s the remains of two hundred and fifty people were found in an ancient burial site at Repton in Derbyshire which historians have dated to the 900s AD. They are pretty sure that these remains were from the Great Heathen Army. This mixture of Vikings seemed to have a different agenda to the ones who landed on the east coasts of Yorkshire and Lincolnshire. These were essentially Danish Vikings. The Vikings who landed on the Wirral in Cheshire and on the west coast of Lancashire where my ancestors probably came from were also different. They were mostly Norwegian Vikings who had arrived in England via Ireland. If knur and spell really was a legacy from the Vikings, it would probably have been from the Danish Vikings and not the Norwegians or the Swedes. However, this is not cut and dried because at one point in the Viking history even the Norwegian Vikings ruled York. Historians tell us that Norwegian Viking, Eric Bloodaxe, was twice King of Northumbria in the mid-900s although they still haven't reached a consensus as to exactly what he did when he was in England. That's a great soubriquet but nowhere near as impressive as Thorfinn Skullsplitter of Orkney! We do know that both Eric's spells as king were short i.e. 947-948 and 952-954. Later on King Cnut of Denmark was also King of Norway (1028 - 1035)! So the whole history of the Vikings is much more complex than I can do justice to in a story about knur and spell. All I can do here is provide food for thought. I can just picture in my mind Bloodaxe playing Skullsplitter at a game of knur and spell and I claim the film rights accordingly! Perhaps Bloodaxe and Skullsplitter are more correctly defined as 'epithets' rather than nicknames.

Apart from their famous runestones and the Icelandic Sagas (poems and stories), the Vikings didn't leave much documentary evidence that I know about. There is much debate and disagreement amongst celebrated historians about just where the Vikings went and what they did. I am not one of those celebrated historians, so my observations don't carry much weight!

There are, of course, plenty of places throughout the Danelaw area where Viking artefacts (coins, weapons, jewellery etc) have been found. These include Cuerdale and Bedale which are mentioned in another chapter. Many of these have also been found in York which was the Viking Danelaw capital for quite a while. In the Viking days York was the second biggest city in England. Only London was bigger. Perhaps the most exciting Viking find ever wasn't any of the previously mentioned items. It was a very large coprolite! In 1972 excavation work was going on in Coppergate, York on a building site where a new bank was to be erected. Imagine the excitement when they discovered a gigantic paleofeces dating back to the ninth century. This well-preserved fossil, which has ever since been colloquially known as 'the Lloyds Bank turd', was in one piece and in perfect condition. Measuring in at eight inches long and two inches wide, it could well be the first bank 'deposit' ever made and is the largest human excrement ever found anywhere in the world. The constipated depositor, whose eyes must have been watering at the time, was believed to be a Viking...maybe even Eric Bloodaxe himself? Whatever the case, the experts do know for sure that this was definitely not bullshit!

From what I can gather there were Danish, Norwegian and Swedish Vikings who came. Mostly Danish and Norwegian and not many Swedish. Most of them came directly from specific areas in Denmark or Norway. But some of them had already been plundering in Holland, France, and Spain before they arrived in Britain and came indirectly from those countries. Most of the Swedish Vikings did their plundering in places east of Sweden. Danish and Norwegian Vikings mostly travelled west or north-west from their homelands.

There were basically two types of Viking. The first ones to arrive just made spasmodic raiding trips. Like the Norwegian Vikings who sacked the monastery at Lindisfarne in Northumbria, killed a load of monks and sailed off into the distance with all their treasures. These were just opportunistic trips by gangs of men looking for easy targets. After that Vikings started to arrive who had a different agenda. They wanted to steal the land away from the locals and settle down there. They brought their women with them and settled all throughout the Danelaw area.

The Norwegian Vikings pinched huge parts of Scotland. All the offshore islands like Orkneys, Hebrides, Shetlands etc, as well as northern parts of Scotland like Caithness and Sutherland. The Norman conquest of England was in 1066 but much of the west of Scotland was still controlled by the Norwegians well into the 1200s. In fact this remained the case until the Battle of Largs in 1263. They also went to Ireland, Iceland, Greenland, and Isle of Man. But, just like today, Irishmen never shy away from a fight and they eventually kicked the Norwegian Vikings out. So, they sailed across to England and settled in the Wirral and on the west coast of what is now Lancashire.

When the Norwegian Vikings landed on the Irish Sea / Fylde coasts they didn't have to do much fighting to get the land because at that time this region of England was wild and remote with hardly anyone living there. In other places both Norwegian and Danish Vikings fought side by side. At other times they fought against each other. Jorvik (modern day York) was capital of the Danelaw and was under Danish rule. However, at one point even York was ruled by Eric Bloodaxe who was a Norwegian Viking.

It is more or less the case that all the places where knur and spell was played were in the part of the Danelaw which was settled by the Danish Vikings. I found only one instance of knur and spell in all the places which were primarily settled by the Norwegian Vikings. This was at Dalry near Ardrossan in Scotland and that only started in the nineteenth century, courtesy of an itinerant Yorkshireman. I found nothing in Ireland, Iceland, Greenland, Isle of man or West Lancashire. However, knur and spell was played in York where Eric Bloodaxe was for a short while. It was also played in Preston and places close to the Ribble estuary where some of the Norwegian Vikings landed when they landed from Ireland on their way to York. Having said that, by studying the place names in all the Danelaw counties, we can find that places which are typically Danish, such as towns and villages ending in 'by', are scattered about everywhere and intermingled with towns which are typically Norwegian. In other words, there appears to be no clear demarcation lines separating the Danes and the Norwegians.

I did read about knur and spell being played at Dukinfield and Stalybridge which are now located in the Manchester Tameside area. Prior to 1974 they were part of east Cheshire. However, this is a long way from the Wirral and is very close to the Yorkshire border where knur and spell was rampant. The only places in West Lancashire where knur and spell got a mention was with the Sutton coal miners near St Helens and there was also some evidence of knur and spell being played at Widnes. Both these towns are only ten or eleven miles away from Liverpool. Widnes is situated on or near the River Mersey which was considered to be the boundary separating the southernmost point of the Danelaw with the old Kingdom of Mercia. Knur and spell was definitely played in the northern part of the Derbyshire Peak District which is near the Yorkshire border and only a handful of miles away from Sheffield which was a knur and spell epicentre. The *Derbyshire Courier,* 25 August 1906 reported a match at Brimington near Chesterfield and others at Norton and Unstone (*Derbyshire Times and Chesterfield Herald*, 16 February 1861). It was also played at Clay Cross, a mining village, which is five miles south of Chesterfield. Baslow (*Derbyshire Courier*, 4 March 1837) and Bakewell in the Derbyshire Peak district also played knur and spell, as did the village of Tansley near Matlock. It was also played in Staffordshire at places such as Biddulph and Walsall.

Biddulph Moor in Staffordshire, where knur and spell was played, is only eight miles north of Stoke-on-Trent. This is in the heart of the Staffordshire Potteries region which began in the 1600s. I don't know if knur and spell was played in the original six small towns which were eventually swallowed up and became Stoke-on-Trent. However, the game of northern spell did feature on a child's porcelain mug which was available from the Staffordshire Potteries during the 1800-1849 period. It is absolutely certain that many of the pot knurs used in the knur and spell game were manufactured in this region. Regent Pottery of Hanley, which is bang in the middle of the Potteries, was a regular advertiser of knurs in the late 1800s and early 1900s in the Yorkshire Post and Leeds Intelligencer newspapers. So too were Normacott Art Potteries of Fenton. In 1916 they were selling one-inch diameter glazed pot knurs at fifteen shillings per thousand as listed in the *Yorkshire Evening Post*. This makes pot knurs a very cheap commodity at less than one farthing each!

There were also plenty of old potteries in Yorkshire. One of these, Leeds Pottery, was founded in Hunslet in 1756. Almost from the start it was a serious rival to Wedgewood. There were also old potteries at Woodlesford and Swillington Bridge which, like Hunslet, are also Leeds suburbs. Yet another was the Rockingham Pottery at Swinton near Rotherham which were also big knur and spell playing areas. No reference to knur making at any of these potteries has been found to date. But they were all located in the centre of massive knur and spell playing regions, so it is highly likely that they would have supplied some knurs. I imagine that knur making would have been a very minor part of their business. Their main items would have been high quality chinaware such as dinner plates and teapots. If they made knurs it would have only been to use up some of their manufacturing waste scrap. The Staffordshire and Yorkshire Potteries took a bad financial hit following the Napoleonic Wars with France (1803-1815). During this period many of the potteries were fighting for survival. It could have been at this time that they started making knurs in a search for alternative products to help fill their equipment. This timeline would certainly match the dates when pot knurs started to appear in newspaper reports about knur and spell matches.

The transition from wooden and stag knurs to pot knurs was a very slow process. It was probably at least one hundred years before wooden and stag knurs completely disappeared. All the long knock distance records were achieved using wooden knurs which had a rough carved surface and were also heavier. The smooth surfaced pot knurs did not lend themselves to big hitting.

Even older than the Staffordshire and Leeds potteries was the pottery at Potovens, a small hamlet just north of Wakefield. It was very close to the modern-day village of Wrenthorpe. Excavation of this site in 1968 revealed pottery kiln activity between 1475 and 1780. Although there is no evidence to date that this pottery made any knurs, the possibility cannot be completely ruled out either. Every single hamlet and village in this area was a strong knur and spell playing area. This includes Potovens, Alverthorpe, Wrenthorpe, Wakefield and Ossett amongst dozens of others. Many of them such as Potovens itself and Alverthorpe don't even exist today. The latter became part of Wakefield as early as 1834. They are both part of England's disappearing village story discussed in more depth elsewhere in this book.

The only places in the south of England where knur and spell was mentioned in *Bell's Life* or *Sporting Life* were as follows. There was a match played in November 1862 at the West London Cricket Ground in the Old Brompton Road between two top Yorkshire exponents of the game.

One of these players was Job 'Nelly' Pearson. He often featured during that era in knur and spell, single wicket cricket and quoits matches. Sometime during the 1860s he moved over to Philadelphia in the USA and ran a saloon there. In 1875 he re-appeared on the English scene and claimed to be the American Quoits champion. That year he lost to the All-England Quoits Champion, George Graham, in a match for four hundred pounds. Whether or not he played knur and spell in the USA while he was there is not known. However, what we do know is that in 2020 there is a folk music group called *Knurr and Spell* which has been operating in the Chapel Hill and The Triangle area of North Carolina for the past ten years. There may be a story behind how they came to get this unusual name. If this had been a Yorkshire group it may not be all that unusual. But for an American group to choose this name it could have more significance. Maybe some old descendant from Job Pearson had moved into that area with his knur and spell stick? Chapel Hill is over four hundred miles away from Philadelphia so that would be stretching the imagination somewhat...but not impossible. At this point the Open Golf Championship in Scotland was in its fifteenth year and was going great guns. The facetiousness is overwhelming! In 1875, played at Prestwick GC, the total purse was twenty-one pounds with eight pounds paid to the winner and thirteen pounds shared between the next seven finishers! The top ten places were filled by Scots. Even a tiddly winks match would have probably attracted bigger crowds and paid more money than golf in 1895! Yes, tiddly winks was yet another game which originated in pubs.

In April 1888 there was a similar exhibition game played at the Essex North London Club in Islington. Both these were obviously exhibition matches to promote the sport in that area. Not many Londoners turned up to watch those matches and so far as I know knur and spell never gained a sizeable foothold in the London area despite a few clubs there. It reminded me of the futile attempts the AFL have had over the years to promote their tinpot game of Aussie Rules football in the UK. They never got more than three men and two dogs watching their games. I am being mean when I say that. A few thousand people did turn up in London to watch AFL. But considering the fifty-six million people in the UK which includes around four hundred thousand Australian ex-pats (two hundred thousand living in London), the AFL exhibition match went down like a damp squib!

Just about the same time that knur and spell was enjoying a mini revival in Lancashire and Yorkshire, some students at the Borough Road College in Isleworth started a knur and spell club which was announced in the *Hammersmith and Shepherd's Bush Gazette* dated 14 October 1960. Rugby nerds will be interested to know that this college is about two miles away from the famous Twickenham rugby ground. I have no idea how long this college club functioned or where they played.

Knur and spell exhibition matches were not the only sports where men from the north of England participated in during the 1800s in the London area. According to the *Sydney Morning Herald* 8 October 1864 there was a big swimming match held on the River Thames. A Manchester man competed against a London professor in a race over two miles from Hammersmith to Putney. The Mancunian picked up the £200 winner's prize. This event had been held annually for several years prior to 1864.

According to the *Buckinghamshire Herald* 26 February 1859 and the *Luton Times Advertiser* of the same date, a lot of people were at Mentmore in Buckinghamshire to watch a knur and spell match. Pearson of Mentmore met Burton of Cheddington in a challenge match. As far as I know this Pearson was not related to the Job Pearson previously mentioned. Knur and spell was not often seen in this part of England even though it was still technically in a former Danelaw area. Mentmore is about forty miles north of London. Both Mentmore and Cheddington are also about forty miles away from both Royston and Therfield Heath where Georgie Villiers played golf in the early 1600s. Knur and spell may have been more popular in Buckinghamshire than the *Herald* and *Advertiser* reporters were aware of. There were several newspaper articles in 1876 which involved separate instances in both Chesham and Denham of holly trees being stolen to make knurs with and the culprits being hauled before the beak. These two places are fifteen to thirty miles south of Mentmore and are much closer to London.

Modern day Buckinghamshire is in fact on the border between the former Danelaw and the Anglo-Saxon kingdom of Wessex. Although there may not have been big Viking settlements in Buckinghamshire, many skirmishes occurred there involving the Vikings. Over a long period Viking weapons, jewellery and other artefacts have been found in many places in Buckinghamshire e.g. Stone Bridge, Castle Hill, Iver, Marlow, Taplow, Wendover, Fingest, Turville etc, many of which are even south of Mentmore and in the area of the Chiltern Hills. The widespread nature of these finds and the amount of jewellery may indicate that many Viking women were probably there, so it perhaps wasn't just a question of fighting on the way through. Maybe they hung around in that area longer than is generally recognised. As recent as 2020 a mass grave burial site was found at Buckingham involving more than forty bodies. There has been some suggestion that these may have been Vikings.

In *Bell's Life* dated 24 April 1859, there was a report on the first ever nurr and spell club formed in London. It was called the Paragon United Amateur Nurr and Spell Club which had been formed by thirty or forty gentlemen living near the Caledonian Road, Holloway. They had apparently organised their first season to play at a site next to the City of London Cricket Ground in Paul's Road, Camden Town. Their club meetings were held at the Caledonian Arms Tavern in Holloway. Caledonia was of course the Roman name for Scotland. I was unable to find anything about how long this club survived or if there was any Scottish connection. However, it would not surprise me if this club had been founded by ex-pat Scots with modest means who wanted to enjoy hitting a little ball with a stick but who could not afford the Blackheath GC way of life. In any case, Camden and Holloway are about ten miles from Blackheath. In 1859 it would have taken quite some time to cross London in a horse and carriage to get to Blackheath. There were no other golf clubs in the south of England at that time.

Which came first, the chicken or the egg? Golf or knur and spell? Well, chicken came from a Germanic/Dutch/Old English background and egg came directly from an Old Norse (Viking) background. I would guess that egg came first. If I take that as a good omen, then my money would be on knur and spell pre-dating golf! But you won't find this written up in any by-law (yet another word borrowed from the Vikings) and even if it did pre-date golf, I can't find any evidence that the Scots had heard of knur and spell. At least I can't find any very *early* evidence that the Scots knew about it. They certainly knew about knur and spell in the early 1800s with regular comments about big Yorkshire knur and spell matches cropping up in Scottish newspapers from that period. I have also seen reference to knur and spell being called 'poor man's golf' in Scottish newspapers dating back to the late 1800s. There is an abundance of evidence that knur and spell was played in all the English counties which bordered on Scotland, so it would be just about impossible for them to never have heard about it. And just to throw a spanner in the works, I even read in the 1874 edition of *The Yorkshire Magazine* that Knur and Spell may have come from the German *Knorren und Spielen*. If this has any credibility it may even date back to when the Saxons landed in England from Germany after the Romans had left in the late 400s. Oh, don't I wish I was a philologist!

Even if knur and spell did date back to Viking days or earlier, there would have been many periods in the Middle Ages when this game or any other game may have struggled. In the early 1300s there was a major famine in England which wiped out about five per cent of the population and this was followed in 1349 by the Black Death which was even more catastrophic with an estimated two or three million people succumbing. Then for much of the 1400s there was the War of the Roses between Lancashire and Yorkshire when forty or fifty thousand people died, and the Tykes gave us a bit of a hiding at the Battle of Towton. In the 1600s many more people than that died during the Civil Wars. I don't know if knur and spell was ever played at Towton. It may well have been because it was certainly played only two miles away at Tadcaster.

Could the following be the missing link? It is well documented that a good proportion of the English population in ancient times were slaves. Slavery had existed in Britain long before the Romans came and although the number of slaves is hotly debated by historians, figures of ten to twenty per cent of the population are often mentioned. Even when the *Domesday Book* was written in 1086 it showed that ten per cent of the English people were still in slavery. Out of a total population of 1.7 million that meant there were at least one hundred and seventy thousand slaves. This was twenty years after William the Conqueror had completed the Norman conquest of England. From this time onward the situation started to change, and slavery had just about disappeared by the year 1200. Of course, that didn't mean the English people abandoned slavery altogether. Having been slaves themselves, they eventually got into slave trading in a big way. In the late 1500s and early 1600s the English monarchs were jealous of all the success that Portugal and Spain were having with their empire building, so they began to build their own empire. The notorious slave trade between Africa and the Caribbean was started and by the 1700s slavery was the biggest contributor to the English economy. It wasn't abolished until the 1830s when a man called William Wilberforce, from my mother's hometown of Hull in east Yorkshire, introduced his famous legislation into the British parliament.

When the Vikings arrived at England in 793 AD they were very much involved in the slave trade. Particularly on their raids in Scotland and Ireland they would take prisoners and sell them as slaves. Dublin was one of the big centres where slaves were sold. They also sold many of their slaves in Iceland and modern technology shows the effect of this very clearly. The DNA of today's Icelandic people includes a very high percentage of both Scottish and Irish blood.

However, for reasons unclear, the Vikings in the Danelaw area of England had begun to free many of their slaves even before the Norman Conquest. Maybe it was because they had been introduced to Christianity and this had already started to change their way of thinking? Whatever the reason for this change, it has been recorded in several places that the freed slaves in the Danelaw area enjoyed a much higher degree of freedom than anywhere else in England. What is more, the Danes had generally assimilated well with the people they had conquered and found a way to live peacefully.

In fact, of the estimated one hundred and seventy thousand slaves still in England after the Normans came, only about six thousand lived in the Danelaw areas. The slave population outside of the Danelaw, especially in the southern counties of England, was four or five times of that inside the Danelaw. The Normans fairly quickly abolished slavery or at least they replaced it with feudalism and serfdom which was maybe a slightly less onerous life for the people involved. The Lancashire and Yorkshire people celebrated in the usual way...by bonking! In the period from 1086 to 1190 the English population increased from 1.7 million to 3.1 million. This was probably one of the largest percentage population increases in English history (more than eighty-one per cent).

The Vikings had a very big influence on English culture long after the Norman Conquest. Indeed, many of the Danish Laws which had been in force pre-1066 were continued for several hundred years after King William took over. In fact many of the words which we still use today in our legal system were Viking words or ideas. The word 'by-law' came from the Vikings. The first time the first semblance of a 'jury' to settle disputes was during the Viking period. They set up democratic assemblies (courts) which they called 'Things' all over England and in any other place they went such as Iceland, Orkneys, or Isle of Man.

Between 1100-1135 Henry I was King of England. This overlapped with David I being King of Scotland (1124-1153). During that time, the area in the Danelaw around the modern-day city of Sheffield, was known as Hallamshire. King David married Maud of Huntingdon, who was the daughter of Walteof, the Earl of Huntingdon and Northampton which was part of the Danelaw. Walteof was the last Anglo-Saxon earl to retain his status after the Normans had conquered England in 1066. Through his marriage to Maud, King David of Scotland effectively gained control of his wife's sizeable land and property in England. This included Hallamshire and large areas around modern-day Sheffield, which had been a very strong area for Danelaw and was also a very strong area for knur and spell. It may have even been the epicentre for knur and spell. Even though he was King of Scotland, David spent over thirty years of his life living in England, which was about half of his life. Much of this would have been in Hallamshire where knur and spell was king!

King David I also made great effort throughout his reign to increase Scotland's territory on the west side of Britain. In 1136 King Stephen of England ceded Carlisle and parts of Cumbria to King David under the Treaty of Durham. But David wasn't content with that. He also had his beady eyes on Westmorland and the northern part of Lancashire. Knur and spell was extremely widespread through all these northern English counties.

Of course they were not called Cumbria, Westmorland and Lancashire in those days. Everything had been part of the kingdom of Northumbria until it started breaking up in the 900s and 1000s. Northumberland today is just a vestige of what the kingdom of Northumbria had been back in the day.

Another very interesting quirk of English and Scottish history which also involves Yorkshire is the following. During his reign, King David of Scotland made many plundering raids into northern England. In 1136, to appease King David, King Stephen of England signed over the town of Doncaster to Scotland. Doncaster is in South Yorkshire and is over one hundred and seventy miles from the Scottish border. This 'giving up' of Doncaster was also officially part of the Treaty of Durham. To this very day, Doncaster has never officially been given back to the English by the Scots. Technically, this town in Yorkshire still belongs to Scotland! Why is this interesting? Because Doncaster was a big knur and spell playing region. Doncaster is also adjacent to ALL the major knur and spell centres in Yorkshire. It is seventeen miles from Barnsley, twenty-one from Wakefield, twenty-three from Sheffield, thirty-three from Leeds, forty-one from both Bradford and York, forty-two from Lincoln, forty-three from Halifax and forty-seven from Hull. If knur and spell did emanate from the Danelaw days, then this is yet another very strong reason why the Scots would certainly have known all about it from very early on.

So, if knur and spell had been played in the Danelaw before the 1100s or in what had been the Danelaw during the 1100s, especially in the Sheffield area, the Scots would most likely have known about it through King David and his entourage. And, if knur and spell had come into England via the Anglo-Saxon route and not via *nurspel*, then the link via the Anglo-Saxon, Walteof, may also be significant. If this had happened, then it would mean that the Scots knew about knur and spell at least two hundred and fifty years before golf started to be played in Scotland. The extra liberty which the freed slaves in the Danelaw enjoyed, may help to explain why knur and spell took hold strongly in the northern counties and not in other parts of England. The beginning of the end for the Danelaw started in 1042, at least two decades before the Norman conquest. But its impact was still felt for a long time after that. Ironically, William the Conqueror, the first Norman King of England, was himself a descendant of Norwegian Vikings!

If I was to try to identify just ONE place in England where knur and spell started, my gut feel would be that Hallamshire could well be that place. Hallam existed long before William the Conqueror and long before the Domesday Book was written. i.e. From Roman times and through both the Anglo-Saxon and Viking periods. I also think that King David of Scotland may well be the link between knur and spell and golf starting in Scotland. He had very strong ties with England. He envied the progress that was happening in England and in Europe generally, and wanted a piece of the action for Scotland. The infra-structure and subsequent amelioration process he set up would have lent itself perfectly to copying all things English, but certainly with the twist of trying to de-Anglicise them somewhat and give them a Scottish flavour. But alas, this is all pure conjecture...no proof!

Even if we forget about knur and spell altogether, another question which still bugs me is this. Anglo-Dutch relations have been going on for over two thousand years. They started even before Caesar's conquest of Britain. Since that time there has been a continual interchange of Dutch and English people which included soldiers, refugees, missionaries, workers, and businesspeople. For example, during the 1100s and 1200s, after the Norman conquest, many Flemish weavers came to live in England. Indeed, the Dutch were instrumental in the formation of the English Guild system during that period. There was also a big collaboration between the English and Dutch during Elizabeth I's reign. Whether it be wool farming, textiles, clocks, printing, draining the fens in East Anglia, steel and knife making...the list goes on. The Dutch helped England develop in so many areas. In fact, at any given time there would have been far more Dutch diaspora living in England than would be living in Scotland. Even today people of Dutch origin living in England still outnumber the Dutch living in Scotland by almost ten to one. With a much bigger Dutch diaspora in England than Scotland, why would colf or *kolf* take off in Scotland and not in England? (the possible answer to this question comes later. Continue reading) Maybe because trap-ball and knur and spell were already well established in Danelaw England?

A fact that we should not lose sight of is the following. If knur and spell is indeed a very ancient game dating back to the Vikings or even the Anglo-

Saxons, then it is possible that both colf, kolf and knur and spell came from the same place. The Anglo-Saxons arrived in England after the Romans left. They came from Germany, Denmark, and Northern Holland. The Vikings in the Danelaw were mostly from Denmark. The games of colf and kolf were mainly from Northern Holland where some of the Anglo-Saxons came from and where Danish Vikings were once in charge. The Angles came from Southern Denmark where the Danish Vikings came from. Germany supplied the Saxons and borders on both Denmark and Northern Holland. Before the Romans arrived, a Celtic tribe called the Brigantes ruled most of the area we know call Yorkshire. They called it Brigantia. These Celts also came to Britain from somewhere in continental Europe but there is much dispute among historians about their exact origin. It was quite some time into Roman occupation before they were finally sent packing. It is widely believed that the Scottish game of shinty, the Irish game of hurling, the Isle of Man game of cammag and the Welsh game of bando, which all involved the use of a crooked stick and a little ball, all go back to Celtic days. The Irish even had a stick and ball game called *cluichi puill* which translated means 'hole-game' and was played over one thousand years ago in Ireland. Who is to say that the modern game of golf was not inspired by one or more of these Celtic games?

If we go back in history even further than the Celts to 6500 BC we arrive at a place with the intriguing name of Doggerland. (No, it has nothing to do with fornication!) This is the date when scientists believe that Britain finally separated (physically not politically) from mainland Europe. The separation was a long process which probably started about twelve thousand years BC when sea-levels started to rise dramatically after the last major Ice Age. Prior to the separation Britain had been a peninsula joined to Europe along the coasts of Holland, Denmark, and Germany. This includes the place where kolf came from and also includes where the Vikings came from who established the Danelaw. Doggerland only received that name in the 1990s and was named after the famous Dogger Bank in the North Sea. This area, which is a large sand bank in a shallow part of the North Sea, is famous for cod and herring fishing. It was named after seventeenth century Dutch fishing boats called doggers. At one stage Dogger Bank was part of a larger area which fully connected modern Britain to Europe and was subsequently named Doggerland. During the process it went through a stage where it was an island in the middle of the North Sea before becoming completely submerged. In recent years archaeologists have been dredging the shallow submerged area around Dogger Bank and have been finding all kinds of artefacts to prove the earlier existence of Doggerland. I don't know much about the people who lived in that area during the Mesolithic or Neolithic periods, but I can't imagine they played with sticks and balls. Having said that I understand that some students believe that the Basque people came from the hunter gatherers and farmers of that era and apparently, they have modern-day DNA evidence indicating a genetic make-up which supports their claims. There is not full agreement however between genetic researchers about just where the Basques or the Basque language originated. I think the jury is still out on that one!

Intriguing to think that the first European golf club ever to be established outside Scotland was very close to the French Basque country at Pau in Southern France with the Pyrenees nearby. It is even more interesting to note that the first golfer from continental Europe to win the Open championship was a Frenchman born in Biarritz in the French Basque country and not far from Pau. His name was Arnaud Massy. He won the Open at Hoylake in 1907. He was also the first man to win the French, Belgian and Spanish Opens. Although he came from the French Basque country I don't know if he was a Basque. His surname doesn't sound like a Basque one. However, his father was a sheep farmer, and many Basques followed this profession...still do! It is also known that Arnaud was a good player of *pelota vasca* which is a traditional sport in the Basque country even to this day. *Pelota, cesta punta* and *frontón* are all versions of the same game that involves hitting a small ball with the hand, a paddle or a curved basket strapped to the arm. After Arnaud Massy we had to wait seventy-two years before another golfer from the continent won the Open in 1979...the late great Severiano who came from the Asturias region of Spain which is very close to the Basque region in the north of the country.

Chapter 20

The Lunt, Lunt Meadows, Lunts and more Lunts

Digressing for a moment, and for the umpteenth time in this book, I should say something more about the first Lancashire and Yorkshire golf clubs and the areas where they are located. West Lancashire GC is one of the ten oldest clubs in England. It is at Blundell Sands on the Irish Sea Coast in the Sefton area of Liverpool. This is about twelve miles south of Royal Birkdale GC. It was founded during a meeting at the Seaforth Hotel in 1873. This part of Lancashire is well and truly 'Lunt territory'. Just four miles east of Blundell Sands is the small village of Lunt which until the 1600s was always referred to as 'The Lunt'.

Prior to the 1600s, and from the late 1100s and early 1200s, it was just a small hamlet. The first documented reference to the village of Lunt was in about 1250 in the records of Cockersand Abbey. The Lunt surname was taken from this hamlet which itself was named by the Vikings. Our branch of this family is known to have originally moved from this area to Colne, Nelson, and Burnley in north east Lancashire in the late 1800s and early 1900s. Following archaeological finds less than ten years ago in the area of Lunt Meadows, it is now known that human activity was occurring in that area about eight thousand years ago during the Mesolithic hunter gatherer period. These finds were made in the area which lies in the flood plain of the nearby River Alt and included primitive flint tools and evidence of permanent habitation. Lunt Meadows has significant peat deposits and is currently a conservation area.

The Lunt surname seems to have first appeared in the late 1200s or early 1300s, but prior to that other variants of the name such as Lund, Lont, Lond and Lount were commonly used. I have never attempted to trace our ancestry back to year dot, but there are lots of mentions of different 'Lunts' dating to at least the 1200s in the village of Lunt and in nearby villages such as North Meols, Thornton, Sefton, Melling, Ince Blundell, Aintree, Great Crosby, Bispham, Homer Green, Marshside, South Hawes, Netherton, Litherland etc. The best source of this information is found in *Townships: British History On-Line*.

For example, in 1292 there was a Simon de Lunt, son of Adam de Lunt, who was defendant in a fishery case. In the early 1300s Richard de Lunt was a notable member of the Lunt village community, who granted his son Henry a messuage and croft in that village. After the Norman conquest French and Latin were the two main languages spoken in England, hence the 'de Lunt'. In 1309 there was a Roger de Lunt. He had a son called Robert who granted his son John a house and curtilage in the village of Lunt. In 1342 there was a John Lunt who had a son Robert. Robert also had a son called Robert who sold some land that year known as the 'Cole Yard' to Richard de Molyneux. Also in the 1300s there was a Richard de Lunt, son of Margery de Lunt who was the daughter of Simon de Lunt. In 1336 there was a Henry de Lunt who was granted a messuage and curtilage in 'The Lunt' in Sefton. A curtilage was an enclosed area attached to a house, like for instance a courtyard. A messuage was a house with land attached. In 1717 a John Lunt registered a leasehold estate there. John, like many people in that area, was a Papist (old name for Roman Catholic). This may go some way to explaining why knur and spell was not popular in West Lancashire. However, a more likely reason is because the Fylde / Irish Sea Coasts / Wirral are where the Norwegian Vikings mostly landed after they had been kicked out of Ireland. Knur and spell appears to have been mostly played in areas settled by Danish Vikings. Another reason why knur and spell may not have taken off in this area was because for hundreds of years before and after the Viking Age, much of this area was very marshy with significant wetland areas and peat deposits.

About four miles away from Lunt, in a different direction to Blundell Sands, lies the village of Aintree. This village was made forever famous in English folklore history in 1829 when a local pub landlord leased some land from the second Earl of Sefton and founded the world renowned Grand National Steeplechase which is a four mile two-and-a-half-furlongs horse race over very high fences. About four hundred years earlier, in 1426, Robert de Ridgate granted land in Aintree to Nicolas del Lunt.

Less than five miles from the village of Lunt, travelling east, is the village of Melling. In 1309 Richard de Lund paid homage in regard to tenements in Melling. In 1342 a Richard de Lunt was trustee in relation to a property transfer in Melling. This Richard de Lunt was the clerk of the Lunt village. In those days a clerk was a highly respected position in the community. In the *History of the Corporation of Old London*, the job of clerk dates from the 1270s. The vast majority of the population were illiterate in those days. Only clerics and clergymen were literate. The word clerk was synonymous with scholar.

Not long after Richard de Lunt effected the Melling deal, all hell let loose in England when the Black Death (bubonic plague) ravaged the country in about 1348. By 1350 a big proportion of the five or six million people living in England would have 'gone for the early bath'. Living conditions in this area of Lancashire during that period would not have been great and for sure they would have seen their full share of cadavers. I don't know if our learned kinsman survived the pandemic or not.

Three hundred and fifty years later another Lunt achieved national notoriety in England. His name was John Lunt, and he was a central player in the infamous Lancashire Plot of 1694. This involved a group of prominent wealthy landowners from the area surrounding Lunt village, including from the Molyneux and Blundell families. These had been French Norman families who were gifted large swathes of land by William the Conqueror following his 1066 victory. They were all staunch Roman Catholics and Jacobite supporters who were intent on displacing King William and restoring King James **II** to the English throne after he had been deposed following the Glorious Revolution of 1688. John Lunt had been born in the Macclesfield area about fifty miles away from Lunt village. He was extremely well travelled back in a time when travel was arduous. He was also a very colourful character who did just about everything during his 'illustrious' career including highway robbery, horse thief, builder's labourer, running pubs, marrying bigamously more than once, and acting as a double agent for the government to expose the wealthy Irish Sea Coast conspirators. In other words, because he hardly ever spoke the truth, he was eminently qualified to work for the government! Hardly ever being a euphemism for never!

There is also a distinct possibility that John Lunt knew an old ancestor of my good friend and poet, Timothy St Julien Barber. Tim can trace his ancestry to early 1625 and is from the same family as John Barber who was Lord Mayor of London in the 1730s. It is known that John Lunt and John Barber not only lived in the same London suburb at the same time, but also lived in the same street. As a young man Barber loved to frequent London pubs and Lunt ran several different pubs in that neighbourhood. Barber was also a strong Jacobite supporter and like Lunt had many high contacts in government circles.

I don't know if our Lunt family descended from any of the aforementioned Lunts. However, a story that has been continually passed down in our family is that there has always been a Lunt called Richard in our family. I have no real idea if this story is true or not, but my youngest son is a Richard, and my brother is a Richard. A grandad and a great grandad were Richards and so on. My only grandson to date on the male side is called Remy Jack, but there is still time if they pull their fingers out. Henry Leonard just arrived October 2020.

Just to emphasize the strong relationship between Lunts and Lancashire consider the following. In the 1881 UK Census there were one thousand nine hundred and twenty-seven people with the Lunt surname. One thousand and twenty-three (fifty-three per cent) of these lived in Lancashire and forty-seven per cent were scattered throughout all the other British Counties. Also in 1881 if we looked at the top twenty parishes where the Lunt name was found, fourteen of those parishes (seventy per cent) were in Lancashire. And this was despite the fact that between 1815 and 1915 there had been considerable migration. This included internal migration where many country people moved out of small villages and hamlets into towns and cities as rapid urbanisation occurred during the Industrial Revolution. It also included external migration where many people emigrated overseas. Mainly to the USA, Australia, and Canada, but also to New Zealand, South Africa, and the West Indies. Many Lunts went to the USA during this time. Lunt village is only a few miles from Liverpool port where regular sailing ships used to depart for New York. In 1820 the sailing time to New York was from twenty-one to twenty-nine days.

A great example of both these kinds of migration of Lunts from the Irish Sea Coast was revealed to me just a couple of years ago while living in the Melbourne area of Australia. Completely out of the blue I received a telephone call from a lady living in Preston, Melbourne. Her name was Jean Lunt Marinović. Jean told me that during some work she had been doing to trace her ancestry, she had discovered that her father had lived in a small, terraced house in Trawden, Lancashire in the very early 1900s. About one hundred years later, she had been thrilled to find that in 2017 a guy called Richard Lunt, my brother, was still living in that very same house.

When she showed me the ancestry work she had done, it transpired that her grandad, James Lunt, was born in North Meols near Southport in 1878, where my forebearers had come from. James married a girl from Leigh in 1908 and by this time they were living in Ince near Wigan. They had a son, Arthur Dean Lunt, in 1911. James's wife, Millicent, died young at only forty-five years of age in 1924. At that point James and Arthur moved into the Colne area to live. Probable reason for this is because James's older brother, my great grandad Richard Lunt (born North Meols in 1872), was already living in Trawden near Colne and was the village blacksmith talked about elsewhere in this book. In 1928 James and Arthur emigrated to Canada. Arthur married in Canada and had a daughter, Jean Lunt, who later married Croation Ante Marinović. James had died in October 1945 having just survived TWO world wars. In 1947 Arthur was awarded an MBE for services to the Canadian Government. James Lunt's father (Jean's great grandad) was called Peter Lunt. He was also born in North Meols in 1846. His father John, born in 1810, also lived in North Meols, as did his father Richard (1772) and his father John (1744). Incidentally, Meols is from an old Norse word meaning 'sandhills' which make some beautiful natural hazards a few miles away at Royal Birkdale GC. Very likely this would have been one of the landing places for the Viking long boats when they fled Ireland.

North Meols is at the mouth of the River Ribble estuary which is about ten miles wide at that point. This river has a strong tidal bore and inland navigation was possible as far as Preston in those days when it used to be dredged. In fact the largest ever haul of Viking treasure, thousands of coins and silver items, was found in 1840 on the banks of the River Ribble at Cuerdale near Walton-le-Dale and Fishwick Bottoms. Largest ever that is until 2012 when an even more impressive hoard of Viking treasure was discovered at Bedale, a small village which is close to both the North Yorkshire Moors National Park and the Yorkshire Dales National Park. Bedale is surrounded in every direction by knur and spell playing places such as Northallerton, Richmond, Masham, Leyburn, Thirsk and many others in Upper Wensleydale. Cuerdale and Bedale are about eighty miles apart.

At the time Jean and I met we were both writing our first books. Mine was about an old Australian champion golfer called Jack Harris. Her book was on a much more serious topic. It was about a genocide which occurred after the end of World War II involving Josip Broz Tito who later served as President of the former Yugoslavia between 1953 and 1980. The book is called *One Day in May – Bleiburg 1945* and covers a very important part of Croatian history.

Getting back to the story after a very long digression, Cleveland GC in Yorkshire is at Redcar on the north east coastline. Long before this club was founded in 1887 knur and spell was played within a few miles of Redcar at places such as Middlesbrough, Guisborough, Hinderwell, Danby, Ainthorpe, Leaholm, Runswick Bay and Whitby. In fact all across the north Yorkshire moors and along Teesside. Clued up Australians will know that this part of England has been very significant in the modern history of their country. Firstly, about nine miles from Cleveland GC is Marton-in-Cleveland where Captain Cook was born. Secondly, only six miles from Cleveland is Eston where Royal Melbourne GC founder member Thomas Brentnall used to live. Thomas did his pre-university schooling at Darlington and Great Ayton. He later went to Durham University and then worked in a Middlesbrough bank before moving to Prestonpans. All the Durham and Yorkshire places he was associated with were big knur and spell playing places. In fact emigrant miners from Durham started up knur and spell competition in Australia's Hunter Valley long before Thomas arrived in Australia and of course long before any Australian golf clubs were founded. Finally, it was also Eston where iron ore was discovered in the 1850s which resulted in the development of a very large steel making industry in the Cleveland area. It was mostly steel from Middlesbrough which was used to build the Sydney Harbour Bridge. Middlesbrough is just five miles from Eston.

.

Chapter 21

Knur and spell and early golf in the Antipodes, Articles of Agreement and handicaps

Because I am now living in Australia, I should mention something about the history of knur and spell in New Holland, Terra Australis Incognita and Van Diemen's Land. I refer to these old names only because when knur and spell first appeared on this continent, Australia did not officially exist as a nation. One of the earliest ideas to rename this land as Australia came from Matthew Flinders when he circumnavigated the continent in 1803. But when his maps were published in 1814, the name Terra Australis was still used. The British Admiralty had agreed to the name 'Australia' by 1824 and from that date the name 'Australia' started to gain traction. But officially, it was not until 1901 that the six mainland states joined up. Until then they were still run separately and referred to by their colonial names. Van Diemen's Land having already changed to Tasmania by 1856.

Knur and spell (aka poor man's golf) was played in Australia many years before clubs like The Australian GC, Royal Sydney GC or Royal Melbourne GC were even contemplated. So, let's not worry about whether The Australian GC or Royal Melbourne GC is the oldest... they both relative youngsters compared with knur and spell! And of course, competitive knur and spell was played long before most other Australian golf clubs started to spring up in the early 1900s. There had been some earlier efforts at getting golf established in Australia before that but nothing substantial. We had Brodie Spark playing an odd game with Captain Ferrier at Grose Farm in around 1840 and David Robertson (brother of the famous Allan Robertson) playing an odd game or two with Captain Kirk at Homebush in 1857 before he returned to Scotland after his brother had died in 1859.

John Dunsmure and Charles Lawrence had also tried to drum up some interest in Sydney during the 1850s and 1860s. There is also strong evidence that golf was played at Flagstaff Hill in Melbourne around 1847/1850 and the infamously disputed case of early golf played at Ratho (Bothwell) in Tasmania. Golf historians surmised that this happened around 1860 but I personally don't agree with their conclusions which were full of conjecture. My view is that the Reid family probably played on their estate for their own amusement long before 1860 even if there was no proper golf course or formal golf played there.

But whatever the case, none of these early efforts to establish golf either in Tasmania or on the mainland amounted to much when it came to organised clubs or competition. They all involved very few players and were very short-lived. Probably the main reason they were short-lived and difficult to get up and running is a very simple practical one. At that time there were no manufacturers of golf clubs or golf balls in Australia. The old wooden shafted golf clubs used in those days were relatively easily damaged during play. They warped with time and the shafts broke relatively easily, especially if not maintained properly. The old golf balls, particularly the featheries used before the gutties appeared around 1850, were even more easily damaged. Leather featheries in wet weather were a complete disaster. Even good golfers who could hit the middle of the club face on a regular basis could easily burn up several expensive golf balls every round they played. Less skilful players (i.e. most of them) who often hit the ball with a glancing blow, caused even more trauma to the ball and consequently would exhaust their stock of balls even faster. Once they had broken a club or two or used up their stock of featheries (or gutties), it was a nightmare situation. The only way they could replace clubs and balls was to send an order to England or Scotland by sailing ship which took several months each way. Besides which there would have been a significant manufacturing lead-time because the clubs were all hand-made. Each club would have taken many hours or even days to make. Until a critical mass of golfers was established in Australia in the 1890s this was a major issue for all the early would-be Australian golfers.

Most of the early attempts at golf start-ups in Australia would have been made using the old featherie golf balls. This undoubtedly would have been the main stumbling block. If you broke a club, it may have been possible to find some local blacksmith or carpenter to repair it or even make a new one. However, once your featheries had gone it would have been a much trickier proposition to find a local featherie golf ball maker. Probably impossible! I suspect that no one ever made a featherie golf ball in Australia...but I could be wrong. Once the guttie balls arrived on the scene, and especially after the introduction of moulds to make your own guttie balls, like the one in Jeparit Museum, things started to change rapidly.

From the early 1890s onwards, golf professionals started to appear who were skilled at golf club making and sports stores started to stock golf balls. Of course, the use of featheries had died out by then and been replaced by the cheaper to produce and longer lasting guttie balls and other balls which were continually evolving.

In a well-documented New Zealand case, the Dunedin / Otago GC had encountered the very same problem when they tried to start up their club in 1869. When a Scottish gentleman called Charles Howden, the father of New Zealand golf, first introduced golf there, he had no problem to find nearly thirty men who wanted to play. However, he was the only guy who owned some clubs. So, they couldn't start up for another one to two years because they had to order the equipment from the old country. No telephones, fax, or internet in those days. Orders would have to be sent by letter in a sailing ship which took several months to arrive. When the order arrived in Scotland it would not be a case of just loading up umpteen sets of golf clubs on to the next sailing ship bound for New Zealand. There was no Ray Drummond golf store holding large stocks of readymade clubs. There were no mass-produced golf clubs. They were all hand-made and each club took many hours or days to make. An order for thirty sets of clubs would have been a large order which may have taken weeks or months to put together. This would be the case even if the 'sets' only consisted of half a dozen clubs. Even arranging payment for such a big order would have been a rigmarole. No touch-button bank transfers or credit card payments in those days! After all this, several more months in a sailing ship to deliver the clubs would be needed.

More than likely this golf equipment supply issue was the trigger point which resulted in Dunedin and former Bothwell schoolteacher, John

Brown Park, asking Alexander Reid Sr's son if he could have the old clubs stored at Ratho in Tasmania. He would have undoubtedly received these old clubs from Tassie much earlier than the new stock arrived from Scotland. They eventually ran the Dunedin club for a few years in the early 1870s. Unfortunately, all the members' golf clubs, which were stored in a room at a pub which served as their clubhouse, disappeared in the mid-1870s when the pub was sold. They were back to square one. No one had any equipment left and there were still no golf club or ball suppliers in New Zealand where they could replace them. Nor were there any in Australia at that time which would have been a much nearer supply source than Scotland if it had been available. The club disbanded and didn't fire up again as Otago GC until the 1890s which is about the same time as golf club manufacture in Australia started to appear. Once a certain critical mass of golfers was reached there was no stopping the progress of golf.

On the other hand, the early Australian knur and spell was a much more widespread activity which involved dozens of players and many different communities. They didn't have the equipment supply problem because they made their own pommels/spells and could even use self-carved wooden knurs if they ran out of the ceramic ones. The epicentre for knur and spell (poor man's golf) in Australia was the Hunter Valley coal mining community mainly around the modern-day city of Newcastle. From at least the early 1870s organised knur and spell was regularly played in villages such as Lambton, Wallsend, Waratah, Plattsburg, Greta, Anvil Creek, Minmi, Hamilton, Teralba and New Lambton etc. And probably in many more of the dozens of places where collieries were located. Immigrants from the Northumberland / Durham coal mining area, in what is now the Tyne and Wear region, had brought the game with them. It is highly likely that they brought and played it quite some time before the 1870s because UK miners had started to emigrate to Australia from the mid-1820s onwards. Lambton was probably the sporting centre of the area in those days and is located about eight kilometres from the centre of Newcastle. However, judging from the range of places where knur and spell was played it was clearly quite popular amongst the mining communities. Minmi and Plattsburg are close to twenty kilometres away from Newcastle and Anvil Creek and Greta are both over fifty kilometres from the city. On unmade roads using a horse and buggy this would have been a decent journey to make. From match reports in Australian newspapers from that period we know that miners in the Hunter Valley were playing with the spring-loaded spell and not the gallows. We also know that they were using wooden knurs and not pot knurs. This knowledge about the type of knurs used in itself probably suggests that play in Australia more than likely occurred prior to 1850, because after that the use of ceramic knurs was rapidly spreading. The description given of the pummels used matched the ones being used at the time in England.

Newcastle itself, which had that name from about 1804, was named after Newcastle in the UK. Many of the surrounding towns and suburbs of Newcastle also were also named after places in Northumberland or Cumberland in the UK. Wallsend was there in the 1850s, Morpeth in 1834, Hexham in the 1820s and Lambton in the early 1860s. Hamilton had a borehole in 1849 and Greta was named after a small river in Cumberland near Keswick in 1842.

Coal had been mined in the Hunter Region from the late 1700s. Initially they used mostly convict labour, but production rates were starting to significantly increase, and more workers were needed. Convict labour had plenty of issues, but they also needed people with more actual mining expertise. Miners from the UK started to trickle out from about 1824. More mines opened, and production continued to expand throughout the 1800s. A large contingent of UK miners arrived in 1840 and even larger numbers arrived in 1850 and 1853. By the end of the 1850s the population of Newcastle and the surrounding mining villages had doubled. About ninety-four per cent of the immigrant miners came from the UK, many of them under assisted passage programmes. These included Welsh, Cornish, Scottish, Northumberland and Durham miners. Approximately half of the miners who came were from the Northumberland and Durham coal fields which were very big areas for knur and spell playing. By 1869 there were almost one thousand eight hundred mining workers in the Hunter mining region and this more than doubled again by 1879. They would probably have brought their knur and spell playing equipment with them from at least as early as 1840 and would have played the game from that time even if it was in an ad hoc manner. We know that organised knur and spell was already thriving in the Hunter region by the mid-1870s, but it more than likely started much earlier than that. In 1900 - 1901 there was another big influx of Geordie miners from Northumberland UK when the Hebburn Colliery started up at Weston / Kurri Kurri in NSW. This mine was surrounded by the other mining places mentioned earlier. Of course it was named after the Hebburn Colliery in the UK on the south bank of the Tyne River just a few miles east of Newcastle. I did not have sufficient time to explore if these 1900 / 1901 miners also played knur and spell in the Hunter. However, there is a very good chance that they did because knur and spell was booming in Geordie-land at the time they left the UK.

Unfortunately, the *Newcastle Morning Herald and Miner's Advocate* (NMHMA) newspaper which reported most of this activity only fired up in 1876 so anything on earlier knur and spell in Australia is still hidden. The *Newcastle Chronicle and Hunter District News* operated from 1858-1866 and the *Newcastle Chronicle* ran from 1866-1876 but I have not had the time to explore these. The *Illustrated Sporting Life* also had a very short burst in 1866.

These were not the only Australian newspapers which presented articles on knur and spell in the mid-1800s. *Bell's Life in London* had sister publications in both Sydney and Melbourne. *Bell's Life in Sydney and Sporting Reviewer* (1845-1860), *Bell's Life in Sydney and Sporting Chronicle* (1860-1870) and *Bell's Life in Victoria and Sporting Chronicle (Melbourne)* (1857-1868) which all regularly gave information about knur and spell being played back in the homeland. e.g. *Bell's Life in Victoria,* 24 January 1863, gave a very full account of the big match played in London played between Kirk Stables and Nelly Pearson. e.g. *Bell's Life in Sydney* dated 13 April 1867, quoted William Jeffery Prowse advising his Australian readers under his penname of 'Nicholas' about his forthcoming *History of Knur and Spell.* Of course, when Prowse wrote this, knur and spell already had a history which went back several hundred years.

The *Empire* newspaper which was published in Sydney from 1850-1875 also regularly wrote about knur and spell. E.g. In January 1862 it gave a full report on a big match which had been played in Doncaster, Yorkshire in November 1861. The *Hobart Courier,* 19 November 1853, was writing about knur and spell.

If Australian newspapers were presenting articles on knur and spell in 1853, they surely must have thought some of their readers had an interest in it?

One old newspaper which I haven't been able to search is the *Maitland Mercury and Hunter River General Advertiser* which was established in 1843. The first Europeans had arrived into the Maitland area between 1818 and 1838 and the town of West Maitland was founded around 1820. There is every chance that information on old knur and spell activity in that area will be found in this publication.

What we must remember is that while most of this mid-1800 Hunter Valley activity with knur and spell was taking place, golf in Australia was virtually unknown. Indeed, even in England at that time golf was also practically unknown. In 1850 there were only TWO golf clubs in England and both of them were not truly English clubs. They were both essentially clubs founded by ex-pat Scots. The first 'English' club didn't fire up until 1864, followed shortly after that by London Scottish GC (another ex-pat club) who still play on Wimbledon Common. Purely by coincidence, as I am writing this bit about London Scottish, the second day of the 2019 Wimbledon tennis tournament is just about to begin and newly crowned world number one lady player, Australian Ash Barty, is about to start her campaign.

When we try to assess how popular a particular sport was in bygone years such as this, we need to take some important factors into account. It is not enough just to search for old newspaper reports because these mostly only report on actual competitions which took place. These competitions would only represent a very tiny fraction of the knur and spell playing which was happening at the time. The same happens today with the modern golf scene. The vast majority of people who play golf do not maintain an official golf handicap. Nor are they actual members at a golf club. Nor do many of them play competition golf. For example, I know for sure that of the many hundreds of players who frequent Wattle Park golf course each week to play golf, probably only about twenty of thirty actually play in the competitions there. The average handicap of a male player who does play competitive golf is probably twenty or higher. But the true average handicap of all male golfers (club members and public golf course players) would be much higher than that. That is IF they maintain a handicap ...and most people who play golf do not do this! The number of social rounds of golf played in Australia where no proper handicap is involved would absolutely dwarf the competitive golf rounds. According to the 2017 R&A report *Golf Around the World* there are 8204 private clubs and 24957 public clubs.

Just like golf, knur and spell had many hackers in addition to its stars of the game. The games which the hackers played would hardly ever be read about in the newspapers. I do have firsthand experience of this. I personally saw knur and spell played in the tiny Lancashire village of Trawden in the 1950s on many occasions. The Trawden villagers were regularly playing social knur and spell. They were not playing in a big money event but more than likely playing for who paid for the beer in the local pub or maybe even just for bragging rights. The same would have been happening at hundreds or even thousands of hamlets and villages all over Lancashire, Yorkshire, and other northern counties. I liken this to what happens in Australia with cricket. Many of Australia's Ashes cricket team probably started off playing backyard or beach-cricket. This is where they first got their love of the game from before they progressed through the ranks. None of those backyard or beach games would ever find their way into a newspaper. The same happened with knur and spell. The thousands of knur and spell references which can be found in old British newspapers are just a very small sample of the knur and spell which was actually being played. No doubt the same would apply to knur and spell in the Hunter Valley in the mid-1800s.

I did of course find plenty of newspaper references where individual Trawdeners played in tournaments held in other towns and villages throughout Lancashire and Yorkshire. In the first quarter of the twentieth century there were also a few challenge matches held in Trawden itself. Quite a few of these matches were held in the fields behind the Rock Hotel (these days called the Trawden Arms), but this was all long before I was born. I lived only about twenty-five metres away from the Rock Hotel until I was about twenty-one years old.

The knur and spell played in the Hunter Valley more or less emulated what had been happening in Northumberland, Durham, Lancashire, and Yorkshire throughout the 1600s, 1700s and 1800s. In 1700 the coal production in England was about three million tonnes. There would have lots of social knur and spell as well as organised competition events. Contests could be between individuals or between teams. There was a strong link to drinking and gambling and sizeable crowds were attracted. A typical example was shown in the *Wetherby News and Central Yorkshire Journal* dated April 1879. This described a match which took place in Tadcaster between two pub teams which had thirteen players on each side. Each player was only allowed five rises and there was no money involved.

There were never any universal rules for knur and spell. Although in England at least, according to the *Barnsley Chronicle* dated 12 April 1873, a notice was posted to all would-be knur and spell players. This advised that a standard form of Articles of Agreement had been drawn up which was suitable for knur and spell matches. This was designed to save time when arranging the big money matches and help to avoid disputes etc. Copies of the form were available for one penny each or nine pence per dozen. Despite not having universal rules, especially when money was involved, knur and spell did have a process to try to ensure that proceedings were conducted in an orderly fashion. Apart from the above-mentioned Articles of Agreement, there was always an independent referee and an independent stakeholder appointed for every serious match. Sometimes the same man would perform both duties. Other times two separate men were employed. These provisions didn't mean that all problems were eradicated. Disputes frequently arose at knur and spell matches particularly in cross-Pennine battles between Lancashire and Yorkshire. It wouldn't be a proper knur and spell match unless there was a dispute!

One of the earliest references to Articles of Agreement, as the way of setting the rules to be applied at a sporting contest, was in 1727. This may even have been the first time ever that Articles were used for this purpose. It was for a two match cricket series between the Duke of Richmond and Mr Alan Brodrick, 2nd Viscount Midleton played in Sussex. Seventeen years after this series, in 1744, the first Laws of Cricket were dreamt up and used, even though they were not written up until 1755. The Laws were revised in 1774 (and many times since then) and have been held since 1788 by the Marylebone Cricket Club (MCC) in London. It is highly likely that the 1744 Laws used the 1727 Articles as a starting point for their rules. Articles of Agreement have also been used for hundreds of years by sea captains and the sailors who manned the ships to fix on-board rules at sea. This probably preceded the cricket application, but I can't be sure.

As far as knur and spell was concerned, signed agreements in writing between various parties participating in the big money challenge matches had been used for quite some time before the above-mentioned standard form appeared on the scene in 1873. At least since 1850 and maybe earlier than that. Almost certainly the idea to use Articles of Agreement in knur and spell would have copied the cricket example, since the two games were always very closely linked. Unfortunately, as far as I know, the next step to draft up universal rules for Knur and Spell was never taken.

When it came to golf I never found any reference to Articles of Agreement being employed in this sport. The first rules of golf came into being in 1744, the very same year as the first cricket rules. I don't know which came first. Almost from the start of golf there were occasional big money matches happening between aristocrats, noblemen or big landowners, but I found nothing mentioned about Articles of Agreement. Even in 1825, long after articles were first used in cricket, there was a big golf challenge played at Montrose Links between Lord Kennedy and a Mr Cruickshank. This involved three matches at five hundred sovereigns each. Although this was a massive amount of cash for that time, there was no reference to any articles. Cruickshank was a big landowner. He owned the Langley Park Estate not far from Montrose in the county of Angus. Cruickshank was not a descendant of any of the landed gentry who were given big slices of land in King David's time. He had made all his money owning or part owning three large sugar plantations on the island of St Vincent in the Caribbean. Over eight hundred slaves were involved in these operations. When the UK government abolished slavery, he not only managed to successfully get all his money out of St Vincent, but he also picked up a lot of money from the British Government as compensation for loss of earnings when he had to let the slaves go. I don't know if the Hunter Valley knur and spell boys ever used Articles of Agreement for any of their matches. I never saw any evidence of this in the reports. I suspect that it didn't happen because all the match reports I saw only ever referred to small handicap events held at pub grounds with small prize money or actual prizes such as 'two pigs' or to individual challenge matches with relatively small stake money. To date I haven't seen any reports about big money knur and spell challenge matches in Australia between two individual players...something that was an everyday occurrence at that time amongst the top English players.

Long before golf competition started in Australia, the Hunter Valley knur and spell boys operated a handicap system whenever they played. However, instead of 'receiving strokes' like a golfer with less ability does when he plays against a better player, the weaker knur and spell player 'received distance' as the equaliser. In a handicap match played in October 1886 at Lambton NSW for ten pounds per corner, the *NMHNA* reported that one player had conceded twenty score (four hundred yards) over twenty rises. In other words, he was betting that he would hit each strike at least twenty yards further than his opponent. He must have had tickets on himself because he lost the match by eighteen-score PLUS the twenty-score handicap! Some of the handicap events played in Yorkshire even as late as 1923 were very big affairs attracting crowds of several thousands. In one played at Lightcliffe near Halifax there were so many entrants that they had to play fourteen heats stretching from July 2 to August 18. The first prize winner on that occasion hit a pot knur two hundred and eighty yards. Not a bad hit for a smooth ball with no dimples and using a very rudimentary hitting implement! Even when scratch knur and spell players challenged each other a handicap system could still be applied. This was because there was no set rule governing the length of the pummel stick they used to hit the knur with. If a player used a pummel which was several inches longer than the mean pummel length, then he would have a pre-agreed number of yards per extra inch of pummel per rise subtracted from his overall distance total. If he used a shorter pummel, he would gain extra yardage accordingly. In an 1863 edition of *Bell's Life*, a knur and spell player from Blackburn in East Lancashire using a very short twenty-seven-inch pummel issued a twenty-five pounds challenge to any player in England. I have read somewhere that the standard pummel length was four feet (forty-eight inches). If that is true it would be a few inches longer than most modern drivers used which clock in at forty-four or forty-five inches, but it would be quite close to the clubs long driving competition players use or even longer. PGA players can go up to forty-eight inches if they want to. Long driving champions use fifty inches with a loft sometimes as low as three degrees. This is almost copying the earlier knur and spell pummels which as far I know did not have any built-in loft at all. I never saw any mention about the overall weight of the pummel being considered. I read that pummel weights were about six ounces, but I don't know if this was typical. If it was, it would be much lighter than a modern driver which checks in at about eleven ounces.

In another handicap match reported in *Bell's Life* 31 May 1863, played at Leeds in Yorkshire, one player gave the other player one score start for every pound he was heavier in weight. He was eighteen pounds heavier, so he conceded eighteen score (three hundred and sixty yards) over thirty rises. This promoted very heavy betting on the contest which was eventually won by the bigger man. Another weight related contest was where a man offered to play anyone in England at knur and spell who weighed the same as him. Since he only weighed forty-five kilos maybe he didn't get too many challengers!

Generally speaking the knur and spell boys were many decades ahead of the golf boys when it came to handicapping better players so that players with less ability could still participate. They were also much more creative when it came to devising different ways of equalisation. The knur and spell boys in the Hunter Valley were also certainly involved in heavy betting on knur and spell matches long before golf started in Australia and their matches would often attract sizeable crowds.

The golf boys had been setting betting odds on different players within individual clubs at least from the 1600s but they didn't have a formal handicapping system. It was well into the 1870s before this started to happen at Royal Devon, Westward Ho GC after the par rating for each hole had been brought into use around 1870. By 1881 they were averaging the best three scores of the year minus the scratch score (course rating) which was established by the club.

As far as other clubs in England were concerned, it would have happened around the same time, but they were all doing their own thing. In the *Blackheath GC Chronicles* published in 1897 (page 121) it said, 'Following the modern golfing custom, the club in 1883 instituted competitions for a monthly medal under club handicap and limited to twenty-one strokes'. In another section of the same *Chronicles* it was obvious that they had been using a handicap system with a twenty-one maximum handicap to run their Calcutta Cup and Singapore Cup competitions from 1875 and 1876 respectively. In fact, in the *Rules of the Blackheath GC* adopted in 1860, Rule X mentioned that 'The competitors to be handicapped by the Secretary and Club-Keeper'. However, from other information in the *BHGC Chronicles* it seems that handicaps were not actually used until the mid-1870s. The idea of a centralised handicap authority was proposed in 1887. A system of course portability for handicaps was developed in 1897 but was only adopted in 1927.

On the other hand, the knur and spell boys had many more variables in their game which could be used for handicapping purposes. Where a hacker golfer just receives a number of 'free' strokes from the better golfer, a hacker knur and spell player could just receive an agreed number of 'free' yards. Or, as in golf, one player may just agree to give his opponent more hits (rises). After that he had a myriad of other variables he could try to build into his handicap agreement. The first would be the type of knurs to be used. Pot knurs (common, ribbed or tinted) weighing half-ounce, three-quarter ounce or one ounce? Or wood knurs (holly, lignum vitae or boxwood) which could be 'green' or pre-dried? Or even staghorn knurs. If he played with wood knurs, he may well choose to use his own knurs which may have his own secret pattern carved on the surface to improve knur flight characteristics. With the pommel he could choose what shaft length he would use (shorter length shafts usually attracted more 'free' yards.) He could also choose which wood his shaft was made from. His pummel head would also have his own secret design combining a mixture of hard and soft woods and even the pummel head width was regularly stipulated. He could often then choose which method he wanted to use to launch the knur (spell or gallows) or he could dispense with both these methods and insist that the knur had to be thrown into the air by hand before being struck by the pummel. If the two combatants were of vastly different stature, sometimes the heavier man had to concede an agreed number of yards for each pound of extra weight. Even the position on the playing field where the players set up their spell or gallows was something often built into the Articles of Agreement.

Big strong men with little or no co-ordination always had a chance to win at knur and spell. They had the opportunity to challenge other players at just the 'long knock' form of the game rather than the 'aggregate score' form. This meant that in say a match of thirty rises (thirty strikes), they could in theory have twenty-nine air swings and then get lucky and hit just one shot out of the park. It was also fairly common for a contest to include BOTH aggregate score AND long knock elements into the pre-match agreement. So the loser of the match on aggregate score still had a chance to pick up a prize for the longest individual knock.

In Northumberland UK, as it was then, the game of knur and spell was often referred to as Collier's golf. Just like the UK, the game of knur and spell in Australia was organised around ordinary everyday pub life. The guys who played it didn't have dedicated club houses or dedicated playing areas. But they did play for significant amounts of money. Elsewhere in Australia, there were reports of Knur and spell being played in Queensland. According to the *Daily Standard* 30 January 1923, knur and spell was played by members of the Yorkshire Society of Queensland in Bowman Park, Paddington, Brisbane. Yorkshireman Richard Cutler promoted the game in Tasmania in a letter to the editor of the *Launceston Examiner* dated February 1883. Obviously, Mr Cutler had not discovered that his Durham neighbours, who had settled in the Hunter Valley, had beaten him to it by many years. On the mainland, the Corio Cricket Club, according to the *Geelong Advertiser* dated 19 June 1871, were given a complete set of knur and spell equipment by a gentleman called Sharpe Brearley Esq. He had told them the knur and spell was a favourite pastime in both Yorkshire and Lincolnshire. This was twenty years prior to Geelong GC starting up. Even in 1923 there was a newspaper report of a game played at Punchbowl, near Bankstown, in Sydney which is only a few miles away from the Homebush site where Robertson and Kirk played.

So far I have not found any evidence that knur and spell was played in New Zealand, but certainly articles about knur and spell did appear in NZ newspapers. As late as 22 July 1919, *The Dominion* newspaper in Wellington wrote a general article on the game as played in England which said , 'Great crowds flock to see the Saturday contests, bets are made, and champion players are heroes little below international centre forwards in the world of football. For the man who can make a drive of 300 yards is a past-master of the game...' Coal mining in New Zealand had started later than the Hunter Valley development. It was the late 1840s before an Englishman began coal mining activities there. It is highly likely that some Yorkshire or Durham miners followed him, so there would be a good chance that knur and spell will bob up somewhere in NZ.

Knur and spell in England went back hundreds of years before it arrived in Australia. In 1780 when Captain Cook sailed from Whitby on the east coast of Yorkshire to discover Australia, he would certainly have known all about knur and spell. Even the ship he arrived in, the HMS Endeavour, was a converted coal carrier! For the first twenty-seven years of his life he lived in North Yorkshire where knur and spell was raging in the 1700s. He was born in Marton-in-Cleveland which was in the heart of the Teeside knur and spell scene. As a boy he lived at Great Ayton which is on the edge of the North Yorkshire Moors National Park. Knur and spell was played at dozens of places across these moors. When he was seventeen, he moved to Staithes on the east coast of Yorkshire, just south of Scarborough (where knur and spell was played) and just a few miles north of Whitby (where knur and spell was also played). Just a few miles west of Scarborough is the tiny village of Snainton (population circa eight hundred) where eminent Yorkshire scientist Sydney Cross Harland was born and died. His biography revealed that as a boy around the early 1900s he played knur and spell there. This particular example is typical of thousands of places where knur and spell was played but nothing ever appeared in the newspapers about it. Staithes is less than two miles away from Hinderwell where knur and spell was also played. It is also just ten miles away from Danby / Ainthorpe and not far from Leaholm and Castleton (also K&S playing places). At Ainthorpe there is a pub called the Fox and Hounds. In the 1500s it was an old coaching house. In the 1700s it added accommodation cottages. In 2018 we can still get a nice beer at the Fox and Hounds. I don't know when this pub first got involved in promoting knur and spell events but in the 1800s they frequently put adverts for knur and spell events in the *Whitby Gazette*, as did many other pubs across the moors. Only twenty-two miles away from Great Ayton, on the southern edge of the North Yorkshire Moors, is the town of Helmsley. In *Bell's Life* dated

20 August 1887, they had an article about some old Helmsley newspaper records from 1787 which mentioned that they played 'dab and shel' (knur and spell) at that time. Maybe a Knur and spell pummel would show up on the ship's manifest for the Endeavour? In most contemporary writeups on the origins of golf, knur and spell rarely if ever gets a mention. I suspect that the very name 'poor man's golf' sealed its fate to a life of obscurity in golfing history.

In fact, one of the men behind the eventual start-up of Royal Melbourne GC (RMGC) in 1891 was also from the North of England and the former Danelaw area. His name was Thomas Brentnall. Thomas was the son of a successful grocer and had been born in the small village of Escomb in County Durham in 1846. He was brought up in nearby Eston in North Yorkshire and given a private education. Both Escomb and Eston are in the very heartland of the coal mining region. One of the very first references to coal being mined in the North East of England was in the famous *Boldon Book* which was commissioned by the Bishop of Durham to assist in the administration of his vast estates and was published in 1183. This book was along the same lines as the even more famous *Domesday Book* which had been published in the previous century. The *Boldon Book* refers to a coal miner in Escomb who supplied coal to the local blacksmiths to use in their forges to make ploughs for the farmers. There was a big expansion of the coal industry in that area during the thirteenth and fourteenth centuries.

After completing his education Thomas took a job in a bank but didn't stay there too long before moving to Prestonpans in Scotland, a small town just east of Edinburgh. There he worked for a colliery which supplied lots of coal to the salt making industry which evaporated sea water in giant pans to make the salt. Very close to Prestonpans is the Royal Musselburgh GC and that is where Thomas got started into golf. He was a member there as early as 1874. However, by 1878 he had emigrated to Australia with his family and taken a job as an accountant. This he did well and later he became the first president of the Institute of Chartered Accountants, Australia. Brentnall had played regular golf dating back almost twenty years before RMGC was conceived, probably more than any of the other RMGC founders. Even in Australia he had been hitting golf balls up and down paddocks in Essendon many years before RMGC was even thought about. When he did this it is unlikely that holes and flags were involved.

The point about the Thomas Brentnall story is that both Escomb and Eston were also in very strong knur and spell playing regions. Knur and spell had probably been played there for at least two hundred years before Brentnall was even born. Although I couldn't find an actual reference to knur and spell being played in Escomb itself, there are dozens of references to the game being in played in other mining villages all within five or ten miles away from Escomb. Places such as Willington, Brandon Village, Esh Winning, Byers Green, Langley Park, Esperley, North Bitchburn, Hetton-le-Hole, Latherbrush / Bishop Auckland, Ushaw Moor, Newton Cap, Waterhouses, St Helen Auckland, Cockfield, Southchurch, Butterknowle, Evenwood, Sunnybrow, Hunwick and throughout the Deerness Valley. It is highly unlikely that knur and spell would not have been played in Escomb too. A coal mine was opened in Escomb in 1837 and according to the 1851 Census the vast majority of the twelve hundred inhabitants worked at the pit. Coal mining in the north east region of England had in fact been carried out in some shape or form from as early as the 1200s and 1300s. Eston was also a strong mining town, but in this case it was primarily ironstone mining. The Eston mine was the chief reason why Teeside in the UK became one of the world's largest iron and steel producers in the 1850 - 1950 period. Five miles away from Eston is Marton-in-Cleveland where Captain Cook was raised.

There is no way Mr Brentnall could not have at least known about the game of knur and spell before he moved to Scotland. He may even have played it himself. In fact it is highly likely that he would have played knur and spell at some point because virtually every young boy in England in the 1800s would have had his own knur and spell gear. Keep in mind also that all these places are only just over one hundred miles away from where golf is said to have started in the Lothians. Note that knur and spell was also played much further north than the Escomb area and much closer to the Scottish border. In fact, the border between Scotland and England runs diagonally from Berwick on Tweed (in England) on the east coast down to around Gretna Green (in Scotland) on the west side. Newcastle on Tyne in England is just about on the same latitude as Gretna Green in Scotland and a big chunk of Northumbria, north of Newcastle, is further north than the southernmost part of Scotland. Knur and spell was certainly played further north than Gretna Green in places such as Bedlington, East Sleekburn and Morpeth which are only about 100 miles from Muirfield GC.

If one Yorkshire man could move to Lothian in the 1800s from a knur and spell / coal mining district to another coal mining region, maybe he was not the first or only one to do it? Coal mining in Prestonpans started in about 1210 and even earlier in Escomb. i.e. long before golf started in Scotland. We already know that many English people migrated to the Lothians in the 1100s during King David's reign. If knur and spell really was a Viking or even an Anglo-Saxon game there is just about zero chance that the Scots didn't at least know all about it.

The truth is that the border between England and Scotland, over many years, has been a moveable feast. On the west side of the country, Carlisle is a sizeable city which today is located close to Scotland but on the English side of the border. This wasn't always the case. At one time Carlisle and other parts of Cumbria were part of Scotland and indeed Carlisle has changed hands between England and Scotland several times since it was founded before the Romans arrived. Carlisle was not in the Domesday Book. It was part of Scotland at the time of the Norman Conquest in 1066. William the Conqueror's son, William Rufus, took Carlisle and Cumberland back for England in 1092. On the east side of the country Berwick-on Tweed was always in dispute. The town is currently in England, but the county of Berwickshire is in Scotland. In 1380 the castle of Roxburgh, which is now in Scotland, was held by the English.

Roxburgh Castle was built around 1128. King David **I** of Scotland had a royal residence there and until 1500 Roxburgh, as a city, was just as important as Edinburgh. It was centrally located on the River Tweed and had royal burgh status. Between 1128 and 1460 it changed hands between England and Scotland several times. In 1334 King Edward **II** of England used it as a base during his battles against the Scots, following the English win at the Battle of Dopplin Moor in 1332. The Scots finally captured the castle back from the English in 1460 and destroyed it. But before that happened, while the English were still in charge, golf was already rearing its head in the Lothians. There can be no question that when golf started in what is now modern-day Scotland in the Lothians, the English still had a massive influence there. Although still classed as a 'borders town', Roxborough on today's map is comfortably on the Scottish side of the border by five or ten miles and is only about forty-two miles from Musselburgh GC.

For hundreds of years, even though peace treaties were in place, great turbulence continued on both sides of the border. It may explain why knur and spell does not appear to have been played in places on or very close to the border. The nearest I found knur and spell being played was thirty miles from the border on the west side and about fifty miles from the border on the east side. I have never seen any reports on knur and spell played in Carlisle itself. However, I have seen mention of knur and spell players from Carlisle and Newcastle etc playing in knur and spell events at several of the big Yorkshire knur and spell epicentres. This would have happened increasingly after 1850 as the railway network between the main cities rapidly expanded and made travel easier.

In the mid-1800s knur and spell playing in the former Danelaw area of England was at its peak. And even before Brentnall was born, miners from that same region had emigrated to Australia to work in the Hunter Valley coal fields. When he arrived in Australia the game of knur and spell was already flourishing in the Hunter Valley. Many years later the golfers at Royal Sydney and Royal Melbourne did eventually manage to catch up with and surpass the Durham coal miners of the Hunter Valley. However, it was probably a further two decades after RSGC and RMGC started up before golf was actually played at Newcastle GC, which was at least forty or fifty years behind the Knur and spell scene in that area.

Why Brentnall didn't opt to play knur and spell and took up golf instead is probably easy to explain. He had come from a relatively privileged background. It would have been quite rare in those days to go to private schools, especially if you lived in the middle of a major coal mining area. He obviously had great aspirations of moving up the social ladder.

The game of golf in both Scotland and England had initially been played mostly by the royals and other wealthy individuals. Although it had become more accessible in Scotland for the lower classes following the introduction of the much cheaper to produce guttie ball in 1849, it remained an elite game in England for at least another hundred years. The guttie ball was not the only reason why golf became more accessible to ordinary people. The Industrial Revolution which began in the late 1700s and early 1800s was a massive driver of both economic and social change. Most of the people I caddied for in the 1950s were owners of Lancashire cotton mills, doctors or other wealthy people. In 1850 golf had been around for about four hundred years but it was still very much in its fledgling state. Knur and spell on the other hand was booming in the former Danelaw Counties of England. The population of those former Danelaw Counties at that time was several times higher than the total population of Scotland. There would have been far more knur and spell 'laikers' in England than there were golfers in both England and Scotland combined. Reflecting the fact, I suppose, that there were far more poor men around to play poor man's golf than there were rich men to play regular golf. Indeed, in Brentnall's own memoirs which were published shortly after he died in 1937, he recalls that when he first played golf at Royal Musselburgh GC in 1874 there were only four recognised golf courses in Great Britain. This recollection of his is definitely not accurate but the fact remains that regular golf at that time was very much a minor sport in England compared to knur and spell (poor man's golf) which was booming. He probably meant just four courses 'in England' in 1874? And even that is questionable, although it wouldn't have been far off the mark!

However, although they were 'salt of the earth people', the knur and spell playing coal miners were rough and tough *hombres* and not exactly the kind of men Brentnall would have fraternised with. Poor man's golf would definitely not have been for him! Knur and spell was not Robinson Crusoe in this regard. The class divide between the upper and lower classes when it came to sharing their leisure time was prevalent in many sports, not just knur and spell and golf. In 1868 the Amateur Athletics Association banned the working classes and the start-up of Rugby League away from the more upper-crust Rugby Union also arose because of upper-class snobbery. Football was also very much a working man's and hooligan's game in those days which the wealthy classes withdrew from. That is until they realised that they could make money out of it! Some crude form of football had been played for at least five hundred years before the world's first football club, Sheffield FC, drew up a set of rules in 1858. The club sold off this hand-written historical set of rules in 2011 for £881,250. (A$1.53 million) A nice little earner indeed!

Thomas Brentnall must have been a fair golfer for his day. In the 17 February 1893 *GOLF A Weekly Record of 'Ye Royal and Ancient' Game* No 127 Vol.V (published in London), it shows that he played in a three-day handicap Bogey competition at Melbourne on 27 December 1892. He was 12 down playing off a 10 handicap. Two players above him tied on 9 down. Then on 7 January 1893 in the monthly medal he was runner-up to Captain Reynolds losing by two strokes. He shot a net 93 also playing off a 10 handicap. Melbourne had only been going as a club for about one year at that stage and this was long before they moved to Black Rock. It looks like Brentnall was in the top two or three golfers in the RMGC in those early days.

There are small historical societies and museums scattered all over the Hunter Valley coal mining region. I have not had an opportunity to explore this possibility, but it would not surprise me if some old knur and spell equipment was held by some of them. Certainly in similar museums all across the north of England many great examples from this ancient game are to be found.

Chapter 22

Four hundred years and gone nowhere

Another very telling indication about how small the game of regular golf was compared with 'poor man's golf' (knur and spell) in the mid- 1800s is to look at the details of the first ever so-called Open championship which was played at Prestwick in October 1860. I say 'so called Open' because as we all know it wasn't truly open at all. The first Open only allowed professional golfers to play. Amateurs had to wait for the second Open in 1861 before they got their chance. The 1860 event, which was reported in the *Glasgow Herald* to be open to Scottish golfers plus a few selected English clubs, attracted just eight entries. This included seven players from Scottish clubs and just one single entry from England. One hundred and sixteen years earlier, in April 1744, when the first Silver Club competition was held on Leith Links and was won by Edinburgh surgeon John Rattray, just ten gentlemen played in this inaugural event. So for well over a century the number of competitors for top golf events was pathetically low and had remained virtually unchanged.

The lone English entrant into the first Open was George Daniel Brown who was supposedly a cockney. The single entry from England is not surprising since there were only two golfs clubs in England existing in 1860. According to the pitifully small write-up of the 1860 Open in the *Glasgow Herald* dated 19 October, Brown came from Blackheath. However, there could be a chance that Brown beat Maurice Flitcroft to the punch by one hundred and sixteen years as the first ever impostor at an Open championship. Firstly, according to the Blackheath GC minutes from that era, the professionals at Blackheath GC from 1851 – 1865 were the two Scottish brothers Willie and Jamie Dunn. Furthermore, close scrutiny of the Blackheath GC minutes for a few years either side of 1860 shows no evidence of the name George Daniel Brown, either as a professional or as an amateur playing in their regular medal competitions. Not only was there no mention of him in the extensive and very detailed *Blackheath GC minutes* but there wasn't even any mention of the first ever 1860 Open championship itself. The minutes covered the period from 1766 when the first provable evidence of Blackheath existence dates to, up to the publishing of these minutes in 1897. For the years 1860 -1897 there was not one single mention of any of the thirty-seven Opens played during that time. Why would this be? Maybe it reflects the fact that Blackheath GC, although being clearly the oldest golfing establishment in England, has never held an Open Championship? Maybe it reflects the disdain shown by the amateur members towards professional golfers? Or maybe at the time they thought the Open championship was just a Mickey Mouse event? (which it was!) Blackheath GC was the only existing London club in 1860. London Scottish GC didn't arrive until 1865. So just where did Brown get his golf experience? Maybe he was a knur and spell ring in? Maybe Brown was just a pseudonym for one of the top knur and spell players? Neither Willie nor Jamie Dunn played in the 1860 inaugural British Open. They both played in 1861. Willie played again at least five times after that even up 1877 but he never ever got a mention for this in the Blackheath GC minutes.

It would be nice if the romantic suggestion that George Brown had been a knur and spell impostor was true, but this idea is very unlikely. When Captain Fairlie sent out his letter from Prestwick GC inviting players to compete in the first Open, he specified that the clubs, such as Blackheath GC, should send someone to represent them who was known to them as a 'respectable caddie'. Prior to 1860 a professional golfer was defined as a person who carried a gentleman's clubs i.e. a caddie. Probably the only way Brown could have known about the Open tournament was if someone from Blackheath GC had told him about it and indeed had put his name forward. Some of the caddies just carried clubs. However, some of them also learned to play as well as carrying clubs. Often the 'gentleman' would get his caddie to play with him in four-ball matches to give himself a better chance of winning a bet. Brown probably fell into this category. The fact that he was never mentioned in the Blackheath GC minutes is not really surprising. There would have been a few dozen caddies at Blackheath GC in 1860, remembering that in those days all members would play with caddies. Also noting that they had both club carriers and forecaddies who went ahead to warn other links users about golfers coming through. Some of them would just be club carriers and others would also be able to play. All of them would have been treated as 'nobodies' by the 'gentlemen' of the club. i.e. they were not the paid retained professionals at the club nor were they members of the club itself. Hence George Brown's name never appeared in the BHGC minutes.

Any knur and spell event held in that era, even if played at the smallest most remote village or hamlet in Yorkshire, would have had better support. For example, in *Bell's London Life and Sporting Chronicle* dated 27 June 1852, a knur and spell event at Northowram was advertised. This is a tiny village a few miles away from Halifax in Yorkshire. The event was held at the Windmill Tavern and nine men from Northowram took part. Stake money had to be sent to the Windmill Tavern in advance. Another better example was given in *Bell's Life in London* dated 7 May 1864. It was the All-England Knur and Spell handicap held at the New Belle Vue Ground, Park Top near Halifax held on 14 May and 28 May. There were seventy-five entries playing for ten pounds first prize, two pounds second prize and one pound third prize with another one pound each day for the longest knock. Almost thirty years later in 1890 the Open only attracted thirty-nine entries and the first professional to finish received just thirteen pounds which was far below what any knur and spell winner would get in that year at almost any tiny village knur and spell event. This was the first year a non-Scottish golfer won the Open. He was John Ball from England, who also happened to be the first amateur to win. Five years later, in 1894, the first non-Scottish professional won the Open at Royal St George's in Kent. It was Englishman, John Henry Taylor, who collected the £30 first prize from the £90 total purse.

The truth is that the Open Championship really WAS a Michael Mouse event from 1860 – 1900. During that forty-year period the Open averaged only forty entrants (8-98) who were predominantly old Scottish golfers, most of whom had little or no chance of winning. For the first twelve championships there was an average field of only thirteen (8-20). In the last decade of that century English players started to appear in larger numbers and from then on things started to look up. The Americans didn't start to turn up at the Open *en masse* until a few years after the First World war in the 1920s but naturally they dominated immediately when they did turn up. Despite the Scots having had about five hundred years extra time to practice, it only took the Americans just over thirty years to totally eclipse the Scots when it came to playing ability. In fact in the past one hundred years, 1921 – 2021, only two Scots have won the Open Championship... Sandy Lyle (1985) and Paul Lawrie (1999), versus forty-four wins for the Americans. Phenomenal!

The fact that the *Blackheath GC minutes* appeared to ignore even the existence of the Open Championship throughout the nineteenth century wasn't because they didn't know what was going on in Scottish golf. They had close contact on a regular basis with many Scottish clubs. In fact, three years before the first Open championship in 1860, they had played in a Great Golf Tournament at St Andrews in July 1857 which was probably the first ever big tournament played on the Old Links. Two-man teams (all amateurs) from eleven different clubs competed (Blackheath, Royal Perth, Edinburgh Burgess, Montrose Royal Albert, Edinburgh Bruntsfield, Prestwick, R & A St Andrews, Dirleton Castle, Innerleven, Musselburgh and North Berwick). In the final, Blackheath defeated R & A St Andrews by seven holes. After receiving the Silver 'Claret Jug' first prize, Blackheath declared themselves the champion golf club of the world. Shortly afterwards the Blackheath members voted to increase their professional Willie Dunn's weekly wage to seventeen shillings and sixpence. His golf tuition to the two Blackheath amateur players who lifted the trophy must have done the trick! About fifteen years later, after Tom Morris Jr was allowed to keep the original championship belt after winning the Open three years running in 1870, the claret jug concept was again brought out of the cupboard. This coincided with the R & A managing to entice the Open championship away from its birthplace club of Prestwick GC where it had been played for the first twelve years of its existence.

This period was several years after the guttie ball had been introduced and golf's popularity was on the increase. Twenty-five years earlier things had been very different. Golf was struggling. Blackheath GC in 1829 only had thirty-six members. This compared to fifty-two members in 1787. Several old golf clubs in Scotland had gone belly up. Old Manchester GC had no more than twelve members.

The biggest golf playing nation in the world at that time was probably India. Major Hugh Lyon Playfair, the founder of Indian golf, had started up Dum Dum GC in Calcutta in 1829. When he gave a report to Blackheath GC, as minuted in 1833, he told them that there were eleven hundred golfers in India. Dum Dum was the only golf club there in 1833. Royal Bombay didn't start until 1842. Since there were only about ten or a dozen golf clubs total in England and Scotland combined at that time, and most of them were struggling for members, it would seem highly likely that golfers in India would have outnumbered both the English and Scottish golfers combined. Albeit they were ex-pat Scottish and English golfers living in India and working for the East India Company. This company had effectively ruled India since 1757. It wasn't until after the Indian Rebellion in 1857 that the British Government assumed control in 1858 under the new British Raj. We must also remember that when we call Blackheath an 'English' club, this is using some poetic license. Yes, it is located in a London suburb near Greenwich. However, for the first two hundred years at least probably every member of this club would have been an ex-pat Scot living and working in the London area. So, it was essentially a Scottish club which just happened to be ensconced in England! It could also be debatable whether Old Manchester GC at Kersal Moor was an English club because it too had mostly ex-pat Scots as members.

We should also realise that if the Open championship was a Michael Mouse event for most of the second half of the 1800s, Blackheath GC themselves had not really set the world on fire either. Although they claim to have existed in some form or other since about 1608, it seems to be only from 1843 that they had a modest club house on Royal Hill. After a few years they moved to another on Blackheath Hill and to yet another nearby in 1865. They were still at the latter in 1897. These days they enjoy a swanky club house at Eltham Lodge which was built in the 1660s, but they didn't go there until 1923. Throughout the 1800s, if they had a good turnout for dinners, they invariably patronised a pub in either Blackheath or Greenwich...favourites being the Green Man, the Ship Inn or the Trafalgar Hotel.

Major Playfair was not as far as I know a member at Blackheath GC. He was probably just a visitor giving Blackheath a progress report on the Dum Dum club. Blackheath had been a very supportive mentor of the Dum Dum club, as they had also been to several start-up clubs in England in the 1800s including Westward Ho and Hoylake. Major Playfair was born in Meigle, near St Andrews. He played his golf at St Andrews and lived there. He was a very good golfer in his own right, having won the St Andrews's Gold Medal in 1818 and again in 1840 at the age of fifty-four. When he left India and retired from the army, Major Playfair returned to St Andrews in about 1832. At the time St Andrews was a rundown town and hardly anyone played golf there. The Old Course was in a very poor state of condition. Over the next twenty years he completely turned this around. He was the driving force which got professional Allan Robertson to re-vamp the Old Course. If I remember correctly, I think he was also behind the idea for St Andrews to have its famous double greens. He was also the main driver in the iconic R & A clubhouse being built in 1854. St Andrews as a golfing society had been going for exactly one hundred years at that point. They had fired up in 1754 with just twenty-two foundation members who all described themselves as either noblemen or gentlemen. All their meetings and functions during those one hundred years had been in taverns or hotels. They had run regular competitions continuously since 1766. Major Playfair also vastly improved the town itself and laid the foundations for what St Andrews is today.

Prior to the clubhouse being built, golf in St Andrews had been going for about four hundred years without really going anywhere. Then over the next hundred years it exploded into the mammoth sport we know today. The R & A club itself expanded from twenty-two members in 1754 to over two thousand five hundred worldwide members today.

Of course, the ancient game of knur and spell was enjoying a boomerooney at that time and would have had many more players than all the English, Scottish and ex-pat golfers in India combined. Sadly, it wasn't an organised sport. There are no accurate statistical records available to prove my conclusion. However, there is plenty of historical newspaper evidence to support my views.

Please don't be fooled when you read about knur and spell as being a quaint old English game just being played in a small, localised part of Northern England. This tends to write off knur and spell as being an insignificant game. Nothing is further than the truth. Although knur and spell was not regularly played in southern England, readers should be aware that the northern counties of Yorkshire, Lancashire, Lincolnshire, Durham, Northumberland, Cumbria, Cheshire, Derbyshire, Staffordshire, Nottinghamshire, Worcestershire and Shropshire, where knur and spell was played, are about fifty thousand square kilometres in total area. This is about the same area as Scotland if we deduct the Scottish Highlands where up to 1850 at least there was only one golf club in existence i.e. Fortrose. Perhaps more importantly, the population of these northern English counties is about THREE TIMES as big as the WHOLE of Scotland...and always was. The ten biggest towns in Yorkshire are Leeds, Sheffield, Bradford, Wakefield, Hull, York, Barnsley, Huddersfield, Doncaster, and Halifax. All these places and the hundreds of towns, villages and hamlets which surrounded them, were knur and spell strongholds and were growing even before the Industrial Revolution started. Add to that the mining communities in Durham, Tyne and Wear and Northumberland plus the textile towns of Lancashire and it is very easy to see why knur and spell completely dwarfed the game of golf in Britain for at least two hundred years and probably much longer than that.

What we must not forget when we look at all the knur and spell playing places is that back in the early to mid-1800s when knur and spell was probably at its peak, many of the small towns, villages and hamlets where it was found, were separate places in their own right. Today, many of them have disappeared or at least do not enjoy a separate existence. As an example, take the city of Leeds in Yorkshire which was a massive knur and spell playing region. If we zoom in on *Google* maps for the Leeds area, we can see at least one hundred and fifty names of small towns, villages and hamlets of what appear to now be suburbs of Leeds. Back in the day all of these were little towns, villages and hamlets in their own right which have since been swallowed up by the big city of Leeds. Virtually all these one-hundred and fifty places played knur and spell. Many of the smaller hamlets have lost their original identity altogether. The only evidence of their existence may be a street, or a road named after them. When we do the same for other big cities and towns in Yorkshire such as Sheffield, Bradford, Barnsley, Wakefield, Hull, York, Halifax, Doncaster, Huddersfield etc we can see the exact same pattern. There were literally thousands of small places where knur and spell was played in addition to the bigger towns and cities.

As an example, to demonstrate just how big knur and spell was, consider the case of Mitchell Brothers. This was a small to medium sized textile mill in the Little Horton area of Bradford. i.e. an inner-city suburb. According to the *Bradford Observer* 22 July 1858, a team of knur and spell players from this company played against a team from another textile mill. Mitchell's selected their team of ten players from twenty-six men who had stuck their hands up. There would have been many more players working at Mitchells. These twenty-six were probably the only ones who fancied their chances. The vast majority of these players would not have been the stars of the game. They would have been the Joe Hackers of the game whose names never or seldom appeared in newspaper reports on the big challenge matches. Bradford's population was over one hundred thousand in the mid-1800s, and this rose to over three hundred thousand by the early 1900s. in 1858 there were over forty textile mills just in the inner suburbs and over one hundred mills in the wider Bradford Parish. Mitchell's were only a small to medium sized operation. Some of the bigger mills would have been several times bigger than Mitchell's. There would have been lots of knur and spell players at every mill. Thus there could have been two thousand players just working at the inner-city Bradford mills and more than double that if we took the whole Bradford Parish. Bear in mind also that knur and spell players didn't just come from the textile industry. They were also found in just about every other occupation as detailed in another chapter. And Bradford is only ONE place where knur and spell was played. There were hundreds if not thousands of others.

Ten miles from Bradford is the big city of Leeds, another massive knur and spell playing area. In 1855 there were forty textile mills there too. When we consider all the textile producing towns throughout Yorkshire we would be looking at nine hundred woollen mills by 1850 -1860. There are thousands of other places throughout the former Danelaw area where the game was played including many sizeable towns. E.g. Hull, York, Lincoln, Sheffield, Leeds, Newcastle, Halifax, Huddersfield, Wakefield, Barnsley, Doncaster, and Manchester. Manchester had a massive cotton industry. Just in Lancashire alone there were two thousand six hundred cotton mills. I could probably fill several more pages with place names, but I think the point is made. Knur and spell playing in the mid-1800s was huge!

We should understand that although the playing of knur and spell had been seen across a very wide area of the Danelaw at least two hundred years earlier, the massive expansion of the game probably occurred from about 1800 or late 1700s onwards and preceded the golf explosion, which we ultimately saw, by roughly one hundred years. The Bradford mill example cited above mirrored this massive expansion. In 1801 there was only ONE textile mill in Bradford!

There are also plenty of places in England which were not swallowed up by big cities. They just disappeared altogether and became 'lost villages or hamlets'. Reasons for this disappearance are varied. They may have struggled to survive in the time the Great Plague was around. They may have been submerged when dams and reservoirs were constructed. The land may have just been bought up by rich landowners who drove the villagers away so that they could develop the area for hunting or other reasons. Sometimes the land was confiscated by the government so that it could be converted into military training grounds. Two such famous 'lost' villages in Yorkshire are Wharram Percy in the Yorkshire Wolds and Whorlton which is close to the North Yorkshire Moors. I don't know if knur and spell was ever played at Wharram Percy. However, it is close to Pocklington, Malton, York, Beverley, Goole, and Hull which were all knur and spell centres. Similarly, Whorlton is close to many knur and spell playing places such as Danby, Northallerton, Ainthorpe, Swainby, Faceby, Guisborough, Helmsley, Hinderwell, Whitby etc. There were also quite a few lost hamlets on Baildon Moor (Low Springs, Moorside, Sconce etc) where we know that knur and spell was played at least from the early 1600s. Little Matlock is a small, vanished hamlet where knur and spell was played. This used to be near the village of Loxley just west of Sheffield. There are hundreds if not thousands of such places all across the north of England and many of them are known to have been knur and spell playing places.

Two of the most noteworthy places where villages disappeared because of reservoir flooding which are in the Danelaw area are Lady Bower reservoir in Derbyshire and Haweswater reservoir in the Lake District. Both these reservoirs were only constructed in the 1930 / 1940s.

Two villages, Ashopton and Derwent, were submerged in Lady Bower which is situated on the Snake Pass on the main road (A57) over the moors between Manchester and Sheffield. Knur and spell had already found its way across the Snake Pass from Yorkshire into many Manchester suburbs well over a century before the dam was made or maybe even earlier. So it is very likely that the game was played in both Ashopton and Derwent.

Two villages, Mardale Green and Measand, also disappeared when Haweswater was constructed by Manchester Corporation in the Lake District. Knur and spell had been extensively played all over the southern Lake District in many remote villages and hamlets dating to at least the 1600s. Mardale Green had a pub called the Dun Bull, so there is a chance that knur and spell was played here. Mardale was in the parish of Shap. This parish is known to have had two thingmounts which date to the Viking era. One was situated in Mardale and the other close to Keld which is nearer to Shap. There is another thingmount at Little Langdale which is just a few miles away. These thingmounts, which could also be called moots, were open-air court meeting places where the Vikings made their laws. Problem was that the Vikings in this part of Cumbria were mostly Norwegian Vikings, probably from the Bergen area on the south-west coast of Norway, who had arrived via the Ireland, Scotland, and Isle of Man route. My overall findings have been that knur and spell was not widely played where these Norwegian Vikings predominated. i.e. knur and spell was overwhelmingly played in the area dominated by Danish Vikings. This could account for why so far I have found very little knur and spell played in the northern part of the Lake district.

Apart from villages disappearing because humans deliberately flooded valleys etc, many seaside town and villages around England have been lost due to coastal erosion problems. Maybe the most serious example of this in the former Danelaw area is the fifty mile stretch of coast in Holderness, between Bridlington and Spurn Point. Experts have estimated that an approximate four-mile-wide area along the whole of this strip, about two hundred square miles of land, has been lost. Erosion probably started in the Roman era or even earlier, but from records we know that much has gone since 1066. Over thirty small towns and villages disappeared in this strip alone. Of course, erosion has not abated. In 2020 coastline in the Holderness region is still being lost at the rate of about two metres per year! Knur and spell was widely played in this area. No doubt many former knur and spell playing towns and villages have been lost in this process over the past few hundred years.

Those of you who know something about English folklore will probably be aware that Loxley is one of the places associated with that likeable rogue, Robin Hood, who was a bit like Ned Kelly in Australian history. The Robin Hood ballads date to the Edward II era in the early 1300s and probably even earlier. In any case long before golf started in Scotland. Although Robin Hood's name is popularly linked to Sherwood Forest and Nottingham, the consensus amongst historians is that he was a south Yorkshireman and spent most of his time there. It may be just another remarkable coincidence, but every single place in Yorkshire ever associated with Robin Hood's name also just happen to be big knur and spell playing places. I wonder if Robin and Little John ever played knur and spell (?) Historians believe that Little John came from the Beverley or Holderness areas of Yorkshire which are also knur and spell regions. Certainly we know from the *Sheffield Daily Telegraph* that knur and spell was played at the Robin Hood and Little John pub at Little Matlock near Stannington in 1881. Their reputed skill at archery and their anti-authoritarian tendencies may have pointed them towards knur and spell. Afterall, there was a strong link between golf and archery in Scotland for hundreds of years and the first golf clubs made were by bowyers. Could a similar thing have happened in England between knur and spell pummels and archery? Stranger things have happened!

It may be worth pointing out at this stage that although knur and spell was only played in the former Danelaw areas, it was not at all unknown in the southern counties of England or for that matter in any parts of Scotland,

Ireland, or Wales. Throughout the 1800s and 1900s, articles about knur and spell frequently appeared in newspapers in every nook and cranny in Britain. However, it is true to say that southerners in general mostly did not have a clue what knur and spell was and for them there was always a mystery surrounding it. This was largely due to the low profile which the knur and spell players tried to maintain to minimise their chances of being hauled before the courts. This arcanum still prevailed at the end of the twentieth century as the game of knur and spell finally drew its last breath.

What we should all be aware of is that in the year 1560 when golf was rearing its head in Edinburgh, the total population of that city was only about twelve thousand people and many of those would have been poor people who had no financial means to play the expensive game of golf. Moreover, all other towns in Scotland in that era were less than half the size of Edinburgh. If we assume that there would only be two per cent rich men, and not all of them would play golf, it probably means that very few people indeed would have started off the golf craze in the Edinburgh and Leith area in those days. Quite a few of those early golfers at Leith were also visiting English royalty plus aristocrats and noblemen from the English parliament in London. Do you remember the Duke of York partnering John Patterson against two English noblemen? We never saw any Scottish newspaper reports from that era about Hamish McHaggisface playing Jock McStrap to decide who was going to buy the haggis.

Chapter 23

Cloth caps, clogs, Aborigines, the rise and fall of knur and spell and stolen holly trees

To my mind there is no doubt whatsoever that knur and spell, at least indirectly, would have played a very big part in the later success of the phenomenon we now know as golf. The rich people in England for over two hundred years would have watched, or at least read about, the cloth cap and clog brigade enjoying themselves playing knur and spell whilst boozing and gambling at the same time. So, when golf clubs in England did eventually start to appear in the second half of the nineteenth century, it was not such a big risk for them. There was a very long and successful tradition of men being fascinated by hitting a little ball with a stick for them to look back on. They could see that the apparently absurd notion of grown men hitting a little ball with a stick and then chasing after it was not going to be a short-lived fad. It was something that had already endured for hundreds of years before in the slightly different format of knur and spell or trap-ball.

Having just mentioned 'cloth cap and clog brigade' it reminds me that something should be said about sporting footwear used over the years. From about the 1850s the Scottish golfers had been making some half-arsed attempt themselves to hammer nails through their shoe and boot soles to give them more grip in wet conditions. In a similar amateurish way to how they had been manually roughing up guttie balls with a hammer to try to affect the ball flight. However, it was the end of the 1800s before shoes specifically designed for golfers, with spikes etc, became available. Compare this with what other sports were doing and we soon find that, as with many other things, the golfers were very slow on the uptake. Cricket shoes with spikes had been commercially available from around the late

1700s or early 1800s. Running shoes and even tennis shoes with spikes had also been around long before the golfers wised up. To my mind it would not have been such a stupid idea for golfers in 1800 to play their game in cricket boots if they wanted to improve their grip! Maybe some of the enlightened ones did?

As for the old knur and spell boys, well they solved the wet weather grip problems hundreds of years before the golfers got their act together. What is more they didn't need specially designed shoes to do it. They played in their everyday footwear...clogs. Clogs had been around for hundreds of years. Morris dancers, who traditionally use clogs, were around in the mid-1400s. From at least the 1600s wooden clogs were particularly favoured by the textile workers of Yorkshire and Lancashire, but they were also popular throughout Britain. The wooden clogs were generally made from either alder or sycamore, but other woods could also be used. They used buffalo skin leather uppers with a clasp fastener. The wet grip secret to these clogs were the clog irons nailed to the bottoms which were a bit like miniature horseshoes. These irons were fixed to both soles and heels. They were about three-eighths of an inch wide and a quarter of an inch thick. There was a groove down the middle to protect the nail heads from excessive wear. The iron was soft enough to be malleable so that it could be hammered to the exact profile of the clog. The clogs made in the north of England were of far superior quality to the all-wooden Dutch clog which many tourists bring back as a souvenir when they go to Holland. A lasting memory I have of wearing the north of England made clogs in my primary school days, late 1940s and early 1950s, was how they fared on winter days when soft snow was on the ground. On such a day there was a very rapid build-up of compacted snow beneath both clogs. In no time at all it was almost like walking on stilts and I was at least six inches taller. Very useful for me because I was always a short arse! The build-up was generally removed by kicking one clog against the other or by stubbing the toe of the clog, which had a metal toe-guard protection, into something hard like a stone wall! The other things I remember is that we could generate sparks by scraping the clogs at speed across the stone pavement surface and that you could hear people coming for quite a distance away because of the clatter made by the clogs on the stone pavements. I can still remember my intrigue at watching the clogs take shape on the clogger's last and how impressed I was by his dexterity.

As far as Australia is concerned, competition knur and spell was played here for many several decades before the Australian Open championship first fired up in 1904 with a first prize of only ten pounds. Even twenty-five years before this, one could probably earn more money playing knur and spell in the Hunter Valley! Golf was definitely less popular than knur and spell in those days and less profitable for the winners. How times have changed!

By an interesting quirk of coincidence, around the same time the Durham miners were playing knur and spell in the Hunter Valley, an Australian sporting team were visiting all the main knur and spell playing towns in the North of England (Sheffield, Leeds, Bradford, Newcastle, North Shields, Blackburn, Halifax, Rochdale, Bury, Keighley, Middlesbrough, Hunslet, Lincoln etc). But they were not there to play knur and spell. The ALL-ABORIGINAL cricket team were the first Australian team from any sport in 1868 to tour England. Amazingly, they did it about fourteen years BEFORE the birth of the famous Ashes. It was an incredibly long tour which lasted from May 25 to October 17. During this time, they played no fewer than forty-seven matches all over the country!

They spent much of their time playing cricket and giving other displays, which included throwing cricket balls, boomerangs, and spears! At a venue in Blackburn, just ten miles from where I was born, they played against an East Lancashire team. Charley Dumas (traditional name Pripumuarraman) reputedly threw a cricket ball close to one hundred and twenty-six metres (or about one hundred and thirty-eight yards as it was in those days). Ten miles in the in the opposite direction from my home, over the border in Yorkshire, they played Keighley CC on 27 July 1868. It was the twentieth match of their tour. Both teams used over-arm bowling, which had only been legalised in 1864. Dick-a-Dick, Sundown, Rd Cap, Mullagh, Jim Crow, Twopenny, Peter, Bullocky, Charley, Cuzens and Mosquito managed an honourable draw in that match. Dick-a-Dick (traditional name Djungadjinganoook or Yanggendyinanyuk) was the son of a Wotjobaluk Chief. He lived at the Ebenezer Mission in Dimboola near Horsham and died there in 1886. I visited there in March 2021. The old Moravian church still stands but is all fenced off.

Knur and spell had been played in the Keighley area at hamlets such as Harehills and Syke Head near Oakworth at least from the 1700s. There are no reports that this pioneering aboriginal team attended any knur and spell event. But this sport was at its peak when they were in England from May to October 1868. It was on a par with cricket and bigger than football, so it would not be surprising if they had at least some exposure to knur and spell. Not forgetting that many of the top English cricketers of the day played knur and spell themselves and also many of the cricket clubs at that time organised knur and spell events. Also remembering that knur and spell was prominently featured in the first ever Wisden cricket almanac in 1864 which Australian cricketers would have seen, and no doubt been intrigued about. In 2018 it will be the one hundred and fiftieth anniversary of that first ground-breaking tour but sadly in all that time only ONE aboriginal man has played test cricket for Australia (Jason Gillespie).

The good news is that two all aboriginal teams, both male and female, toured England in 2018 to commemorate the 1868 tour. During the 2018 tour a board was unveiled at Victoria Park Cemetery in East London to tell the story of that first team and to honour King Cole (traditional name Bripumyarramin) who had died during the 1868 tour. It is also good to know that Jason Gillespie is currently Head Coach at the Sussex Cricket Club after earlier having done a stint with the Yorkshire Cricket Club. For a very good analysis of this first sporting tour of England read *Strangers in a Strange Land...The 1868 Aborigines and other Indigenous Performers in Mid-Victorian Britain* by David Sampson which was a thesis submitted to the University of Technology, Sydney in 2000.

According to a 2007 abridged report by EIGCA (European Institute of Golf Course Architects), there were fifty-seven golf courses in England in 1888. This number had risen to one thousand eight hundred and fifty by 1914. In 1888 knur and spell 'laikers' would have outnumbered golf players in England by several orders of magnitude. Despite golf taking off after the first Open Championship in 1860, the number of advertisements in the *Yorkshire Post* between 1870 and 1920 actually indicate that knur and spell also increased in popularity during that period. Even in 1920 pub adverts in the *Yorkshire Post* for knur and spell matches accounted for fifty-six per cent of all pub activity adverts at that time. Winners of knur and spell matches in the 1920s would regularly receive one hundred pounds prize money. The 1920 winner of the 55th Open golf championship at Royal Cinque Ports GC in Deal won just seventy-five pounds. Although golf courses and golf clubs in England were burgeoning at that time, knur and spell in Yorkshire and East Lancashire probably held its own with golf up at least up until the start of World War II in terms of prize money and number of participants.

It is irrefutable that knur and spell (poor man's golf), for much of its history, was played in England by far more people than golf and in far more individual locations. However, as we all know, knur and spell's greater popularity didn't last forever. At the end of the nineteenth century knur and spell still enjoyed a big lead over golf, but by the end of the twentieth century knur and spell was practically unknown. In the same period golf had gone through the roof. So why did the game of golf kick on and knur and spell become obsolete? There is no single answer to this question.

By the 1900s both games had been going for hundreds of years. The evolution of golf was a very slow process. It took about four hundred years before a ball was developed around 1850 which the ordinary working man could afford to buy. That was probably the single most important change for golf. In the hundred years that followed the number of golf courses in the world increased from about twelve to over thirty thousand. There were many other factors which had an influence on this speed-up in development. The Industrial Revolution had started in the late 1700s and by 1850 railways in England and Scotland were everywhere, backed-up by a wide network of horse-drawn vehicles which connected small villages and towns with the main train stations. Curiously enough, the first horse drawn stage coach to appear in the UK was in 1610 and it ran between Edinburgh and the port of Leith...thus connecting the city with the Leith Links golf playing area. St Andrews in Scotland opened up their rail-link in 1852 and no doubt this played a big part in the future success of that city. St Andrews, under Old Tom Morris, were also the first golf club in around 1875 to completely separate the teeing ground from the putting green. Golf artisans turned into club professionals and as golf exploded, hundreds of Scottish golfers started to find employment as professionals at new start-up clubs all around the world.

With the replacement of the featherie ball, golf club design started to change. The long-nosed clubs made by the artisans which had been widely used and designed to be at least a bit user friendly towards the featherie ball, were gradually phased out as the so-called 'bulger' clubs started to appear in the 1880s and 1890s. This happened in just a few decades after having ruled the roost for several hundred years. The guttie ball, and golf balls developed after that, were much more tolerant of iron clubs and by the early 1900s a typical set of clubs generally had far more iron clubs in it than wooden ones. This change also started to bring in large commercial enterprises such as Dunlop, Spalding, Slazenger etc as demand for golf balls and golf equipment generally began to skyrocket. Gradually over time these companies grew to dominate the golf club and golf ball manufacturing side of the game at the expense of the club based professional. Hand-crafted golf clubs mostly disappeared as mass-produced equipment became available.

In the early days, most of the golf clubs probably didn't have their own dedicated golf courses to play on. Golfers usually played on common land which was shared with the public for other activities such as picnicking or taking their dog for a walk. Farmers would also be grazing their animals there which served to keep the grass short. Leith links in Edinburgh was one such place. At its peak there were several dozen golfing societies all playing their games there. Blackheath GC in the London area was another such club. They played on Greenwich Hill before moving to their current site. To try to keep the peace when sharing the links with the general public they always played wearing red jackets so that the public could identify them as golfers. They also played with a forecaddie whose job it was to go ahead to where they intended to hit the ball. His job was not just to keep an eye on where the ball went to make sure it was not lost. He also had to warn any members of the public that golfers were coming through and to watch out for flying missiles. In Blackheath in 1856 the forecaddie wore a red cap and carried a red flag. Even in 1889 BHGC had a local rule which said 'Golfers must wait for people and conveyances to pass out of their way before playing. It is not sufficient to call fore'. As late as 1908 Blackheath golfers at Greenwich still played with a forecaddie who was absolutely a *sine qua non*. By this time the forecaddie was actually carrying two red flags which he operated in a rather semaphoric manner to indicate to his player that the coast was clear. Much resembling, I suppose, the bizarre antics of an AFL goal umpire in 2021. Eventually as the numbers of golfers and public users significantly increased it became too dangerous to share the playing space, so they had to find a dedicated area.

It is interesting to note from the newspapers of the 1885 to 1900 period, that although golf was starting to explode, and even though Blackheath was the oldest club in England, their average turn-out at monthly medal events was still only twenty to twenty-five players. This was a pathetically low number compared to what was happening at knur and spell handicap events over that period in every nook and cranny of the north of England. However, on 24 April 1845 the *Kentish Gazette* reported that only fifteen players contested the summer medal at Blackheath, so the 1890 figures did at least show a nice percentage increase!

The rise and fall of knur and spell followed quite a different path to golf. Whereas golf had survived from about 1450-1850 on the backs of royalty, aristocrats, rich landowners, and some other rich citizens such as Kincaid the Edinburgh surgeon, knur and spell had grown steadily from at least the early 1600s and probably earlier. Supported primarily by the working classes, knur and spell continued to grow throughout the 1700s and the first half of the 1800s. Unlike golf, knur and spell did not go through the struggling period in the first third of the 1800s. By 1850, knur and spell was far bigger than all the golf in Scotland and England combined. It had far more participants than golf and was played in hundreds if not thousands more places. It was able to do this despite very little publicity. Moreover, much of the publicity it did get was negative. Players being fined for playing knur and spell on Sundays. People being killed by being hit by flying knurs or by heads detaching from pummels. Landlords being fined for allowing illegal gambling on their premises. Players being hauled before the courts because they had chopped down someone's holly or boxwood trees to make knurs with etc. There were even regular disputes amongst players as to how matches should be conducted which occasionally ended up in a bout of fisticuffs.

Stolen boxwood or holly trees was a big problem throughout the 1800s. Mostly the theft of these trees was from large country estates owned by rich landowners or titled people. Bryam Park occupied by Sir John Ramsden and the Ramsden family since 1628 was one such place. This was a few miles east of Wakefield and just south of York. Coxhoe Hall in County Durham which had been around since 1300 was another. The famous poet Elizabeth Barrett Browning was born there in 1806. Becca Hall near Lotherton-cum-Aberford (a few miles east of Leeds) was built in 1783 and for a while a Colonel Markham lived there. It was bought in 2011 by the sister of the famous wilderness survivor Bear Grylls. Sandbeck Park in Maltby which was built in 1626 was another happy hunting ground for boxwood and holly trees. This was the family seat of successive Earls of Scarborough. Thrybergh Hall was built in 1811 as a private residence for the Fullerton family. These days it serves as the opulent clubhouse for Rotherham GC which founded in 1903. Esholt Hall near Shipley in Yorkshire was built by Sir Walter Calverley in the early 1700s. It was then owned by the Stansfield family from 1755 until the early 1900s. Blackwell Hall / Grange near Darlington in county Durham dates to the late 1600s. It was the home of the High Sheriff of Durham. Aireville Hall at Gargrave near Skipton was built in 1836 for a rich mill owner. Abbey House at Kirkstall near Leeds was originally built as the gatehouse to Kirkstall Abbey in the 1100s. Later it was converted to a private residence and in the mid-1880s George Beecroft and family lived there. Gledstone House near Skipton was built around 1770. Throughout the 1800s it was occupied by the Roundell family. Yet another was Burley Hall in Burley-in-Wharfedale which is close to Ilkley, Otley, and Bradford. This hall had been built around 1630 and re-built after a fire in 1832.

All these places and many more like them throughout northern England were regular plundering grounds for would-be boxwood or holly tree thieves to enable them to satisfy the big market demand for wooden knurs. Many of the rogues successfully absconded with their booty, but lots of others ended up in the English Court system as dozens of old newspaper reports will attest to!

Again, unlike golf, cost of playing was never an issue with knur and spell. Most of the equipment used was self-made or at least made in someone's garage or garden shed. The working part of the game, the knurs, were always considerably cheaper than the featherie golf balls. This applied when hand-made holly, boxwood or stag horn knurs were used, but even more so when ceramic knurs were used. Maybe the fact that most of the equipment, apart from the ceramic knurs, were either self-made or supplied via a cottage industry contributed to the demise of the sport.

A very good typical example of the cottage industry supplied equipment was detailed in the *Yorkshire Evening Post*, 24 August 1926. This gave the history of a man called 'Jimmy' Robinson who lived in Hunslet which is now part of modern-day Leeds. Jimmy died in about 1914. The story was told by his son Harry who had helped his dad to make the gear since he was about six or seven years old. About fifty years earlier Jimmy had been taught how to make knur and spell tackle by a man called 'Mousey' Liversedge from Hunslet. Jimmy himself rarely played knur and spell but he supplied equipment to many of the top players. He made knurs, spells, pommel sticks and heads in his workshop in the cellar of his home. Most of his customers were in Lancashire or Yorkshire but he also sold to Billy Davies who was a famous knur and spell player living in Wales. Although he had a Welsh sounding name, Billy was a Yorkshire man born in Castleford. He was a glass blower who had moved to Wales and taken the game with him. Billy wasn't the only Yorkshireman to take knur and spell into Wales. According to the *Wrexham Advertiser* 8 October 1864, a man called Edward Manners, who had been born in Knaresborough in 1830, introduced the game in the north Welsh town of Wrexham.

The spells Jimmy made had an iron bed (not wood) with spike legs which fixed it to the ground for stability. It had a steel spring with a cup at the end to project the knur into the air. A bridge with a brass screw served to regulate the spring. A spell cost one pound to twenty-five shillings in those days. Not an insignificant cost in the 1800s.

The knurs which Jimmy and his son made were either from boxwood or lignum vitae. Even by the 1870s holly was probably already proving difficult to get hold of. The wood knurs were nearly as big as a golf ball and had either crude dimples or criss-cross lines carved on them. They were about one ounce in weight or slightly more. Individual customers had their own preferences when it came to weight. Some wanted the knurs to weigh an ounce plus one shilling. Some wanted it to weigh an ounce and fifteen pence (which was made up of an ounce plus a shilling piece and one three-penny bit). Others wanted an ounce plus eighteen pence (an ounce plus a shilling piece plus a sixpenny piece). Wooden knurs took quite some time to make and sold for sixpence each. At these kind of weights, the wooden knurs were clearly more than twice as heavy as the common pot knurs which were generally only half an ounce. Thus the extra weight and the rough surface characteristics of the wooden knurs obviously more than compensated for the greater wind resistance, because the wooden knurs could be hit considerably further than the lighter weight and lower wind resistance pot knurs.

When the knurs were finished, they were soaked in oil for a few weeks. The boxwood knurs had to be hardened by pickling in a salt and sand preparation. Obviously, the knurs when soaked in anything would absorb the medium and would increase in weight. I don't know if the weight check was done before or after this conditioning process.

Jimmy's brand of pummel heads were mostly combinations of hornbeam and maple woods. To get the wood as hard as possible it was pressed in a two-stage process. The first part of the pressing was done at a forge. The job was finished off in a gas press in his cellar. This was a manually operated affair and highly secret 'homemade technology.' The pressed wood was glued to the face and also pegged to hold it in place.

The splice of the head was made from old pick handles (hickory) and the shaft from ash. The pummel stick was made by Jimmy planing down the grain and the head was held in place using a wax band and gutta percha. The shafts varied in length from forty-two inches to fifty-four inches and there was a cotton band at the top to give a good grip.

The shaft was very fine piece of work. According to Jimmy's son it would apparently 'crack almost like a whiplash' after it had been shaved down ready to fix the spliced head. It would rival even the superb craftmanship of the best surviving hickory golf club maker in Australia, my good friend Ross Baker! Although there were many newspaper reports throughout the long history of knur and spell about heads flying off pommel sticks or of shafts breaking, Jimmy's son was very proud of the fact that users of Robinson-made knur-sticks had never experienced either splice or shaft failure when hitting or lost a pummel head.

Throughout the north of England there was a wide network of 'Jimmies' beavering away in their cellars, garages and garden sheds making spells, knurs, and pummels in order to make some extra cash on the side. Every single one of them would have his own idea of just how these items should be made and what the best raw materials were. Our Jimmy was using ash for his shafts, but by 1870 many of the makers would have switched to hickory. There was no governing body which set the rules for the game and for the equipment used. Any kind of wood could be used to make the pummel heads, the knurs, and the shafts. The knurs could also be made of stag horn, ceramic, stone or even metal. This kind of complexity was probably great for the betting aspect of the game but ultimately, I suspect that it didn't help the game to survive. By the time I became aware of knur and spell in the late forties and early 1950s, the big money knur and spell challenge matches had already become a thing of the past.

Whereas golf eventually evolved to a stage where expensive dedicated golf courses and club houses were necessary, knur and spell never had this cost element. In the early days both golf and knur and spell both revolved around pubs. Unfortunately, knur and spell never managed to break this nexus. It never had dedicated grounds and it never had dedicated club houses. Nor did the equipment used ever become fully commercialised. Some of the fancy spells used to elevate the knur prior to hitting were professionally made. So too were the kiln fired ceramic knurs, although they were never made specifically for knur and spell. They were made for other uses and knur and spell players just latched on to their availability. As soon as most of these other uses dried up, so did the ceramic knur supply. The minimum order size for pottery makers to make them specially was just too high.

In 1958 the Worcester Porcelain Company did offer to supply porcelain spheres to the few remaining knur and spell players from their manufacturing facility in Glamorgan, South Wales. However, maybe the size of their standard spheres was not suitable or maybe the number of players still playing the game was too small to hold their interest. Or maybe their spheres were not robust enough and shattered too often?

The original stag horn knurs disappeared first. Then the lignum vitae, holly and box-wood knurs also became much harder to get. Lignum vitae was imported and was an expensive wood. Boxwood and holly grew in England, but people started to get more and more annoyed as players illegally chopped down their trees. More court cases and fines resulted and eventually 'free supply' of these woods also started to dry up. Eventually the much cheaper ceramic knurs also became harder to get. Probably because their use to prevent furring in hard water areas was made redundant as water softening chemicals came into vogue for use in factory boilers...usually salt-based ion-exchange systems.

Not having their own ground to play on also began to give problems. Playing knur and spell in built up areas was too dangerous and city councils started to bring in byelaws to forbid the playing of knur and spell in inner city areas, public parks etc. As early as May 1935 the *Sheffield Independent* newspaper was reporting that there were notices at the entrances to Sheffield Parks announcing penalties for anyone caught playing knur and spell. Farmers got tired of thousands of spectators trampling over their fields, damaging crops, damaging gates, and dry-stone walls. Also leaving gates open which allowed cows and other animals to escape. Playing on the moors probably continued the longest but some councils even banned this as the early 'greenies' began to pop their heads up.

The complexity of all the different knur types which could be used would not have helped the game overall. However, maybe the chief reason knur and spell didn't survive is because it never had a central governing body or a unified set of rules. Had it been better organised it would probably still be around today. To support this view, we only need to look at the case of hornussen (Swiss farmers golf) which was briefly mentioned earlier in this story. Hornussen, like knur and spell, is essentially also a long driving competition. Like knur and spell, it also goes back at least to the early 1600s and most likely earlier than that. Another similarity between knur and spell and hornussen is that they were both very popular in the 1800s. Hornussen was especially strong in Emmental and Entlebuch.

Switzerland is a small country. In area it is significantly smaller that the Danelaw knur and spell playing counties of England and with about three million fewer people. The difference was that hornussen was properly organised. A Swiss Federal Hornussen Association was up and running by 1902 and today they have well over two hundred clubs and over seven thousand members. An international Hornussen Association was founded in 2012 to promote the sport world-wide and today they have more than twenty clubs in the USA. Had knur and spell done the same, at the end of the 1800s or early 1900s, they may well have also survived.

Golf had laid down a set of rules as early as 1744 and these rules have been constantly evolving ever since to keep pace with changes in equipment, changes in course design and also reflecting the spread of golf from Scotland to almost every other country in the world. The first ever consolidated code of rules was issued by the R & A in 1899 and the first unified rules between the R & A and the USGA arrived in 1952. The best summary of the changes which occurred between 1744 and 2016 can be seen in the paper issued by the R & A / USGA in 2016 entitled *A Brief History of Revisions to the Rules of Golf: 1744 to Present.* Knur and spell suffered the consequences of never having had a proper organised structure.

Still better examples of very ancient stick and ball games which survived because they had strong organisations are shinty in Scotland and hurling in Ireland. These similar Gaelic games probably date to at least one thousand years before golf started. When football, cricket, rugby, athletics etc began to form governing bodies during Queen Victoria's reign, shinty and hurling did the same thing. Because of that they are still thriving in 2020. On the other hand, the Isle of Man played a similar stick and ball game for hundreds of years called 'cammag'. But like knur and spell they did not formalise their organisation and consequently they vanished despite, again like knur and spell, having a few revival efforts. The Gaels were a sub-branch of the Celtic people who arrived in Britain in the 500s BC.

Apart from all these factors, there was a whole raft of developments outside of knur and spell which had a big impact. As we know, towards the end of the nineteenth century golf was expanding very quickly after having languished in the doldrums for the previous four hundred years. But golf wasn't alone. Football, which had been around even longer than golf and had languished for maybe five or six hundred years, suddenly start to take off with the formation of the first football league in the late 1800s. Cricket, which had been around as long as golf, had started to take off in the 1700s and 1800s but it too had a big surge in the late 1800s as Test Match cricket began. Rugby had been around at least since the 1600s without making much progress but following the lead of cricket and football and producing a set of standard rules, it too grew fast. So much so that even before 1900 rugby had split into the two codes of Union and League. Other lower profile sports were also springing up everywhere.

All these developments gave both players and spectators a much wider choice about where they spent their leisure time. Couple that with the fact that people in Britain were better off financially than they had been before the Industrial Revolution, so they could better afford to participate in some of the more expensive options than knur and spell. Apart from having more money to spend on their leisure time, they also had more leisure time to spend their money on. Although there was a wide range of working hours throughout the 1800s across different occupations, factory hours for many people were very long. The 1833 *Factory Act* specified sixty-nine hours for a six-day working week. This reduced to sixty hours in 1847 with the *Ten Hours Act*. In the 1870s it was nine hours per day and by 1919/1920 it was eight hours per day with forty-seven hours per week maximum. This dropped to forty-five hours per week in the 1946/1949 period and today is significantly less than that. It is maybe interesting to note that with the 1847 and 1850 Factory Acts that Manchester was the first big city in England to reduce working hours by allowing workers to stop work at two o'clock on Saturday afternoons!

On further reflection, it was apparent that the final demise of knur and spell also probably followed the fate of the British coal, textile, and steel industries where a sizeable cohort of the players came from. All these industries had been declining prior to WW2. There was a further big surge in mill closures between 1960 and 1970 and by the early 1980s it was all over red rover. The same thing happened with the coal industry which was finally kyboshed by Margaret Thatcher following the 1984 - 1985 major strike. Thatcher's battle with the miners had nothing to do with the poor economics of the coal industry *per se*. Grimethorpe Colliery still made over one million pounds profit in the year before it was closed! She had a vehement ideological desire to crush trade unionism, no matter what the industry was, with scant regard to any social impact. In the early 1980s there were about one hundred and seventy-five coal mines in the UK. Today fewer than ten survive. In fact the last decent sized coal mine in England closed in August 2020. At its peak in 1913 there were about two thousand six hundred coal mines in the UK employing over one million people. The UK still uses about eight million tonnes per year of coal, but this is mostly imported from Russia. Much of this is used in the steel and cement making industries, but over the past few decades the UK steel industry has also declined dramatically and will be following coal into oblivion shortly. As one might imagine the UK's CO2 emissions have dropped dramatically as the much lower energy requirement from their lost manufacturing industries kicked in. Of course this has had little or no effect on world emissions because the slack is just taken up by other developing countries. In 2020 China now has well over fifty per cent of the world's steel production. They make considerably more than the USA and EU combined! I hope that western countries don't need to ramp up warships and tanks production quickly in the near future! With a forty-six per cent share China also dominate world coal production by a massive margin. Even in 2020 both China and Russia are still planning very big coal production expansions. Russia is targeting a twenty-five per cent share of the global coal market by 2035. They just love it when countries like the UK and Australia shut down all their manufacturing industries! Looks to me like a touch of the 'short and curlies' will soon be the order of the day... or already is! There is a very old well known Chinese proverb which says that 'he that puts all his eggs in one basket inevitably ends up with egg on his face!' Human greed hath no limitations!

The other thing which I am sure didn't help knur and spell was it being constantly referred to as 'poor man's golf'. The connotations conveyed by this description were not exactly subtle. Poor men didn't like being called poor men, even if they were poor! Many men who had just modest aspirations of climbing up the social ladder did not wish to be associated with something that was known as a poor man's game. Even linking a game to an occupation like 'collier's golf' with the miners or 'Swiss farmer's golf' with hornussen was much more preferable. Apart from this 'unflattering' description of knur and spell, another factor which would not have helped was its constant ridiculing in the southern press. Not of course in *Bell's Life* and *Sporting Life* newspapers, but certainly in the daily tabloids.

With the benefit of hindsight, we can probably say that had it survived knur and spell would probably have been better equipped than golf for the modern era. In 2019 many golf clubs are struggling. As far as I can see, the two main problems they have are as follows. Firstly, it is a very time-consuming game. To play eighteen holes of golf can often take five hours. Add to that time taken to drive to and from the course and also add any time spent at the nineteenth hole. In an age of instant gratification, this kind of time expenditure is difficult to justify. As I see it, the cost of membership at a golf club is not the major issue. The time element is the main factor at play. Secondly, as memberships are dropping, clubs are selling their land to housing developers. They then either build another course further out in the sticks where land is cheaper, or they amalgamate with another club. Both are relatively short-term band-aid solutions. Moving out to a course many miles out of the city only makes the travelling time problem much worse!

Knur and spell never had either of these two problems. Even in the 1800s knur and spell competitions could be played over anything from three rises to one hundred rises depending on how many entrants there were to the competition. In other words, it could be infinitely variable to suit the time available! The other major advantage for knur and spell was that it did not need the vast amount of land which is required for a golf course. Golf courses can be anywhere from seventy-five acres to one hundred and fifty acres whereas knur and just needed about as the same land used for a short par four. i.e. Approximately five per cent as much land as a golf course and probably significantly less than this because of the all the 'wasted' land in between holes on a golf course. Needless to say, the cost of maintaining a knur and spell field would be only a tiny fraction of the money spent on golf course upkeep! Knur and spell never used fancy machines to keep the grass in their playing fields short. The course maintenance team was always comprised of sheep, cows and goats.

The big land cost and high maintenance cost issues with golf courses are things which will be difficult to solve, and which will only get worse as time goes by. The only way I could see this problem being at least slowed down is by reducing the number of holes on a golf course to nine holes or even less, as was the case for the vast majority of golf's existence. The time element is something which could be tackled by looking at different formats of the game.

Cricket is perhaps the best example of this. They never had the big land requirement which golf has, but the time element in traditional five-day cricket was much worse than in golf. So, they came up with limited overs ODI's and Twenty20 as played in the Australian Big Bash League as alternatives to the five-day game.

Tennis is another game which will probably have to address the time element of the game in future. Starting a five-set match at nine o'clock in the evening and finishing in the early hours of the morning, or even in the middle of the night, is ridiculous and certainly not fair to the players involved. Have the tennis organisers never heard of biorhythms? Maybe they will need to stop giving players a free serve every time they serve? Why should the very tall players be given such a massive advantage which often gives them thirty or forty free points every match? Maybe they will also need to abolish the net serve rule and make it rub-of-the green as in general play? These two changes alone would speed-up tennis enormously.

By the 1950s and 1960s when I first became interested in all these things, knur and spell was already on its last legs. There were a few attempts at revival, but all these were doomed to fail even before they started. This was because in 1967, the MP for Blackburn, Barbara Castle, introduced the breathalyser into the UK to curb drink driving. Knur and spell had always been very closely linked to pubs with the associated heavy drinking and gambling. After the breathalyser came in, the whole nature of British pub life began to change dramatically. In tandem with the breathalyser there were constant alcohol tax increases over a long period. Prior to the breathalyser the social life of many working-class people had revolved around activities at the pub for hundreds of years. But over the next twenty years this was transformed, and traditional English pub life disappeared forever. In droves, people stopped going to the pub for a full night out.

If they went out at say seven o'clock in the evening for a night out, they had already reached their limit on the breathalyser for driving home by 8 o'clock. So, what could they do for the next three hours? Beer prices had gone through the roof because of high taxes, so they started to go out for just the last hour between ten and eleven o'clock closing time. Many pubs didn't survive and were closed down. Most of the ones which did survive turned themselves mainly into eating places and many of the old pub games such as cribbage (a card game), dominoes, darts, knur and spell etc began to disappear or at least diminish sharply. In the county of Yorkshire alone, the number of establishments appearing on the 'lost pubs' list as of 5 November 2020 was three thousand three hundred and twenty-two! Just as a matter of interest, the first man ever to be fined in court for drink driving was a London taxi driver. It was in 1897 and he was driving a horse and carriage! I don't know if it was the man or the horse or both who had been drinking too much!

I suppose at the end of the day we can only be amazed at just how long the anachronistic game of knur and spell survived. Even in the 1950s, when I first tried to play the game, I could clearly see that it was a game which belonged to another age. It was only due to the dedication of the likes of Billy Baxter, Stuart Greenfield, Len Kershaw and a handful of likeminded Yorkshiremen that the game managed to stagger on for another forty or fifty years before it fizzled out.

It's an interesting perspective, but even though knur and spell was actually booming in the mid-1800s, newspapers in England outside of the big knur and spell playing areas, would often publish articles about its demise. For example, the *Leicestershire Mercury* dated 8 October 1842 reported 'The field games of old England have almost entirely passed away. Football, throwing the quoits, spell and knor, archery – have become obsolete and forgotten, like old fashion in apparel, or a custom known only in name'... How wrong could they get it? Football is now probably the biggest sport in the world. Quoits and archery are still very popular and spell and knor peaked and then struggled on for another one hundred and fifty years after that article was written! A stark reminder that we should all take much of what is written in newspapers, or in books like this one for that matter, with a pinch of salt. Or at least we should seriously question them.

We may never know if knur and spell preceded golf. The *Dictionary of Archaisms and Provincialisms,* compiled by James Orchard Halliwell in the 1800s, lists obsolete phrases, proverbs, and ancient customs from the 1300s. It does include knur and spell. This may suggest that knur and spell came before golf. But the reliability of this particular glossary is probably still open to scrutiny. However, even though knur and spell had just about completely disappeared by the end of the twentieth century, it is safe to say that it certainly left a legacy which remains to this day. Knur and spell was essentially a long driving competition which began many hundreds of years ago. Even today most golfers still get a thrill when they hit a booming drive. Throughout the days when Jack Harris played tournament golf there was often a long driving competition held in association with some of the events he played. In 1963 the incomparable Jack Nicklaus won the US PGA Championship long driving competition with a strike of three hundred and forty-one yards. Fifty-five years ago, with old technology balls and clubs, he was hitting longer than the average PGA tour player does in 2018. The last official knur and spell World Championship took place in 1991. Just a few years before that the World Annual Long Driving Golf Championship had started up in 1975 and has continued every year since. The fascination man has with hitting a little ball a long way exists from time immemorial and it ain't going to evaporate any time soon! Who needs a hole? For the sake of modern-day political correctness please don't answer that question!

Chapter 24

Let's hear it for the royals, rich landowners, Bell's Life and Freemasons

Whether or not knur and spell preceded golf or vice versa can probably be debated *ad infinitum*. However, what cannot be denied is the massive influence that the Royal families of both England and Scotland have played in the successful development of golf from the earliest beginnings. When James **II** of Scotland banned the playing of both golf and football in 1457 he effectively guaranteed a bright future for these two games. Just think about when you tell your children not to do something. They invariably do the opposite. And that is exactly what happened. The law was impossible to enforce even though the ban was re-affirmed in 1471 by James **III** and yet again in 1491 by James **IV**. Finally, James **IV** realised that if you can't beat them it is best to join them. In 1502 he ordered the first ever 'set' of six golf clubs to be custom made for him by a bow-maker in Perth and the ban was lifted. No doubt the signing of the Treaty of Perpetual Peace between England and Scotland in 1502 had some bearing on his action. Mary Queen of Scots later played golf at St Andrews and it was James **VI** of Scotland (James **I** of England) who granted the patent for featherie balls to be made in 1618 because he was spending too much on imported Dutch made balls. James **I**'s son Charles **I** also played golf as did his grandson Charles **II**. James **II** of England (James **VII** of Scotland) also played golf. There are records in the *National Library of Scotland* of his playing golf at Leith Links in 1682 when he was Duke of York before becoming king in 1685. All these royal links to golf and their aristocratic connections in the early days virtually ensured that many things would be written about golf and paintings depicting golf would be commissioned. This would not have happened to the same degree if it was just any old Joe Hacker playing the game. It certainly didn't happen with knur and spell even though it was a game played by far more people.

The royal connection went missing in the eighteenth century when the House of Stuart passed over to the House of Hanover after Queen Anne died in 1714. Then along came King William **IV** and granted the first ever 'Royal Status' to Perth GC in 1833 and shortly after to St Andrews GC in 1834. The Industrial Revolution was in full swing. The guttie ball came along in about 1849 and the first Open championship popped up in 1860. Sixty-odd more golf clubs have gained royal status since then. Sixty of those are in the UK or in Commonwealth countries with only a handful in other countries. The bulk were granted in the late 1800s by Queen Victoria. But since then King Edward **VII**, King George **V**, King George **VI**, and his daughter Queen Elizabeth **II** have all done their share of granting.

The first royal captain of the R & A was **HRH** twenty-one years old Edward Prince of Wales who later became King Edward **VII**. He was elected captain of R & A St Andrews in 1863. This was the first year when the famous 'driving in' ceremony started at St Andrews. Only problem was that he wasn't there to actually do the 'driving in'. He delegated the job to one of his lackeys. To mark the occasion, it was announced in the *Ayrshire Express* 12 September 1863, that Mr Robert Forgan, clubmaker, St Andrews, has just completed a set of nine clubs for **HRH** the Prince of Wales. Looks like it had taken about three hundred and fifty years for a set of clubs to jump from six to nine clubs! After that the number of clubs used by golfers burgeoned. Between 1863 and 1938 it grew to thirty or more clubs. The USGA recognised that this was starting to get ridiculous, so they brought in the fourteen club maximum in 1938 and this has remained the case ever since. The R & A followed their lead in 1939.

The queen's uncle, Edward **VIII**, who abdicated in 1936 to marry American divorcee Wallis Simpson, was also a keen golfer. When he was in exile in Paris after his abdication, he was a regular visitor at St Cloud GC in Paris where Melbourne golfer Jack Harris played in the French Open in 1960. In fact, Edward was a spectator at the championship on the day Jack Harris played with fellow Australian Murray Crafter and Murray smashed the St Cloud course record. Edward and Wallis spent all their exile in a villa in the *Bois de Boulogne* which is less than five kilometres from St Cloud GC. Princess Diana and Dodi Fayed made a brief visit to that villa on that fateful day in August 1997. The royal family have their own 'royal household' golf courses i.e. a nine-holes course at Windsor Castle and a nine-holes course at Balmoral in Aberdeenshire. Prince Andrew, Duke of York, is probably the best golfer in the royal family in 2018. In 2004, which was the two hundred and fiftieth anniversary, he was the last royal captain of the R & A. Without the continued royal patronage at each stage of its evolution, golf would probably not have developed into what it is today. I wonder if Prince Andrew's old mate, Jeffrey Epstein, ever played golf?

The granting of 'royal' status by King William from 1833 came as a timely shot in the arm for golf. With the hiatus from royal patronage during the 1700s and early 1800s, exacerbated by the profligate spending of some of the golf clubs, golf had been on a steady decline in Scotland. In the late 1700s the forerunner to the R & A went bankrupt. In the early 1800s the Burgess Golf Society was very close to going down the gurgler and in 1833 even the Honourable Company of Edinburgh Golfers (now Muirfield GC) had to sell all their clubhouse chattels to try to remain afloat. Paintings, furniture, silverware...it all had to go. One year later the clubhouse itself also had to be sold. These clubs survived but many other clubs sank without trace. The ones which did survive were kept going by the weavers of St Andrews and by a group of rich landowners who were also into heavy gambling. These guys were not themselves great golfers. They just gambled on all kind of sporting activities.

Although they gambled big and regularly put-up big stake money for the artisans of the day like Robertson, Morris, Park, Herd, Dunn, Strath etc, the newspaper coverage they got in Scotland was meagre. However, around the time of the first Open in 1860, or even by the mid-1850s, things began to change as news of the big challenge matches started to get national coverage in English publications such as *Bell's Life, Sporting Chronicle and Sporting Life.* These were the newspapers which the English sporting gamblers relied upon to keep themselves informed. *Bell's* was well established having started in 1822. By the time the first Open was held they had been covering sports such as horse racing, boxing matches, knurr and spell, wrestling, arrow throwing, pidgeon shooting, dog racing, hare coursing, quoits, pedestrianism, and other sports for almost forty years. This additional much wider exposure to the national gambling community gave golf an even bigger economic boost than the 'royal' status had done. The artisan club and ball makers mentioned above, mostly went on to be the first golf professionals at golf clubs and then on to golf course design. Knur and spell managed to stay ahead of golf in England for at least another sixty years after the 1860 Open, but the die was cast, and the writing was already on the wall.

After mentioning the important part which the royal family played in the evolution of golf over the years, it would be remiss of me if I didn't also give some recognition to the role of freemasons in the early development of golf. What is often claimed to be the oldest Masonic Lodge in the world is Lodge of Edinburgh #1 (Mary's Chapel) which dates to 1599. The early masonic activity involving the craft of stonemasonry and guilds etc had gone back earlier than that. However, the face of freemasonry began to significantly change from 1717 when the Scottish stonemasons decided to allow merchants and professional people other than stonemasons to join their lodges or to set up their own lodges. These non-stonemason members were known as speculative members. From the time that freemasons got involved in golf, purpose-built golf clubhouses started to appear. It is well known that freemasons had a very heavy involvement in the setting up of at least five of the first six golf clubhouses to be built in Scotland. The very first golf clubhouse to be built may well have been the one at Bruntsfield links in East Lothian, not long after the 'speculative rule' change in freemasonry. Prior to these golf clubhouses being built, members of golf associations often used to meet in pubs. When the first clubhouse for the Honourable Company of Edinburgh Golfers was built near to Leith Links in 1768, every single member of the club at that time was a freemason. They had been playing at Leith since at least 1744. In 1853 the foundation stone for the R & A clubhouse at St Andrews was laid by a freemason and in the early years at least several captains of their club were freemasons. Until 1789 Blackheath GC in London was a freemasons-only club. I don't know what involvement, if any, freemasons had at Carnoustie GC, but I do know that before Lodge Dalhousie was built in 1882 they used to convene at Simpson's Golf Arms Inn which may indicate that they also had an interest in golf. Musselburgh GC was said to be the only one of the oldest clubs which did not appear to have freemason involvement. However, the Honourable Company moved from Leith to Musselburgh in 1836 and shared the links with several other golf associations. They even built their own clubhouse there in 1865. So, even if Musselburgh GC itself did not have freemason members, Musselburgh links certainly had lots of freemasons playing on it. The Honourable Company did not move to their current home of Muirfield until 1891.

One of the basic rules of joining most freemason lodges is you must be a man. No women allowed. I don't know which wag suggested the acronym GOLF meaning Gentlemen Only Ladies Forbidden, but it is a cracker. Muirfield GC remained that way for two hundred and seventy-three years until they finally voted to allow women members in 2017. They had voted against women members as recent as 2016 but were dragged screaming and kicking into the modern age only after the R & A had deleted Muirfield as a venue from the Open Championship rota list. They are back on the rota list now but at the time of writing I understand that Muirfield GC still has no women members. Ostensibly because they have a long waiting list of people who wish to join, and women have to wait their turn just like everyone else. The R & A could be accused of playing the 'holier than thou' game because they themselves only voted to allow lady members in 2014 and over two years later they still didn't have a changing room for ladies in their main clubhouse. As far as I know ladies still have to change and shower in the Forgan House building which is quite some distance from the main club and of course means that ladies and men members change in separate buildings. Royal St Georges GC, another club on the Open rota, only allowed lady members from 2015. Several other Scottish clubs still retain their men only policy. These include Royal Burgess GC which is one of the six oldest clubs and which of course was very heavily dominated by freemasons.

Knur and spell on the other hand was never designated as a 'men only' sport. It just panned out that way. Virtually every young boy had his own knur and spell equipment long before he was legally old enough to go into a pub. Women could have played if they wanted to and very occasionally they did this on holiday and gala occasions when the sport was played at times like Shrove Tuesday as a whole village activity with no serious money being involved. For these village community days, sometimes very small monetary prizes could be given such as five pounds to the winner, three pounds for second and one pound for third. These prizes would be paid for by a small entrance fee such as sixpence or one shilling. At other times the promoter, usually a village pub landlord, would offer actual prizes such as a copper kettle, a handsome Chinese pig, a case clock valued at three pounds, some new knur and spell equipment, a silver or gold watch, a single barrelled gun, a fat goose, a fancy snuff box or on more than one occasion a pound of tobacco! On one occasion at a challenge match between two men, the loser had to buy dinner for forty people. The dinner consisted of a giant pie which contained amongst other things one leg of mutton, one tongue, four rabbits, two necks of mutton, nine oxtails and two beast neers (kidneys).

On the 4 January 1868, the *Knaresborough Post* reported on a knur and spell match between Janice and Thomas Scarborough playing against William Parker and Thelma Myers. However, in the big knur and spell challenge matches which were always associated with lots of drinking and gambling, it was very much a male dominated sport. Women would be anxiously waiting at home to see if their husbands would return from the moors sober without having gambled away all the housekeeping money!

There were also plenty of newspaper match reports between teenage boys and youths. Generally no stake money was mentioned in these reports, but it wouldn't surprise me if the older men were still placing bets. The most surprising match report I read in this regard was in the Leeds Times 27 July 1861. It was a match at Odsall Common, Wibsey, Bradford between John Haigh and Benjamin Mack. Haigh was nine years old, and Mack was only five years old!

The previously mentioned Blackheath GC in London had in their early days a group of masons playing there who called themselves the Knuckle Club. The Knuckle Club formed in 1789, disbanded in 1825 and became the Blackheath Winter golf Club. They played like this until 1844 when they became part of the parent Blackheath GC. Between 1789 and 1825 they did the Full Monty as far as freemasonry was concerned. They had secret handshakes, coded passwords, dressing up like the most worshipful Grand

Poo-Bah and all the bizarre and clandestine initiation ceremonies etc. In this club he was actually called the 'Grand Knuckle'. However, no one ever knew why this group formed in the first place. Whatever the reason for the formation was they didn't want other people to know about it. Just before they disbanded, they deliberately destroyed the first four pages of their club minutes which may have thrown some light on why they existed. This was an act which of course made outsiders even more suspicious of what they had been up to. Over the years there has been many conspiracy theories on this subject. One which resonates with me concerns Australia. Blackheath has always been a suburb of London which was known as the stock-broker belt. Several prominent members of the Knuckle Club have been linked with ship owning families who set up the process with the British Government to ship convicts to Australia between 1788 and 1868. During the time the Knuckle Club were operating, the club kept a 'betting book' among the members. A great many of the bets placed had nothing to do with golf at all. They would bet on stock price movements, job promotions and demotions, results of battles in the war, ship movements, court trial results etc. All things where you could easily imagine that someone had some inside information or was in a position of influence. The Blackheath parent organisation, which probably had mostly mason members, had anecdotally been in existence since 1608. But any written evidence of the period from 1608 to 1787 was also lost. Apparently destroyed in a fire. Seems to be a pattern here (?) This early BHGC documentation may have gone missing during the time of the Jacobite uprisings or just after them. It had probably been deliberately destroyed to protect Jacobite supporters within the club who feared being incriminated and arrested for high treason.

From 1770 up until the Knuckle Club disbanded there were many significant things happening which would lend themselves to wheeling and dealing. Captain Cook first landed in Botany Bay in August 1770. In between this date and 1787/88 when Commodore Arthur Phillip went back with the First Fleet which included over one thousand convicts, the American War of Independence had started in 1775. This quickly put a stop to convicts being shipped from the UK to the American cotton and tobacco plantations etc and to the trans-Atlantic Slave trade. Although the

African slaves already in America by then were kept in slavery for many years after that.

In England, the Committee for the Abolition of the Slave Trade was formed in 1787...not long before the Knuckle Club formed. This led to the Slave Trade Act in 1807 and eventually to the Slavery Abolition Act in 1833. However, when the First fleet went to Australia in January 1788 it was to set up a colony. Arthur Phillip needed plenty of 'free labour' to help him do this. After the Abolition Committee had been formed in 1787 it was anyone's guess when full Abolition would get through. So, the ban on convicts to America came just at the right time. He had a plentiful supply of convicts who were sentenced to many years of hard labour and did all the heavy lifting jobs in the new colony...for nothing! Of course, the real crooks in Britain who had committed serious crimes (murder etc) were not sent to Australia. Most of them were hanged. Between 1750 and 1775 there were about seven hundred people hanged in London alone. In 1770, in England, there were no less than two hundred and twenty-two crimes for which the penalty was death by hanging. One of those crimes was cutting down a tree. However, I never read about anyone actually being hanged for cutting down a holly or boxwood tree to make knurs with!

The people who came to Australia were mostly poor people convicted of very petty crimes such as stealing a loaf of bread because they were hungry or maybe urinating in the street. For sure there would have been a 'well organised system' in England to ensure that this supply of free labour didn't dry up. One can imagine that such a system could not operate openly. Everything would need to be done in a very secretive and furtive manner. I wonder who may have been the ideal candidates to run such an operation? Probably not the Boy Scouts! From 1788 to 1868 somewhere between 160,000 and 170,000 convicts were sent to Australia.

Transportation levels peaked in the early 1830s just after the Knuckle Club had disbanded and destroyed the important pages in their club records! By the time they disbanded many of the original founders of this club had already died. Any original members still alive would most likely have been getting long in the tooth. Don't we just love conspiracy theories?

We do know from the *Legacies of British Slave-Ownership* website that at least one of the BHGC members, William Innes, who was Blackheath

GC captain in 1778, had some kind of involvement with the slave business. When he died in 1795 there were several slave owner creditors named in his will. It appeared that some of these were Jamaican slave owners. By whichever means Innes amassed his money he certainly did it very successfully to the tune of more than £150,000 which in today's money would be over sixty million pounds. As far as I could see William Innes was never a member of the Knuckle Club, but his nephew Alexander Innes certainly was. Surprise! Surprise! According to the Blackheath Chronicle minutes, it was in fact the very same Alexander Innes, who, when the Knuckle Club disbanded in 1825, destroyed the first few pages of the Knuckle Club Minutes so that no one could ever see why this off-shoot club had been formed in the first place. Good one Sandy! He had another nephew, Joseph Innes, who died in Jamaica in 1779.

These were not the only Blackheath GC members who had an involvement in what we would these days regard as 'shady business'. The star Blackheath GC performer in that respect was prominent BHGC committee member Duncan Campbell. Not only was he a plantation owner in Jamaica which employed lots of slaves, but in Blackheath he was also in charge of the prison hulks transporting convicts to Australia. For much more detail on this subject suggested reading would be *Convict Transportation and the Metropolis, The Letter Books and Papers of Duncan Campbell* from the State Library of NSW. *The Duncan Campbell Letter Books-The Blackheath Connection* website by Dan Byrnes is also a must read. Other BHGC members who get an honourable mention are George Macaulay, William Curtis and Alexander Dalrymple.

So, when we look back at modern Australia's early history there are TWO deplorable things which we should never forget. i.e. The brutal treatment of the indigenous peoples of Australia which resulted in the loss of many thousands of lives AND, simultaneously, the one hundred and seventy thousand British 'convicts' who were effectively sent to Australia as slaves and who were also treated very badly. The majority of these 'convicts' had been sentenced for petty crimes such as stealing a pair of knickers from someone's washing line. You got seven years for this particular offence, which was ridiculous, especially if the knickers didn't even fit you properly! During the two hundred and fifty-eight years that transportation to the Americas or Australia took place, the political scene in England was dominated by either the Tories or the Whigs (originally called the Whiggamores and later to become the Liberals).They were the ones who were calling the shots! So, it is not really surprising that bad things occurred! They didn't care about hurting other people, no matter whether it be the aboriginals of Australia or their own British people! What's in it for me was their only mantra... and still is! In a nutshell, the privileged aristocrats begat the Whigs and the Whigs begat the Liberals. I rest my case. No further explanation becomes necessary except to state that despite the intervening two hundred plus years the leopard still has the same spots.

Even though women committed about as many petty crimes as men, that had nothing to do with the so-called justice system. The people running the show in Australia wanted mostly men as their slaves because they were the best at working farms or mines and building roads etc. Consequently only about twenty thousand women were transported versus one hundred and fifty thousand men. i.e. They could make much more money by having men there instead of women.

Woe betide anyone who was so brazen as to speak out against the Tories and Whigs. Off to Australia with you my boy! Life was very hard for these transportees once they got to Australia. But first they had to survive the four or five months at sea, in a tiny, cramped sailing ship, under atrocious hygiene conditions. Hundreds did not survive the long voyage and died at sea. Many more arrived in Australia in a very sickly condition and died soon after arrival.

Today, in 2019, all the discussion about what happened in modern Australia's early days is always centred on the atrocities and wrong doings which were perpetrated on the aboriginals. Without doubt that is something which should be properly addressed and is long overdue. As with most things, historians are always at loggerheads when they attempt to put numbers on what happened. Before the arrival of the Europeans, estimates of the indigenous population seem to vary between about eight hundred thousand and one and a quarter million. Similarly, estimates of the number of aboriginals who died in the conflicts also vary widely. I have seen numbers as high as sixty-six thousand or even higher.

To my mind, however, it should not only be the Australian aboriginals who deserve more recognition for all the maltreatment which was perpetrated on them. The large number of British 'convicts' who were sent to an absolute hellhole against their will, also deserve much more consideration. During the transportation years over eight hundred convict ships arrived into Australia. On every ship several people died during the long and hazardous voyage which in those days was extremely treacherous because the Suez Canal was not opened until 1869. Thousands died en route. E.g. Forty-three from seven hundred and seventy-five died on the First fleet in 1787. Two-hundred and sixty died from one thousand on the Second Fleet in 1789. Ninety-five from three hundred died in 1799. Many more than this arrived in Australia, still alive but in extremely bad health, having picked up all kinds of diseases during the trip. Many of these new arrivals died young because medical support for them in Australia was crap. Over two thousand five hundred convicts also died in fights against aboriginals, after being forced unwillingly into this situation. They didn't want the conflict situations they found themselves in, but if they didn't do as their Tory and Whig masters ordered they would get flogged by the cat-o'-nine-tails or even worse.

We should also acknowledge that one hundred and seventy thousand only represented a tiny fraction of the total number of people who were adversely affected by this transportation policy. About seven times more men than women were sent to Australia. Many thousands of families in the UK were split up. Not only were men separated from their wives and children but also from their parents, grandparents, and friends. The overall number of British people affected by this policy would easily equal the number of aboriginals disenfranchised and more than likely could well exceed it.

We must also remember that all these convicts were dumped into a hostile environment which was totally strange to them. Just the hot summer climate without the benefit of modern air conditioning would have been a big challenge. Never mind the poisonous snakes and deadly spiders etc. The aboriginals on the other hand had survived here for many thousands of years and did not struggle with the weather or the wildlife. But they did have their land stolen from them and then often had to work as slaves for little or no pay just to be able to stay on that land! This situation continued well into the 1900s, especially in the sugar and cotton plantations of Queensland and the big outback cattle stations.

Today in modern Australia about twenty per cent of the population (more than five million people) are descended from convicts and about two million British people are descended from transported convicts. The reality is that the convict transportation policy from England probably had a more far-reaching effect than is generally recognised. Especially when we remember that between fifty thousand and one hundred and twenty thousand British convicts were also transported to North America to work as slaves in the tobacco plantations for many years before the American Civil War stopped it.

All the numbers mentioned above are rubbery. They change whichever source of information we look at. But nevertheless this will not change the thrust of the point being made. These days descendants of transported convicts almost look on this as a badge of honour, but there was nothing at all glamorous about the tough life their ancestors were compelled to endure. If we want to try and right the big wrong done to the Australian aboriginals we should also do the same for the big numbers of reluctant first European arrivals and their descendants who were also treated abominably.

I personally have no direct experience or knowledge about freemasonry. I only know what I have read on the inter-net. However, I must say that over ninety per cent of what I have read paints freemasonry in a negative light. Most police organisations are anti-freemasonry. The Catholic Church are also anti-freemasonry. This may seem like the kettle calling the pan black because of all the paedophile priests in the Catholic Church and the even worse cover-ups from a high level. My gut feeling is that it probably takes one to know one!

My reading did include many articles by freemasons themselves trying to convince the world that they were just a bunch of old guys getting together for a chin wag and some conviviality over dinner and drinks in the process of doing charitable works. But none of this sounded convincing. After all, there must be ten thousand different organisations in the world which one could join if that is all you want to do, without the need for all the secrecy, paraphernalia and *polvo de toro*. Pablo Escobar, the Colombian drug baron, did plenty of charitable work too. But where did he get all his money from in the first place?

I don't know what influence Freemasons have on golf clubs in 2019. However, I am aware that 'logo' golf balls are widely available on-line with all manner of Masonic symbols stamped on them. The same applies to the other very secretive group which started out in the 1700s as an organisation breaking away from the Freemasons i.e. the Illuminati. I doubt if they also had logos on wooden knurs or on common pot knurs!

Chapter 25

The publicans have it

I have talked about the roles which both royalty and freemasons played in the development of golf from its earliest days, but the unsung heroes of this story have to be the publicans. Long before golf club houses started to be built, golfers were holding their meetings in pubs. Eating and drinking was a very big part of the early golfing experience. We only need to look at the great detail in the *Blackheath GC Chronicle club minutes* to realise just how important this part played or much earlier than that with the Thomas Kincaid notes. Indeed, even long before golf associations in Scotland had their own course to play on, the pub was the only central point. In the early days golfers played on places such as Leith Links. There would be no charge to play there because it was common land enjoyed by all the people. At its peak there were probably twenty or thirty associations of golfers all playing on the same piece of land after which they would each retire to their preferred watering hole. Probably only a handful of original pubs associated with golf in Scotland still survive in the same place as they were centuries ago. But that doesn't detract from just how important they were at the time.

The amazing thing about the old-time British pubs was that they not only played an integral part in the early development of golf, but they did the same thing for most other sports as well! Take for instance the sport of horse racing. This sport from its outset was set up as an ideal outlet for gambling. The first ever recorded bookmaker appeared at Newmarket Racecourse in Suffolk around 1795. For the next fifty years illegal betting shops and elite London gaming clubs quickly went out of control. The government responded with the Gaming Act in 1845 and then the Betting Act in 1853. This more or less restricted gambling to on-course betting through bookmakers at racetracks. This was not a big issue for the wealthy people in the country because they could afford to use the railway network which was expanding rapidly. Most racecourses were near to a train station. However, the ordinary working man could not afford to swan around the country on trains going to racecourses. Whenever they wanted to place a bet they did it illegally at their local pub via a massive network of 'bookies runners'. This situation continued until 1961 when the first high-street betting shops in England were legalized by Harold McMillan's Conservative Government. Over twenty years before this (pre-1940) as much as five hundred million pounds per year (close to nine hundred million A$) was being gambled away on horse racing. The pubs would not benefit directly from the gambling money handed to the runners, but they would benefit enormously as the punters spent lots of time in the pubs drinking as they placed their bets with the runners. When the high-street betting shops opened in 1961 this would have been a very big blow to pubs. Unfortunately for them, they received an even bigger blow in 1966 when the breathalyser was introduced. This sounded the final death knell for many traditional British pubs which had existed as a major centre for community life for hundreds of years. Up until the 1960s most pubs had generally only offered simple food to their clients. Ploughman's lunch (bread and cheese), pie and mushy peas or stew and hard were the usual fare. The 'hard' in this last-mentioned treat was made from oatmeal. It was thin, flexible, and somewhat resembled an Indian poppadam or a piece of Roti bread. If you didn't require such an exotic dish you generally just nibbled on an assortment of different flavoured potato crisps or a small dish of salted peanuts. After the 1960s the pubs which survived re-invented themselves primarily as fully-fledged eating places and / or bed and breakfast places. Depending on the location most pubs converted to cheap-end family bistro type places or more haute cuisine up-market restaurant type places. A few pubs in remote village locations struggled on as 'drinking' places, but they received the final knock-out punch in 2007 when the UK banned smoking inside pubs. This was followed in 2011 by an English ban on the sale of cigarettes from vending machines in public places, including pubs. You can still buy just a beer at these places, but they would not survive on their drinks trade alone. Since this ban, the number of pubs in the UK has dropped by twenty-five per cent. In fact since 2001 over thirteen thousand pubs have closed down in the UK. In some areas of England the closure of public houses is far higher. Take for instance the borough of Hyndburn which is in East Lancashire around the town of Accrington. This is a seventy-three square kilometre region with a population of about eighty thousand. Prior to 2001 there were ninety-five pubs in this borough. Today in 2019 there are about forty-five pubs left. This is more than double the rate of pub loss elsewhere in the country. It doesn't need much research to understand why this should be. The percentage of Muslims in Hyndburn is just over ten per cent which is more than double the five per cent average across the country as a whole. Muslims don't drink alcohol and they don't go inside pubs. With all the forecasts being that by 2050 the number of Muslims in England will equal the number of Christians and by 2100 there will be far more Muslims in England than Christians. We can only suppose that the pubs which are still surviving today are going to be on a sticky wicket in future. Luckily all this didn't directly affect me so far. In two weeks' time I will turn seventy-six, but I have still never had a bet on a racehorse (apart from picking a number in the office for the Grand National or the Melbourne Cup), nor have I ever been inside a betting shop. And in 2050 I won't be here to find out if all the predictions are true or not!

The two other major sports in England, football, and cricket, were also closely linked to pub life. Most English villages had village greens where cricket was often played. Every village green had a pub or two alongside of it. Some pubs had their own cricket teams which played in local junior leagues.

In 1863 a group interested in drafting the first set of laws for what eventually became the Football Association met in the Freemasons Tavern near Covent Garden in London. Most of the group agreed on the proposed laws and eventually morphed into the Football Association (soccer). Ones who didn't agree with the proposed laws broke away from the group and went on to form the Rugby Union Code. Again both rugby teams and football (soccer) teams often had strong links with pubs. In the 1960s when I had digs in Denton near Manchester I played scrumhalf on Saturdays for the Old Aldwinians Rugby Football club. Our regular meeting place was the Old Pack Horse pub near Guide Bridge, Audenshaw. Then, provided I wasn't injured, I played fullback on Sunday mornings for the Red Lion pub football (soccer) team at Crown Point, Denton.

Back in the 1700s and 1800s, long before I ever visited a pub, the pub landlords were major promoters or at least big supporters of just about every sport that was going around. Whether it be knur and spell, golf, trap-ball, quoits, cockfighting, bear baiting, rackets, arrow throwing, cricket, rabbit or hare coursing, pedestrianism, athletics, prize fighting (bare knuckle boxing), wrestling, shooting (pidgeons, starlings, sparrows), road bowling, curling, bowling alleys, single wicket cricket etc, they had their hands in every pie. All these sports involved big monetary challenge matches and attracted big crowds with heavy gambling. 'Heavy gambling' is of course a relative term. It depends on who is doing the gambling. For example if an ordinary working man had a five pounds bet in 1850 that would mean that he was probably spending several weeks' wages. So if he lost it, he would be in Richard's Pasture or Dicky's Meadow if you prefer. I never did find out who Dicky was! I wonder if this old Lancashire expression, which seems to have been very popular in the mid-1800s, originated as a result of men and boys sneaking into farmers' fields without permission to play games of knur and spell and getting into trouble as a consequence. Whereas if an aristocrat had a one thousand pounds wager in 1850 and lost it, he wouldn't blink an eyelid. He would still be eating his turtle soup for an entree!

There was always a field attached to the pub where the event could be staged. Some had athletic tracks. Others had cockfighting pits, boxing rings, bowling alleys or rackets courts.

The other important point to note about pub landlords in the 1800s is that many of them were not just entrepreneurial promoters of all these sports. Often they themselves were active participants in many of the sports. They also got involved in coaching and training of other participants. In some of the bigger establishments they could even have a stable of runners or prize fighters etc who were domiciled at the pub itself.

All these mainly outdoor activities were in addition to a wide range of indoor games such as cards, dominoes, darts, pool, snooker, billiards, pitch and toss etc. And that was just the game / sport side of things. Pubs also offered all round entertainment with piano players, singers, comedians etc.

where people would spend the full evening having a big singsong. Tennis was probably the big modern game which did not appear to have much connection with pubs throughout its history, although it still had plenty of royal attention in its early days from French, Scottish and English kings and had been going hundreds of years in various forms.

Another thing which pubs did, and probably still do, is provide a central meeting place for all kinds of community activities which generally don't involve monetary challenges or gambling. Cycling clubs, Morris dancer teams, bird watching clubs, angling clubs, hiking clubs, dwile flonking groups etc often assemble, have meetings, and take refreshment at pubs. If you have never been flonked by a dwile according to this 400-year-old East Anglian harvest time custom you haven't lived! Another game which is popular in pubs is chess. In 2019, most chess clubs in England are pub based. Collectively these activities involve lots of people. For example, if we look at the number of UK golfers in 2019 and discount the ones who play just once per year, we will soon discover that just with the fishing sector alone there are about twice as many recreational anglers in the UK than there are golfers! There are more cyclists than golfers in the UK too!

Yet another activity which closely identified itself with pub culture, and which was so big that it deserves special mention, was the musical society scene throughout the UK. There were thousands of brass bands, male choral societies, handbell ringers, campanologists etc, many of which based their club headquarters, band room practices, meeting point on competition days etc at one of their local pubs. Just in the Yorkshire mill areas alone there were about four hundred of these clubs by the late 1800s and throughout the UK maybe up to forty thousand brass bands. At its peak in the late 1800s brass band playing membership in the UK would have completely dwarfed golf club membership. Only a few hundred brass bands have survived into the modern era. Membership at one of these clubs was strictly amateur. Brass band players were all working men who enjoyed this as a hobby or pastime. They also liked to partake of the amber liquid just like the Morris dancers etc and, because of the fierce rivalry between opposing bands, it was another area which also attracted its fair share of gamblers. In common with many of the other pub centred activities such as knur and spell, prize fighting, pedestrianism etc, brass bands also had their star performers who became legends in their local areas. Some of the brass band players also played knur and spell. For a very detailed history of this sector of the community read *The Popular Musical Societies of the Yorkshire Textile District 1850 – 1914* by David Russell in his doctoral thesis dated November 1979 for York University.

In the first half of the 1980s my brother Richard and his wife Irene used to run the Fleece Inn on the steep cobbled main street running through Haworth in Yorkshire in the Worth Valley. This pub was built around 1756. It was one of the pubs where Branwell Brontë, the ill-fated brother of the famous Brontë sisters, used to get his favourite tipple of gin in the late 1830s and 1840s. In Rick's time there, a team of Morris Dancers were regular visitors. He would rub his hands whenever they arrived because they were prolific drinkers! Knur and spell was played on the moors close to Haworth and in every hamlet and small village around Haworth. Branwell himself may have dabbled at this sport.

After their stay at the Fleece Inn, Rick and Irene also ran the Rock Hotel in Trawden for a few years which was only about twenty-five yards away from where we had been brought up as children. This pub had been built in about 1895 and is now called the Trawden Arms. Knur and spell was definitely played in the pub grounds in the late 1800s and early 1900s. There had been a pub in Trawden since at least the early 1700s called the Black Rock Inn. This pub closed in 1895 and its license was transferred to the newly built Rock Hotel. Today the old Black Rock Inn building houses a gift shop and a coffee shop. The old pub beer cellar from the Black Rock Inn still exists in its original form and serves as a store room for the gift shop. The Rock Hotel (Trawden Arms) was originally built on or close to the place where the old Trawden cornmill had been. This mill, which was mostly used for grinding oats, had been built in 1566 until it was finally demolished around 1880. During the time of its operation oats would have been the staple diet for most Trawdeners. Land for the cornmill had been granted by Queen Elizabeth I in the 1500s. Her successor, James I, he of early golf and featherie golf-ball fame, also extracted an annual rent for this land in the early 1600s. The mill was water-powered by Trawden brook which emanates from the nearby Boulsworth Hill and which still runs today a few metres behind Trawden Arms. By the time I was born in the 1940s, the cornmill race, the water channel diverted from the beck to power the mill stone, had long since disappeared. The full name for Trawden is Trawden Forest. In King James I's day it would still have been a big hunting area which would no doubt have been of great interest to his majesty.

An interesting fact about the Black Rock Inn in Trawden was that in 1841 it was listed in the *Quarterly Magazine and Literary Journal of the United Ancient Order of Druids* as being a location for one of their lodges. (lodge # 47) This was a splinter group from the Ancient Order of Druids founded in London in 1781 at the King's Arms Tavern in the West End. It operated as a benevolent group which operated under the motto of 'justice, philanthropy and brotherly love'. One of its more famous members in the 1900s was Sir Winston Churchill. It was never a religious group. About the same time there was also a group in Trawden who called themselves the Grand United Order of Oddfellows. This society had been founded in Manchester in 1798. The Druids used to ponce about with long white beards and wearing long white gowns with pointed hoods looking like the Ku Klux Klan. I wonder if the Druids and Oddfellows both played knur and spell and went road bowling? What a sight that would have been!

Another very old activity with strong connections to pubs is hunting where participants dress up in fancy red coats and ride horses in pursuit of a pack of scent hounds who are chasing a fox, a hare, or other wild animals. This 'sport', if that is an appropriate name for it, was banned in England and Wales in 2005. However, since then it has continued more or less unabated, and many pubs all around the country still host an annual Hunt. They even try to justify this by calling it 'pest-control!' There are pubs all over the UK which are named after this particular sport e.g. Hare and Hounds, Fox and Hounds, Huntsman etc. The same thing happens with the other so-called sport which involves slaughtering animals and birds with shot guns. e.g. Dog and Gun, Dog and Partridge, Red Grouse, The Pheasant, Dog and Duck, Blue Boar, The Shooters etc. Even if the pubs have no direct involvement in these sports they still are generally very supportive of them. They buy lots of the slaughtered birds and animals for serving up in their restaurants. In the old days pubs were also the places where poachers would find their customers for the game they had surreptitiously knocked off from the local lord of the manor's estate.

The wide interaction between pubs and the general populace described above didn't end there. Over the years pubs had a far greater influence on daily lives than that. All kinds of other activities were often conducted in and around pubs. Pub rooms were routinely used to all sorts of events such as town planning meetings, inquests by the coroner on deceased people, cotton mill shareholder meetings and public auctions of private properties whether it be residential or farms / farmland / farm machinery and Oddfellows' or Druids' meetings. According to the *Burnley Advertiser* April 1861 there was even a firm of visiting surgeon dentists from Manchester who used to hold a weekly dental session in the Red Lion pub in Colne main street. Also in the 1860s, another man from Manchester used to visit Colne twice per week and give dancing lessons in an upper room in the Red Lion pub. There has been a long tradition of holding wedding and funeral wake receptions in pubs and that continues in 2019. In May 1884 there was even a canary exhibition held in the Walton Arms pub at Colne as reported in the *Burnley Express*. Seventy-five pairs of birds were entered.

Pubs were also the designated pick-up and drop-off points for the horse drawn omnibus service which operated daily between Burnley and Colne. In 1855 this service would start at the Parkers Arms pub in Burnley and terminate at the Red Lion pub in Colne, also stopping at pubs in other towns and villages *en route*. Colne railway station had opened in 1848 but was probably too expensive for many people to use.

Most of the pubs in those days had stables for the horses attached to the pub. Some of the enterprising pub landlords had started the first ever 'Rent-a-Car' service in the 1800s.i.e. Poorer people who couldn't afford to buy or maintain a horse and buggy could hire one from their local pub. At the Rock Hotel in Trawden (now Trawden Arms) the stables had disappeared long before I was born in 1943. After the second world war they had been converted into a cabinet making and French polishing business. This was later replaced by a carpenter's joinery. In 2019 the old stable yard now has a few self-contained accommodation units belonging to the pub which service the local hiking community.

Pub landlords were already charging spectators to watch knur and spell matches, and other sporting activities, as early as 1840 or even earlier. Whereas, as far as I could ascertain, the first-time gate money was taken at a golf match appears to have been in 1892 when two Scottish professionals, Douglas Rolland and Jack White, played each other at Cambridge. This was another indication of just how far ahead of golf knur and spell was in the 1800s.

So we can see that the three very different sets of bedfellows (royalty, freemasons, and publicans), all had a profound influence on how golf developed in the UK. All the time they were doing this the leaders of the opposition, the churches, and chapels, were doing their very best to stop it happening. To be fair to them, it probably wasn't done because they were entirely against recreational activities *per se*. It was primarily because they could see all the harm caused by drinking and gambling addictions, which often led to family violence and higher crime rates in general.

Royalty and aristocracy were also patrons of other sports such as horse racing, cricket, trap-ball, prize fighting and cockfighting. This was mostly for gambling purposes, although they did own racehorses and breed their own fighting cocks. The publicans were maybe the real stars because they were into just about everything, and this involved participating, promoting, and hosting. They were the true facilitators.

Apart from all the above-mentioned contributions pubs made to life in the UK, they have also made an amazing part in recording the development of the nation throughout history. Starting back in the Roman days pubs started to erect signs outside of their establishments. This continued right through the Saxon, Viking, and Norman days and in 1393 it was even made compulsory by King Richard for all pubs to have a sign outside. Because prior to 1500 many people were illiterate, the signs generally had the name of the pub and also a picture to fit this name. Every aspect of life in the UK can still be seen in these pubs signs. Themes depicted can be religion, royalty, new inventions, any kind of occupation, famous people, military , maritime, humour and just about any other subject, including all the sports mentioned throughout this book. A complete snapshot of British life going back two thousand years has been recorded in pub signs.

Every pub sign has a fantastic story to tell. It is so sad that pubs are closing down at an unprecedented rate and much of this history will be lost. One of the oldest pubs still surviving in England is the Bingley Arms at Bardsley which is a suburb of Leeds in Yorkshire. This pub dates back to the mid-900s and boasts a yew tree in its beer garden which was already there before the pub was built. For a long time in its early history it was called the Priests Arms. Leeds was always a very big area for knur and spell playing and many other old sports. No doubt this pub would have a great story to tell if only it could speak.

Chapter 26

Did those English chappies really invent golf?

When we talk about Vikings, Anglo-Saxons, golf, and knur and spell, we must never lose sight of one very important fact. During the Viking and Anglo-Saxon eras, the part of modern Scotland which was unquestionably the birthplace of golf as we know it was actually NOT in Scotland at all. IT WAS PART OF ENGLAND! Up until the eleventh century all the area called Lothian in current day south-east Scotland belonged to the English Kingdom of Northumbria which stretched from Humberside up to the Firth of Forth. It had been that way for four or five hundred years. The Danelaw and the Kingdom of Northumbria overlapped. The Danelaw extended much further south than Humberside but only went as far north as Teesside. From Teesside to Lothian it was still ruled by the English. That means that Leith links, Musselburgh GC, Muirfield GC and even the capital Edinburgh, where golf first sprung up, were ALL in England when the Vikings and Anglo-Saxons before them were around. St Andrews, which is north of the Firth of Forth and these days is considered as the home of golf, didn't come on the scene until later at least as far as golf clubs and golf societies are concerned. Of course, they all didn't necessarily have those names in that era. The name Edinburgh didn't show up until King David I's royal charter in 1124-1127 and it is definitely an Anglian name and not a Scottish one. Most of the place names in the Lothians are also of Anglo-Saxon and not Scottish origin.

The old Kingdom of Northumbria also just happened to include most of the counties where knur and spell was ever played. So, IF knur and spell really did come from the Vikings or the Anglo-Saxons then it would mean that both golf and knur and spell had actually started in the very same place (i.e. the former Kingdom of Northumbria). Even if knur and spell had started earlier than the Vikings and went back to Anglo-Saxon days the same would apply because Northumbria existed from about 653 AD. It is clear that IF knur and spell had been played before golf started, then the people in the Lothian area would definitely have known about it since they lived in the same kingdom. If I wanted to be very mischievous, I could suggest that even if golf didn't come from the Saxons, the Vikings or the Dutch, then many of the people of Lothian who first kicked off the golf craze in the 1400s would have been able to trace their ancestors back to the Kingdom of Northumbria. They would have had English ancestry! So, was it really the English who first invented golf? Wash your mouth out you little Sassenach...I can already hear the moans and groans.

Historians believe that the English language predominated from the 500s in the Lothians and that the Gaelic-Celtic language spoken by the Scots was never the main one in this region of Scotland. Even in post-Roman days Lothian was dominated by British speakers. There still appears to be debate and controversy amongst historians about exactly when the Lothians were annexed by the Scots. The Battle of Carham, in or around 1018 when King Malcom of Scotland beat Uhtred, son of Walteof, Earl of Northumbria, is often mentioned as the date. However, in the *Anglo-Saxon Chronicle* of 1091 it mentions that 'King Malcom of Scotland went with his army out of Scotland into Lothian' and King David **I** of Scotland (1124-1153) regularly referred to the people of Lothian as 'English subjects' of the king.

The *Melrose Chronicle* for 1216 still talked about Scots being men from NORTH of the Firth of Forth. Even in 1300 Scotia was said to be the land of the Scots and was geographically north of the Firth of Forth. Whereas Lothian was south of the Firth of Forth and was the land of the English.

For sure, things on the ground in that area of Scotland would not have changed quickly. Conflict continued for several centuries after that. Three hundred years later in the seventeenth century, 'moss-troopers', which was a euphemism for Scottish robbers, were still making plundering raids in the border areas between Scotland and England. i.e. into Cumberland, Westmorland, and Northumberland. This was such an issue at the time that the English government ordered many of the border towns and villages to maintain teams of bloodhounds as slough dogs to help track down the intruders. Cross-border raids were not all in one direction. There were some English retaliation raids too. Certainly, even in the 1600s, the places close to both sides of the England / Scotland border would have seen much lawlessness and would not have been ideal places to play any kind of sport. Between 1795 -1797 famous English poet William Wordsworth, who lived in the middle of knur and spell playing country, wrote his one and only play about this subject. It was called the *Borderers* and was set in the time of Henry **III**.

In the early 1300s King Edward **I** of England had already taken control of Scotland again and that gave rise to two Scottish Wars of Independence in the 1300s. Famous names such as William Wallace and Robert the Bruce are associated with many of the battles which took place. When the Scots beat the English at the Battle of Bannockburn near Stirling in 1314 they maybe thought that Independence was secure, but it had to wait until 1328 and the Treaty of Northampton for full ratification by the English. But the fighting didn't stop there. In fact, conflict continued for a long time after the dates when the first playing of golf in Scotland is said to have occurred.

In 1400, King Henry **IV** of England marched an army into Scotland and camped near Leith in Lothian. On this occasion there was not so much as a whimper of resistance when Henry marched through the Lothians with his men. Maybe the people there still regarded themselves as 'English' even in 1400? In the 1500s there was much hostile activity. The Scots were beaten at Flodden in 1514, and again at Solway Moss near Gretna Green in 1542. The English also invaded and sacked southern Scotland in 1544 -1545 and yet again beat the Scots in the Battle of Pinkie Cleugh not far from Musselburgh GC in 1547. In the same year, 1547, Edward Seymour, 1st Duke of Somerset and Lord Protector of England, captured Hume Castle at Greenlaw which is about ten miles into Scotland from the current border. It was not before *The Treaty of Edinburgh* in 1560 that the English completely pulled out of Scotland. This of course means that the English army and government officials pulled out. Lots of English people would continue to live there. All this was long after 1450 AD when the first reports of golf being played can be found.

If in 2018 it can be shown by DNA checks that many people living in England show traces of Viking and Anglo-Saxon blood, we can be absolutely certain that when golf started up in Leith in the 1400s many of the people there would have still had a big wodge of English blood in them. Dilution of DNA would have remained low for a long time because the mobility of people wasn't anything like it is today. We should also remember that even the northern most parts of modern Northumbria, where knur and spell was certainly played and which ends at Berwick on Tweed, is only about fifty miles away from Leith, Musselburgh and Gullane where the earliest golf is said to have begun.

The area known today as east Lothian, where Musselburgh GC, Muirfield GC and Bruntsfield GC are all located, was in fact known as Haddingtonshire until 1921. Although the Battle of Carham was in 1018, this area was subject to enormous influence by the English long after this battle. As the long trouble between the English and the Scots progressed, this area continued to be the favourite entry point for invading English armies and remained so for several centuries after 1018. And until long after golf was thought to have started in Scotland in the mid-1400s. In 1216 King John's army destroyed Haddington town. In 1296 King Edward's army took charge of Dunbar. Even as late as 1650 Oliver Cromwell's English army again took Dunbar. Haddington is about eight miles from Muirfield GC, and Dunbar is about fifteen miles away.

Berwick-on-Tweed on the English / Scottish border has changed hands between the two countries many times. When golf was firing up in the mid-1400s Berwick was actually in Scotland. But along came Richard Duke of Gloucester in 1482 and ever since it has been an English town. The name Berwick is not a Scottish one. It had Old English origins and was founded as an Anglo-Saxon settlement. Even today in 2019 only a small percentage, maybe twenty-five per cent, of the Berwick population think of themselves as Scottish. The remainder think they are English or just Berwickers. The latter being people who don't align strongly with either England or Scotland.

It is very true, even today, that although political boundaries may change and different unions formed, people already living in those areas never lose their sense of identity. The Principality of Wales came under the English in 1284. The union between Wales/England/Scotland dates to 1707 and the Kingdom of Ireland didn't join in until 1801. Over the past two thousand years there has been as many as sixteen different states from which today's set-up has slowly evolved. But it matters not one iota that our passports say that we are all British. England last existed as a separate country over two hundred and fifty years ago, but I am still first and foremost an Englishman, a man from Aberystwyth is still a proud Welshman and someone from Aberdeen is still a fierce Scot. We never or rarely refer to ourselves as 'UK or British' men! And if anyone still doubts where true individual allegiances lay, then just go to a Six Nations rugby international at Twickers, Cardiff Arms Park (Principality Stadium), Murrayfield or Lansdowne Road (Aviva Stadium) and you will soon get the drift. The sound of thousands of Welsh miners giving a stirring rendition of *Sosban Fach* at the Arms Park ground prior to a match against England still rings in my ears! *Diolch yn fawr* boyos! Of course, when any of us were playing against the French, that was a different matter, and we closed ranks! *Allez Les Bleus* was never my favourite rugby chant! I can still remember how my heart pounded when, fuelled by an excess of Guinness at Jurys Hotel prior to the game, I cheered for the Irish against the French in the great Willie John McBride's last game at Lansdowne Road, Dublin, in 1975. What a legend he was!

The case for the English inventing golf is even stronger than I first thought! By the time King David I of Scotland was crowned in 1124 it had been over one hundred years since the Battle of Carham. At that stage Scotland had not progressed very far. But David was intent on changing all that and he may be the true father of modern Scotland. He spent much of his life in England, and he wanted to bring into Scotland all the progressive things he saw happening there. But he was one smart cookie. Although the Picts, Caledoni and other tribes had been instrumental in halting the Anglo-Saxon plan to conquer the whole of Scotland, he obviously had doubts about whether they were equipped to do things other than fight. They were good at wielding swords and medieval war clubs, throwing spears, and pulling long bows, but how would they go at building towns and running institutions? History shows us that the Scots would in fact have been very good at the latter, but King David had doubts at the time. In England he obviously moved in high circles and had lots of aristocratic friends throughout the country. Soon after he became king, he decided to colonise the Lowlands of Scotland, south of the Forth of Firth, by powerful

English aristocratic families. Many dukes, lords, earls, and barons among them. To persuade them to move north he gifted them large parcels of land and also used them to occupy most of the high offices in his government. In fact, many of the famous family names in today's modern Scotland, which we think of as being quintessentially Scottish, were not Scottish at all. Names such as Moreville, Bruce, Murray, Home, Stewart, Hamilton, Cunningham, Ridel, Lindsay, Percy, Olifard (Oliphant), Gifford, de Quincey, Ramsay, Hay, de Rollo, Berkeley (Barclay), Gordon, Montgomerie, Fraser, Fitz-Alan, Grant, and Sinclair. They could all trace their family origins back to Yorkshire, Cumbria, Durham, Northamptonshire, Gloucestershire, Shropshire, Hampshire, Essex and indeed to places all over England and even Wales. And it was mainly these guys who could afford to play most of the golf in the early days. This was fifty or sixty years after the Norman Conquest had occurred. So, undoubtedly many of the families would have been of French (Norman) origin who would have been rewarded with land estates in England by William the Conqueror. Many of the Normans also had Viking ancestry. Even John Balliol who became King of Scotland (1292-1296) was the son of an English baron who lived at Barnard Castle in County Durham (of course, Barnard Castle just happened to be a big knur and spell playing area!) Later, John's son, Edward, was also crowned king for a short time during which he ceded all the Lothians area to King Edward III in 1333. Of course, as we all know, golf in those days was a rich man's sport. The majority of golfers in the early days, or at least a big chunk of them, would have come from these rich and powerful aristocratic families, most of whom had English ancestry, or Norman before that. In any case definitely not Scottish!

Two other names we link closely with Scotland are Dr Alexander Carlyle and John Home. Golf history buffs will know that both these two gentlemen are also famous because they played an early game of golf at Molesey Hurst (or more correctly in Hampton), London, in 1758. At least they hit a few golf balls there as described in *Carlyle's autobiography*. Carlyle and Home did not live in London. They both lived in or close to Edinburgh. They were in London as invited guests at the home of a famous English actor of the time called David Garrick. Garrick's villa and also the shrine (or should that be folly) he had built to celebrate William

Shakespeare, known as Garrick's Temple, can still be seen today. They are both on the north side of the River Thames in Hampton. They are not in Molesey or Hurst Park. The area where both Carlyle and Home hit golf balls was not a golf course, but just a big lawn area on the side of the Thames river which Garrick had private access to. The reason they were visiting London was because just a few months earlier, in 1757, Garrick had been involved with the performance at Drury Lane theatre of a play called *Douglas* which Home had penned a few years earlier. Garrick, under the mentorship of Irishman Charles Macklin, revolutionised English acting through the 1700s. Macklin is reputed to have lived to one hundred and six. One of his funniest creations in 1781 was in '*Man of the World*', in the person of Sir Pertinax Macsycophant. Clearly, this is the gentleman who most of the current MPs in Australia followed as a role model.

Carlyle at least was said to be a reasonably proficient golfer. One of the golf clubs (sticks) which either Carlyle or Homes (or both) used that day was presented to the Blackheath GC in 1828 and can still be seen in their clubhouse as part of a display of old golf clubs from the 1700s. There is a photo of all these clubs in the *Chronicles of Blackheath Golfers* by WE Hughes published in the late 1800s.

The club presented on July 28, 1828 to the BHGC by club member Charles Cunningham was said to be the putter which John Home had used in the 1758 'game' at Molesey Hurst (Hampton). The club had been gifted to Charles Cunningham by a gentleman called Carlyle Bell who lived in Edinburgh. Bell was a clerk and cashier to the commissioners at the College of Edinburgh. In 1828 and 1829 both Charles Cunningham and Carlyle Bell were writers to the signet and joint town-clerks of the City of Edinburgh. In 1806 Bell had married Joan, the daughter of the Reverend Robert Home, minister of Polwarth. The wedding took place at Kilduff House which was the home of John Home who at the time was eighty-three. John Home died two years later. Kilduff House is at the small village of Athelstaneford which is about seven miles south of Muirfield GC. John Home had married Robert Home's sister. Then in 1821 Carlyle Bell married again. This time to Jean Dickie who was the daughter of Charles Cunningham. It appears that the 'Douglas' club came into Cunningham's possession via this circuitous Home connection. In the *Morning Post* 10

March 1828, it was reported that Cunningham had been runner-up in the Gold Medal competition at BHGC shooting one hundred and fifteen strokes over twenty-one holes. He averaged between seven and eight strokes per hole on a track which included twelve holes between 170 and 380 yards, six holes just over 500 yards and three holes just over 400 yards. The course had zero man made sand bunkers and comprised only natural hazards.

As far as I could ascertain John Home didn't marry until he was forty-eight and does not appear to have had any issue. This particular golf club which is still held at BHGC in Eltham could be historically very significant. Because when John Home played at Garrick's place in 1758 he was already thirty-six years old. It is unlikely that he took a brand-new putter with him just for the occasion. It is very possible that he had already owned this putter for ten or twenty years. In the late 1730s / early 1740s he had attended Edinburgh University which is only two or three miles away from Leith Links. Many a young Scot picked up the golfing craze when they were at university. Since, as far as I know, the jury is still out as regards the provenance of the Old Troon clubs, this old club at BHGC may in fact prove to be the oldest existing golf club anywhere in the world. Probably at least a hundred years younger than the oldest existing knur and spell stick, but *c'est la vie!*

What is also quite interesting about both Alexander Carlyle and John Home is that although they both lived and were brought up in east Lothian, they had not been born there. They both came from the border region of Scotland and both from only about fifteen miles away from England. Carlyle was born in Cummertrees, Dumfriesshire in 1722. Home was born in Ancrum, Roxburghshire in the same year. Carlyle's antecedents had come from Cumbria in England. They had properties there and also in Yorkshire. Knur and spell was of course extensively played in both Cumbria and Yorkshire. They had been there since before the Norman Conquest and for centuries had pledged their allegiance to the English kings. However, they crossed over the border and somehow acquired land there before eventually switching allegiance to the Scottish King Robert the Bruce in the 1274 – 1328 period. It has to be noted that amongst the English and Scottish noblemen in those troublesome times there was often a frequent switching of sides depending on which way the political wind was blowing. It had nothing to do with patriotism. It was all about trying to pick a winner in an effort to protect their vast unearned wealth.

Home's family progress was more difficult to trace. However, he was known to be a relative of the Earls of Home who had descended from an Anglo-Saxon Earl of Northumbria called Gospatric who had fled England in 1066 to get away from William the Conqueror. The Earls of Home had acquired chunks of land in Berwickshire in the 1200s. John Home's father, Alexander, was town clerk of Leith. Alexander's great grandad was a direct descendant of Sir James Home. Apart from Ancrum, many of the Home family came from the Polwarth, Greenlaw and Fogo areas which are all about ten miles from the English border in the Scottish Lowlands. So both Carlyle and Home could trace their forebearers back to England and did not come from a long Scottish ancestry line. It may be also worth noting that both of these gentlemen were against the Jacobites in the 1745 uprising.

When we are thinking about this part of modern Scotland we should not forget that what is probably the most famous and most important Anglo-Saxon icon found anywhere in the UK, can be found in Ruthwell Church which is only three miles away from Cummertrees. The Ruthwell Cross dates to circa 800 AD when all this area was part of Northumbrian England. It is over five metres high and is inscribed in both Latin and Old English. These inscriptions include passages from England's oldest known poem, the *Dream of the Rood*. Thirty-five miles away, in St Cuthbert's Church at Bewcastle, which is just a few miles over the border into England, is found another very similar Anglo-Saxon Cross from the same period. This cross is slightly smaller but nevertheless just as impressive.

The feudal tenure system which King David adopted from the Norman English, which involved vassals and their superiors, lasted over eight hundred years in Scotland. Over that period, it did undergo many changes. However, it was not fully abolished in Scotland until the *Abolition of Feudal Tenure Act (Scotland) 2000* which came into effect in 2004.

Perhaps the most significant thing King David did was to establish the burgh system which were autonomous trading areas. These were initially populated by English and Flemish merchant classes. They retained the English language and English culture for centuries after their formation.

During this colonisation period many ordinary English families also moved north. The modern suburb of Ingliston (Englishtown) in Edinburgh was a place where many English settlers went. There are many other places throughout Lothian which were named after places in England where they had come from. This process continued after David died in 1153 when many of his successors such as Malcolm **IV**, William **I** and Alexander **II** continued the trend.

The well-heeled and well-connected immigrants didn't just go to the Lothians. They were in all the neighbouring shires of the Scottish Lowlands (Roxburghshire, Selkirkshire, Berwickshire, Peeblesshire and to some extent also to the shires immediately west of these). It may not be surprising that the first twelve Open golf championships were held in Ayrshire at Prestwick GC in the Sottish Lowlands. In fact, after the one hundred and fortieth Open championship is held in 2018 at Carnoustie, we will be able to say that seventy-five per cent of ALL Opens have been held south of the Firth of Forth. And of the remaining twenty-five per cent, only two courses north of the Firth of Forth have hosted the Open. St Andrews (29) and Carnoustie (8). Whereas five different clubs in the Lothians and Ayrshire have hosted Opens (i.e. Muirfield, Musselburgh, Troon, Prestwick, and Turnberry). The people in the Lowlands of Scotland had little to do with the those in the Highlands whom they regarded as heathen and barbaric. According to the *Scottish Golfing History* site, of the clubs which still survive today, only ONE of the first twenty golf clubs founded before 1850 (Fortrose GC) is situated in the Highlands of Scotland. Fortrose is about fifteen miles north of Inverness. Every other old Scottish club at that time was a Lowland club. In the days when golf started, the Scottish Highlands were much more densely populated than they are today. The people there were mostly Gaelic speakers, and they had a very low standard of living. The Lowlands development during and after King David's time mostly passed them by. Even during the reign of King James **VI** of Scotland (1603-1625) the people in the Highlands were still *persona non grata*. He still portrayed the citizens in the Highlands as 'lawless barbarians' and his Scottish Parliament wanted to abolish the Gaelic language. To achieve this, under the Statutes of Iona in 1609, he made it law that Highland clan chiefs send their heirs to Lowland Scotland to be educated in English speaking schools. They got a boost in the early Industrial Revolution (late 1700s and early 1800s) but by about 1840 most of them had started to migrate. Some went to the growing industrial towns and cities in Northern England or even in the Scottish Lowlands. Even greater numbers left Scotland altogether and emigrated to Canada, USA, or Australia. By the time golf exploded in the late 1800s many of them had already flown the coop. For a fantastic, detailed account of how all this transpired, the George Chalmers book first published in 1807 titled *Caledonia or An Account Historical and Topographic of North Britain From Most Ancient to Present Times* is a must read.

An even more interesting thing happened just after King David died. In 1154 King Henry **II** in England decided that there were too many Flemish people from Flanders living in England. He kicked them out and many of them found a safe haven in the Lothians. The hamlet of Flemington just south of Glasgow is a place where many of them first went. In those days Flanders, where they had come from, was a major trading area. The Flemings were very industrious and entrepreneurial. They were ideal people to help kickstart David's dream for Scotland by starting up businesses and generating trade. The numbers of Flemings who arrived in Lothian during that period were significantly high. So much so that they were initially able to gain the right to be governed by their own law! These days Flanders is known as the Dutch speaking area of Belgium. In former days a part of that area was under Dutch control. Dutch, kolf, Lothians? The plot thickens! It appears that an ideal scenario was being set up for what happened in Scotland just a few generations after. Dutch speaking inhabitants and a wealthy landed gentry who didn't have to work and could spend their time just counting their money, playing golf, boozing and gambling. Perfecto! Needless to say that this colonisation by King David would have also strengthened the knur and spell claim. If this game had come down by the Vikings or the Saxons, then many of the English people who moved to Lothian from Yorkshire, Lancashire, Cumbria, Lincolnshire etc, both ordinary and aristocratic, would have known about it. Another very significant thing King David did was in 1123 AD. He donated the links land in St Andrews to be common land used by all people for a multitude of purposes. It could be from this date that ordinary people there started hitting little wooden balls with homemade crooked sticks. It took several hundred years after that however for golf to evolve to the stage where golf clubs and golf societies were formed.

So, we don't have to worry if there was very much English blood remaining in the Anglo-Saxon descendants living in Lothian at the time golf started there. The English bloodstock was topped up and considerably increased in the 1100s, 1200s, 1300s and even 1400s. It is probably safe to say that English, Saxon and Norman blood would have predominated in the Lothians and neighbouring shires at the time golf started! Most of the true Scots, the Picts and Caledoni, were living north of the Firth of Forth and mostly did not mix with the people in the Lowlands.

The Angles of the Kingdom of Northumbria had aspired to expand their territory way further north than the Firth of Forth. In 685 AD they had fought their way almost as far north as Forfar in the present-day county of Angus. This is geographically significantly further north than Edinburgh and even north of St Andrews. But that is as far as they got. The fierce Picts who lived north of the Firth of Forth defeated the Angles at the Battle of Dun Nechtain. This put paid to the Northumbrian plans and they retreated into the Lothians where they stayed for several hundred more years. Even today the influence of the Angles can still be seen in that part of Scotland. In 855 AD the Anglo-Saxons and Cumbrian Britons held Stirling, the gateway to the Scottish Highlands. During that period, they built the first stone bridge over the Forth river.

Before the Kingdom of Northumbria was created in 653 AD, there had been two separate Kingdoms called Bernicia (north of Teesside) and Deira (south of Teesside). The Anglo-Saxons unified them. It is interesting to note that some of the modern-day knur and spell playing areas, predominantly the Durham coal mining towns and villages, were in the former Bernicia part of the Kingdom of Northumbria. Whereas most of the knur and spell playing places were in the former Deira part which was later absorbed into the Danelaw. This may lend some credence to the suggestion from some people that knur and spell was an old Anglo-Saxon game which existed even before the arrival of the Vikings.

The Anglo-Saxon period was not the first time the Lothians had been a part of England. After the Romans had built Hadrian's Wall they built another wall stretching from the Firth of Forth to the Firth of Clyde. This was called Antonine's Wall. It was started in 142 AD and completed in 154 AD. It was abandoned after only eight years. When the Romans first conquered the Lothians, the area was not inhabited by Scots. It was populated by the Votadini tribe. These were Celtic people who had lived there throughout the Iron Age dating back to 800 BC. The Votadini continued to occupy this area until the Romans left Britain in about 410 AD. They were able to live quite well amongst the Romans and acted as a kind of safety blanket between the Romans and the barbarous tribes north of the Firth of Forth. According to Roman records the Votadini were a British tribe. So, let's face it. If we go back two thousand three hundred years before golf appeared in Scotland, the area around the Lothians where golf evolved was mostly inhabited by non-Scottish people. So *och aye the noo* you little Scottish jockeys! (Whatever that means!)

Chapter 27

Did golf come after knur and spell?

An English monk called Bede who lived in the Kingdom of Northumbria wrote his famous *Ecclesiastical History of the English People* in 731 AD. Maybe this could throw some light on the subject? The Venerable Bede was probably the most famous scholar of the Anglo-Saxon period. If the plebeians were knocking little wooden balls around when he was busy with his quill, he may well have recorded it somewhere.

It would be useful to know just when the playing of knur and spell at Easter time first started. We know that since the seventeenth century it was common for knur and spell to be played on Shrove Tuesday etc. We know that Pope Gregory **I** the Great was thought to have been associated with the Ash Wednesday custom at the start of Lent in the 540-604 AD period. We also know from the William Fitzstephen Chronicles that trapball (the short form of knur and spell) was played in England in the 1100s on Shrove Tuesdays. Fitzstephen never specifically mentioned knur and spell as far as I know. However, he was a London based chronicler who wrote chiefly about the megalopolis. It is conceivable, and in fact highly probable, that he may not have had any idea what was happening in the small hamlets and villages of Yorkshire. Indeed, even in the mid-1800s when knur and spell in the former Danelaw area was at its peak, and daily newspapers were everywhere, most people in London or throughout the south of England still had not the faintest idea what knur and spell was. This was despite the fact that travelling around England and Scotland had been made considerably easier than Fitzstephen's day through the booming railway network.

Whether or not the Scots had heard about knur and spell in England before they started to play golf from 1450 onwards is difficult to establish.

However, golf was very much a fringe sport in Scotland until after the guttie ball was introduced around 1850. Even in the first Open championship in 1860 only seven professional Scottish golfers took part, and it remained a very small event for most of the 1800s. What we do know from Scottish newspapers of the 1800s is that the Scots knew all about the raging game of knur and spell in England long before the explosion in the game of golf which started to happen from the late 1800s onwards. An interesting perception of how the Scots themselves saw the game of golf in the 1800s was given by the *Dundee Evening Telegraph* dated 7 October 1878. In an article entitled *Golf at St Andrews*, it was suggested that the majority of the human race rank golf as somewhere between hockey and knur and spell. I don't know if this article was written by a Scot or if they were quoting another publication. But for those who don't know, Dundee is a Scottish city which is not far from both St Andrews and Carnoustie. Even the very heartland of Scottish golf was regularly getting reports of knur and spell matches played in England. The *Edinburgh Evening News* dated 26 May 1874, reported on a knur and spell match for two hundred pounds played at Queen's Ground, Barnsley between Messrs Brown and Hitchen. By comparison, in 1874 the Open Championship was played at Musselburgh. The total prize fund was twenty pounds from which the winner received a paltry eight pounds.

The other thing that would make it absolutely certain that the Scots knew all about knur and spell long before the big leap forward post 1850 is to consider the number of Scots actually living in England. In the 1851 Census the number of Scots living in English towns and cities right across the country was somewhere between a half and one and a half per cent. However, in the northern English towns, where knur and spell was booming, this percentage was much higher. Newcastle, which was a very strong knur and spell area, had nearly seven per cent Scots .i.e. at least five times the national average. Sunderland had over three per cent and Carlisle was as high as nine per cent. Most towns and cities in the north of England saw a very big jump in population in the first half of the nineteenth century because of the industrial revolution. Big knur and spell centres such as Leeds and Manchester were typical. Between 1801 and 1851 the population of Leeds jumped from 53,000 to 172,000. Many of this increase were Scots.

Likewise Manchester jumped from 70,000 to 303,000 in the same period. It would be amazing if some of those Scots did not play knur and spell. At the very least they would have had to be both blind and deaf not to have known all about it. We must also remember that if some of those Scots had been golf players before they left Scotland to live in northern England, there was virtually nowhere in England where they could continue to play their sport. Apart from small ex-pat clubs at BHGC in London and OMGC in Salford, there were no other English golf courses in existence. So why not play knur and spell which was very similar to hitting a golf ball, albeit considerably more challenging? They would have no difficulty to find somewhere to play knur and spell. It was played in just about every hamlet, village and town throughout the whole of the Danelaw area. Literally in thousands of places all across the north of England!

Was knur and spell ever played in Scotland? Yes, it certainly was Stanley! In the *Ardrossan and Saltcoats Herald* dated 30 August 1901 there was an article about an old Yorkshire man called James Wilson. He had lived and worked most of his life in Dalry in the Garnock Valley in Ayrshire. He died in the late 1890s, just a few years after retirement, and was buried there. Apparently, 'English Jim' as he was affectionately known by the locals, introduced knur and spell into Scotland 'many years ago' and it was played there for several years before dying out. I can't be sure what 'many years ago' actually means. However, in the *Ardrossan and Saltcoats Herald* dated 1 October 1864, there was a very detailed explanation of just how knur and spell players set up their equipment at the start of a match... this referred to the spring-loaded spell method of launching the ball and not the gallows arrangement. This is likely to have been around the time when knur and spell was introduced into that region of Scotland and it was obviously prior to the big expansion of golf which happened in the late 1800s. I could not find the names of any Scots who Jim played with, but it is highly unlikely that he played by himself. Whether or not any Scots played knur and spell with Jim at this time is somewhat irrelevant. The truth is that knur and spell was played in Scotland BEFORE the explosion of golf took off in the late nineteenth century and that is an undisputable fact! What is more, it was played just a handful of miles away from the birthplace of the Open Championship, Prestwick GC.

Although it is difficult to pinpoint exactly when knur and spell was introduced in Dalry, it is safe to say that knur and spell was played many decades before there was a golf course there. The earliest mention of any golf course in Dalry was in 1907 which is several years after James Wilson died. There was a nine-hole public golf course there from the 1920s but that disappeared around the 1960s. The Ardrossan and Saltcoats GC suffered exactly the same fate. It started around 1910 as a nine-hole course and also disappeared in about 1950 after expanding to eighteen holes, retracting to nine, expanding again to eleven holes and then back to nine again. There are still existing today some very good golf courses close by. Ardeer GC is only four miles from Dalry and Irvine GC is only seven miles from Dalry. However, they fired up in 1880 and 1887 respectively so chances are they also came well AFTER knur and spell in that region.

There were also other attempts to introduce knur and spell into other areas of Scotland. For example, the *Dundee Evening Telegraph* dated 27 May 1919, talked about the late Henry Gould Dixon of Dundee. Henry was also a Yorkshire man born in 1840 who had done his apprenticeship as a cutler and saw maker in Sheffield in the 1850s. By age twenty-one, in 1861, he was already established in his own iron monger / tool merchant / fancy wares business in Willison Street, Dundee. By January 1863 he had moved around the corner to 33 Murraygate and by 1872, according to *The Dundee Directory,* he had already moved to a more prominent location at 41 High Street where he ran the British Sports Repository. He stayed there until he died in 1914, by which time he had lived well over fifty years in Dundee and become a very prominent citizen of that town. Among other things he sold penny farthing bicycles and held various patents for hollow frames, saddles and tyres. According to the *Piper o' Dundee* publication 17 June 1896 he also had the agency for the Daimler 'horseless carriage' which was one of the earliest motor vehicles. As late as 1922, eight years after Henry had died, the *Dundee High School Magazine* were still advertising 'Dixon's Showrooms' at 41 High Street as a supplier of all kinds of games and toys for children (train sets, Meccano sets, dolls etc). In 1924 the business was transferred to his sole surviving son, Charles Alfred Dixon.

Over the fifty plus years journey Henry certainly had a great diversity of businesses and his legacy lived on long after he had died. Dundee's population in those days was in excess of one hundred and fifty thousand and, from his earliest days there, Henry did his utmost to introduce knur and spell into the region having played it as a boy and youth in Yorkshire. Before he left Yorkshire he would have seen just how big the game of knur and spell was in England and would probably have seen an opportunity to make a quid by introducing it into Scotland where golf still had to find its feet. This is very interesting because Dundee is located well north of the Firth of Forth and is further north than St Andrews. It is situated on the north bank of the River Tay and is equidistant from both Carnoustie GC and St Andrews GC, each being about thirteen miles away...in different directions. These are the only two clubs north of Edinburgh which have ever hosted the Open Championship. This is yet another perfect indication that even in the very heart land of Scottish golf, knur and spell was already known to the Scots long before the golf explosion occurred. The High Street location where Dixon had his main store is not many yards away from where, in modern day Dundee, there is a larger-than-life statue of my favourite childhood comic hero, Desperate Dan. I suspect that James Wilson and Henry Dixon would not have been the only Yorkshiremen playing knur and spell in Scotland. They probably were not the first either! I am sure that a little more digging in the right places would reveal much more information about knur and spell in Scotland.

Geographically the Dalry location for Scottish knur and spell is also very interesting. Dalry is located only six or seven miles away from both Ardrossan and Saltcoats, both of which are only about seventeen or eighteen miles from Prestwick GC where the first twelve Open championships were played between 1860 and 1871 and they are even nearer to Troon GC. It is also very close to Irvine, where ex-pat Scot, prominent Sheffield citizen, famous poet and newspaper proprietor, James Montgomerie was born. Sheffield had been a very big knur and spell region long before Montgomerie was born and was raging there at the time Montgomerie was in circulation. There is no doubt whatsoever that when golf really started to take off in the late 1800s the Scots already knew all about knur and spell. They already knew just how big knur and spell was in all the northern counties of England! No doubt that the success of knur and spell in England at that time would have spurred on the Scots to do something similar with golf.

Even more interesting is that Dalry is only about four miles away from Kilwinning which in those days is where Eglinton Castle stood proud. The 13th Earl of Eglinton who lived there was a mad keen sportsman. He was very fond of playing golf and regularly played with James Ogilvie Fairlie who was a mentor to old Tom Morris after Tom had been fired from St Andrews by Allan Robertson after the guttie versus featherie dispute. Old Tom even named one of his sons James Ogilvie Fairlie in 1856 as a sign of respect to his mentor. Fairlie had been a founding member of Prestwick GC in 1851. He was also the main organiser of the first ever Open Championship in 1860. A very capable golfer in his own right, he played in the 1861 Open as an amateur and finished eighth. According to the *Ardrossan and Saltcoats Herald* dated 11 October 1862, Colonel Fairlie of Coodham had also won the Prestwick, North Berwick, and St Andrews autumn medals in succession. A feat which had probably never been achieved previously. James died in 1870 at age sixty-one. His good pal, the 13th Earl of Eglinton, who also had the title of Baron Ardrossan, died at St Andrews in October 1861 at age forty-nine. His death was quite sudden and unexpected. On the afternoon of the day he died he had been playing golf at St Andrews and was apparently in robust health. However, at dinner that evening with his golfing mates, he suffered a seizure and did not recover. The Earl was well known and respected as a champion of the health and happiness of the general populace. It would not be any great surprise if we ever found out that he knew all about knur and spell being played in Dalry which was very close to his ancestral family seat. It was actually the Earl of Eglinton, aka Archibald Montgomerie, who donated the famous Championship Belt which was played for at the first and subsequent Open golf contests until it was won outright by Young Tom Morris (older brother of James Ogilvie Fairlie Morris). James Ogilvy Fairlie had been born in Calcutta, India in 1809. He lived at Coodham near Symington in South Ayrshire which is only about thirteen miles from Kilwinning and likewise close to Dalry. In 1839, when he was thirty years old, he had taken part in the famous Eglinton Jousting Tournament at

Eglinton Castle. It wouldn't surprise me to learn that James Ogilvie Fairlie had heard about knur and spell too...maybe from his good mate Archie!

Apart from golf, Archie Montgomerie was also a very big rackets enthusiast. This was another big sport in England and Scotland throughout the 1800s and is still going today. As early as 1840 Archie had a rackets hall built at Eglington Castle and by 1860 he had employed a professional rackets player. This player was a pub landlord in Bristol where he also had a rackets court attached to his pub. In 1848 Archie had staked a big rackets match in Birmingham to the tune of eight hundred sovereigns (£840). The Eglinton Castle rackets court still exists in 2020 and is the oldest surviving rackets court anywhere in the world. Cricket, horse racing / breeding, archery, croquet, curling and the Eglinton Hunt were also on Archie's sporting calendar.

Sacré bleu! Knur and spell, 'poor man's golf', was played very close to the same place, and around the same time, where modern golf as we know it made its big step forward after the first Open in 1860! i.e. Prestwick. Who'd a thowt it? Sounds like a good name for a pub! Whoops, it already IS an established pub name! Who would have thought it? In 2020 there are still many pubs and inns all around England with this name! It was also played in 1861 very close to the place which subsequently came to be regarded as the home of golf i.e. St Andrews.

Old Tom Morris would turn in his grave! Although Old Tom went back to St Andrews in 1865, the Open championship continued to be played only at Prestwick until 1873. It was sometime after the father of the Open, James Fairlie, died in 1870, that St Andrews GC managed to wrest the Open domination away from Prestwick. Leith, Musselburgh, Perth, and St Andrews may have been the places where golf first started in the 1400s, but it had gone nowhere in four hundred years until Fairlie organised the first Open in 1860 at Prestwick.

In 1866, long before the big explosion in golf occurred, several London newspapers, including the *London Evening Standard* and the *Penny Illustrated,* reported on arrangements in the park at Stirling Castle for all the athletic games of the Highlands, 'not even forgetting knur and spell', to take place. I could not find any details or confirmation that this actually happened. Stirling is about fifty-five miles south of Dundee where our friend Henry Dixon was already playing his knur and spell in 1866.

St Andrews had been transforming itself from the mid-1830s when Major Hugh Playfair came back from his time in India. While Playfair made big changes to the layout of the town itself, Allan Robertson and Tom Morris made big strides forward on the golf side of things.

The Society of St Andrews Golfers had gone bankrupt in 1799. The town council had then started to allow rabbit farming on the St Andrews links, and this continued until 1821, at which time the old links was in a very dilapidated and rundown state. Allan Robertson had been appointed as ball-maker and Hugh Philp as club-maker in 1819. Tom Morris arrived in 1835 as a fourteen-year-old apprentice to Allan Robertson. The Society of St Andrews Golfers were still struggling until the mid-1830s when they got a big boost from King William **IV** who coincidentally also happened to be the Duke of St Andrews. He granted them royal status when they became the Royal & Ancient Golf Club of St Andrews. At this point they didn't have a club house and still continued to conduct all their meetings in local pubs. The clubhouse only came in 1854. This was very timely because the guttie ball had arrived in 1848 and by early 1850s had already mostly replaced the featherie balls. This ball change had a massive influence on the future fortunes of St Andrews and on the future of golf itself because it markedly changed the makeup of the golf playing community.

An interesting insight into what golf was like in Scotland in the early 1800s can be seen by reading the section about golf in *The Scotsman's Library; being a Collection of Anecdotes and Facts Illustrative of Scotsmen and Scotland* by James Mitchell, of the University of Aberdeen; Correspondent Member of the Society of Scottish Antiquaries, published in 1825. It was printed in London for a company in Edinburgh.

This book is seven hundred and forty pages long but only includes less than half a page of uninspiring information about golf. Considering that it is written by a Scot the writeup says very little of interest about the game. It does mention that there are four or five different kinds of clubs which are used according to where the ball is situated. It also mentions that the gentlemen golfers are dressed in old Scottish dress and are accompanied by a 'servant' (interestingly no mention of the word caddie) to carry their clubs.

One can only surmise from the way that this was written that the author had little idea what golf was all about even though he was an educated Scot. Although it was published in 1825 we can probably assume that it was prepared a few years before that. Research for such a book in those days would be a long and tedious process with no click of a button access to archival material. The lack lustre description of the game given probably matched the very poor condition of the St Andrews links at the time.

In 1754 the Society of St Andrews Golfers had started with just twenty-two noblemen, landed gentry and professors. When James Sorley, one of Scotland's best-known golf journalists, wrote an article in the *St Andrews Citizen* dated 22 July 1911 entitled *The Early Days of St Andrews Golf Club*, it painted a very interesting picture of how much the golf community had changed. Sorley was born in St Andrews in 1886 and he died young at age thirty-six in 1922. At age nineteen he tied in the captain's cup at the St Andrews club for players under twenty. In 1908 he was match secretary at the St Andrews club. He initially became a golf professional and before the 1914 war started, he was professional and golf club-maker at Rothey Park GC in Leicestershire. Prior to that he had written regular articles for the Citizen newspaper and after the war he returned to be a full-time writer. Sorley lived and breathed golf. He was very well connected and respected in the St Andrews community where he was the 'Don Lawrence' of the day. For non-Australian readers, Don Lawrence was one of Australia's most famous sports writers. He has also been credited with coining the nickname 'Golden Bear' which he gave to Jack Nicklaus when he first came to Australia in the early 1960s.

The 1911 article was very interesting because it gave a full list of all the 'original' St Andrews members who had joined the 'new club'. He defined 'original' as those who joined the club 'between the beginning of the club in 1843 and the year 1860'. Of course, he wasn't talking about the R & A GC of St Andrews. He was talking about the St Andrews GC which had started off life as the Mechanics GC. Nevertheless, for me, the list is still very interesting.

There were eighty-nine members on the list which to me is not a lot of people considering we are talking about a seventeen-year period. The list gave the names of all the members and their occupations. It did not give the dates they joined the club.

The occupational makeup of the club was the thing which stood out. There were eleven tailors, eight cabinet-makers, six joiners, six gardeners, four plumbers, four shoemakers, four innkeepers, four merchants, four bakers, three golf ball makers, two painters, two tinsmiths, two slaters, two plasterers, two masons, two valets, two bank clerks, an engineer, a smith, an upholsterer, a residenter, a hairdresser, an umbrella maker, a weaver, a glazier, a caddie, a saddler, a grocer, a café owner, an architect, a stationer, an ostler, a groom, a coal agent, an iron monger and a clubmaker.

The sole clubmaker member on the list was Robert Forgan who, in 1856, took over the club making business of his uncle, Hugh Philp, and became the biggest golf club maker in Scotland. The three ball makers on the list were Allan Robertson, his assistant Tom Morris and David Gressix. Robertson and Morris, who had been with the R & A since 1818 and 1835 respectively, jumped ship when the new Mechanics GC was formed in 1843. I couldn't find anything else about David Gressix.

I suspect that many of these members may well have joined after 1848 when the guttie ball first reared its head. This is because the price of golf balls came down from three or four shillings per ball to about one shilling per ball. This represented a price reduction of about seventy-five per cent for golf balls.

When we look at this massive price reduction for golf balls, we must also consider that, in addition, the guttie balls were much more durable than featheries.

Although there was a high percentage of 'tradies' making up this new club we must also remember that it cost them nothing at all to play on the St Andrews golf course. The course remained 'free' for local residents after that until 1946. Incredibly it was free to play there for ANYONE until 1913! Even today locals pay just a small fraction of what visitors from out of town are charged.

Taking this into account I almost feel that I should revise my earlier thoughts about only rich men being able to afford to play golf in Scotland in the early days. With playing on the course being free for everyone, the cost of equipment could always be mitigated. One doesn't need a full set of clubs to play golf and one doesn't need brand new clubs. Any number of cheap second-hand clubs is good enough to get started. As for expensive golf balls. Forget about that! Just get out on the course after all the toffs have been playing, most of whom had not much idea how to play, and there was bound to be lots of finders.

I can personally vouch for these suggestions. When I started to play golf in the late 1950s, I had a half-share in half a bag of old clubs for which I and a mate paid two pounds between us. Some had steel shafts, and some had hickory shafts. We only had six irons and a putter...no woods. The balls we played with were all finders. Our biggest cost was finding the green fees every week. I vividly remember one very traumatic Saturday afternoon in 1959. It was two days after my sixteenth birthday at two o'clock in the afternoon. I had arrived at the course only to discover, to my dismay, that I had forgotten to take some old balls from the box underneath my bed. Bugger, I had to buy some second-hand balls to play with! That was the first and last time I ever bought any golf balls. Sixty years have passed since that time and during all those years I have only ever played with finders, or new balls other people gave me for birthdays, Xmas or trade-day handouts. I play with any brand of ball I find. It has no impact whatsoever on my score. I would like to claim that I had an early awakening to saving the environment by doing my bit on recycling. However, the truth is that I was very poor at the time and these days I am just tight-fisted! Most days I play with just one club, my driver, and generally shoot less than my age off the stick on our short par sixty-four course. Other people on the course often laugh at me when they see me playing with just one club. However, while researching for this book I learned that Allan Robertson, the world's best golfer in the 1840s and 1850s, often used to play challenge matches at St Andrews playing, like me, just his driver (no putter). Of course, he was a professional golfer and even with just his driver he could go around St Andrews in about ninety. For that era this was a very good score bearing in mind that he was playing with misshapen featherie leather balls and having to putt on crappy surfaces which under no circumstances deserved to be called 'greens'. If anyone is still in doubt about this particular strategy I would suggest a visit to the British Golf Museum at St Andrews. While there, make sure that you look at the 'driver-putter' which legendary club-maker Hugh Philp made for Colonel Fairlie, the father of the Open Championship. Tom Morris borrowed this club from Fairlie in 1864 to win his third Open Championship at Prestwick GC.

It was with this old bag of clubs that I probably played my best ever round of golf. It was around the 1972 / 1973 period. Dad had been recently diagnosed with a terminal illness and we had decided to take him on short holiday to North Wales. One of the places we went to was Criccieth in the Gwynedd area which has great views of the Snowdonia mountain range. There is a very old castle there which had been built in the 1200s and stands above Tremadog Bay. There was also a very inviting golf course in Criccieth. Dad wasn't feeling well enough to play so I just rocked up and was going to play by myself. However, another guy had just arrived with the same intention, so we met up on the first tee. He spent little time telling me that he had recently won the Ford Fiesta golf tournament in Majorca. I had no idea what that meant but it sounded very impressive. With my old bag of clubs and playing in a pair of runners I felt somewhat inferior and quite intimidated. He generously gave me the honour on the first tee and off we went. I didn't have any woods in the bag, so I used my old two iron to drive with and also to make most of the long fairway shots. By the time we reached the eighteenth tee I still had the honour. I didn't lose one hole. I was pulling shots out of my backside all the way around. Chipping in out of bunkers, making thirty-foot putts and generally playing out of my skin. I shot three over the card off the stick on a course I had never seen before! Prior to that I had never scored better than eighty even on the courses near home which I knew well. There was a road which ran alongside the golf course and dad had been driving up and down that road and stopping at various places where he could often see us teeing off. He told me afterwards that he thought I must have been doing OK because he had noticed that I was always teeing off first. The man upstairs was certainly looking after me that day! Of course I was brought back down to earth very quickly after that round as my golfing prowess was all downhill from there!

Criccieth GC had been founded in 1905. One of its founding members was David Lloyd George the famous British prime minister. The course is no longer there. It was closed a few years ago. Criccieth is also not many miles away from the Isle of Anglesey where I used to do some crewing in my mid to late twenties on a two-man Fireball racing dinghy at Red Wharf Bay near Pentraeth. Fireballs operate with a centreboard and we spent much of our time trying to get the boat upright after capsizing! They were a bit more 'hairy' to sail than the very sedate GP14 which my old mate Len May at Rotunda used to potter around in.

It would be exciting if the proof for all this postulation about Knur and spell, Vikings and Anglo-Saxons could be found. However, I am afraid that the three years I spent learning Latin at school in the 1950s did not equip me well enough to be able to decipher ancient church records! Though it did teach me how to conjugate the present tense of the Latin verb to love (*amo, amas, amat, amamus, amatis, amant*) and my old school motto, *Festina Lente*, did serve me well during the long research process! I will therefore just have to be satisfied with the knowledge that for several hundred years knur and spell was undeniably a far more popular game in England than golf and when at its peak was also far bigger than the game of golf in Scotland.

Of all the games which have stuck their hands up over the years as possible forerunners to the game of golf, knur and spell and its junior version, trap-ball, have to be at least considered. Knur and spell was a game played for hundreds of years, in hundreds if not thousands of locations across the Danelaw. Many of these locations were just across the Scottish border and often less than one hundred miles away from Leith. Trap-ball, which has been shown to pre-date golf, was also very extensively played in England. None of the other games mentioned come close to having that pedigree. It was played by players who spoke the same language as the people in the Lothians where golf evolved. The fact that knur and spell and trap-ball already existed from a very early date could help to explain why colf didn't take off in England, even though England was much nearer to Holland than Scotland and even though there were far more Dutch ex-pats living in England than in Scotland.

There is no evidence to date which indicates that the Vikings brought knur and spell with them when they first invaded England in 799 AD. However, my gut feel is that many of the Viking legacies such as beer drinking, conversion to Christianity and early freeing of slaves, dry stone wall making etc, probably facilitated the early playing of knur and spell and other games such as road bowling and trap-ball. Trap-ball was a short form version of knur and spell which was played in England long before golf appeared in Scotland. The chances are that knur and spell also preceded golf in Scotland, but there is no proof to date. Social golf groups probably started in Scotland from about 1640, but actual golf clubs didn't appear until the early 1700s. So at the very least, knur and spell in England and golf in Scotland developed in tandem. And to repeat what I have said several times already elsewhere in this book, throughout the 1800s and into the early 1900s, knur and spell in England was far bigger than golf in Scotland.

Chapter 28

Why?

What I find so intriguing is the fact that in nearly all the write-ups about the origins of golf, knur and spell rarely gets a mention. Golf historians often wax lyrical about continental games such as colf, kolf, soule, chole and jeu de crosse. They even give the old English game of cambucca a look-in and the Chinese game of chuiwan. For some strange reason, the very ancient game of knur and spell (aka poor man's golf) is *persona non grata* as far as the golf authorities are concerned. This is despite the fact that we know from Scottish newspapers even in the early 1800s that the Scots knew all about knur and spell. This is also despite the fact that of all the stick and ball games mentioned above, knur and spell was the one played geographically closest to Scotland by thousands of players and probably the only one played in Scotland itself. Prior to the explosion of golf in the late 1800s knur and spell was also a very much bigger game than golf. Why therefore would knur and spell be mostly ignored? I think I know the answer to that question. As Sherlock Holmes would have said 'when you have eliminated the impossible, whatever remains, however improbable, must be the truth?' In some cases knur and spell is not only mostly ignored, but often, even when it is briefly mentioned, it is totally misrepresented.

A great example of this is the book called the *Same Old Game* by Michael Roberts published in 2011 which comes in two volumes totalling over eight hundred pages. This is a book mostly about football, but it also contains much about stick and ball games. In these two massive tomes there is lots of very interesting information on many sports apart from football, including some very obscure Icelandic sports. However, despite the fact that knur and spell in England was even bigger than football in the 1800s, there is only two or three lines about it in the two volumes. And what little information is given is totally inaccurate i.e. It talks about Nor (knur) and spell as being a croquet-like game, which is akin to saying that football is like dwile flonking. A perfect example to demonstrate that even seasoned sports writers in the twenty-first century have no idea about knur and spell, despite a wealth of information about the game being readily available on line.

Another great example is Michael Flannery and Richard Leech's *Golf Through the Ages...600 years of Golfing Art*. This is a beautifully illustrated book which has a wealth of interesting information, particularly from continental Europe. It concludes that golf was really a game which began in France which was probably fine-tuned by the Dutch before it reached Scotland. Unless I missed it, nothing is said about the Romans playing with little leather balls long before the French. Nor does it appear to say anything about knur and spell. It does mention wooden balls being used in a variety of different games, but nothing about the hand carved knurs which the English were using for many centuries.

I am not a golf historian. However, I cringe when I hear golf historians parrot on about 'primary evidence'. Often primary evidence is difficult to find, and predictions based on probabilities should not be so easily dismissed. A perfect example of this is the Periodic Table for chemical elements.

Prior to 1789 there were only eleven elements known to man. By the time Lavoisier came along in 1789 there were twenty-nine known elements. This had risen to sixty-three by 1869 when Russian scientist Dmitri Mendeleev published his table. Deming's 1923 list had eighty-six, Seaborg's 1945 list had ninety-five and in 2019 there are one-hundred and eighteen elements known to man. The amazing thing is that quite a few of the most recent elements on the table do not exist naturally and have only ever been synthesized in a laboratory.

At each stage of this long evolution scientists of the day were predicting the existence of other elements even though they had not been discovered yet. Mendeleev himself predicted eight elements which had not yet been found. They were predicting where in the Group Table the missing elements would be found, even though they had no 'primary evidence' at that stage to back themselves up. They were even predicting the properties which these unknown elements would have. Can you imagine where the world would be today if the scientists had listened to historians? Go on gut feel, go on probabilities, and then seek and ye shall find!

I cringe even more when golf historians quote a so-called piece of primary evidence which is so obviously mostly opinion and does not stand up to even the most rudimentary scrutiny. Such a piece of evidence was the Jane William's letter in the 1890s about early golf in Tasmania. So much was written and conjectured from that letter which had nothing at all to back it up. As far as I can see, the only thing mentioned in that letter which subsequently has been substantiated was the bit about some old golf clubs being sent to a schoolteacher in Dunedin. This piece of confirmed history alone could have revealed so much more information if the right questions had been asked. However, judging by what was written about this letter, those questions were obviously never asked.

It is even more frustrating when the same golf historians examine another piece of 'primary evidence' on the same subject, only to proceed to extract bits of information which support their original story, while at the same time choosing to ignore other contradictory bits of information in that same primary evidence which do not support the original story. If this was to be done, then at least some explanation as to why they have chosen to reject or just plain ignore the non-supporting evidence would need to be included. Just pick out the bit which supports your story and quote that? Nice one Cyril! The best description I can conjure up for this quality of chronicling is that it resembles a modicum of crappage! It is rather like when conducting laboratory tests and the initial results do not meet the specifications. No problem! Just keep on repeat testing until you get the result you want! Brilliant!

When we start to look seriously at where the games of golf and knur and spell came from it becomes a very complicated matter. This is because the evolution of the United Kingdom over the last two thousand years or more has been a complete mishmash. Romans, Anglo-Saxons, Vikings, Normans, Frisians etc. Even this breakdown is not straightforward. The Angles and the Saxons came from different parts of Europe. When they settled in England they were not just one Anglo-Saxon community. The Angles came from the south of Denmark and mostly settled north of the Humber. The Saxons were a Germanic tribe who settled mostly in the south of England, but not always. The Vikings likewise were not one community. They were mostly Danish and Norwegian Vikings with an odd Swede tagging along for the ride. Sometimes they fought side by side and at other times they fought against each other. They tended to settle in different areas but not exclusively. The Normans came from Normandy in northern France. Many of them were descended from Vikings who had settled in France around 911 AD. The Frisians came from the northern coast of the Netherlands and settled in places such as Frizinghall in Bradford, Frieston in Lincolnshire, and all over Kent. There are in fact over twenty places in England where the Frisians settled. Most of these places are in the former Danelaw area. Whether or not the Frisians had been fighting as mercenaries for their Viking rulers, or earlier still for their Roman masters, is not fully clear. There could be a good chance that they were coerced into this role. Either way they still left a significant legacy.

All my Australian golfing and cricketing mates will be dead chuffed to learn that the Ashes Series record all-time bowling performance of forty-six wickets was achieved by a man from Frizinghall. Yes, you have guessed correctly. It was the great Jimmy Laker who included a nineteen wickets for ninety runs haul in that tally during the 1956 Old Trafford test match with his amazing off-spin bowling. Another relatively unknown fact about Jimmy is that during that tour he took ten wickets in a single innings TWICE on different grounds. Once in a test match and once playing for Surrey against the Australian touring side. A feat never achieved by any other test cricketer in the history of the game. Not on covered wickets, nor on un-covered wickets.

It was really hard to differentiate between the Angles, Saxons, Dutch, Scandinavians, Frisians, and Normans at that time. They all came from areas close to each other and before any of them invaded England they had been warring and then mixing with each other for a long time. Not only that. Even once they had arrived in England they didn't all stay in their own separate areas. Yes, they may have had areas where one or other of them had the highest population density. But it was not uncommon for Saxon, Viking, or Norman settlements to be relatively close to each other. The same also applied in some cases to Norwegian Viking and Danish Viking settlements. All this just added to the complexity.

Much of modern-day Scotland was part of England for hundreds of years. Some of modern-day England was part of Scotland for a short time. The Dutch have had a big influence on all aspects of English life going back to before the Romans arrived. On top of all this there were always different religious groups stirring the pot and vying for dominance.

If we accept the favourites colf and kolf as being the most likely forerunners to modern-day golf, we can almost duplicate the above comments for colf etc. The Netherlands had been an even bigger hotchpotch of invaders and migrants than the UK. What is more, all the usual suspects were involved. The Romans from Italy, the Jutes from Denmark, the Franks from France, the Vikings from Denmark and Norway, the Saxons from Germany and of course the Spanish all had a go. The Romans, Saxons and Danish Vikings were all common to both the Netherlands where colf was played and to the Danelaw where knur and spell was played.

Despite all this discombobulation, I have come to the firm opinion that knur and spell was probably a game dating back to the Viking period. It was a game played almost entirely in the former Danelaw area of England. The densest knur and spell playing regions coincided precisely with the densest Danish Viking settlement regions. Where there were no Viking settlements, there was little, or no knur and spell played. On and near to the west Lancashire coast, which was predominantly settled by Norwegian Vikings, there appeared to be no knur and spell played.

In some areas, such as north of the Tyne and up to the Scottish border, Viking settlements were few and accordingly knur and spell playing was sparse. This area was still mostly Saxon, still called Northumbria and not part of the Danelaw. Population density here was low compared to elsewhere in the country and remains so today. Anglo-Saxons in this area had proved very difficult for the Vikings to keep under control. After the sacking of Lindisfarne monastery, St Cuthbert and the monks fled south. In 877 AD Danish King Guthred granted the exiled monks a big chunk of land south of the River Tyne but north of the River Tees. This was initially around Chester-le-Street and later around Durham. This area served as a kind of buffer zone which essentially kept the Vikings mostly separated from the Anglo-Saxons in the northern parts of Northumbria and allowed both to live in relative peace. There were far more Viking settlements in this Chester-le Street / Durham area and correspondingly much more knur and spell playing. This is even though that area was also a strong Anglian area. In fact, in Escomb which is just outside Bishop Auckland, where early Royal Melbourne GC player Thomas Brentnall came from, there is a very old Anglo-Saxon church dating back to around 675 AD. This is one of only three such churches still remaining in England.

At this point I should stress that the Vikings I am talking about are the ones who came to England during the first Viking Age i.e. during the years 793 AD to 954 AD. I am not talking about the Vikings who came in the second Viking Age between 990 AD and 1066 AD. During the latter of these two periods, Danish Viking kings actually ruled all of England, including north of the Tyne, and not just the former Danelaw area. The most successful of these was King Canute who reigned from 1016 – 1035 AD. Canute was the first Viking to become a Christian king. Although Canute and his successors lived in the south of England, his rule had virtually no impact on the places where the majority of the Vikings settled. If we check the work done by *mySociety* in conjunction with the British Museum we can see around two thousand place names in England where Vikings settled. Well over four hundred (twenty per cent)) of those places are found in Yorkshire, which is easily the highest percentage of any county. Consequently, we find that Yorkshire was also by far the biggest knur and spell playing county. The other ten northern counties had fewer Viking settlements with correspondingly less knur and spell playing. There are a handful of places in Ireland, Scotland, Wales and southern England but over ninety-seven percent of all Viking settlements are to be found in the former Danelaw area, which is north of the old Roman road, Watling Street. These places would have all been settled in the 793 – 954 period and they are the places where ninety-nine percent of all the knur and spell playing places in the UK are found. Most of the lasting settlements in the Danelaw region by Danish farmers were probably established in just one generation. i.e. In the forty- or fifty-year period which spanned the end of the 800s and the early 900s. Maybe their early conversion to Christianity facilitated the process? I know little or nothing about interpreting place name information. Maybe an expert toponymist could throw further light on this matter?

Prior to 874 AD the Danelaw had been occupied by several different Viking leaders who tended to squabble amongst each other. However, Guthrum managed to consolidate the Danelaw around 874 AD. Then, after several unsuccessful attempts to oust King Alfred of Wessex, culminating in Guthrum's defeat at the battle of Edington in 878 AD, both leaders agreed to a Peace Treaty in about 880 AD. This document essentially specified the boundaries of each other's land holdings and also laid the framework for peaceful trading between the two. The old Roman road, Watling Street, was used to denote the southernmost boundary of the Danelaw. The treaty also demanded that Guthrum had to convert to Christianity. He was baptised in 878 AD and changed his name to Athelstan. He should not be confused with King Alfred's grandson who was also called Athelstan and who became the first King of England in 927 AD.

Assuming that my thoughts are correct, and if knur and spell really does date back to Danelaw days, then it would obviously have been played in England long before golf reared its head in Scotland. If that was the case, there is no way that the Scots would not have known all about it.

Whether or not the Scots took knur and spell as the basis for golf is impossible to know. However, in the 1800s, long before golf exploded, knur and spell was undoubtedly a far more popular game than golf. It is highly likely that knur and spell at the very least had an indirect effect on golf's development.

Although the onomastic evidence pointing knur and spell to the Danish Vikings seems to me to be overwhelmingly strong, which if it was true would date knur and spell in England to a time long before golf started in Scotland, the Scots themselves never or very rarely give knur and spell a mention when they talk about golf's origins. That in itself makes me extremely suspicious. Why would they do that? Why would they completely ignore a similar stick and ball game which in its heyday was far bigger than golf and which was played for hundreds of years on their own doorsteps by thousands of players who spoke the same language? I could perhaps understand if the Scot's had given knur and spell some consideration and then given reasons why they dismissed it. However, just to say little or nothing at all about knur and spell seems very strange. It certainly appears that discussion of the game of knur and spell is anathema to the Scots!

In 1817 the famous poet and writer Samuel Taylor Coleridge introduced the concept of 'suspension of disbelief' into literary circles. This is where someone accepts something in their mind to be true even though they know full well that it is false. With the Scots and knur and spell the reverse appears to have happened. They seem to have chosen to deny the existence of knur and spell even they know quite well that it did exist and for centuries was far bigger than their miniscule game of golf.

The only explanation I can think of for what I can only conclude to be 'an intentional disregard' of knur and spell, is that golf was a rich man's sport for most of the five or six hundred years of its existence. The people who played it would have hated to think that their 'royal' game could have maybe stemmed from a game mostly played by poor men. There must have been a 'simulated ignorance' about the existence of knur and spell by the Scots.

It certainly appears that, as far as knur and spell in concerned, the Scots have been trapped in a perpetual 'liminal space' from which they have never emerged. I can only suggest that they remember the words of French philosopher Blaise Pascal which he uttered in the 1600s... 'Somewhere, something incredible is waiting to be known'.

The irony is that the rich Scots who played golf also needed 'poor' men to assist them in the pursuit of their sport. Of course, these poor men were never treated as equals. They were just tolerated. There was always a master and servant relationship, and the 'poor' men were always kept in their place. For the first four hundred years the 'servants' were called club-makers, hole cutters, ball makers, caddies, and fore-caddies etc. They were paid pitifully low wages. If we closely examine the *Blackheath GC minutes* for the 1700s and early 1800s we can see that much more money was spent on just one weekly club dinner with exotic treats such as whole turtles and copious amounts of claret than what they paid their 'servants' for a whole year's wages.

It wasn't until 1850 - 1860, four hundred years into golf's evolution, that the words 'golf professional' started to creep into the golfing vocabulary. Even then the so-called professionals were always regarded very strictly as servants by the club members. The amateur / professional divide was created and to this day is very strictly adhered to. There is probably nowhere more enlightening than the *Blackheath GC Chronicles* (published in 1897) to illustrate the disdain shown by amateur golfers towards professionals. In the period of history covering the forty-odd years after the guttie ball was introduced and the emergence of the so-called professionals, they only get the briefest of mentions. Although Blackheath professionals played in the Open Championship many times during that period there is no mention whatsoever about the Open in the club minutes. On the other hand, everything that happened in that club which related to the amateur club members found its way into the club minutes. If an amateur golfer farted three times while putting out on the last green, there would be a report on it in the minutes, and probably a special medal created to play for into perpetuity!

After the emergence of these professionals it was probably another one hundred years before golfers were able to make a decent living by playing golf. Until then most of their income came from teaching golf and making and repairing golf clubs. During the 1920s the top US player was Walter Hagen who won eleven majors. Not bad considering that the US Masters did not exist in those days, the US PGA also didn't exist for the first three years of his PGA career, and he lost the opportunity to play in nine other majors when he was at the peak of his powers because the tournaments were cancelled during the First World War. The US Masters only started in 1934 and Hagen was already forty-two years old by then. Had all these things not happened, Hagen would almost certainly have finished with more majors than Jack Nicklaus. Walter Hagen's strike rate in majors is over nineteen per cent. This is by far the highest strike rate of any professional golfer in post WWI history! Another star player who played in the Hagen era was Gene Sarazen. His strike rate was about six per cent. Jack Nicklaus's strike rate was just about eleven per cent. Tiger Wood's strike rate is currently just over seventeen per cent but could easily drop to below fourteen per cent by the time he finishes his career. Arnold Palmer's was nearly five per cent and Gary Player's was six per cent. Ben Hogan's was over fifteen per cent and Sam Snead's was just under six per cent. Hagen was definitely in rarefied atmosphere! So too was Ben Hogan when you consider that his strike rate was achieved even though over a thirty-three-year major playing career he only played once in the British Open at Carnoustie in 1953 ...and won it! He also missed the opportunity to play in thirteen majors because of WW2. When he missed these thirteen majors it was from 1940 -1945 when he was aged twenty-eight to thirty-three and would have been at his peak.

The top Australian player when Hagen played was Joe Kirkwood. Neither Joe nor Walter could earn a good living just playing golf tournaments. Eventually they teamed up and toured the world playing exhibition matches and doing trick shots. Things really only started to change significantly after television came along in the early 1950s and sports management groups appeared from around 1960. That is things changed for a select few professionals who managed to get on to one of the various world golf tours. The vast majority of club-based professionals around the world still earn their living teaching golf or managing golf shops.

Although things have improved for the above mentioned 'servants' over the past one hundred years, the old social class division culture has certainly not completely disappeared. There are still plenty of golf clubs around the world which steadfastly and stubbornly cling on to the *status quo*. A very good insight into what it was like in Australia as regards the 'master' and 'servant' relationship can be gleaned from the book *BRIAN 'Just Magnificent' TWITE* which was published in 2018. Brian joined Metropolitan GC in Melbourne as their golf professional in 1955 from the prestigious Sunningdale GC in England. Sixty-four years later, at the age of ninety-two, he is still very much associated with the club and still plays there several times each week. In his book Brian recalls that even as late as the mid-1970s he addressed club members by their full titles while in return they just called him 'Twite'. Sounds like there was not even the courtesy of being called 'mister' Twite. To use Brian's own words, he knew his place. In Brian's case Metropolitan GC proved to be a very happy place for him and he has spent his whole working life in Australia at that club. This was not always the case for many other golf professionals at other clubs.

The same kind of story can be told for Bud Russell who was a young Scottish professional who arrived at Barwon Heads GC in 1930 from the Lowlands of Scotland where he had trained under the legendary Jack

White. Bud retired in 1987 after fifty-seven years' service. He had been serving the club for well over thirty years before he was even allowed to enter the members' clubhouse!

It is true that today there are many public golf courses where anyone can play. It is also true that living standards for many people have greatly improved which has enabled many working-class men to be able to afford to play at private clubs.

However, there are still lots of exclusive clubs around the world where eyebrows would be raised if a group of bogans turned up looking for a game.

In most Asian countries golf is still primarily a rich man's game and playing golf is still very expensive. Try joining a club in Tokyo and see how much you would need to fork out. Go for a game in Dubai or Abu Dhabi and be prepared to take out a mortgage.

Even in developed countries like the USA, UK, and Australia there are still many golf clubs which do their utmost to keep out the so called 'riff-raff'.

They do this in several ways. High joining fees and high annual subscriptions is an obvious way which eliminates many people. Most of the top clubs also have a rigid interview process which weeds out many of the undesirables. These are not the only restrictions applied. Many of these top clubs will also have a waiting list of people who wish to become members. I personally know several members at Royal Melbourne GC who only maintain their membership for 'status' reasons and who often only play there once or twice per year.

When Scot Alistair McDonald moved to Colne in the late 1950s / early 1960s from Dingwall in the Scottish Highlands he enquired about membership at Colne GC. Colne was dominated by the cotton industry in those days and was very much a working-class area. He was shocked to find that one of the prerequisites of membership at that time was that he would have to provide them with proof of his bank balance! This was exactly the same time when I was doing my caddying at Colne GC as a young teenager, but I was blissfully unaware of this kind of thing. I was more than happy to walk away each time with my half a crown reward for pulling the trolley and climbing walls to find the errant and battered balata covered balls, usually out of bounds in the lush meadows on the other side of Cockhill Lane.

There are many clubs where no matter how much money you have, you will find it difficult to play there, let alone become a member. In all the thousands of rounds of golf I have played, I am yet to actually meet someone who has played at Augusta National GC in the USA (the home of the US Masters tournament).

There are also plenty of golf courses all around the world which have been built by private individuals just for play by their families and invited friends. David Evan's Cathedral Lodge GC, Lloyd William's Capitol GC and the late Kerry Packer's Ellerston GC immediately come to mind.

If 'poor' men are kept out of many golf clubs, spare a thought for the ladies. In 2019 there are still plenty of golf clubs around the world which don't allow lady members full stop. For most of golfing history, even the clubs which did allow lady members only allowed them to join as associate members who didn't have full playing rights, couldn't vote on club matters and who could only play at certain times in the week, which didn't interfere with the times when the men preferred to play! Consequently, in 2019, only twenty per cent or less of golf club members are women. It was the Commonwealth Franchise Act 1902 which gave women the right to vote in Federal Elections. However, over a hundred years later many of Australia's top golf clubs still had their heads stuck in a sand bunker. It is only after they have seen participation rates of women in golf sharply decline that they are slowly coming around to extracting the digit.

Golf club culture has changed a lot since the very early days but there is still a lot of room for improvement. The old 'nose in the air' mentality still exists at many of the old established clubs. Or as my friend Tim's mum used to say, 'They have their collars made out of their shirt-tails!' There is no doubt in my mind that, over the years, this has been a big part of why knur and spell, poor man's golf, has been kept out of the golf origin conversation.

Since the title of this book is 'poor man's' golf, which is often referred to as 'collier's' golf, it may be appropriate to say a few words about miner's golf in Scotland. From the early 1900s mining communities in Scotland, began to take an interest in playing golf. This was generally done through Miner's Welfare groups. Blantyre Miner's Welfare GC, which is a few miles south east of Glasgow was established in 1972 was still operating in 2019. A nine-holes course was started in Blantyre as early as 1913 but this course was liquidated in 1918. Stoneyburn Miner's Welfare GC near Whitburn and Bathgate had a nine-holes course in 1921, but this packed up just after WW2. Craigend Miner's Welfare GC at Maddiston near Falkirk which opened nine-holes in 1925 has also disappeared. What was possibly the first eighteen-holes course for miner's was announced in 1946 by the Fauldhouse Miner's Welfare Committee and was linked to the Whitrigg Colliery at Whitburn. I am unsure if this was the same course as the Greenburn GC which started in 1953 in Fauldhouse and still exists today. All these places are not far from Uddingston which is located in the centre of the Scottish coalfields. Golf and Miner's Welfare Groups were not limited to Scotland. It was also happening across the UK. Even though, thanks to Margaret Thatcher, most of the UK coal industry does not exist anymore, some of the golf courses which were laid down in those days still operate. An example of this is Backworth GC, another nine-holes course, which is close to Newcastle and about three miles north of West Moor and eight miles south of Bedlington. The Backworth Colliery Miner's Welfare Scheme purchased Backworth Hall in 1934 which had been built in the late 1700s for Ralph William Grey. In 2021 the Hall still serves as the club house for Backworth GC. Knur and spell was played at Newcastle, West Moor and Bedlington throughout the 1800s. It would not surprise me if the Backworth miner's, and maybe even the Scottish Miner's Welfare groups, had also played knur and spell before they switched to golf in the 1900s. The Scottish Miners would certainly have known all about knur and spell from their coal mining counterparts in English collieries via National Coal Mining Associations.

All the talk about knur and spell and Vikings or Anglo-Saxons is of course purely circumstantial. I have never seen any evidence which shows that the Vikings or the Anglo-Saxons played knur and spell before they arrived in England. However, whether or not knur and spell dates back to the Vikings is immaterial. Whether or not knur and spell came after the Vikings but before 1450 AD is also irrelevant. Whether or not knur and spell just developed in tandem alongside golf doesn't matter either.

For me, the big question is why did the Scots, in all their spouting about the origins of golf, not at least make knur and spell part of the discussion?

They have waffled on for years about colf, kolf and just about every other ball and stick game under the sun. So why would they never or rarely mention a ball and stick game which was played just a few miles from their border with England by thousands of players in thousands of places? Knur and spell did exist and did exist in a big way. That part of the story is not circumstantial. It is a proven fact. The Scots could have just about stood on the Cheviot Hills any day of the week and watched knur and spell being played by their closest neighbour, the Auld Enemy. In their debate about golf's origins, why would they choose to ignore a golf-like game which even in the 1800s was far bigger than golf itself? It is impossible that the Scots didn't know all about knur and spell. In fact, there is a mountain of evidence to show that the Scots did know all about knur and spell. The mind boggles!

Another possible explanation of why the Scots may have switched their minds off when it comes to knur and spell may be very deep rooted and may go back about three hundred and forty years. Before expounding on yet another wild idea, please allow me to first explain where the concept came from.

When we look at many of the issues in the modern world, it doesn't take long to realise that many of them can be traced back to events which happened many centuries earlier. Take for instance the conflict between the UK and the Irish Republican Army (IRA) which was very problematical in the twentieth century. This issue had stemmed from the time when King Henry **VIII** had decided to break away from the Pope in the 1500s and also to set up a Protestant colony enclave in Northern Ireland. Another example of a very old situation which has been festering for at least one thousand years is the one between Christians and Muslims which raised its head in relatively recent times through Osama bin Laden / al- Qaeda and after that with the Islamic State of Iraq and Syria (ISIS). Holy wars / jihads etc had been going on at least since the First Crusade in 1096 which was instigated by Pope Urban **I**. The Second, Third and Fourth Holy Wars had quickly followed in 1147, 1189 and 1202 under the instruction from Popes Eugene **III**, Gregory **VIII** and Innocent **III**.

In like fashion it would not surprise me if the Scottish reticence to discuss knur and spell also went back a long way and had its genesis in the first international golf match between the Duke of York and Scot John Patterson against the two English noblemen around the late 1600s. Let's first refresh ourselves about why this golf match came about. The two English nobles were insisting that 'the English had invented golf' and obviously must have had some good reason why they had formed that opinion. I suspect that this statement would have stirred up something in the Scottish psyche which would make them want to knock this idea on the head and bury it without trace before it could gain any traction. This would be especially the case since we know with great certainty that knur and spell in England was already thriving in the former Danelaw area at the time this first international match occurred. Since knur and spell in England at that time would have been far bigger than golf in Scotland, and the Scots would have known that, such a reaction would be very understandable. They would absolutely have hated to think their game of golf, which to them was almost a religion, may have emanated from knur and spell, and they would have obstinately resisted such an outrageously blasphemous idea...and in 2020 this would still be the case! The strange thing about the infamous 'first international match' in 1681 / 1682 is how anyone could think that playing a golf match would decide the issue about where the game originated! But this is what is said to have happened, and the event found its way into Scottish legendary folklore and possibly the story about where the game was discovered has been perpetuated ever since!

I am not for one moment suggesting that we should only apply the Law of Parsimony to our detective work when we delve into the history of golf or knur and spell. Just keep an open mind. Sometimes Occam's Razor will get the job done. Other times Hickam's Dictum may be more appropriate. Neither approach should be ignored.

Chapter 29

This will really piss off the Scots!

At the very beginning of this long diatribe on the origins of golf, I commented that there is general agreement that golf as we know it today was developed by the Scots. Maybe I got that wrong? Maybe I should have said that golf 'as it used to be played' prior to 1850 was developed by the Scots.

The truth is that modern golf in 2019 is very different to the golf which was played five hundred years ago or even the golf which was played in 1850. Since 1850 everything about golf has changed dramatically. The golf clubs are different, the golf balls are different, the golf courses, especially the greens, are different, the golf course maintenance procedures are different, the golf teaching methods are different, and so it goes on. Virtually none of the enormous changes which have occurred over the last one hundred and twenty years were invented by the Scots. We may safely say that golf has been re-invented mostly by the Americans and the English!

For a start let's think about the first dedicated commercial shop which sold golf clubs and golf equipment in St Andrews, Scotland. Surely it had to be a Scot who opened that. Incorrectamundo! It was a cockney from London called George Daniel Brown who opened the shop in 1861 / 1862. Unfortunately, Brown was not a local. He was, as we say in Lancashire 'an off-com'd un', and he couldn't make a success of it. It was later sold and became the Old Tom Morris Golf Shop in about 1866, which is still there today in the line of buildings across the road from the eighteenth green on the Old Course. Before Brown opened his shop, golf club and golf ball makers just sold their wares from their workshops or from their homes.

Mowing machines to keep greens in good shape were invented in England in 1830 but didn't become widespread on golf courses until the late 1800s. The first motorised mowing equipment also came from England in 1902. The first gas powered mower was from the USA in 1919.

Most of the information available on the creation and maintenance of golf greens in the early 1900s was from English grass seed companies. In fact, in 1914, the English grass seed supplier, Suttons of Reading, were claiming to already have over a century of experience in the business. Most, if not all of this, would not have been golf course business. It would have been for Buckingham Palace, big country mansion lawns for the rich people and large public parks! I don't suppose that anyone will be surprised to learn that all the fancy irrigation systems for both greens and fairways were also invented by non-Scottish companies...mostly American. What about those manually operated water / brush devices which are scattered all across most golf courses which are used to clean golf balls during the game? I don't recall ever seeing one which was made in Scotland!

The Scots had used piles of sand to tee up with for four hundred and fifty years before both the English and Americans invented the first wooden tees which were stuck in the ground in the 1890s. The Scots kept their heads stuck in the sand bucket for another thirty years. They were very tight with their money. They didn't like the massive expense of buying a wooden golf tee! God forbid! A gross (one hundred and forty-four) of tees cost one shilling which meant you had to pay one whole farthing for three tees! Or you could buy twelve tees for one penny! Why spend a farthing or a penny when you could get a bucket of sand for nothing? Very frugal young fellows those tight-fisted Scots! The American-made 'ReddyTee' didn't get accepted by the general golfing community until the 1920s. It was only after super star golfers Walter Hagen of the USA and Joe Kirkwood of Australia began to regularly use them that they became the norm.

The Americans probably invented the first commercial steel shafts in about 1925 to replace hickory which in any case had all come from America. Steel shafts had in fact been invented in the USA in the late 1800s but not commercialised. A Scottish blacksmith called Thomas Horsburgh did have a patent granted in 1894 for a solid iron shaft. Unfortunately this proved unsuitable for use because the weight to shaft diameter ratio was out of kilter. A Derbyshire man sold hickory shafts reinforced with steel wire steel ribs in 1902. In 1912 an Oldbury engineer in the Midlands area of the UK had also made a tubular steel golf shaft when working for a bicycle frame manufacturing company. We could argue all day about exactly who invented the steel golf shaft, but we can safely say with great certainty that it wasn't the Scots! Carbon-fibre graphite shafts were first from America in 1969. The first steel-headed driver came in 1979 from TaylorMade, a US firm. The first titanium driver came in 1990 from Mizuno, a Japanese company.

Even the idea of a matching set of golf clubs had nothing at all to do with the Scots. Back in the hickory days it was not uncommon for just about every club in a golf players arsenal to be made by a different maker. Virtually every club would have different flex and different weight etc. The golf clubs were not numbered like they are today. They all had different names such as mashie, niblick, spoon, jigger, cleek etc. This only started to change around 1925 when American companies like Wilson, Spalding and McGregor got in on the act. The irons were the first to change and for a while both the old name and the new number were stamped on the clubs. By 1940 all the old names had more or less disappeared apart from on the woods which lingered on for another ten years or so.

The first wound ball (Haskell) to replace the crude guttie balls in 1899 was American. The first moulded-in dimples on golf balls were English in 1908. None of the many golf ball innovations since the early 1900s came from Scotland. The 1.68-inch diameter golf ball was a US invention and had been used there since the 1930s. A very big breakthrough came in the mid-1960s when the soft and easily damaged balata golf ball covers were mostly replaced by the very tough and cut resistant Surlyn resin from the Du Pont company in the USA. Surlyn is an iononer resin which is a copolymer of ethylene and methacrylic acid. The softer urethane covers on the current top brand balls came after that but not from Scotland. The first slip-on rubber grip for golf clubs to replace leather came in about 1953 from the USA. American Sam Snead was the first to popularise the use of golf gloves quickly followed by fellow Americans Jack Nicklaus and Arnold Palmer. The first pull-carts came from the USA in the 1940s. The first powered golf cart also came from the USA in around 1962. None of the modern golf bags or golf shoes come from Scotland. The first golf bags didn't appear until the late 1800s and probably came from England or the USA. The Scots, or their caddies, had carried their golf clubs by hand for the first four hundred and fifty years or so. They had obviously been far too tight to consider buying a bag to put them in. Sports shoes with spikes for sports other than golf (e.g. Cricket) had been around in England for almost one hundred years before the Scots decided that hammering nails into their shoes was not a very smart idea. The first golf shoes with screw-in metal spikes didn't arrive until about 1891 and these were quickly followed in about 1906 by the highly successful Saddle Oxford shoes which were introduced by the US based Spalding Company. Plastic spikes for golf shoes came in the 1990s and spike-less golf shoes with moulded-in dimples from about 2010. Needless to say that neither of these was a Scottish invention. The Stimpmeter for measuring the speed of greens was designed by an American. The first golf magazine was published in London in 1890. These days many golfers use modern GPS technology for such things as range finders and shot tracker devices. Apart from these there are plenty of other fancy teaching devices like swing speed meters etc. None of these were invented by the Scots. I could keep going for another half an hour, but I think you get the picture. To be brutally honest, golf in Scotland hadn't really progressed very far over four hundred years until the Americans and the English got involved from the late 1800s onwards. In the last hundred years it has literally gone off the planet!

The Scots did invent those annoying sand bunkers! For about four hundred years there were no man-made sand bunkers. All the sand on a golf links course used to be just a naturally occurring hazard. However, although sand bunkers don't appear to have changed much in the last hundred years, there has in fact been continual change over the past one hundred and twenty years in the way new sand bunkers have been constructed. These changes have generally been aimed at better drainage and better ways to prevent erosion. Most of these changes are of course beneath the surface and hence not readily apparent to the player. Most of the changes in this area e.g. The use of geo-fabrics etc, were not invented by the Scots.

The Scots were also using a very simple scorecard to record their scores from an early date. Maybe the oldest surviving example of such a card is the one dated 1820 which was played on Leith Links. No hole lengths, par ratings or hole indices were shown in those days. Just the score for each hole as each individual stroke had been ticked off. In 1820 a score of 84 for twice around the five-hole course had been recorded. As we can imagine, most refinements to the scorecards after that came from none-Scottish sources. For example the Stableford method of scoring, which is probably the most popular scoring system ever invented for amateur golfers, was finally introduced in about 1932 at Wallasey GC by an Englishman from Oldbury in Worcestershire. At that stage he had been trialling and refining it for about thirty years.

The first professional golfers' association in the world, the 'British' PGA, was founded in 1901 by an Englishman, John Henry Taylor from the Royal North Devon GC. It began life as the London & Counties Professional Golfers' Association and is now headquartered in Birmingham.

As far as professional golf was concerned most of the golf developments relating to TV coverage probably came via the Americans. For example, the first time that individual players scores relative to 'over' or 'under' par were used on TV to enable fans to easily see in 'real time' who was leading the tournament, was in 1960. This was one of a multitude of innovations introduced by CBS TV producer Frank Chirkinian from Philadelphia in Pennsylvania. The first use of detailed shot yardage distances during tournament play was also by an American, Deane Beman, in 1954. Jack Nicklaus only started worrying about yardage notes from about 1961.

We can also be very confident that many of the incidental items in a golfer's bag such as golf umbrellas, forks to repair pitch marks, marker pens to identify golf balls etc, were all invented outside of Scotland.

Finally, we must come to the most important thing in a Scottish golfer's bag of tricks. What about the whisky in his hip flask which he may take a wee nip from on a very cold day to ward off the winter chills or maybe to relax his nerves when standing over a crucial short putt? Surprising to many, we find that the three oldest whisky distilleries in the world are not located in Scotland. The two oldest are in Ireland and the next oldest is in the USA! Let's not worry about whether it is whisky or whiskey! I can't bear this. It is enough to make my porridge go cold and my left-handed spurtle get dry rot! Yes, the Scots do love and eat a lot of porridge but even that probably originated in Ireland! I have to admit however that the first distillery to receive a royal warrant was a single malt Highland whisky called Royal Brackla which was granted by King William **IV** in 1833, about the same time he started handing out 'royal status' warrants to golf clubs. This distillery is at Nairn which is about sixteen miles east of Inverness.

We can probably argue the toss about who invented golf and who developed the golf equipment etc until the cows come home. But there is one thing which the Scots must be given a great deal of credit for. They were definitely the ones who first spread golf all around the world. All the first golf clubs or golf playing groups outside of Scotland such as Blackheath, Old Manchester, Dum Dum in India, Pau in south-west France, Mauritius in the Indian Ocean, Corinth in Greece, Dunedin in New Zealand, Bothwell in Tasmania etc were all started up by ex-pat Scots or groups of people like the British India Company or British Army who had lots of Scots in their ranks. Then in the second half of the 1800s and the early 1900s when golf professionals started to appear and began to be employed by emerging golf clubs all around the world, the vast majority of these early golf professionals came from the well-established Scottish clubs. Wherever these early professionals went, whether it be the USA, England, Australia, South Africa etc, they made and supplied golf clubs and taught the game. They were also very prominent in the golf course design of most of the early golf clubs.

When it came to bringing golf to the attention of the general public, however, the two biggest changes happened in the 1950s and 1960s. These changes occurred more or less just as the game of knur and spell was drawing its last breath. By a strange coincidence, both changes involved men from the state of Illinois in the USA.

George May was a golf promoter who ran the Tam O' Shanter GC just outside Chicago at a place called Niles. The World Championship of golf was held there from 1946 to 1957. Australian golfers Ossie Pickworth, Norman von Nida and Peter Thomson all played there in the early 1950s. Although the US Open championship had been shown on TV in 1947, it had only been on local TV in St Louis. However, in 1953 the Tam O' Shanter World Championship was broadcast on TV nationwide all-around America for the first time ever. It was on TV for only one hour, but it was so well received that the die was cast for the mammoth golfing circus which we see today. Then, in 1960, along came another man from Chicago called Mark McCormack. He recognised the tremendous potential of linking sports stars with product sponsorship and television viewing rights when he created IMG, the world's first sports management group. Up until that point top golfers had struggled to make a good living just by playing golf as opposed to teaching and club making. His first deal was made with Arnold Palmer and after just three years Arnie's annual income had jumped from fifty thousand dollars to five hundred thousand dollars. Today IMG is a massive media distribution group. Apart from golf they handle top stars from many different sports as well as top entertainers etc. In 2013 the group was sold for well over two billion dollars. McCormack also initiated a world ranking system for golfers. This became the Official World Golf Ranking System in 1986. Although neither of these changes had anything to do with the Scots, they could maybe claim some indirect kudos because McCormack is a Scottish surname, Tam O' Shanter was the name of a Scot in one of Robbie Burn's most famous poems and one of the first pioneers of early television was a Scot by the name of John Logie Baird. Interesting that Scotland's favourite poet wrote this poem in 1790 in the town of Ayr which is just three miles away from Prestwick where the British Open golf championship was born seventy years later and not far away from Dalry where knur and spell was played at the same time. As I write this section the 2019 Open Championship is just about to start at the Royal Portrush GC in Northern Ireland. The last time it was hosted by that club was in 1951 when the English Ryder Cup player Max Faulkner won his one and only major. Max was a regular visitor to Australia in the 1950s along with a whole posse of other British Ryder Cup players. Keysborough GC's teaching professional, Jack Harris, took twenty-five British Ryder Cup scalps during that decade, plus three US Ryder Cup scalps as well. Max Faulkner was one of Jack Harris's regular 'victims'.

In 2014 *Golf WRX* published a list of the fifteen best inventions in golf history. Thirteen out of fifteen listed were non-Scottish inventions. The other two shown were not really inventions. They were just rule changes (stymie and fourteen club rules) about which maybe the R & A and USGA both had a say.

Chapter 30

Now is the time to say goodbye. Goodbye! Farta**ta**! Fartata**ta**! (As Peter Cook and Dudley Moore would say)

Over many years the origins of golf have been researched and written about by hundreds if not thousands of historians. By comparison the game of knur and spell has had relatively little attention. I didn't start out writing this book with the deliberate intention of being contentious. It just seemed to develop into a polemic as I gradually uncovered more about knur and spell and also learned more about the history of golf. Hopefully the paltry contribution presented in this book will spark more activity in this area and much more about knur and spell will eventually surface. The best information anywhere in the world on the history of golf in Scotland is to be found on the *Scottish Golf History* website. They have unearthed many gems of information on golf and continue to do so. Perhaps, in future, something similar may appear for knur and spell.

The object of this book has not been to prove that knur and spell was a game stemming from the Vikings. Like Sherlock Holmes, I have merely tried to find an explanation for the facts observed by a process of induction using a raft of generalizations. Was it a Viking game? The inductive argument for this is still quite weak.

If we forget about the Vikings, and just ask the question did knur and spell play any part in the evolution of golf, either directly or indirectly, then the case for this is significantly stronger. The fact that the Scots and the golf historians have habitually omitted knur and spell from the golf evolution conversation, to my simple mind, only serves to strengthen the argument.

Having said all this, I must come clean. I know perfectly well that modern golf was invented by an esteemed gentleman from North Korea called Kim Jong-Il, shortly before he shot eleven holes-in-one on his first ever round of golf! Silly me. I could have saved myself a lot of research and saved any readers (all two of them) having to wade through all my prattling! In December 2011, when Kim Jong-Il died, the golfing world mourned the loss of this superstar golfer. The amazing thing was that he was fifty-two years old when he shot his 38 under par 34 at the 7041 metre Pyongyang GC in 1994. I don't suppose that he played every shot with his driver like me. Then I really would be impressed! Maybe Kim invented knur and spell too? (Ha ha)

I wonder what Jack Harris would have thought about all this. Perhaps he would have thought that it was just a load of old balls ...or even gnarly knurs! Some things are for sure. Jack Harris would have made a magnificent knur and spell player. I still don't know exactly when or where the games of golf and knur and spell began! Knur and spell was a much bigger and more popular game in the UK than golf throughout the 1800s! I can show this book to my three-year-old granddaughter Freja and our pet schnoodle, Archie, without being told that it is a pile of rubbish, and still get a cuddle and a pat!

Afterword

When I completed this book the only sensation I felt was numbness. Much of the book was written during the Covid lockdowns which deprived us all of many of the everyday social exchanges we thrive on.

In January 2021 we were just seeing some light at the end of the tunnel when devastating news from the UK told us that Covid had taken my dear old mum.

We were unable to return to the UK and still we have been unable to scatter mum's ashes around the oak tree in her garden which my eldest daughter, Jennifer, had given her grandma as a sapling almost forty years ago.

The massive void in our lives is all consuming.

We can certainly relate to WH Auden's words....

> 'The stars are not wanted now: put out every one;
> Pack up the moon and dismantle the sun:
> Pour away the ocean and sweep up the wood;
> For nothing now can ever come to any good.'

But mum had a great long life and all we have to do to cheer up is to close our eyes and listen to her playing Ludwig Van Beethoven's *Für Elise* on her piano.

God bless you mum.

Acknowledgements

In no particular order I need to thank the following people for all the invaluable help they have given me in putting this book together.

Jonathan Lunt
Susanna Kouyias
Jennifer Simon
Richard Lunt
Mike Shaw
Timothy St Julien Barber
Ross Baker
Andrew Mason
Steve Rogerson
Russell Holdsworth
Ricky Lunt
Danny Hey
Stephen Coupe
Mark Kouyias
Barbara Boyes
Oswyn Parry
Alistair MacDonald
Sylvie Blair

And to all the other family and friends who have given me support and encouragement throughout the process despite having to listen to all my long boring stories...THANK YOU.

9 780645 22